MCSA

Windows Server® 2016

Complete Study Guide

MCSA
Windows Server® 2016
Complete Study Guide
Exam 70-742

William Panek

SYBEX®
A Wiley Brand

Senior Acquisitions Editor: Kenyon Brown
Development Editor: Kim Wimpsett
Technical Editors: Rodney R. Fournier and Chris Crayton
Senior Production Editor: Christine O'Connor
Copy Editor: Judy Flynn
Editorial Manager: Mary Beth Wakefield
Production Manager: Kathleen Wisor
Executive Editor: Jim Minatel
Book Designers: Judy Fung and Bill Gibson
Proofreader: Nancy Carrasco
Indexer: Jack Lewis
Project Coordinator, Cover: Brent Savage
Cover Designer: Wiley
Cover Image: Getty Images Inc./Jeremy Woodhouse

This book is dedicated to the three ladies of my life, Crystal, Alexandria, and Paige

Acknowledgments

I would like to thank my wife and best friend, Crystal. She is always the light at the end of my tunnel. I want to thank my two daughters, Alexandria and Paige, for all of their love and support during the writing of all my books. The three of them are my support system and I couldn't do any of this without them.

I want to thank all of my family and friends who always help me when I'm writing my books. I want to thank my brothers Rick, Gary, and Rob. I want to thank my great friends Shaun, Jeremy, and Gene.

I would like to thank all of my friends and co-workers at StormWind Studios. I want to especially thank the team who I work with on a daily basis and that includes Tom W, Dan Y, Corey F, Ronda, Dan J, Jessica, Dave, Tiffany, Tara, Ashley, Brittany, Doug, Mike, Vince, Desiree, Ryan, Ralph, Dan G, Tyler, Jeff B, Shayne, Patrick, Noemi, Michelle, Zachary, Colin, and the man who makes it all possible, Tom Graunke. Thanks to all of you for everything that you do. I would not have been able to complete this book without all of your help and support.

I want to thank everyone on my Sybex team, especially my development editor Kim Wimpsett, who helped me make this the best book possible, and Rodney R. Fournier, who is the technical editor of many of my books. It's always good to have the very best technical guy backing you up. I want to thank Christine O'Connor, who was my production editor, and Judy Flynn for being the Copy Editor.

I want to also thank Chris Crayton who is my Technical Proofreader. Special thanks to my acquisitions editor, Kenyon Brown, who was the lead for the entire book. Finally, I want to thank everyone else behind the scenes that helped make this book possible. It's truly an amazing thing to have so many people work on my books to help make them the very best. I can't thank you all enough for your hard work.

About the Author

 **William Panek** holds the following certifications: MCP, MCP+I, MCSA, MCSA+ Security and Messaging, MCSE-NT (3.51 & 4.0), MCSE 2000, 2003, 2012/2012 R2, MCSE+Security and Messaging, MCDBA, MCT, MCTS, MCITP, CCNA, CCDA, and CHFI. Will is also a four time and current Microsoft MVP winner.

After many successful years in the computer industry, Will decided that he could better use his talents and his personality as an instructor. He began teaching for schools such as Boston University and the University of Maryland, just to name a few. He has done consulting and training for some of the biggest government and corporate companies in the world including the United States Secret Service, Cisco, United States Air Force, and US Army.

In 2015, Will became a Sr. Microsoft Instructor for StormWind Studios (www.stormwindstudios.com). He currently lives in New Hampshire with his wife and two daughters. Will was also a Representative in the New Hampshire House of Representatives from 2010 to 2012. In his spare time, he likes to do blacksmithing, shooting (trap and skeet), snowmobiling, playing racquetball, and riding his Harley. Will is also a commercially-rated helicopter pilot.

Contents at a Glance

Contents

Table of Exercises

Introduction

This book is drawn from more than 20 years of IT experience. I have taken that experience and translated it into a Windows Server 2016 book that will help you not only prepare for the MCSA: Windows Server 2016 exams but also develop a clear understanding of how to install and configure Windows Server 2016 while avoiding all of the possible configuration pitfalls.

Many Microsoft books just explain the Windows operating system, but with *MCSA: Windows Server 2016 Complete Study Guide*, I go a step further by providing many in-depth, step-by-step procedures to support my explanations of how the operating system performs at its best.

Microsoft Windows Server 2016 is the newest version of Microsoft's server operating system software. Microsoft has taken the best of Windows Server 2003, Windows Server 2008, and Windows Server 2012 and combined them into the latest creation, Windows Server 2016.

Windows Server 2016 eliminates many of the problems that plagued the previous versions of Windows Server, and it includes a much faster boot time and shutdown. It is also easier to install and configure, and it barely stops to ask the user any questions during installation. In this book, I will show you what features are installed during the automated installation and where you can make changes if you need to be more in charge of your operating system and its features.

This book takes you through all the ins and outs of Windows Server 2016, including installation, configuration, Group Policy Objects, auditing, backups, and so much more.

Windows Server 2016 has improved on Microsoft's desktop environment, made networking easier, enhanced searching capability, and improved performance—and that's only scratching the surface.

When all is said and done, this is a technical book for IT professionals who want to take Windows Server 2016 to the next step and get certified. With this book, you will not only learn Windows Server 2016 and ideally pass the exams, but you will also become a Windows Server 2016 expert.

The Microsoft Certification Program

Since the inception of its certification program, Microsoft has certified more than 2 million people. As the computer network industry continues to increase in both size and complexity, this number is sure to grow—and the need for proven ability will also increase. Certifications can help companies verify the skills of prospective employees and contractors.

The Microsoft certification tracks for Windows Server 2016 include the following:

MCSA: Windows Server 2016   The MCSA is now the lowest-level certification you can achieve with Microsoft in relation to Windows Server 2016. It requires passing three exams: 70-740, 70-741, and 70-742.

MCSE: Cloud Platform and Infrastructure   The MCSE certifications, in relation to Windows Server 2016, require that you become an MCSA first and then pass two additional exams. The additional exams will vary depending on which of the two MCSE tracks you choose. For more information, visit Microsoft's website at www.microsoft.com/learning.

How Do You Become Certified on Windows Server 2016?

Attaining Microsoft certification has always been a challenge. In the past, students have been able to acquire detailed exam information—even most of the exam questions—from online "brain dumps" and third-party "cram" books or software products. For the new generation of exams, this is simply not the case.

Microsoft has taken strong steps to protect the security and integrity of its new certification tracks. Now prospective candidates must complete a course of study that develops detailed knowledge about a wide range of topics. It supplies them with the true skills needed, derived from working with the technology being tested.

The new generations of Microsoft certification programs are heavily weighted toward hands-on skills and experience. It is recommended that candidates have troubleshooting skills acquired through hands-on experience and working knowledge.

Fortunately, if you are willing to dedicate the time and effort to learn Windows Server 2016, you can prepare yourself well for the exam by using the proper tools. By working through this book, you can successfully meet the requirements to pass the Windows Server 2016 exams.

MCSA Exam Requirements

Candidates for MCSA certification on Windows Server 2016 must pass at least the following three Windows Server 2016 exams:

- **70-740:** Installation, Storage, and Compute with Windows Server 2016
- **70-741:** Networking with Windows Server 2016
- **70-742:** Identity with Windows Server 2016

For those who have a qualifying certification, they can take the Upgrading exam "Upgrading Your Skills to MCSA: Windows Server 2016" (Exam 70-743). The objectives for this exam span the three individual exams. This book covers all of the objectives for the Upgrading exam. For details about the exam, visit Microsoft's website at www.microsoft.com/learning.

Microsoft provides exam objectives to give you a general overview of possible areas of coverage on the Microsoft exams. Keep in mind, however, that exam objectives are subject to change at any time without prior notice and at Microsoft's sole discretion. Visit the Microsoft Learning website (www.microsoft.com/learning) for the most current listing of exam objectives. The published objectives and how they map to this book are listed later in this Introduction.

 For a more detailed description of the Microsoft certification programs, including a list of all the exams, visit the Microsoft Learning website at: www.microsoft.com/learning.

Tips for Taking the Windows Server 2016 Exams

Here are some general tips for achieving success on your certification exam:

- Arrive early at the exam center so that you can relax and review your study materials. During this final review, you can look over tables and lists of exam-related information.

- Read the questions carefully. Do not be tempted to jump to an early conclusion. Make sure you know *exactly* what the question is asking.

- Answer all questions. If you are unsure about a question, mark it for review and come back to it at a later time.

- On simulations, do not change settings that are not directly related to the question. Also, assume the default settings if the question does not specify or imply which settings are used.

- For questions about which you're unsure, use a process of elimination to get rid of the obviously incorrect answers first. This improves your odds of selecting the correct answer when you need to make an educated guess.

Exam Registration

At the time this book was released, Microsoft exams are given two ways. You can take the exam live online or through the more than 1,000 Authorized VUE Testing Centers around the world. For the location of a testing center near you, go to VUE's website at www.vue.com. If you are outside of the United States and Canada, contact your local VUE registration center.

Find out the number of the exam that you want to take and then register with the VUE registration center nearest to you. At this point, you will be asked for advance payment for the exam. The exams are $165 each, and you must take them within one year of payment. You can schedule exams up to six weeks in advance or as late as one working day prior to the date of the exam. You can cancel or reschedule your exam if you contact the center at least two working days prior to the exam. Same-day registration is available in some locations, subject to space availability. Where same-day registration is available, you must register a minimum of two hours before test time.

When you schedule the exam, you will be provided with instructions regarding appointment and cancellation procedures, ID requirements, and information about the testing center location. In addition, you will receive a registration and payment confirmation letter from VUE.

Who Should Read This Book?

This book is intended for individuals who want to earn their MCSA: Windows Server 2016 certification.

This book will not only help anyone who is looking to pass the Microsoft exams, it will also help anyone who wants to learn the real ins and outs of the Windows Server 2016 operating system.

What's Inside?

Here is a glance at what's in each chapter:

Chapter 1: Installing Active Directory   In the first chapter, I will explain the benefits of using Active Directory. I will explain how Forests, Trees, and Domains work and I will also show you how to install Active Directory.

Chapter 2: Administer Active Directory   This chapter shows you how to create accounts in Active Directory. I will show you how to do bulk imports into Active Directory and also how to create and manage groups. I will also show you how to create and manage service accounts.

Chapter 3: Maintaining Active Directory   In this chapter I explain how to configure Active Directory components like an RODC, DFSR, and trusts. I will also show you how to configure and use Active Directory snapshots.

Chapter 4: Implementing GPOs   This chapter will show you how to implement and configure Group Policy Objects (GPOs).

Chapter 5: Understanding Certificates   This chapter takes you through the different ways to create and manage configure certificates. I will show you how to install and configure a Certificate Server.

Chapter 6: Configure Access and Information Protection Solutions   You will see the different ways that you can setup and configure Active Directory Federation Services. I will also show you how to configure a Web Application Proxy.

What's Included with the Book

This book includes many helpful items intended to prepare you for the MCSA: Windows Server 2016 certification.

Assessment Test   There is an assessment test at the conclusion of the Introduction that can be used to evaluate quickly where you are with Windows Server 2016. This test should be taken prior to beginning your work in this book, and it should help you identify areas in which you are either strong or weak. Note that these questions are purposely more simple than the types of questions you may see on the exams.

Objective Map and Opening List of Objectives   Later in this Introduction, I include a detailed exam objective map showing you where each of the exam objectives are covered. Each chapter also includes a list of the exam objectives that are covered.

Helpful Exercises   Throughout the book, I have included step-by-step exercises of some of the more important tasks that you should be able to perform. Some of these exercises have corresponding videos that can be downloaded from the book's website. Also, in the following section I have a recommended home lab setup that will be helpful in completing these tasks.

Exam Essentials   The end of each chapter also includes a listing of exam essentials. These are essentially repeats of the objectives, but remember that any objective on the exam blueprint could show up on the exam.

Chapter Review Questions   Each chapter includes review questions. These are used to assess your understanding of the chapter and are taken directly from the chapter. These questions are based on the exam objectives, and they are similar in difficulty to items you might actually receive on the MCSA: Windows Server 2016 exams.

> The Sybex Interactive Online Test Bank, flashcards, videos, and glossary can be accessed at http://www.wiley.com/go/sybextestprep.

Interactive Online Learning Environment and Test Bank

The interactive online learning environment that accompanies this study guide provides a test bank with study tools to help you prepare for the certification exams and increase your chances of passing them the first time! The test bank includes the following elements:

Sample Tests   All of the questions in this book are provided, including the assessment test, which you'll find at the end of this Introduction, and the chapter tests that include the review questions at the end of each chapter. In addition, there is a practice exam. Use these questions to test your knowledge of the study guide material. The online test bank runs on multiple devices.

Electronic Flashcards   One set of questions is provided in digital flashcard format (a question followed by a single correct answer). You can use the flashcards to reinforce your learning and provide last-minute test prep before the exam.

Glossary   The key terms from this book and their definitions are available as a fully searchable PDF.

Videos   Some of the exercises include corresponding videos. These videos show you how the author does the exercises. There is also a video that shows you how to set up virtualization so that you can complete the exercises within a virtualized environment. The author also has videos to help you on the Microsoft exams at www.youtube.com/c/williampanek.

Recommended Home Lab Setup

To get the most out of this book, you will want to make sure you complete the exercises throughout the chapters. To complete the exercises, you will need one of two setups. First, you can set up a machine with Windows Server 2016 and complete the labs using a regular Windows Server 2016 machine.

The second way to set up Windows Server 2016 (the way I set up Server 2016) is by using virtualization. I set up Windows Server 2016 as a virtual hard disk (VHD), and I did all the labs this way. The advantages of using virtualization are that you can always just wipe out the system and start over without losing a real server. Plus, you can set up multiple virtual servers and create a full lab environment on one machine.

I created a video for this book showing you how to set up a virtual machine and how to install Windows Server 2016 onto that virtual machine.

How to Contact Sybex/Author

Sybex strives to keep you supplied with the latest tools and information you need for your work. Please check the website at www.wiley.com/go/sybextestprep, where I'll post additional content and updates that supplement this book should the need arise.

You can contact me by going to my website at www.willpanek.com. You can also watch free videos on Microsoft networking at www.youtube.com/c/williampanek. If you would like to follow information about Windows Server 2016 from Will Panek, please visit Twitter @AuthorWillPanek.

Certification Objectives Maps

Table I.1 provides the objective mappings for the 70-742 exam. In addition to the book chapters, you will find coverage of exam objectives in the flashcards, practice exams, and videos on the book's companion website at www.wiley.com/go/sybextestprep.

TABLE I.1   70-742 exam objectives

Objective	Chapter
Install and configure Active Directory Domain Services (AD DS) (20–25%)	
Install and configure domain controllers	1

Objective	Chapter
Install a new forest, add or remove a domain controller from a domain, upgrade a domain controller, install AD DS on a Server Core installation, install a domain controller from Install from Media (IFM), resolve DNS SRV record registration issues, configure a global catalog server, transfer and seize operations master roles, install and configure a read-only domain controller (RODC), configure domain controller cloning.	1
Create and manage Active Directory users and computers	2
Automate the creation of Active Directory accounts; create, copy, configure, and delete users and computers; configure templates; perform bulk Active Directory operations; configure user rights; implement offline domain join; manage inactive and disabled accounts; automate unlocking of disabled accounts using Windows PowerShell; automate password resets using Windows PowerShell.	2
Create and manage Active Directory groups and organizational units (OUs)	2
Configure group nesting; convert groups, including security, distribution, universal, domain local, and domain global; manage group membership using Group Policy; enumerate group membership; automate group membership management using Windows PowerShell; delegate the creation and management of Active Directory groups and OUs; manage default Active Directory containers; create, copy, configure, and delete groups and OUs.	2
Manage and maintain AD DS (15–20%)	
Configure service authentication and account policies	2
Create and configure Service Accounts, create and configure Group Managed Service Accounts (gMSAs), configure Kerberos Constrained Delegation (KCD), manage Service Principal Names (SPNs), configure virtual accounts, configure domain and local user password policy settings, configure and apply Password Settings Objects (PSOs), delegate password settings management, configure account lockout policy settings, configure Kerberos policy settings within Group Policy.	2
Maintain Active Directory	3
Back up Active Directory and SYSVOL, manage Active Directory offline, perform offline defragmentation of an Active Directory database, clean up metadata, configure Active Directory snapshots, perform object- and container-level recovery, perform Active Directory restore, configure and restore objects by using the Active Directory Recycle Bin, configure replication to Read-Only Domain Controllers (RODCs), configure Password Replication Policy (PRP) for RODC, monitor and manage replication, upgrade SYSVOL replication to Distributed File System Replication (DFSR).	3

TABLE I.1 70-742 exam objectives *(continued)*

Objective	Chapter
Configure Active Directory in a complex enterprise environment	3
Configure a multi-domain and multi-forest Active Directory infrastructure; deploy Windows Server 2016 domain controllers within a pre-existing Active Directory environment; upgrade existing domains and forests; configure domain and forest functional levels; configure multiple user principal name (UPN) suffixes; configure external, forest, shortcut, and realm trusts; configure trust authentication; configure SID filtering; configure name suffix routing; configure sites and subnets; create and configure site links; manage site coverage; manage registration of SRV records; move domain controllers between sites; configure account policies.	3
Create and manage Group Policy (25–30%)	
Create and manage Group Policy Objects (GPOs)	4
Configure a central store; manage starter GPOs; configure GPO links; configure multiple local Group Policies; back up, import, copy, and restore GPOs; create and configure a migration table; reset default GPOs; delegate Group Policy management; detect health issues using the Group Policy Infrastructure Status dashboard.	4
Configure Group Policy processing	4
Configure processing order and precedence, configure blocking of inheritance, configure enforced policies, configure security filtering and Windows Management Instrumentation (WMI) filtering, configure loopback processing, configure and manage slow-link processing and Group Policy caching, configure client-side extension (CSE) behavior, force a Group Policy update.	4
Configure Group Policy processing	4
Configure software installation, configure folder redirection, configure scripts, configure administrative templates, import security templates, import a custom administrative template file, configure property filters for administrative templates.	4
Configure Group Policy preferences	4
Configure printer preferences, define network drive mappings, configure power options, configure custom registry settings, configure Control Panel settings, configure Internet Explorer settings, configure file and folder deployment, configure shortcut deployment, configure item-level targeting.	4

Exam objectives are subject to change at any time without prior notice and at Microsoft's sole discretion. Please visit Microsoft's website (www .microsoft.com/learning) for the most current listing of exam objectives.

Assessment Test

1. What is the maximum number of domains that a Windows Server 2016 computer configured as a domain controller may participate in at one time?

   A. Zero

   B. One

   C. Two

   D. Any number of domains

2. Which of the following file systems are required for Active Directory?

   A. FAT

   B. FAT32

   C. HPFS

   D. NTFS

3. Which of the following services and protocols are required for Active Directory? Choose all that apply.

   A. NetBEUI

   B. TCP/IP

   C. DNS

   D. DHCP

4. Which of the following PowerShell commands allows you to view Active Directory users?

   A. Get-ADUser

   B. Get-User

   C. View-User

   D. See-ADUser

5. Which of the following PowerShell commands allows you to enable an active directory account after it's been locked out?

   A. Release-ADAccount

   B. Enable-ADAccount

   C. Unlock-ADAccount

   D. Enable-Account

6. You need to create a new user account using the command prompt. Which command would you use?

   A. dsmodify

   B. dscreate

   C. dsnew

   D. dsadd

7. What kind of trust is setup between one domain and another domain in the same forest?

A. External trust

B. Forest trust

C. Shortcut trust

D. Domain trust

8. You need to deactivate the Global Catalog option on some of your domain controllers. At which level in Active Directory would you deactivate GlobalCatalogs?

A. Server

B. Site

C. Domain

D. Forest

9. You want to allow the new Sales Director to have permissions to reset passwords for all users within the sales OU. Which of the following is the best way to do this?

A. Create a special administration account within the OU and grant it full permissions for all objects within Active Directory.

B. Move the user's login account into the OU that he or she is to administer.

C. Move the user's login account to an OU that contains the OU (that is, the parent OU of the one that he or she is to administer).

D. Use the Delegation of Control Wizard to assign the necessary permissions on the OU that he or she is to administer.

10. You need to create OUs in Active Directory. In which MMCs can you accomplish this task? Choose all that apply.

A. Active Directory Administrative Center

B. Active Directory Sites and Services

C. Active Directory Users and Computers

D. Active Directory Domains and Trusts

11. You want a GPO to take effect immediately, and you need to use Windows PowerShell. Which PowerShell cmdlet command would you use?

A. Invoke-GPUpdate

B. Invoke-GPForce

C. Invoke-GPResult

D. Invoke-GPExecute

12. GPOs assigned at which of the following level(s) will override GPO settings at the domain level?

A. OU

B. Site

C. Domain

D. Both OU and site

13. A system administrator wants to ensure that only the GPOs set at the OU level affect the Group Policy settings for objects within the OU. Which option can they use to do this (assuming that all other GPO settings are the defaults)?

    A. The Enforced option

    B. The Block Policy Inheritance option

    C. The Disable option

    D. The Deny permission

14. To disable GPO settings for a specific security group, which of the following permissions should you apply?

    A. Deny Write

    B. Allow Write

    C. Enable Apply Group Policy

    D. Deny Apply Group Policy

15. You want to configure modifications of the Certification Authority role service to be logged. What should you enable? (Choose all that apply.)

    A. Enable auditing of system events.

    B. Enable logging.

    C. Enable auditing of privilege use.

    D. Enable auditing of object access.

    E. You should consider enabling auditing of process tracking.

16. You need to add a certificate template to the Certificate Authority. What PowerShell command would you use?

    A. Get-CSTemplate

    B. Add-CSTemplate

    C. Add-CATemplate

    D. New-Template

17. You need to see all of the location sets for the CRL distribution point (CDP). What PowerShell command would you use?

    A. View-CACrlDistributionPoint

    B. See-CACrlDistributionPoint

    C. Add-CACrlDistributionPoint

    D. Get-CACrlDistributionPoint

18. You have a server named Server1 that runs Windows Server 2016. You need to configure Server1 as a Web Application Proxy. Which server role or role service should you install on Server1?

A. Remote Access

B. Active Directory Federation Services

C. Web Server (IIS)

D. DirectAccess and VPN (RAS)

19. You have installed Active Directory Federation Services server and the Web Application Proxy. Which two inbound TCP ports should you open on the firewall? Each correct answer presents part of the solution.

A. 443

B. 390

C. 8443

D. 49443

20. You need to modify configuration settings for a server application role of an application in AD FS. What PowerShell command do you use?

A. Add-AdfsServerApplication

B. Set-AdfsServerApplication

C. Get-AdfsServerApplication

D. Install-AdfsServerApplication

Answers to Assessment Test

1. **B.** A domain controller can contain Active Directory information for only one domain. If you want to use a multidomain environment, you must use multiple domain controllers configured in either a tree or a forest setting. See Chapter 1 for more information.

2. **D.** NTFS has file-level security, and it makes efficient usage of disk space. Since this machine is to be configured as a domain controller, the configuration requires at least one NTFS partition to store the Sysvol information. See Chapter 1 for more information.

3. **B, C.** TCP/IP and DNS are both required when installing Active Directory. See Chapter 1 for more information.

4. **A.** The Get-ADUser command allows you to view Active Directory user accounts using PowerShell. See Chapter 2 for more information.

5. **C.** Administrators can use the Unlock-ADAccount command to unlock an Active Directory account. See Chapter 2 for more information.

6. **D.** The dsadd command allows you to add an object (user's account) to the Active Directory database. See Chapter 2 for more information.

7. **C.** Shortcut trusts are trusts setup between two domains in the same forest. See Chapter 3 for more information.

8. **B.** The NTDS settings for the site level are where you would activate and deactivate Global Catalogs. See Chapter 3 for more information.

9. **D.** The Delegation of Control Wizard is designed to allow administrators to set up permissions on specific Active Directory objects. See Chapter 3 for more information.

10. **A, C.** Administrators can create new Organizational Units (OUs) by using either the Active Directory Administrative Center or Active Directory Users and Computers. See Chapter 3 for more information.

11. **A.** You would use the Windows PowerShell Invoke-GPUpdate cmdlet. This PowerShell cmdlet allows you to force the GPO to reapply the policies immediately. See Chapter 4 for more information.

12. **A.** GPOs at the OU level take precedence over GPOs at the domain level. GPOs at the domain level, in turn, take precedence over GPOs at the site level. See Chapter 4 for more information.

13. **B.** The Block Policy Inheritance option prevents group policies of higher-level Active Directory objects from applying to lower-level objects as long as the Enforced option is not set. See Chapter 4 for more information.

14. **D.** To disable the application of Group Policy on a security group, you should deny the Apply Group Policy option. This is particularly useful when you don't want GPO settings to apply to a specific group, even though that group may be in an OU that includes the GPO settings. See Chapter 4 for more information.

15. B, D. To enable AD FS auditing, you must check the boxes for Success Audits and Failure Audits on the Events tab of the Federation Service Properties dialog box. You must also enable Object Access Auditing in Local Policy or Group Policy. See Chapter 5 for more information.

16. C. The Add-CATemplate command allows an administrator to add a certificate template to the CA. See Chapter 5 for more information.

17. D. Administrators can use the Get-CACrlDistributionPoint command to view all the locations set for the CRL distribution point (CDP). See Chapter 5 for more information.

18. A. To use the Web Application Proxy, you must install the Remote Access role. See Chapter 6 for more information.

19. A, D. To use a Web Application Proxy and AD FS, you should set your firewall to allow for ports 443 and 49443. See Chapter 6 for more information.

20. B. The Set-AdfsServerApplication command allows an administrator to modify configuration settings for a server application role of an application in AD FS. See Chapter 6 for more information.

MCSA
Windows Server® 2016
Complete Study Guide

Chapter

1

Installing Active Directory

THE FOLLOWING 70-742 EXAM OBJECTIVES ARE COVERED IN THIS CHAPTER:

✓ **Install and configure domain controllers**

- This objective may include but is not limited to: Install a new forest; add or remove a domain controller from a domain; upgrade a domain controller; install AD DS on a Server Core installation; install a domain controller from Install from Media (IFM); resolve DNS SRV record registration issues; install and configure a read-only domain controller (RODC); configure domain controller cloning

One of the most important tasks that you will complete on a network is setting up your domain. To set up your domain properly, you must know how to install and configure your domain controllers.

After I show you how to install and configure your domain controller, you'll explore the concept of *domain functional levels*, which essentially determine what sorts of domain controllers you can use in your environment. For instance, in the Windows Server 2008 domain functional level, you can have Windows Server 2008/2008 R2, Windows Server 2012/2012 R2, and Windows Server 2016 domain controllers, but the functionality of the domain is severely limited. Also, you CAN NOT have any domain controllers below the domain function level (no domain controllers below 2008 in this example).

Once you understand how to plan properly for your domain environment, you will learn how to install Active Directory, which you will accomplish by promoting a Windows Server 2016 computer to a domain controller. I will also discuss a feature in Windows Server 2016 called a *read-only domain controller (RODC)*, and I will show you how to install Active Directory using Windows PowerShell.

For these exercises, I assume you are creating a Windows Server 2016 machine in a test environment and not on a live network.

Verifying the File System

When you're planning your Active Directory deployment, the file system that the operating system uses is an important concern for two reasons. First, the file system can provide the ultimate level of security for all the information stored on the server itself. Second, it is responsible for managing and tracking all of this data. The Windows Server 2016 platform supports three file systems:

- File Allocation Table 32 (FAT32)
- Windows NT File System (NTFS)
- Resilient File System (ReFS)

Although ReFS was new to Windows Server 2012, NTFS has been around for many years, and NTFS in Windows Server 2016 has been improved for better performance.

If you have been working with servers for many years, you may have noticed a few changes to the server file system choices. For example, in Windows Server 2003, you could choose between FAT, FAT32, and NTFS. In Windows Server 2016, you could choose between FAT32, NTFS, and ReFS (see Figure 1.1).

FIGURE 1.1   Format options on Windows Server 2016

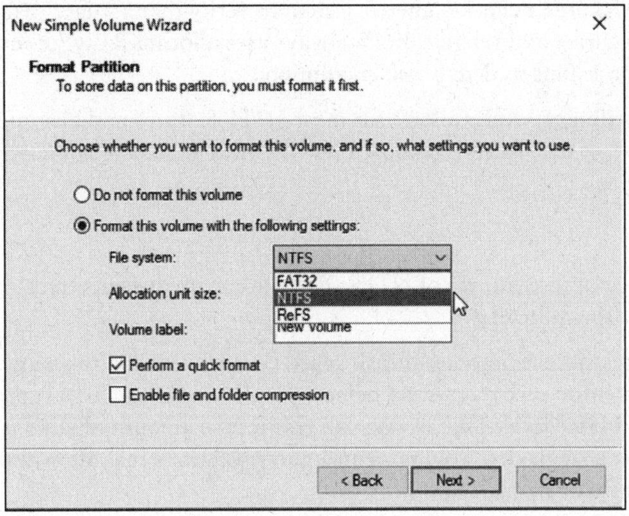

Resilient File System (ReFS)

Windows Server 2016 includes a file system called *Resilient File System (ReFS)*. ReFS was created to help Windows Server maximize the availability of data and online operation. ReFS allows the Windows Server 2016 system to continue to function despite some errors that would normally cause data to be lost or the system to go down. ReFS uses data integrity to protect your data from errors and also to make sure that all of your important data is online when that data is needed.

One of the issues that IT members have had to face over the years is the problem of rapidly growing data sizes. As we continue to rely more and more on computers, our data continues to get larger and larger. This is where ReFS can help an IT department. ReFS was designed specifically with the issues of scalability and performance in mind, which resulted in some of the following ReFS features:

Availability   If your hard disk becomes corrupt, ReFS has the ability to implement a salvage strategy that removes the data that has been corrupted. This feature allows the healthy data to continue to be available while the unhealthy data is removed. All of this can be done without taking the hard disk offline.

Scalability   One of the main advantages of ReFS is the ability to support volume sizes up to 2^{78} bytes using 16 KB cluster sizes, while Windows stack addressing allows 2^{64} bytes. ReFS also supports file sizes of $2^{64}-1$ bytes, 2^{64} files in a directory, and the same number of directories in a volume.

Robust Disk Updating   ReFS uses a disk updating system referred to as an *allocate-on-write transactional model* (also known as *copy on write*). This model helps to avoid many hard disk issues while data is written to the disk because ReFS updates data using disk writes to multiple locations in an atomic manner instead of updating data in place.

Data Integrity   ReFS uses a check-summed system to verify that all data that is being written and stored is accurate and reliable. ReFS always uses allocate-on-write for updates to the data, and it uses checksums to detect disk corruption.

Application Compatibility   ReFS allows for most NTFS features and also supports the Win32 API. Because of this, ReFS is compatible with most Windows applications.

NTFS

Let's start with some of the features of NTFS. There are many benefits to using NTFS, including support for the following:

Disk Quotas   To restrict the amount of disk space used by users on the network, system administrators can establish *disk quotas*. By default, Windows Server 2016 supports disk quota restrictions at the volume level. That is, you can restrict the amount of storage space that a specific user uses on a single disk volume. Third-party solutions that allow more granular quota settings are also available.

File System Encryption   One of the fundamental problems with network operating systems (NOSs) is that system administrators are often given full permission to view all files and data stored on hard disks, which can be a security and privacy concern. In some cases, this is necessary. For example, to perform backup, recovery, and disk management functions, at least one user must have all permissions. Windows Server 2016 and NTFS address these issues by allowing for *file system encryption*. Encryption essentially scrambles all of the data stored within files before they are written to the disk. When an authorized user requests the files, they are transparently decrypted and provided. By using encryption, you can prevent the data from being used in case it is stolen or intercepted by an unauthorized user—even a system administrator.

Dynamic Volumes   Protecting against disk failures is an important concern for production servers. Although earlier versions of Windows NT supported various levels of Redundant Array of Independent Disks (RAID) technology, software-based solutions had some shortcomings. Perhaps the most significant was that administrators needed to perform server reboots to change RAID configurations. Also, you could not make some configuration changes without completely reinstalling the operating system. With Windows Server 2016 support for *dynamic volumes*, system administrators can change RAID and other disk configuration settings without needing to reboot or reinstall the server. The result is greater data protection, increased scalability, and increased uptime. Dynamic volumes are also included with ReFS.

Mounted Drives   By using *mounted drives*, system administrators can map a local disk drive to an NTFS directory name. This helps them organize disk space on servers and increase manageability. By using mounted drives, you can mount the C:\Users directory to an actual physical disk. If that disk becomes full, you can copy all of the files to another, larger drive without changing the directory path name or reconfiguring applications.

Remote Storage   System administrators often notice that as soon as they add more space, they must plan the next upgrade. One way to recover disk space is to move infrequently used files to external hard drives. However, backing up and restoring these files can be quite difficult and time-consuming. System administrators can use the *remote storage* features supported by NTFS to off-load seldom-used data automatically to a backup system or other devices. The files, however, remain available to users. If a user requests an archived file, Windows Server 2016 can automatically restore the file from a remote storage device and make it available. Using remote storage like this frees up system administrators' time and allows them to focus on tasks other than micromanaging disk space.

Self-Healing NTFS   In previous versions of the Windows Server operating system, if you had to fix a corrupted NTFS volume, you used a tool called Chkdsk.exe. The disadvantage of this tool is that the Windows Server's availability was disrupted. If this server was your domain controller, that could stop domain logon authentication.

To help protect the Windows Server 2016 NTFS file system, Microsoft now uses a feature called self-healing NTFS. *Self-healing NTFS* attempts to fix corrupted NTFS file systems without taking them offline. Self-healing NTFS allows an NTFS file system to be corrected without running the Chkdsk.exe utility. New features added to the NTFS kernel code allow disk inconsistencies to be corrected without system downtime.

Security   NTFS allows you to configure not only folder-level security but also file-level security. NTFS security is one of the biggest reasons most companies use NTFS. ReFS also allows folder- and file-level security.

Setting Up the NTFS Partition

Although the features mentioned in the previous section likely compel most system administrators to use NTFS, additional reasons make using it mandatory. The most important reason is that the Active Directory data store must reside on an NTFS partition. Therefore, before you begin installing Active Directory, make sure you have at least one NTFS partition available. Also, be sure you have a reasonable amount of disk space available (at least 4 GB). Because the size of the Active Directory data store will grow as you add objects to it, also be sure that you have adequate space for the future.

Exercise 1.1 shows you how to use the administrative tools to view and modify disk configuration.

Before you make any disk configuration changes, be sure you completely understand their potential effects; then perform the test in a lab environment and make sure you have good, verifiable backups handy. Changing partition sizes and adding and removing partitions can result in a total loss of all information on one or more partitions.

If you want to convert an existing partition from FAT or FAT32 to NTFS, you need to use the CONVERT command-line utility. For example, the following command converts the C: partition from FAT to NTFS:

```
CONVERT c: /fs:ntfs
```

EXERCISE 1.1

Viewing the Disk Configurations

1. Right-click on the Start button and then choose Computer Management.

2. Under Storage, click Disk Management (see Figure 1.2).

FIGURE 1.2   Disk Management

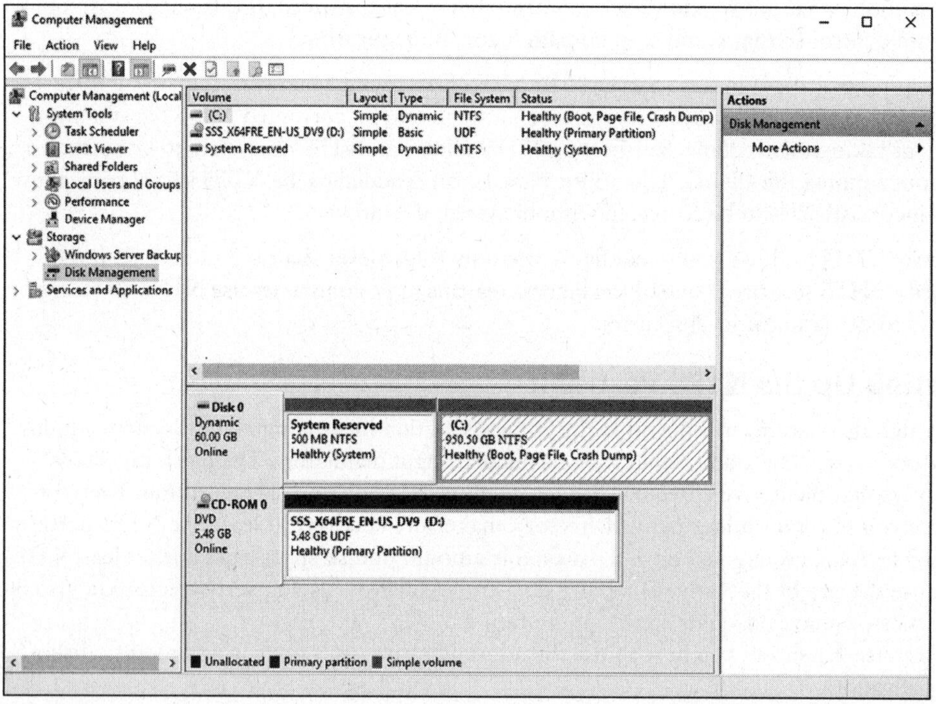

The Disk Management program shows you the logical and physical disks that are currently configured on your system.

3. Use the View menu to choose various depictions of the physical and logical drives in your system.

4. To see the available options for modifying partition settings, right-click any of the disks or partitions. This step is optional.

5. Close Computer Management.

Verifying Network Connectivity

Although a Windows Server 2016 computer can be used by itself without connecting to a network, you will not harness much of the potential of the operating system without network connectivity. Because the fundamental purpose of a network operating system is to provide resources to users, you must verify network connectivity.

Basic Connectivity Tests

Before you begin to install Active Directory, you should perform several checks of your current configuration to ensure that the server is configured properly on the network. You should test the following:

Network Adapter At least one network adapter should be installed and properly configured on your server. A quick way to verify that a network adapter is properly installed is to use the Computer Management administrative tool. Under Device Manager, Network Adapters branch, you should have at least one network adapter listed. If you do not, use the Add Hardware icon in Control Panel to configure hardware.

TCP/IP Make sure that TCP/IP is installed, configured, and enabled on any necessary network adapters. The server should also be given a valid IP address and subnet mask. Optionally, you may need to configure a default gateway, DNS servers, WINS servers, and other network settings. If you are using DHCP, be sure that the assigned information is correct. It is always a good idea to use a static IP address for servers because IP address changes can cause network connectivity problems if they are not handled properly.

Internet Access If the server should have access to the Internet, verify that it is able to connect to external web servers and other machines outside of the local area network (LAN). If the server is unable to connect, you might have a problem with the TCP/IP configuration.

LAN Access The server should be able to view other servers and workstations on the network. If other machines are not visible, make sure that the network and TCP/IP configurations are correct for your environment.

Client Access Network client computers should be able to connect to your server and view any shared resources. A simple way to test connectivity is to create a share and test whether other machines are able to see files and folders within it. If clients cannot access the machine, make sure that both the client and the server are configured properly.

Wide Area Network Access   If you're working in a distributed environment, you should ensure that you have access to any remote sites or users who will need to connect to this machine. Usually, this is a simple test that can be performed by a network administrator.

Tools and Techniques for Testing Network Configuration

In some cases, verifying network access can be quite simple. You might have some internal and external network resources with which to test. In other cases, it might be more complicated. You can use several tools and techniques to verify that your network configuration is correct.

The Windows Server 2016 exams will include a lot of PowerShell commands. One easy way to start getting familiar with PowerShell is to use it whenever you need to run a network configuration command. All of the following commands work in PowerShell.

Using the `Ipconfig` **Utility**   By typing **ipconfig/all** at the command prompt, you can view information about the TCP/IP settings of a computer. Figure 1.3 shows the types of information you'll receive.

FIGURE 1.3   Viewing TCP/IP information with the `ipconfig` utility

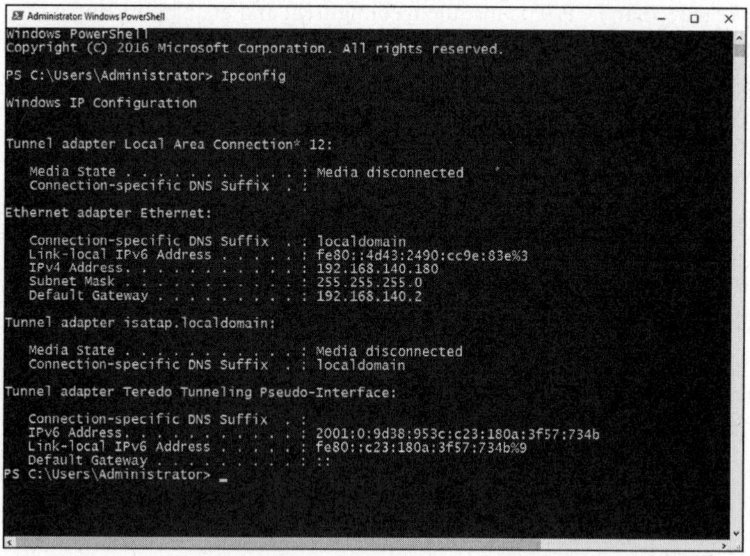

```
Administrator: Windows PowerShell                                    —  □  ×
Windows PowerShell
Copyright (C) 2016 Microsoft Corporation. All rights reserved.

PS C:\Users\Administrator> Ipconfig

Windows IP Configuration

Tunnel adapter Local Area Connection* 12:

   Media State . . . . . . . . . . . : Media disconnected
   Connection-specific DNS Suffix . :

Ethernet adapter Ethernet:

   Connection-specific DNS Suffix . : localdomain
   Link-local IPv6 Address . . . . . : fe80::4d43:2490:cc9e:83e%3
   IPv4 Address. . . . . . . . . . . : 192.168.140.180
   Subnet Mask . . . . . . . . . . . : 255.255.255.0
   Default Gateway . . . . . . . . . : 192.168.140.2

Tunnel adapter isatap.localdomain:

   Media State . . . . . . . . . . . : Media disconnected
   Connection-specific DNS Suffix . : localdomain

Tunnel adapter Teredo Tunneling Pseudo-Interface:

   Connection-specific DNS Suffix . :
   IPv6 Address. . . . . . . . . . . : 2001:0:9d38:953c:c23:180a:3f57:734b
   Link-local IPv6 Address . . . . . : fe80::c23:180a:3f57:734b%9
   Default Gateway . . . . . . . . . : ::
PS C:\Users\Administrator> _
```

Using the Ping **Command**   The ping command was designed to test connectivity to other computers. You can use the command simply by typing **ping** and then an IP address or hostname at the command line. The following are some steps for testing connectivity using the ping command.

Ping Other Computers on the Same Subnet   You should start by pinging a known active IP address on the network to check for a response. If you receive one, then you have connectivity to the network.

Next check to see whether you can ping another machine using its hostname. If this works, then local name resolution works properly.

Ping Computers on Different Subnets   To ensure that routing is set up properly, you should attempt to ping computers that are on other subnets (if any exist) on your network. If this test fails, try pinging the default gateway. Any errors may indicate a problem in the network configuration or a problem with a router.

When You Don't Receive a Response

Some firewalls, routers, or servers on your network or on the Internet might prevent you from receiving a successful response from a ping command. This is usually for security reasons (malicious users might attempt to disrupt network traffic using excessive pings as well as redirects and smurf attacks). If you do not receive a response, do not assume that the service is not available. Instead, try to verify connectivity in other ways. For example, you can use the TRACERT command to demonstrate connectivity beyond your subnet, even if other routers ignore Internet Control Message Protocol (ICMP) responses. Because the display of a second router implies connectivity, the path to an ultimate destination shows success even if it does not display the actual names and addresses.

Using the TraceRT **Command**   The TraceRT command works just like the ping command except that the TraceRT command shows you every hop along the way. So if one router or switch is down, the TraceRT command will show you where the trace stops.

Browsing the Network   To ensure that you have access to other computers on the network, be sure that they can be viewed by clicking Network. This verifies that your name resolution parameters are set up correctly and that other computers are accessible. Also, try connecting to resources (such as file shares or printers) on other machines.

   By default, Network Discovery is turned off. To browse the network, you must first enable Network Discovery from the Control Panel in the Network and Sharing Center ➤ Advanced Sharing settings.

Browsing the Internet   You can quickly verify whether your server has access to the Internet by visiting a known website, such as www.microsoft.com. Success ensures that you have access outside of your network. If you do not have access to the web, you might need to verify your proxy server settings (if applicable) and your DNS server settings.

By performing these simple tests, you can ensure that you have a properly configured network connection and that other network resources are available.

Understanding Domain and Forest Functionality

Windows Server 2016 Active Directory uses a concept called *domain and forest functionality*. The functional level that you choose during the Active Directory installation determines which features your domain can use.

About the Domain Functional Level

Windows Server 2016 will support the following domain functional levels:

- Windows Server 2008
- Windows Server 2008 R2
- Windows Server 2012
- Windows Server 2012 R2
- Windows Server 2016

Which function level you use depends on the domain controllers you have installed on your network. This is an important fact to remember. You can use any version of Windows Server as long as those servers are member servers only. You can only use Domain Controllers as low as your function level.

For example, if the Domain Function Level is Windows Server 2012 R2, then all domain controllers must be running Windows Server 2012 R2 or higher. You can have Windows Server 2008 R2 member servers but all of your domain controllers need to be at least 2012 R2.

> Windows Server 2016 no longer supports the Windows Server 2003 function levels. With Windows Server 2003 being no longer supported, the Windows Server 2003 function levels have been removed.

Table 1.1 shows the features available in Windows Server 2008, Windows Server 2008 R2, Windows Server 2012, Windows Server 2012 R2, and Windows Server 2016 domain function levels.

TABLE 1.1   Comparing domain functional levels

Domain Functional Feature	Windows Server 2008	Windows Server 2008 R2	Windows Server 2012	Windows Server 2012 R2	Windows Server 2016
Privileged access management	Disabled	Disabled	Disabled	Enabled	Enabled
Authentication assurance	Disabled	Enabled	Enabled	Enabled	Enabled
Fine-grained password policies	Enabled	Enabled	Enabled	Enabled	Enabled
Last interactive logon information	Enabled	Enabled	Enabled	Enabled	Enabled
Advanced Encryption Services (AES 128 and 256) support for the Kerberos protocol	Enabled	Enabled	Enabled	Enabled	Enabled
Distributed File System replication support for Sysvol	Enabled	Enabled	Enabled	Enabled	Enabled
Read-only domain controller (RODC)	Enabled	Enabled	Enabled	Enabled	Enabled
Ability to redirect the Users and Computers containers	Enabled	Enabled	Enabled	Enabled	Enabled
Ability to rename domain controllers	Enabled	Enabled	Enabled	Enabled	Enabled
Logon time stamp updates	Enabled	Enabled	Enabled	Enabled	Enabled
Kerberos KDC key version numbers	Enabled	Enabled	Enabled	Enabled	Enabled
Passwords for InetOrgPerson objects	Enabled	Enabled	Enabled	Enabled	Enabled
Converts NT groups to domain local and global groups	Enabled	Enabled	Enabled	Enabled	Enabled
SID history	Enabled	Enabled	Enabled	Enabled	Enabled
Group nesting	Enabled	Enabled	Enabled	Enabled	Enabled
Universal groups	Enabled	Enabled	Enabled	Enabled	Enabled

About Forest Functionality

Windows Server 2016 forest functionality applies to all of the domains in a forest. All domains have to be upgraded to Windows Server 2016 before the forest can be upgraded to Windows Server 2016.

There are five levels of forest functionality:

▪ Windows Server 2008

▪ Windows Server 2008 R2

▪ Windows Server 2012

▪ Windows Server 2012 R2

▪ Windows Server 2016

Windows Server 2008, Windows Server 2008 R2, Windows Server 2012, Windows Server 2012 R2, and Windows Server 2016 have many of the same forest features. Some of these features are described in the following list:

Global Catalog Replication Enhancements   When an administrator adds a new attribute to the global catalog, only those changes are replicated to other global catalogs in the forest. This can significantly reduce the amount of network traffic generated by replication.

Defunct Schema Classes and Attributes   You can never permanently remove classes and attributes from the Active Directory schema. However, you can mark them as defunct so that they cannot be used. With Windows Server 2003, Windows Server 2008/2008 R2, Windows Server 2012/2012 R2, and Windows Server 2016 forest functionality, you can redefine the defunct schema attribute so that it occupies a new role in the schema.

Forest Trusts   Previously, system administrators had no easy way of granting permission on resources in different forests. Windows Server 2003, Windows Server 2008/2008 R2, Windows Server 2012/2012 R2, and Windows Server 2016 resolve some of these difficulties by allowing trust relationships between separate Active Directory forests. Forest trusts act much like domain trusts, except that they extend to every domain in two forests. Note that all forest trusts are intransitive.

Linked Value Replication   Windows Server 2003, Windows Server 2008/2008 R2, Windows Server 2012/2012 R2, and Windows Server 2016 use a concept called *linked value replication*. With linked value replication, only the user record that has been changed is replicated (not the entire group). This can significantly reduce network traffic associated with replication.

Renaming Domains   Although the Active Directory domain structure was originally designed to be flexible, there were several limitations. Because of mergers, acquisitions, corporate reorganizations, and other business changes, you may need to rename domains. In Windows Server 2003, Windows Server 2008/2008 R2, Windows Server 2012/2012 R2, and Windows Server 2016 you can change the DNS and NetBIOS names for any domain. Note that this operation is not as simple as just issuing a rename command. Instead, there's a specific process that you must follow to make sure the operation is successful. Fortunately, when you properly follow the procedure, Microsoft supports domain renaming even though not all applications support it.

Other Features   Windows Server 2008/2008 R2, Windows Server 2012/2012 R2, and Windows Server 2016 also support the following features:

- Improved replication algorithms and dynamic auxiliary classes are designed to increase performance, scalability, and reliability.

- *Active Directory Federation Services (AD FS)*, also known as *Trustbridge*, handles federated identity management. *Federated identity management* is a standards-based information technology process that enables distributed identification, authentication, and authorization across organizational and platform boundaries. The ADFS solution in Windows Server 2008, Windows Server 2008 R2, Windows Server 2012, Windows Server 2012 R2, and Windows Server 2016 helps administrators address these challenges by enabling organizations to share a user's identity information securely.

- *Active Directory Lightweight Directory Services (AD LDS)* was developed for organizations that require flexible support for directory-enabled applications. AD LDS, which uses the Lightweight Directory Access Protocol (LDAP), is a directory service that adds flexibility and helps organizations avoid increased infrastructure costs.

- Active Directory Recycle Bin (Windows Server 2008 R2 Forest level or higher) provides administrators with the ability to restore deleted objects in their entirety while AD DS is running. Before this, if you deleted an Active Directory object, you needed to recover it from a backup. Now you can recover the object from the AD recycle bin.

  Many of the concepts related to domain and forest functional features are covered in greater detail later in this book.

Planning the Domain Structure

Once you have verified the technical configuration of your server for Active Directory, it's time to verify the Active Directory configuration for your organization. Since the content of this chapter focuses on installing the first domain in your environment, you really need to know only the following information prior to beginning setup:

- The DNS name of the domain

- The computer name or the NetBIOS name of the server (which will be used by previous versions of Windows to access server resources)

- In which domain function level the domain will operate

- Whether other DNS servers are available on the network
- What type of and how many DNS servers are available on the network

 DNS is a requirement of Active Directory. You can install DNS during the Active Directory installation. For more information about DNS, please read *MCSA Windows Server 2016 Study Guide: Exam 70-742, 2nd Edition* (Sybex, 2017), or Chapter 11 in the *MCSA Windows Server 2016 Complete Study Guide: Exam 70-740, Exam 70-741, Exam 70-742, and Exam 70-743, 2nd Edition,* by William Panek (Sybex, 2017).

However, if you will be installing additional domain controllers in your environment or will be attaching to an existing Active Directory structure, you should also have the following information:

- If this domain controller will join an existing domain, you should know the name of that domain. You will also either require a password for a member of the Enterprise Administrators group for that domain or have someone with those permissions create a domain account before promotion.

- You should know whether the new domain will join an existing tree and, if so, the name of the tree it will join.

- You should know the name of a forest to which this domain will connect (if applicable).

Installing Active Directory

Installing Active Directory is an easy and straightforward process as long as you plan adequately and make the necessary decisions beforehand. There are many ways that you can install Active Directory. You can install Active Directory by using the Windows Server 2016 installation disk (Install from Media (IFM)), using Server Manager, or using Windows PowerShell. But before you can do the actual installation, you must first make sure that your network is ready for the install.

In the following sections, you'll look at the benefits and required steps to install the first domain controller in a given environment.

New to Active Directory

As with any new version of Windows Server, Microsoft has made some improvements to Active Directory. The following changes have been made to Windows Server 2016 Active Directory:

Privileged Access Management   Privileged access management (PAM) allows you to alleviate security concerns about the Active Directory environment. Some of these security issues include credential theft techniques (pass-the-hash & spear phishing) along with other types of similar attacks. PAM allows an administrator to create new access solutions that can be configured by using Microsoft Identity Manager (MIM).

Azure AD Join   Azure Active Directory Join allows you to setup an Office 365 based Azure network and then easily join your end-users systems to that domain.

Microsoft Passport   Microsoft Passport allows your users to setup a key-based authentication that allows your users to authenticate by using more than just their password (biometrics or PIN numbers). Your users would then log on to their systems using a biometric or PIN number that is linked to a certificate or an asymmetrical key pair.

Read-Only Domain Controllers

Windows Server 2016 supports another type of domain controller called the *read-only domain controller (RODC)*. This is a full copy of the Active Directory database without the ability to write to Active Directory. The RODC gives an organization the ability to install a domain controller in a location (onsite or offsite) where security is a concern.

RODCs need to get their Active Directory database from another domain controller. If there are no domain controllers setup yet for a domain, RODCs will not be available (the option will be greyed out). Implementing an RODC is the same as adding another domain controller to a domain. The installation is exactly the same except that when you get to the screen to choose Domain Controller options, you check the box for RODC. Again, this is ONLY available if there are other domain controllers already in the domain.

Adprep

When you are adding a new user to Active Directory, you fill in fields such as First Name, Last Name, and so on. These fields are called *attributes*. The problem is that when you go to install Windows Server 2016, its version of Active Directory has newer attributes than the previous versions of Active Directory. Thus, you need to set up your current version of Active Directory so that it can accept the installation of Windows Server 2016 Active Directory. This is why you use Adprep. Adprep is required to run in order to add the first Windows Server 2016 domain controller to an existing domain or forest.

You would need to run `Adprep /forestprep` to add the first Windows Server 2016 domain controller to an existing forest. `Adprep /forestprep` must be run by an administrator who is a member of the Enterprise Admins group, the Schema Admins group, and the Domain Admins group of the domain that hosts the schema master.

You would need to run `Adprep /domainprep` to add the first Windows Server 2016 domain controller to an existing domain. Again, to achieve this command, you must be a member of the Domain Admins group of the domain where you are installing the Windows Server 2016 domain controller.

`Adprep /rodcprep` must be run to add the first Windows Server 2016 RODC to an existing forest. The administrator who runs this command must be a member of the Enterprise Admins group.

One feature that is new to the Windows Server 2016 Active Directory installation process is that, if needed, Adprep will automatically be executed during the normal Active Directory Domain Services installation.

Active Directory Prerequisites

Before you install Active Directory into your network, you must first make sure that your network and the server meet some minimum requirements. Table 1.2 will show you the requirements needed for Active Directory.

TABLE 1.2 Active Directory requirements

Requirement	Description
Adprep	When adding the first Windows Server 2016 domain controller to an existing Active Directory domain, Adprep commands run automatically as needed.
Credentials	When installing a new AD DS forest, the administrator must be set to local Administrator on the first server. To install an additional domain controller in an existing domain, you need to be a member of the Domain Admins group.
DNS	Domain Name System needs to be installed for Active Directory to function properly. You can install DNS during the Active Directory installation.
NTFS	The Windows Server 2016 drives that store the database, log files, and SYSVOL folder must be placed on a volume that is formatted with the NTFS file system.
RODCs	Read Only Domain Controllers can be installed as long as another domain controller (Windows Server 2008 or newer) already exists on the domain. Also the Forest functional level must be at least Windows Server 2003.
TCP/IP	You must configure the appropriate TCP/IP settings on your domain, and you must configure the DNS server addresses.

The Installation Process

Windows Server 2016 computers are configured as either member servers (if they are joined to a domain) or standalone servers (if they are part of a workgroup). The process of converting a server to a domain controller is known as *promotion*. Through the use of a simple and intuitive wizard in Server Manager, system administrators can quickly configure servers to be domain controllers after installation. Administrators also have the ability to promote domain controllers using Windows PowerShell.

The first step in installing Active Directory is promoting a Windows Server 2016 computer to a domain controller. The first domain controller in an environment serves as the starting point for the forest, trees, domains, and the operations master roles.

Exercise 1.2 shows the steps you need to follow to promote an existing Windows Server 2016 computer to a domain controller. To complete the steps in this exercise, you must have already installed and configured a Windows Server 2016 computer. You also need a DNS server that supports SRV records. If you do not have a DNS server available, the Active Directory Installation Wizard automatically configures one for you.

EXERCISE 1.2

Promoting a Domain Controller

1. Install the Active Directory Domain Services by clicking the Add Roles And Features link in Server Manager's Dashboard view.

2. At the Before You Begin screen, click Next.

3. The Select Installation Type screen will be next. Make sure that the Role-Based radio button is selected and click Next.

4. At the Select Destination Server screen, choose the local machine. Click Next.

5. At the Select Server Roles screen, click the check box for Active Directory Domain Services.

6. After you check the Active Directory Domain Services box, a pop-up menu will appear asking you to install additional features. Click the Add Features button.

7. Click Next.

8. At the Select Features screen, accept the defaults and click Next.

9. Click Next at the information screen.

10. Click the Install button at the Confirmation Installation screen.

11. The Installation Progress screen will show you how the installation is progressing.

12. After the installation is complete, click the Close button.

13. On the left side window, click the AD DS link.

14. Click the More link next to Configuration Required for Active Directory Domain Services.

EXERCISE 1.2 *(continued)*

15. Under the Post-Deployment Configuration section, click the Promote This Server To A Domain Controller link.
16. At this point, you will configure this domain controller. You are going to install a new domain controller in a new domain in a new forest. At the Deployment Configuration screen, choose the Add A New Forest radio button. You then need to add a root domain name. In this exercise, I will use `StormWindAD.com` (see Figure 1.4). Click Next.

FIGURE 1.4 New Forest screen

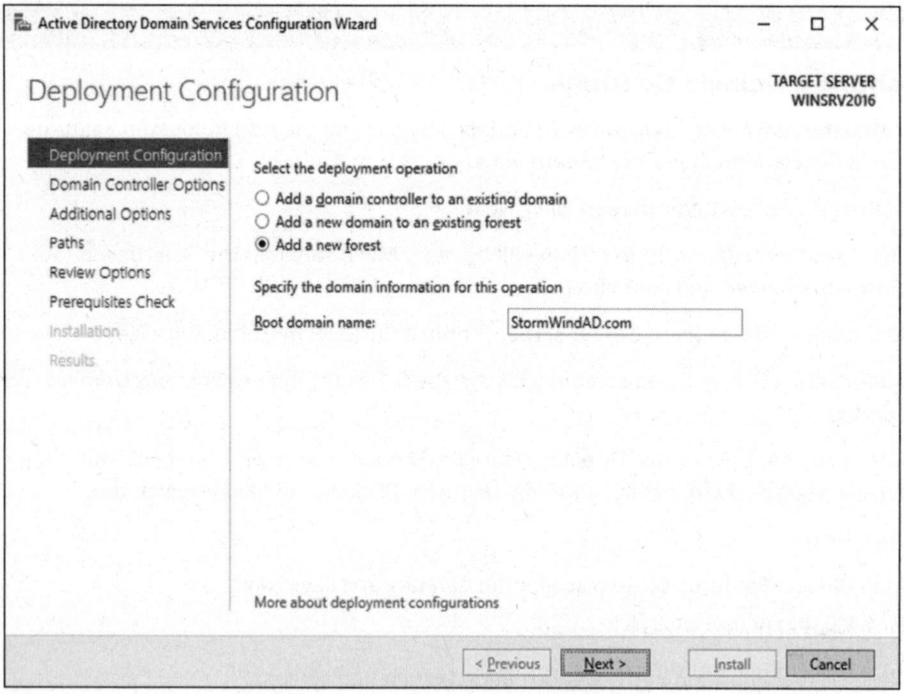

17. At the Domain Controller Options screen, set the following options (see Figure 1.5):
    - Function levels: Windows Server 2012 R2 (for both)
    - Verify that the DNS and Global Catalog check boxes are checked. Notice that the RODC check box is greyed out. This is because RODCs need to get their Active Directory database from another domain controller. Since this is the first domain controller in the forest, RODCs are not possible. If you need an RODC, complete

the previous steps on a member server in a domain where domain controllers already exist.

- Password: **P@ssw0rd**

Then click Next.

FIGURE 1.5   Domain Controller Options

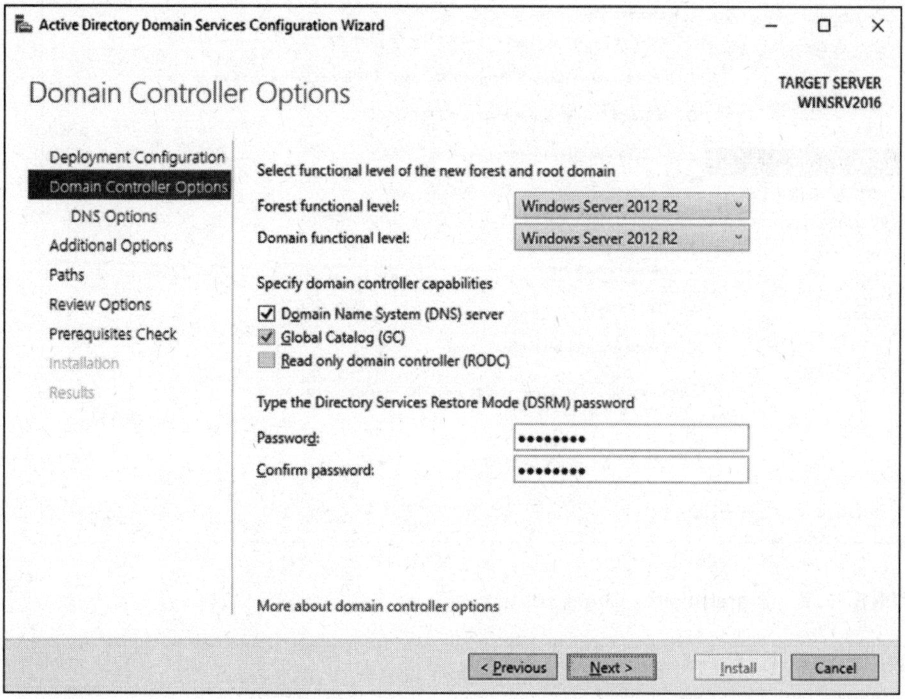

18. At the DNS screen, click Next.

19. At the additional options screen, accept the default NetBIOS domain name and click Next.

20. At the Paths screen, accept the default file locations and click Next.

21. At the Review Options screen (see Figure 1.6), verify your settings and click Next. At this screen, there is a View Script button. This button allows you to grab a PowerShell script based on the features you have just set up.

22. At the Prerequisites Check screen, click the Install button (as long as there are no errors). Warnings are OK just as long as there are no errors (see Figure 1.7).

EXERCISE 1.2 *(continued)*

FIGURE 1.6 Review Options screen

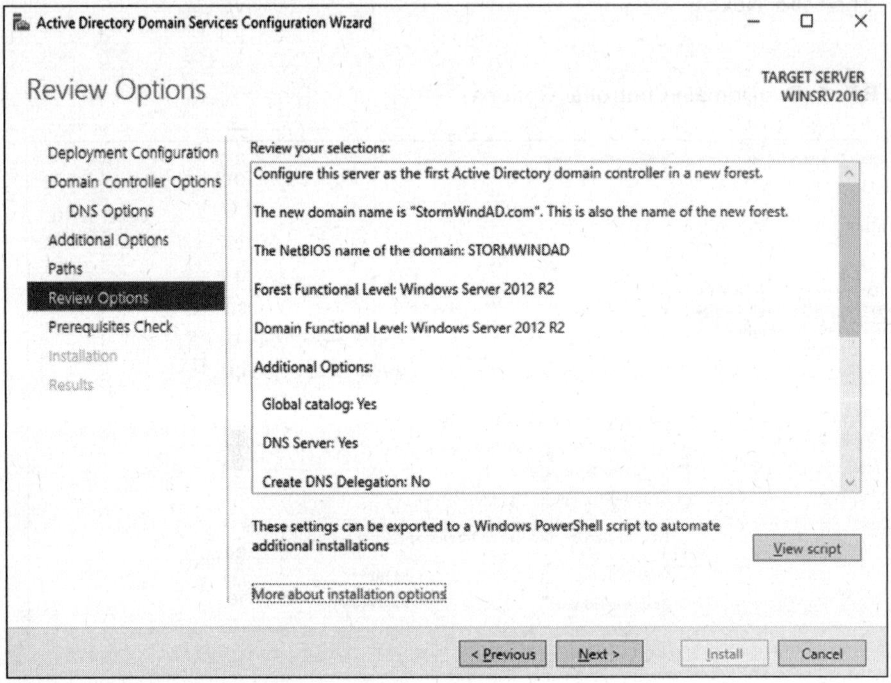

FIGURE 1.7 Prerequisites Check screen

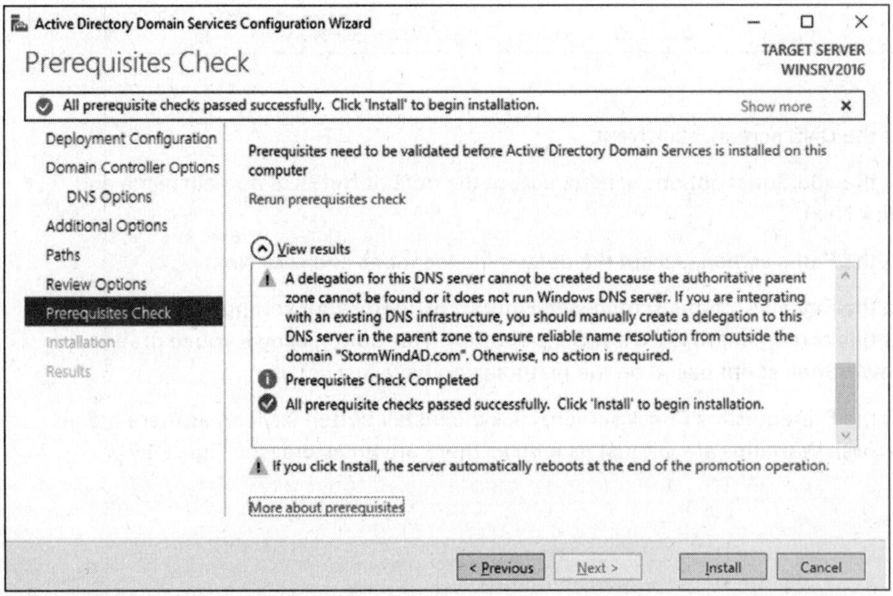

23. After the installation completes, the machine will automatically reboot. Log in as the administrator.

24. Close Server Manager.

25. Click the Start button on the keyboard and choose Administrative Tools.

26. You should see new MMC snap-ins for Active Directory.

27. Close the Administrative Tools window.

In Exercise 1.3, you will learn how to install Active Directory on a Server Core installation. You will use Windows Server 2016 Datacenter Server Core. Before actually installing AD DS, you will learn how to configure the computer name, the time, the administrator password, and a static TCP/IP address, and then you will install DNS.

Exercise 1.3 will have you install Active Directory onto a Datacenter Server Core server using Microsoft PowerShell. If you need to install Active Directory onto any Windows Server 2016 server using PowerShell, it's the same steps in this exercise.

EXERCISE 1.3

Installing AD DS on Server Core Using PowerShell

1. At the Server Core command prompt, type **cd\windows\system32** and press Enter.

2. Type **timedate.cpl** and set your date, local time zone, and time. Click OK.

3. Type **Netsh** and press Enter.

4. Type **Interface**, and press Enter.

5. Type **IPv4,** and press Enter.

6. Type **Show IP** and press Enter. This will show you the current TCP/IP address and the interface with which the TCP/IP address is associated.

7. As you can see, interface 12 is my Ethernet interface. To change this interface, type the following command and press Enter:

```
Set address name="12" source=static address=192.168.0.165
mask=255.255.255.0 gateway=192.168.0.1
```

I used 192.168.0.x for my address. You can replace the address, mask, and gateway based on your local settings.

8. Type **Show IP** and press Enter. You should see that the new address is now manual and set to the IP address you set.

9. Type **Exit** and press Enter.

10. Type **Net User Administrator *** and press Enter.

EXERCISE 1.3 *(continued)*

---

11. Type in your password and then confirm the password. I used P@ssw0rd for my password.

12. Type the following command and press Enter:

    Netdom renamecomputer %computername% /newname:ServerA

13. Type **Y** and press Enter.

14. Type **Shutdown /R /T 0** and press Enter. This will reboot the machine. After the reboot, log back into the system.

15. Type **PowerShell** and press Enter.

16. At the PowerShell prompt, type **Add-WindowsFeature DNS** and press Enter. This will add DNS to the server.

17. At the PowerShell prompt, type **Add-WindowsFeature AD-Domain-Services** and press Enter.

18. At the PowerShell prompt, type **Import-Module ADDSDeployment**.

19. At the PowerShell prompt, type **Install-ADDSForest**.

20. Type in your domain name and press Enter. I used Sybex.com.

21. Next you will be asked for your Safe mode administrator password. Type in **P@ssw0rd** and then confirm it.

22. Type **Y** and press Enter.

Active Directory will install, and the machine will automatically reboot.

Now that we have installed Active Directory onto two different types of systems, let's take a look at how to install an RODC. In Exercise 1.4 I will show you how to add a RODC to a domain. To do this exercise, you need another domain controller in the domain.

EXERCISE 1.4

Creating an RODC Server

1. Install the Active Directory Domain Services by clicking the Add Roles And Features link in Server Manager's Dashboard view.

2. At the Before You Begin screen, click Next.

3. The Select Installation Type screen will be next. Make sure that the Role-Based radio button is selected and click Next.

4. At the Select Destination Server screen, choose the local machine. Click Next.

5. At the Select Server Roles screen, click the check box for Active Directory Domain Services.

6. After you check the Active Directory Domain Services box, a pop-up menu will appear asking you to install additional features. Click the Add Features button.

7. Click Next.

8. At the Select Features screen, accept the defaults and click Next.

9. Click Next at the information screen.

10. Click the Install button at the Confirmation Installation screen.

11. The Installation Progress screen will show you how the installation is progressing.

12. After the installation is complete, click the Close button.

13. On the left side window, click the AD DS link.

14. Click the More link next to Configuration Required for Active Directory Domain Services.

15. Under the Post-Deployment Configuration section, click the Promote This Server To A Domain Controller link.

16. At this point, you will configure this domain controller. You are going to install a new domain controller in an existing domain. At the Deployment Configuration screen, choose the Add A Domain Controller to an existing Domain. You then need to add the name of another domain controller in that domain.

17. At the Domain Controller Options screen, set the following options:

    ▪ Verify that the RODC check box is checked.

    ▪ Password: **P@ssw0rd**

    Then click Next.

18. At the Paths screen, accept the default file locations and click Next.

19. At the Review Options screen, verify your settings and click Next. At this screen, there is a View Script button. This button allows you to grab a PowerShell script based on the features you have just set up.

20. At the Prerequisites Check screen, click the Install button (as long as there are no errors). Warnings are OK just as long as there are no errors.

21. After the installation completes, the machine will automatically reboot. Log in as the administrator.

22. Close Server Manager.

Deploying Active Directory in Windows Azure

Well, before I jump into this topic, I must first explain what I am talking about. Windows Azure is a Microsoft cloud platform that allows you to put your server data into the cloud. Deploying Active Directory with Infrastructure as a Service (IaaS) means you are using virtualization for the deployment.

So, to put this in a nutshell, this type of install is actually not too far off from the install you already did. You create a virtual server and then install Active Directory. Then you upload that virtual server to the cloud.

Now that you understand what this section is about, let's talk about some of the tasks that are different from the normal way you install Active Directory virtually. There are three main differences when installing Active Directory IaaS on Windows Azure.

Windows Azure virtual machines may need to have connectivity to the corporate network. Microsoft states that you don't have to have connectivity to your onsite corporate network, but you will lose functionality. Thus, Microsoft recommends that you set up connectivity, and to do that, you must use Windows Azure Virtual Network. Windows Azure Virtual Network includes a site-to-site or site-to-point virtual private network (VPN) component capable of seamlessly connecting Windows Azure virtual machines and onsite machines.

Static IP addresses are *not* supported on Windows Azure virtual machines.   Normally, when setting up a server, we all use static IP addresses. This is actually required on a DHCP server, DNS server, and so on. But when you deploy Active Directory IaaS in Windows Azure, you must use Dynamic TCP/IP addressing, and this requires that you set up Windows Azure Virtual Network.

IP addresses for Windows Azure virtual machines are attached to Windows Azure Virtual Network, and that TCP/IP address persists for the lifetime of the virtual machine. Because of this, the Windows Server Active Directory requirements for IP addressing are met, and the requirements for DNS are also met if you want the server to have both roles.

Windows Azure allows for two distinct disk types for virtual machines.   The selection of the virtual machine disk type is important when deploying domain controllers. Windows Azure allows both "operating system disks" and "data disks." Most of the time you will use data disks when installing Active Directory on the virtual machine. Data disks use write-through caching, guaranteeing durability of writes, and this is important to the integrity of any Windows Server active machine. There are some other factors of which you should be aware when choosing your disk type. Please check Microsoft's website for more details when choosing a disk type.

Installing Additional Domain Controllers by Using Install from Media

There may be times when you need to install additional domain controllers without having a lot of additional replication traffic. When you can install a domain controller without the need of additional replication traffic, the installation is much quicker. This is the perfect time to install an additional domain controller by using the Install from Media (IFM) method.

Windows Server 2016 allows you to install a domain controller using the IFM method by using the `Ntdsutil` utility. The `Ntdsutil` utility allows you to create installation media for an additional domain controller in a domain. One issue that you must remember is that any objects that were created, modified, or deleted since the IFM was created must be replicated. By creating the IFM as close (time wise) as the installation of the domain controller guarantees that all objects will be created at the time the domain controller is installed.

One other way that you can also create the IFM is by restoring a backup of a similar domain controller in the same domain to another location.

Verifying Active Directory Installation

Once you have installed and configured Active Directory, you'll want to verify that you have done so properly. In the following sections, you'll look at methods for doing this.

Using Event Viewer

The first (and perhaps most informative) way to verify the operations of Active Directory is to query information stored in the Windows Server 2016 event log. You can do this using the Windows Server 2016 Event Viewer. Exercise 1.5 walks you through this procedure. Entries seen with the Event Viewer include errors, warnings, and informational messages.

To complete the steps in Exercise 1.5, you must have configured the local machine as a domain controller.

EXERCISE 1.5

Viewing the Active Directory Event Log

1. Open Administrative tools by pressing the Windows key and choosing Administrative Tools.

2. Open the Event Viewer snap-in from the Administrative Tools program group.

3. In the left pane, under Applications And Services Logs, select Directory Service.

4. In the right pane, you can sort information by clicking column headings. For example, you can click the Source column to sort by the service or process that reported the event.

5. Double-click an event in the list to see the details for that item. Note that you can click the Copy button to copy the event information to the Clipboard. You can then paste the data into a document for later reference. Also, you can move between items using the up and down arrows. Click OK when you have finished viewing an event.

6. Filter an event list by right-clicking the Directory Service item in the left pane and selecting Filter Current Log. Note that filtering does not remove entries from the event logs—it only restricts their display.

7. To verify Active Directory installation, look for events related to the proper startup of Active Directory, such as Event ID 1000 (Active Directory Startup Complete) and 1394 (Attempts To Update The Active Directory Database Are Succeeding). Also, be sure to examine any error or warning messages because they could indicate problems with DNS or other necessary services.

8. When you've finished viewing information in the Event Viewer, close the application.

Gaining Insight Through Event Viewer

Despite its simple user interface and somewhat limited GUI functionality, the Event Viewer tool can be your best ally in isolating and troubleshooting problems with Windows Server 2016. The Event Viewer allows you to view information that is stored in various log files that are maintained by the operating system. This includes information from the following logs:

Application Stores messages generated by programs running on your system. For example, SQL Server 2012 might report the completion of a database backup job within the Application log.

Security Contains security-related information as defined by your auditing settings. For example, you could see when users have logged onto the system or when particularly sensitive files have been accessed.

System Contains operating system-related information and messages. Common messages might include a service startup failure or information about when the operating system was last rebooted.

Directory Service Stores messages and events related to how Active Directory functions. For example, you might find details related to replication here.

DNS Server Contains details about the operations of the DNS service. This log is useful for troubleshooting replication or name-resolution problems.

Other Log Files Contain various features of Windows Server 2016 and the applications that may run on this operating system, which can create additional types of logs. These files allow you to view more information about other applications or services through the familiar Event Viewer tool.

Additionally, developers can easily send custom information from their programs to the Application log. Having all of this information in one place really makes it easy to analyze operating system and application messages. Also, many third-party tools and utilities are available for analyzing log files.

Although the Event Viewer GUI does a reasonably good job of letting you find the information you need, you might want to extract information to analyze other systems or applications. One especially useful feature of the Event Viewer is its ability to save a log file in various formats. You can access this feature by clicking Action ➢ Save As. You'll be given the option of saving in various formats, including tab- and comma-delimited text files. You can then open these files in other applications (such as Microsoft Excel) for additional data analysis.

Overall, in the real world, the Event Viewer can be an excellent resource for monitoring and troubleshooting your important servers and workstations.

In addition to providing information about the status of events related to Active Directory, the Event Viewer shows you useful information about other system services and applications. You should routinely use this tool.

Using Active Directory Administrative Tools

After a server has been promoted to a domain controller, you will see that various tools are added to the Administrative Tools program group, including the following:

Active Directory Administrative Center   This is a *Microsoft Management Console (MMC)* snap-in that allows you to accomplish many Active Directory tasks from one central location. This MMC snap-in allows you to manage your directory services objects, including doing the following tasks:

- Reset user passwords
- Create or manage user accounts
- Create or manage groups
- Create or manage computer accounts
- Create or manage organizational units (OUs) and containers
- Connect to one or several domains or domain controllers in the same instance of Active Directory Administrative Center
- Filter Active Directory data

Active Directory Domains and Trusts   Use this tool to view and change information related to the various domains in an Active Directory environment. This MMC snap-in also allows you to set up shortcut trusts.

Active Directory Sites and Services   Use this tool to create and manage Active Directory sites and services to map to an organization's physical network infrastructure.

Active Directory Users and Computers   User and computer management is fundamental for an Active Directory environment. The Active Directory Users and Computers tool allows you to set machine- and user-specific settings across the domain. This tool is discussed throughout this book.

Active Directory Module for Windows PowerShell   *Windows PowerShell* is a command-line shell and scripting language. The Active Directory Module for Windows PowerShell is a group of cmdlets used to manage your Active Directory domains, Active Directory Lightweight Directory Services (AD LDS) configuration sets, and Active Directory Database Mounting Tool instances in a single, self-contained package. The Active Directory Module for Windows PowerShell is a normal PowerShell window. The only difference is that the Active Directory PowerShell module is pre-loaded when you choose the Active Directory Module for Windows PowerShell.

A good way to make sure that Active Directory is accessible and functioning properly is to run the Active Directory Users and Computers tool. When you open the tool, you should see a configuration similar to that shown in Figure 1.8. Specifically, you should make sure the name of the domain you created appears in the list. You should also click the Domain Controllers folder and make sure that the name of your local server appears in the right pane. If your configuration passes these two checks, Active Directory is present and configured.

FIGURE 1.8   Viewing Active Directory information using the Active Directory Users and Computers tool

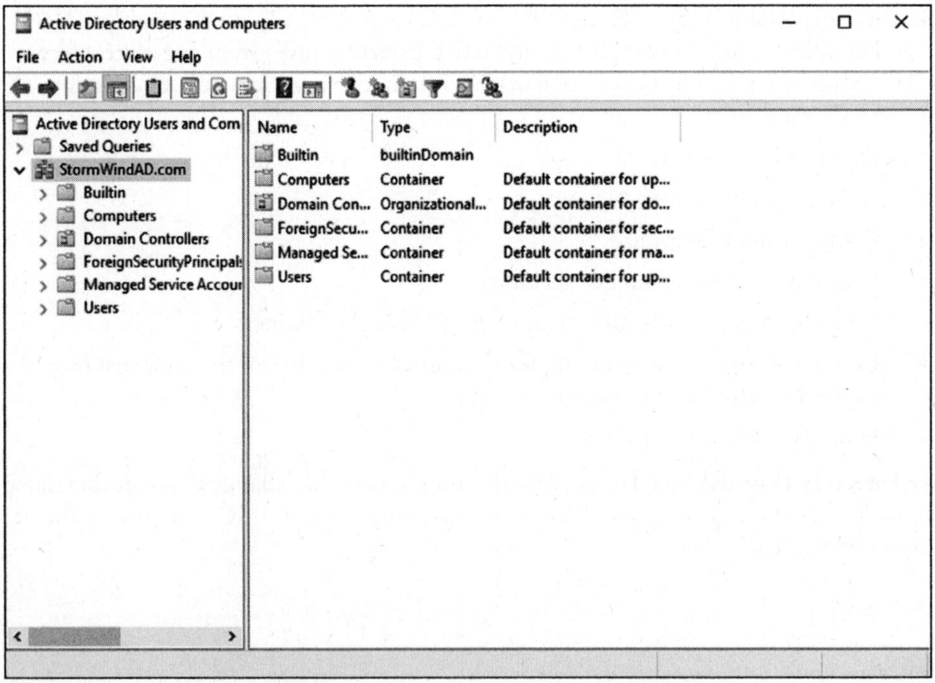

Testing from Clients

The best test of any solution is simply to verify that it works the way you had intended in your environment. When it comes to using Active Directory, a good test is to ensure that clients can view and access the various resources presented by Windows Server 2016 domain controllers. In the following sections, you'll look at several ways to verify that Active Directory is functioning properly.

Verifying Client Connectivity

If you are unable to see the recently promoted server on the network, there is likely a network configuration error. If only one or a few clients are unable to see the machine, the problem is probably related to client-side configuration. To fix this, make sure that the client computers have the appropriate TCP/IP configuration (including DNS server settings) and that they can see other computers on the network.

If the new domain controller is unavailable from any of the other client computers, you should verify the proper startup of Active Directory using the methods mentioned earlier in this chapter. If Active Directory has been started, ensure that the DNS settings are correct. Finally, test network connectivity between the server and the clients by accessing the network or by using the ping command.

Joining a Domain

If Active Directory has been properly configured, clients and other servers should be able to join the domain. Exercise 1.6 outlines the steps you need to take to join a Windows 7, Windows 8/8.1, or Windows 10 computer to the domain.

To complete this exercise, you must have already installed and properly configured at least one Active Directory domain controller and a DNS server that supports SRV records in your environment. In addition to the domain controller, you need at least one other computer, not configured as a domain controller, running one of the following operating systems: Windows 7, Windows 8, Windows 8.1, Windows 10, Windows Server 2008, Windows Server 2008 R2, Windows Server 2012, Windows Server 2012 R2, or Windows Server 2016.

Once clients are able to join the domain successfully, they should be able to view Active Directory resources using the Network icon. This test validates the proper functioning of Active Directory and ensures that you have connectivity with client computers.

 Exercise 1.6 is being done from a Windows 10 Enterprise computer.

EXERCISE 1.6

Joining a Computer to an Active Directory Domain

1. Right-click on the Start menu and choose System.

2. Go to the section called Computer Name. On the right side, click the Change Settings link.

3. Next to the section To Rename This Computer Or Change Its Domain Or Workgroup, click the Change button.

4. In the Member Of section, choose the Domain option. Type the name of the Active Directory domain that this computer should join. Click OK.

5. When prompted for the username and password of an account that has permission to join computers to the domain, enter the information for an administrator of the domain. Click OK to commit the changes. If you successfully joined the domain, you will see a dialog box welcoming you to the new domain.

6. You will be notified that you must reboot the computer before the changes take place. Select Yes when prompted to reboot.

Creating and Configuring Application Data Partitions

Organizations store many different kinds of information in various places. For the IT departments that support this information, it can be difficult to ensure that the right information is available when and where it is needed. Windows Server 2016 uses a feature called *application data partitions*, which allows system administrators and application developers to store custom information within Active Directory. The idea behind application data partitions is that since you already have a directory service that can replicate all kinds of information, you might as well use it to keep track of your own information.

Developing distributed applications that can, for example, synchronize information across an enterprise is not a trivial task. You have to come up with a way to transfer data between remote sites (some of which are located across the world), and you have to ensure that the data is properly replicated. By storing application information in Active Directory, you can take advantage of its storage mechanism and replication topology. Application-related information stored on domain controllers benefits from having fault-tolerance features and availability.

Consider the following simple example to understand how this can work. Suppose your organization has developed a customer Sales Tracking and Inventory application. The company needs to make the information that is stored by this application available to all of its branch offices and users located throughout the world. However, the goal is to do this with the least amount of IT administrative effort. Assuming that Active Directory has already been deployed throughout the organization, developers can build support into the application for storing data within Active Directory. They can then rely on Active Directory to store and synchronize the information among various sites. When users request updated data from the application, the application can obtain this information from the nearest domain controller that hosts a replica of the Sales Tracking and Inventory data.

Other types of applications can also benefit greatly from the use of application data partitions. Now that you have a good understanding of the nature of application data partitions, let's take a look at how you can create and manage them using Windows Server 2016 and Active Directory.

Creating Application Data Partitions

By default, after you create an Active Directory environment, you will not have any customer application data partitions. Therefore, the first step in making this functionality available is to create a new application data partition. You can use several tools to do this:

Third-Party Applications or Application-Specific Tools   Generally, if you are planning to install an application that can store information in the Active Directory database, you'll receive some method of administering and configuring that data along with the application. For example, the setup process for the application might assist you in the steps you need to take to set up a new application data partition and to create the necessary structures for storing data.

 Creating and managing application data partitions are advanced Active Directory–related functions. Be sure that you have a solid understanding of the Active Directory schema, Active Directory replication, LDAP, and your applications' needs before you attempt to create new application data partitions in a live environment.

Active Directory Service Interfaces   ADSI is a set of programmable objects that can be accessed through languages such as Visual Basic Scripting Edition (VBScript), Visual C#, Visual Basic .NET, and many other language technologies that support the Component Object Model (COM) standard. Through the use of ADSI, developers can create, access, and update data stored in Active Directory and in any application data partitions.

The LDP Tool   You can view and modify the contents of the Active Directory schema using LDAP-based queries. The LDP tool allows you to view information about application data partitions.

Ldp.exe is a graphical user interface (GUI) tool that allows an administrator to configure Lightweight Directory Access Protocol (LDAP) directory service. Administrators have the ability to use the LDP tool to administer an Active Directory Lightweight Directory Services (AD LDS) instance. To use the LDP tool, you must be an administrator or equivalent.

Ntdsutil   The ntdsutil utility is the main method by which system administrators create and manage application data partitions on their Windows Server 2016 domain controllers. This utility's specific commands are covered later in this chapter.

NOTE   Creating and managing application data partitions can be fairly complex. Such a project's success depends on the quality of the architecture design. This is a good example of where IT staff and application developers must cooperate to ensure that data is stored effectively and that it is replicated efficiently.

You can create an application data partition in one of three different locations within an Active Directory forest:

- As a new tree in an Active Directory forest
- As a child of an Active Directory domain partition

    For example, you can create an Accounting application data partition within the Finance.MyCompany.com domain.

- As a child of another application data partition

    This method allows you to create a hierarchy of application data partitions.

As you might expect, you must be a member of the Enterprise Admins or Domain Admins group to be able to create application data partitions. Alternatively, you can be delegated the appropriate permissions to create new partitions.

Now that you have a good idea of the basic ways in which you can create application data partitions, let's look at how replicas (copies of application data partition information) are handled.

Managing Replicas

A *replica* is a copy of any data stored within Active Directory. Unlike the basic information that is stored in Active Directory, application partitions cannot contain security principals. Also, not all domain controllers automatically contain copies of the data stored in an application data partition. System administrators can define which domain controllers host copies of the application data. This is an important feature because, if replicas are used effectively, administrators can find a good balance between replication traffic and data consistency. For example, suppose that three of your organization's 30 locations require up-to-date accounting-related information. You might choose to replicate the data only to domain controllers located in the places that require the data. Limiting replication of this data reduces network traffic.

Replication is the process by which replicas are kept up-to-date. Application data can be stored and updated on designated servers in the same way basic Active Directory information (such as users and groups) is synchronized between domain controllers. Application data partition replicas are managed using the *Knowledge Consistency Checker (KCC)*, which ensures that the designated domain controllers receive updated replica information. Additionally, the KCC uses all Active Directory sites and connection objects that you create to determine the best method to handle replication.

Removing Replicas

When you perform a *demotion* on a domain controller, that server can no longer host an application data partition. If a domain controller contains a replica of application data partition information, you must remove the replica from the domain controller before you demote it. If a domain controller is the machine that hosts a replica of the application data partition, then the entire application data partition is removed and will be permanently lost. Generally, you want to do this only after you're absolutely sure that your organization no longer needs access to the data stored in the application data partition.

Using *ntdsutil* to Manage Application Data Partitions

The primary method by which system administrators create and manage application data partitions is through the ntdsutil command-line tool. You can launch this tool simply by entering **ntdsutil** at a command prompt. The ntdsutil command is both interactive and context sensitive. That is, once you launch the utility, you'll see an ntdsutil command prompt. At this prompt, you can enter various commands that set your context within the application. For example, if you enter the domain management command, you'll be able to use domain-related commands. Several operations also require you to connect to a domain, a domain controller, or an Active Directory object before you perform a command.

 For complete details on using ntdsutil, see the Windows Server 2016 Help and Support Center.

Table 1.3 describes the domain management commands supported by the ntdsutil tool. You can access this information by typing in the following sequence of commands at a command prompt:

```
ntdsutil
domain management
Help
```

TABLE 1.3   ntdsutil domain management commands

ntdsutil Domain Management Command	Purpose
Help or ?	Displays information about the commands that are available within the Domain Management menu of the ntdsutil command.
Connection or Connections	Allows you to connect to a specific domain controller. This will set the context for further operations that are performed on specific domain controllers.

TABLE 1.3   ntdsutil domain management commands *(continued)*

ntdsutil Domain Management Command	Purpose
Create NC *PartitionDistinguishedNameDNSName*	Creates a new application directory partition.
Delete NC *PartitionDistinguishedName*	Removes an application data partition.
List NC Information *PartitionDistinguishedName*	Shows information about the specified application data partition.
List NC Replicas *PartitionDistinguishedName*	Returns information about all replicas for the specific application data partition.
Precreate *PartitionDistinguishedNameServerDNSName*	Pre-creates cross-reference application data partition objects. This allows the specified DNS server to host a copy of the application data partition.
Remove NC Replica *PartitionDistinguishedNameDCDNSName*	Removes a replica from the specified domain controller.
Select Operation Target	Selects the naming context that will be used for other operations.
Set NC Reference Domain *PartitionDistinguishedName DomainDistinguishedName*	Specifies the reference domain for an application data partition.
Set NC Replicate NotificationDelay *PartitionDistinguishedName FirstDCNotificationDelay OtherDCNotificationDelay*	Defines settings for how often replication will occur for the specified application data partition.

The ntdsutil commands are all case insensitive. Mixed case was used in the table to make them easier to read. NC in commands stands for "naming context," referring to the fact that this is a partition of the Active Directory schema.

Figure 1.9 provides an example of working with ntdsutil. The following commands were entered to set the context for further operations:

```
ntdsutil
domain management
connections
connect to server localhost
```

```
connect to domain ADTest
quit
list
```

FIGURE 1.9   Viewing ntdsutil commands on the local domain controller

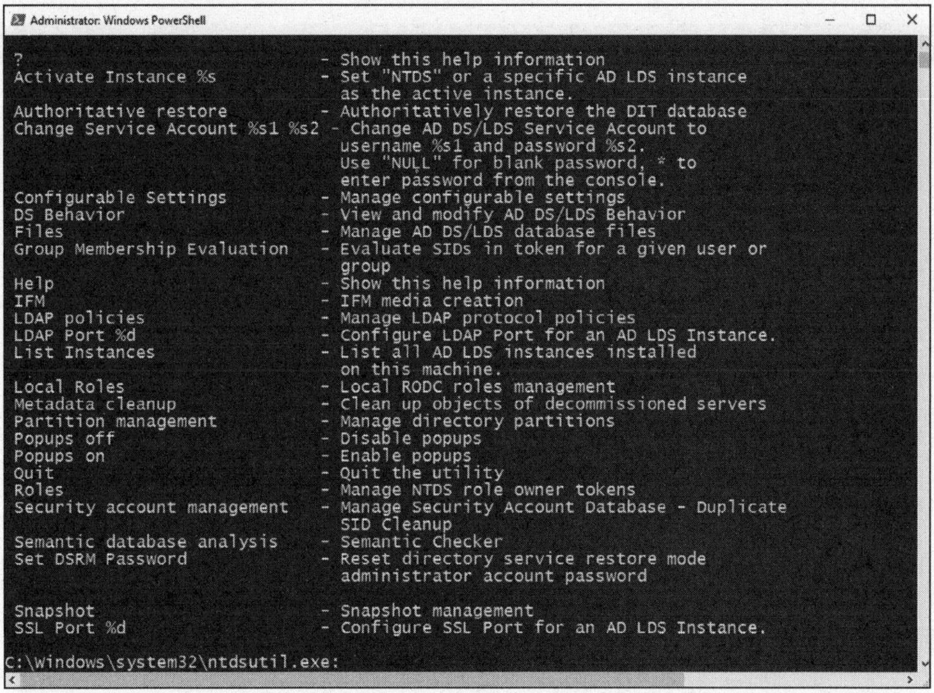

Configuring DNS Integration with Active Directory

There are many benefits to integrating Active Directory and DNS services:

- You can configure and manage replication along with other Active Directory components.

- You can automate much of the maintenance of DNS resource records through the use of dynamic updates.

- You will be able to set specific security options on the various properties of the DNS service.

Exercise 1.7 shows the steps that you must take to ensure that these integration features are enabled. You'll look at the various DNS functions that are specific to interoperability with Active Directory.

Before you begin this exercise, make sure that the local machine is configured as an Active Directory domain controller and that DNS services have been properly configured. If you instructed the Active Directory Installation Wizard to configure DNS automatically, many of the settings mentioned in this section may already be enabled. However, you should verify the configuration and be familiar with how the options can be set manually.

EXERCISE 1.7

Configuring DNS Integration with Active Directory

1. Open Administrative Tools by pressing the Windows key and choosing Administrative Tools.

2. Open the DNS snap-in from the Administrative Tools program group.

3. Right-click the icon for the local DNS server and select Properties. Click the Security tab. Notice that you can now specify which users and groups have access to modify the configuration of the DNS server. Make any necessary changes and click OK.

4. Expand the local server branch and the Forward Lookup Zones folder.

5. Right-click the name of the Active Directory domain you created and select Properties.

6. On the General tab (see Figure 1.10), verify that the type is Active Directory–Integrated and that the Data Is Stored In Active Directory message is displayed. If this option is not currently selected, you can change it by clicking the Change button next to Type and choosing the Store The Zone In Active Directory check box on the bottom.

FIGURE 1.10   General Tab of DNS zone properties

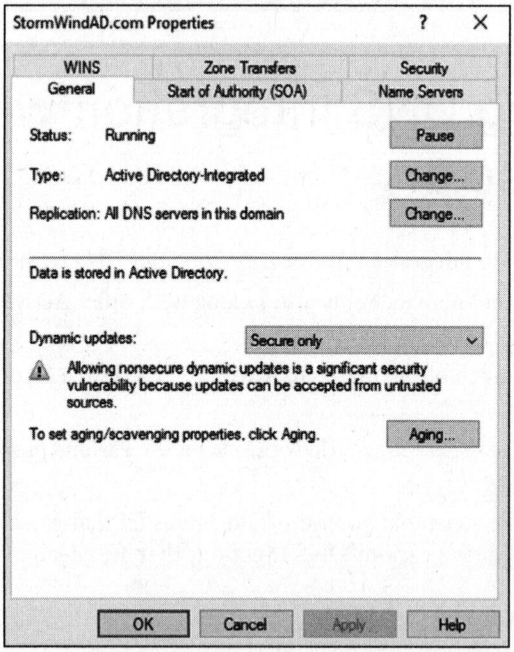

7. Verify that the Dynamic Updates option is set to Secure Only. This ensures that all updates to the DNS resource records database are made through authenticated Active Directory accounts and processes.

   The other options are Nonsecure And Secure (accepts all updates) and None (to disallow dynamic updates).

8. Finally, notice that you can define the security permissions at the zone level by clicking the Security tab. Make any necessary changes and click OK.

Summary

This chapter covered the basics of implementing an Active Directory forest and domain structure, creating and configuring application data partitions, and setting the functional level of your domain and forest.

You are now familiar with how you can implement Active Directory. We carefully examined all of the necessary steps and conditions that you need to follow to install Active Directory on your network. First you need to prepare for the Domain Name System because Active Directory cannot be installed without the support of a DNS server.

You also need to verify that the computer you upgrade to a domain controller meets some basic file system and network connectivity requirements so that Active Directory can run smoothly and efficiently in your organization. These are some of the most common things you will have to do when you deploy Active Directory.

The chapter also covered the concept of domain functional levels, which essentially determine the kinds of domain controllers you can use in your environment.

You also learned how to install Active Directory, which you accomplish by promoting a Windows Server 2016 computer to a domain controller using Server Manager. You also learned how to verify the installation by testing Active Directory from a client computer.

This chapter was limited in scope to examining the issues related to installing and configuring the first domain in an Active Directory environment.

Exam Essentials

Know the prerequisites for promoting a server to a domain controller. You should understand the tasks that you must complete before you attempt to upgrade a server to a domain controller. Also, you should have a good idea of the information you need in order to complete the domain controller promotion process.

Understand the steps of the Active Directory Installation Wizard. When you run the Active Directory Installation Wizard, you'll be presented with many different choices. You should understand the effects of the various options provided in each step of the wizard.

Be familiar with the tools that you will use to administer Active Directory.   Three main administrative tools are installed when you promote a Windows Server 2016 to a domain controller. Be sure that you know which tools to use for which types of tasks.

Understand the purpose of application data partitions.   The idea behind application data partitions is that since you already have a directory service that can replicate all kinds of security information, you can also use it to keep track of application data. The main benefit of storing application information in Active Directory is that you can take advantage of its storage mechanism and replication topology. Application-related information stored on domain controllers benefits from having fault-tolerance features and availability.

Review Questions

You can find the answers in the Appendix.

1. You are the system administrator of a large organization that has recently implemented Windows Server 2016. You have a few remote sites that do not have very tight security. You have decided to implement read-only domain controllers (RODCs). What forest and function levels does the network need for you to do the install? (Choose all that apply.)

    A. Windows Server 2016

    B. Windows Server 2008 R2

    C. Windows Server 2012 R2

    D. Windows Server 2008

2. What is the maximum number of domains that a Windows Server 2016 computer configured as a domain controller may participate in at one time?

    A. Zero

    B. One

    C. Two

    D. Any number of domains

3. A system administrator is trying to determine which file system to use for a server that will become a Windows Server 2016 file server and domain controller. The company has the following requirements:

    - The file system must allow for file-level security from within Windows 2016 Server.

    - The file system must make efficient use of space on large partitions.

    - The domain controller Sysvol must be stored on the partition.

    Which of the following file systems meets these requirements?

    A. FAT

    B. FAT32

    C. HPFS

    D. NTFS

4. For security reasons, you have decided that you must convert the system partition on your removable drive from the FAT32 file system to NTFS. Which of the following steps must you take in order to convert the file system? (Choose two.)

    A. Run the command CONVERT /FS:NTFS from the command prompt.

    B. Rerun Windows Server 2016 Setup and choose to convert the partition to NTFS during the reinstallation.

    C. Boot Windows Server 2016 Setup from the installation CD-ROM and choose Rebuild File System.

    D. Reboot the computer.

5. Windows Server 2016 requires the use of which of the following protocols or services in order to support Active Directory? (Choose two.)

   A. DHCP

   B. TCP/IP

   C. NetBEUI

   D. IPX/SPX

   E. DNS

6. You are promoting a Windows Server 2016 computer to an Active Directory domain controller for test purposes. The new domain controller will be added to an existing domain. While you are using the Active Directory Installation Wizard, you receive an error message that prevents the server from being promoted. Which of the following might be the cause of the problem? (Choose all that apply.)

   A. The system does not contain an NTFS partition on which the Sysvol directory can be created.

   B. You do not have a Windows Server 2016 DNS server on the network.

   C. The TCP/IP configuration on the new server is incorrect.

   D. The domain has reached its maximum number of domain controllers.

7. Your network contains a single Active Directory domain. The domain contains five Windows Server 2008 R2 domain controllers. You plan to install a new Windows Server 2016 domain controller. Which two actions would you need to perform? (Each correct answer presents part of the solution. Choose two.)

   A. Run adprep.exe /rodcprep at the command line.

   B. Run adprep.exe /forestprep at the command line.

   C. Run adprep.exe /domainprep at the command line.

   D. From Active Directory Domains and Trusts, raise the functional level of the domain.

   E. From Active Directory Users and Computers, prestage the RODC computer account.

8. You are the network administrator for a large company that creates widgets. Management asks you to implement a new Windows Server 2016 system. You need to implement federated identity management. Which of the following will help you do this?

   A. Active Directory Federation Services

   B. Active Directory DNS Services

   C. Active Directory IIS Services

   D. Active Directory IAS Services

9. You are the system administrator responsible for your company's infrastructure. You think you have an issue with name resolution, and you need to verify that you are using the correct hostname. You want to test DNS on the local system and need to see whether the hostname server-1 resolves to the IP address 10.1.1.1. Which of the following actions provides a solution to the problem?

A. Add a DNS server to your local subnet.

B. Add the mapping for the hostname server-1 to the IP address 10.1.1.1 in the local system's HOSTS file.

C. Add an A record to your local WINS server.

D. Add an MX record to your local DNS server.

10. You have one Active Directory forest in your organization that contains one domain named WillPanek.com. You have two domain controllers configured with the DNS role installed. There are two Active Directory Integrated zones named WillPanek.com and WillPanekAD.com. One of your IT members (who is not an administrator) needs to be able to modify the WillPanek.com DNS server, but you need to prevent this user from modifying the WillPanekAD.com SOA record. How do you accomplish this?

A. Modify the permissions of the WillPanek.com zone from the DNS Manager snap-in.

B. Modify the permissions of the WillPanekAd.com zone from the DNS Manager snap-in.

C. Run the Delegation Of Control Wizard in Active Directory.

D. Run the Delegation Of Control Wizard in the DNS snap-in.

Chapter

2

Administer Active Directory

THE FOLLOWING 70-742 EXAM OBJECTIVES ARE COVERED IN THIS CHAPTER:

✓ **Create and manage Active Directory users and computers**

- This objective may include but is not limited to: Automate the creation of Active Directory accounts; create, copy, configure, and delete users and computers; configure templates; perform bulk Active Directory operations; configure user rights; implement offline domain join; manage inactive and disabled accounts; automate unlocking of disabled accounts using Windows PowerShell; automate password resets using Windows PowerShell.

✓ **Create and manage Active Directory groups and organizational units (OUs)**

- This objective may include but is not limited to: Configure group nesting; convert groups, including security, distribution, universal, domain local, and domain global; manage group membership using Group Policy; enumerate group membership; automate group membership management using Windows PowerShell; delegate the creation and management of Active Directory groups and OUs; manage default Active Directory containers; create, copy, configure, and delete groups and OUs.

✓ **Configure service authentication and account policies**

- This objective may include but is not limited to: Create and configure Service Accounts; create and configure Group Managed Service Accounts (gMSAs); configure Kerberos Constrained Delegation (KCD); manage Service Principal Names (SPNs); configure virtual accounts; configure domain and local user password policy settings; configure and apply Password Settings Objects (PSOs); delegate password settings management; configure account lockout policy settings; configure Kerberos policy settings within Group Policy.

In previous chapters, you learned how to install Active Directory, but you still haven't been introduced to the lower-level objects that exist in Active Directory.

In this chapter, you will look at the structure of the various components within a domain. You'll see how an organization's business structure can be mirrored within Active Directory through the use of organizational units for ease of use and to create a seamless look and feel. Because the concepts related to organizational units are quite simple, some system administrators may underestimate their importance and not plan to use them accordingly. Make no mistake: One of the fundamental components of a successful Active Directory installation is the proper design and deployment of organizational units.

You'll also see in this chapter the actual steps you need to take to create common Active Directory objects and then learn how to configure and manage them. Finally, you'll look at ways to publish resources and methods for creating user accounts automatically.

Active Directory Overview

One of the fundamental design goals for Active Directory is to define a single, centralized repository of users and information resources. Active Directory records information about all of the users, computers, and resources on your network. Each domain acts as a logical boundary, and members of the domain (including workstations, servers, and domain controllers) share information about the objects within them.

The information stored within Active Directory determines which resources are accessible to which users. Through the use of permissions that are assigned to Active Directory objects, you can control all aspects of network security.

Throughout this chapter, you'll learn the details of security as it pertains to Active Directory. Note, however, that Active Directory security is only one aspect of overall network security. You should also be sure that you have implemented appropriate access control settings for the file system, network devices, and other resources. Let's start by looking at the various components of network security, which include working with security principals and managing security and permissions, access control lists (ACLs), and access control entries (ACEs).

When you are setting up a network, you should always keep in mind that 90 percent of all hacks on a network are internal. This means internal permissions and security (as well as external security) need to be as strong as possible while still allowing users to do their jobs.

Understanding Active Directory Features

Active Directory is the heart and soul of a Microsoft domain, and I can never talk enough about the roles and features included with Active Directory. Let's take a look at some of the advantages of Windows Server 2016 and Active Directory.

Active Directory Certificate Services   Active Directory Certificate Services (AD CS) provides a customizable set of services that allows you to issue and manage public key infrastructure (PKI) certificates. These certificates can be used in software security systems that employ public key technologies.

Active Directory Domain Services   Active Directory Domain Services (AD DS) includes new features that make deploying domain controllers simpler and lets you implement them faster. AD DS also makes the domain controllers more flexible, both to audit and to authorize access to files. Moreover, AD DS has been designed to make performing administrative tasks easier through consistent graphical and scripted management experiences.

Active Directory Rights Management Services   Active Directory Rights Management Services (AD RMS) provides management and development tools that let you work with industry security technologies, including encryption, certificates, and authentication. Using these technologies allows organizations to create reliable information protection solutions.

Kerberos Authentication   Windows Server 2016 uses the Kerberos authentication protocol and extensions for password-based and public-key authentication. The Kerberos client is installed as a security support provider (SSP), and it can be accessed through the Security Support Provider Interface (SSPI).

Kerberos Constrained Delegation   Kerberos constrained delegation (KCD) is an authentication protocol that administrators can set up for delegating client credentials for specific service accounts. For example, KCD may be a requirement for services in SharePoint 2016. If you are planning on using SharePoint 2016 Analysis Services and Power Pivot data, you will need to configure KCD. KCD allows a service account to impersonate another service account and this allows access to specific resources.

Managed Service Accounts   The *Managed Service Accounts* is a Windows Server 2016 account that is managed by Active Directory. Regular service accounts are accounts that are created to run specific services such as Exchange and SQL Server. Normally when an administrator creates a service account, it's up to that administrator to maintain the account (including changing the password). Managed Service Accounts are accounts that administrators create, but the accounts are managed by Active Directory (including password changes). To create Managed Service Accounts, you must use the `New-ADServiceAccount` PowerShell command. You must use PowerShell in order to create a Managed Service Account.

Group Managed Service Accounts   The group Managed Service Account (gMSA) provides the same functionality within the domain as Managed Service Accounts, but gMSAs extend their functionality over multiple servers. These accounts are very useful when a service account needs to work with multiple servers, as with a server farm (for Network Load Balancing).

There are times when the authentication process requires that all instances of a service use the same service account. This is where gMSAs are used. Once group Managed Service Account are used, Windows Server 2016 will automatically manage the password for the service account. The network administrator will no longer be responsible to manage the service account password.

Security Auditing   Security auditing gives an organization the ability to help maintain the security of an enterprise. By using security audits, you can verify authorized or unauthorized access to machines, resources, applications, and services. One of the best advantages of security audits is to verify regulatory compliance.

TLS/SSL (Schannel SSP)   Schannel is a security support provider (SSP) that uses the Secure Sockets Layer (SSL) and Transport Layer Security (TLS) Internet standard authentication protocols together. The Security Support Provider Interface (SSPI) is an API used by Windows systems to allow security-related functionality, including authentication.

Windows Deployment Services   Windows Deployment Services allows an administrator to install Windows operating systems remotely. Administrators can use Windows Deployment Services to set up new computers by using a network-based installation.

Understanding Security Principals

Security principals are Active Directory objects that are assigned *security identifiers (SIDs)*. An SID is a unique identifier that is used to manage any object to which permissions can be assigned. Security principals are assigned permissions to perform certain actions and access certain network resources.

The following basic types of Active Directory objects serve as security principals:

User Accounts   User accounts identify individual users on your network by including information such as the user's name and their password. User accounts are the fundamental unit of security administration.

Groups   There are two main types of groups: security groups and distribution groups. Both types can contain user accounts. System administrators use security groups to ease the management of security permissions. They use distribution groups, on the other hand, solely to send email. Distribution groups are not security principals.

Computer Accounts   Computer accounts identify which client computers are members of particular domains. Because these computers participate in the Active Directory database, system administrators can manage security settings that affect the computer. They use computer accounts to determine whether a computer can join a domain and for authentication purposes. As you'll see later in this chapter, system administrators can also place restrictions on certain computer settings to increase security. These settings apply to the computer and, therefore, also apply to any user who is using it (regardless of the permissions granted to the user account).

Note that other objects—such as OUs—do not function as security principals. What this means is that you can apply certain settings (such as Group Policy) on all of the objects within an OU; however, you cannot specifically set permissions with respect to the OU itself. The purpose of OUs is to organize other Active Directory objects logically based on business needs, add a needed level of control for security, and create an easier way to delegate.

You can manage security by performing the following actions with security principals:

- You can assign them permissions to access various network resources.

- You can give them user rights.

- You can track their actions through auditing (covered later in this chapter).

The major types of security principals—user accounts, groups, and computer accounts—form the basis of the Active Directory security architecture. As a system administrator, you will likely spend a portion of your time managing permissions for these objects.

 It is important to understand that, since a unique SID defines each security principal, deleting a security principal is an irreversible process. For example, if you delete a user account and then later re-create one with the same name, you'll need to reassign permissions and group membership settings for the new account. Once a user account is deleted, its SID is deleted. This is why you should always consider disabling accounts instead of deleting them.

An Overview of OUs

An *organizational unit (OU)* is a logical group of Active Directory objects, just as the name implies. OUs serve as containers (see Figure 2.1) within which Active Directory objects can be created, but they do not form part of the DNS namespace. They are used solely to create organization within a domain.

FIGURE 2.1   Active Directory OUs

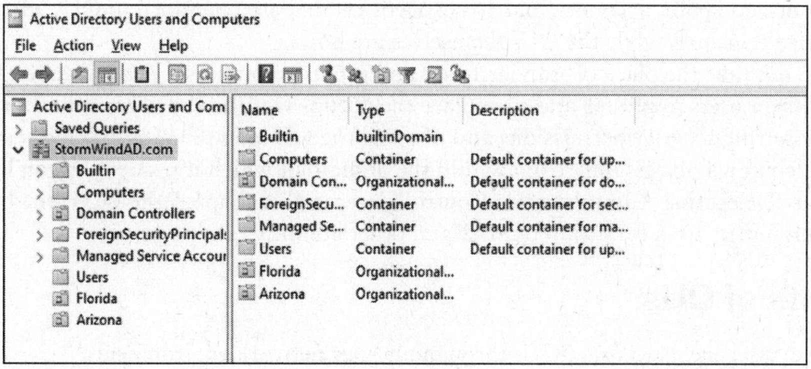

Active Directory Users and Computers			
File Action View Help			
Active Directory Users and Com	Name	Type	Description
Saved Queries	Builtin	builtinDomain	
StormWindAD.com	Computers	Container	Default container for up...
Builtin	Domain Con...	Organizational...	Default container for do...
Computers	ForeignSecu...	Container	Default container for sec...
Domain Controllers	Managed Se...	Container	Default container for ma...
ForeignSecurityPrincipal:	Users	Container	Default container for up...
Managed Service Accoun	Florida	Organizational...	
Users	Arizona	Organizational...	
Florida			
Arizona			

OUs can contain the following types of Active Directory objects:

- Users
- Groups
- Computers
- Shared Folder objects
- Contacts
- Printers
- InetOrgPerson objects
- Microsoft Message Queuing (MSMQ) Queue aliases
- Other OUs

Perhaps the most useful feature of OUs is that they can contain other OU objects. As a result, system administrators can hierarchically group resources and objects according to business practices. The OU structure is extremely flexible and, as you will see later in this chapter, can easily be rearranged to reflect business reorganizations.

Another advantage of OUs is that each can have its own set of policies. Administrators can create individual and unique Group Policy objects (GPOs) for each OU. GPOs are rules or policies that can apply to all of the objects within the OU.

Each type of object has its own purpose within the organization of Active Directory domains. Later in this chapter, you'll look at the specifics of User, Computer, Group, and Shared Folder objects. For now, let's focus on the purpose and benefits of using OUs.

The Purpose of OUs

OUs are mainly used to organize the objects within Active Directory. Before you dive into the details of OUs, however, you must understand how OUs, users, and groups interact. Most important, you should understand that OUs are simply containers that you can use to group various objects logically. They are not, however, groups in the classical sense. That is, they are not used for assigning security permissions. Another way of stating this is that the user accounts, computer accounts, and group accounts that are contained in OUs are considered security principals while the OUs themselves are not.

OUs do not take the place of standard user and group permissions. A good general practice is to assign users to groups and then place the groups within OUs. This enhances the benefits of setting security permissions and of using the OU hierarchy for making settings.

An OU contains objects only from within the domain in which it resides. As you'll see in the section "Delegating Administrative Control" later in this chapter, the OU is the finest level of granularity used for group policies and other administrative settings.

Benefits of OUs

There are many benefits to using OUs throughout your network environment:

- OUs are the smallest unit to which you can assign directory permissions.
- You can easily change the OU structure, and it is more flexible than the domain structure.

- The OU structure can support many different levels of hierarchy.
- Child objects can inherit OU settings.
- You can set Group Policy settings on OUs.
- You can easily delegate the administration of OUs and the objects within them to the appropriate users and groups.

Now that you have a good idea of why you should use OUs, take a look at some general practices you can use to plan the OU structure.

Planning the OU Structure

One of the key benefits of Active Directory is the way in which it can bring organization to complex network environments. Before you can begin to implement OUs in various configurations, you must plan a structure that is compatible with business and technical needs. In the following sections, you'll learn about several factors that you should consider when planning for the structure of OUs.

Logical Grouping of Resources

The fundamental purpose of using OUs is to group resources (which exist within Active Directory) hierarchically. Fortunately, hierarchical groups are quite intuitive and widely used in most businesses. For example, a typical manufacturing business might divide its various operations into different departments as follows:

- Sales
- Marketing
- Engineering
- Research and Development
- Support
- Information Technology (IT)

Each of these departments usually has its own goals and mission. To make the business competitive, individuals within each of the departments are assigned to various roles. The following role types might be used:

- Managers
- Clerical staff
- Technical staff
- Planners

Each of these roles usually entails specific job responsibilities. For example, managers should provide direction to general staff members. Note that the very nature of these roles suggests that employees may fill many different positions. That is, one employee might be a manager in one department and a member of the technical staff in another. In the modern workplace, such situations are quite common.

All of this information helps you plan how to use OUs. First the structure of OUs within a given network environment should map well to the business's needs, including the political and logical structure of the organization as well as its technical needs. Figure 2.2 shows how a business organization might be mapped to the OU structure within an Active Directory domain.

FIGURE 2.2   Mapping a business organization to an OU structure

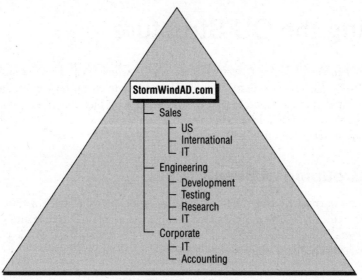

StormWindAD.com Domain

When naming OUs for your organization, you should keep several considerations and limitations in mind:

Keep the Names and Descriptions Simple   The purpose of OUs is to make administering and using resources simple. Therefore, it's always a good idea to keep the names of your objects simple and descriptive. Sometimes, finding a balance between these two goals can be a challenge. For example, although a printer name like "The LaserJet located near Bob's cube" might seem descriptive, it is certainly difficult to type. Also, imagine the naming changes that you might have to make if Bob moves (or leaves the company)!

Pay Attention to Limitations   The maximum length for the name of an OU is 64 characters. In most cases, this should adequately describe the OU. Remember, the name of an OU does not have to describe the object uniquely because the OU is generally referenced only as part of the overall hierarchy. For example, you can choose to create an OU named "IT" within two different parent OUs. Even though the OUs have the same name, users and administrators are able to distinguish between them based on their complete pathname.

Pay Attention to the Hierarchical Consistency   The fundamental basis of an OU structure is its position in a hierarchy. From a design standpoint, this means you cannot have two OUs with the same name at the same level. However, you can have OUs with the same name at different levels. For example, you could create an OU named "Corporate" within the North America OU and another one within the South America OU. This is because the fully qualified domain name includes information about the hierarchy. When an administrator tries to access resources in a Corporate OU, they must specify which Corporate OU they mean.

For example, if you create a North America OU, the Canada OU should logically fit under it. If you decide that you want to separate the North America and Canada OUs into completely different containers, then you might want to use other, more appropriate names. For example, you could change North America to "U.S." Users and administrators depend on the hierarchy of OUs within the domain, so make sure that it remains logically consistent.

Based on these considerations, you should have a good idea of how best to organize the OU structure for your domain.

Understanding OU Inheritance

When you rearrange OUs within the structure of Active Directory, you can change several settings. When they are moving and reorganizing OUs, system administrators must pay careful attention to automatic and unforeseen changes in security permissions and other configuration options. By default, OUs inherit the permissions of their new parent container when they are moved.

By using the built-in tools provided with Windows Server 2016 and Active Directory, you can move or copy OUs only within the same domain. You cannot use the Active Directory Users and Computers tool to move OUs between domains. To do this, use the *Active Directory Migration Tool (ADMT)*. This is one of the many Active Directory support tools.

Delegating Administrative Control

I already mentioned that OUs are the smallest component within a domain to which administrative permissions and group policies can be assigned by administrators. Now you'll take a look specifically at how administrative control is set on OUs.

Delegation occurs when a higher security authority assigns permissions to a lesser security authority. As a real-world example, assume that you are the director of IT for a large organization. Instead of doing all of the work yourself, you would probably assign roles and responsibilities to other individuals. For example, if you worked within a multidomain environment, you might make one system administrator responsible for all operations within the Sales domain and another responsible for the Engineering domain. Similarly, you could assign the permissions for managing all printers and print queue objects within your organization to one individual user while allowing another individual user to manage all security permissions for users and groups. In this way, you can distribute the various roles and responsibilities of the IT staff throughout the organization.

Businesses generally have a division of labor that handles all of the tasks involved in keeping the company's networks humming. Network operating systems (NOSs), however, often make it difficult to assign just the right permissions; in other words, they do not support very granular permission assignments. Sometimes, fine granularity is necessary to ensure that only the right permissions are assigned. A good general rule of thumb is to provide users and administrators with the minimum permissions they require to do their jobs. This way, you can ensure that accidental, malicious, and otherwise unwanted changes do not occur.

 You can use auditing to log events to the Security log in the Event Viewer. This is a way to ensure that if accidental, malicious, and otherwise unwanted changes do occur, they are logged and traceable.

In the world of Active Directory, you delegate to define responsibilities for OU administrators. As a system administrator, you will occasionally be tasked with having to delegate responsibility to others—you can't do it all, although sometimes administrators believe that they can. You understand the old IT logic of doing all of the tasks yourself for job security, but this can actually make you look worse.

 You can delegate control only at the OU level and not at the object level within the OU.

If you do find yourself in a role where you need to delegate, remember that Windows Server 2016 was designed to offer you the ability to do so. In its simplest definition, *delegation* allows a higher administrative authority to grant specific administrative rights for containers and subtrees to individuals and groups. What this essentially does is eliminate the need for domain administrators with sweeping authority over large segments of the user population. You can break up this control over branches within your tree, within each OU you create.

 To understand delegation and rights, you should first understand the concept of *access control entries (ACEs)*. ACEs grant specific administrative rights on objects in a container to a user or group. A container's access control list (ACL) is used to store ACEs.

When you are considering implementing delegation, keep these two concerns in mind:

Parent-Child Relationships The OU hierarchy you create will be important when you consider the maintainability of security permissions. OUs can exist in a parent-child relationship, which means that permissions and group policies set on OUs higher up in the hierarchy (parents) can interact with objects in lower-level OUs (children). When it comes to delegating permissions, this is extremely important. You can allow child containers to inherit the permissions set on parent containers automatically. For example, if the North America division of your organization contains 12 other OUs, you could delegate permissions to all of them at once (saving time and reducing the likelihood of human error) by placing security permissions on the North America division. This feature can greatly ease administration, especially in larger organizations, but it is also a reminder of the importance of properly planning the OU structure within a domain.

Inheritance Settings   Now that you've seen how you can use parent-child relationships for administration, you should consider *inheritance*, the process in which child objects take on the permissions of a parent container. When you set permissions on a parent container, all of the child objects are configured to inherit the same permissions. You can override this behavior, however, if business rules do not lend themselves well to inheritance.

Applying Group Policies

One of the strengths of the Windows operating system is that it offers users a great deal of power and flexibility. From installing new software to adding device drivers, users can make many changes to their workstation configurations. However, this level of flexibility is also a potential problem. For instance, inexperienced users might inadvertently change settings, causing problems that can require many hours to fix.

In many cases (and especially in business environments), users require only a subset of the complete functionality the operating system provides. In the past, however, the difficulty associated with implementing and managing security and policy settings has led to lax security policies. Some of the reasons for this are technical—it can be tedious and difficult to implement and manage security restrictions. Other problems have been political—users and management might feel that they should have full permissions on their local machines, despite the potential problems this might cause.

That's where the idea of group policies comes in. Simply defined, *group policies* are collections of rules that you can apply to objects within Active Directory. Specifically, Group Policy settings are assigned at the site, domain, and OU levels, and they can apply to user accounts and computer accounts. For example, a system administrator can use group policies to configure the following settings:

- Restricting users from installing new programs
- Disallowing the use of the Control Panel
- Limiting choices for display and Desktop settings

Creating OUs

Now that you have looked at several different ways in which OUs can be used to bring organization to the objects within Active Directory, it's time to look at how you can create and manage them.

Through the use of the *Active Directory Users and Computers administrative tool*, also called the *MMC (Microsoft Management Console)*, you can quickly and easily add, move, and change OUs. This graphical tool makes it easy to visualize and create the various levels of hierarchy an organization requires.

Figure 2.3 shows a geographically based OU structure that a multinational company might use. Note that the organization is based in North America and that it has a corporate office located there. In general, the other offices are much smaller than the corporate office located in North America.

FIGURE 2.3   A geographically based OU structure

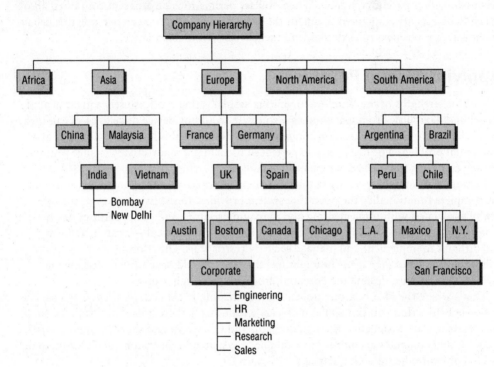

It's important to note that this OU structure could have been designed in several different ways. For example, I could have chosen to group all of the offices located in the United States within an OU named "U.S." However, because of the large size of these offices, I chose to place these objects at the same level as the Canada and Mexico OUs. This prevents an unnecessarily deep OU hierarchy while still logically grouping the offices.

One nice feature when creating an OU is the ability to protect the OU from being accidentally deleted. When you create an OU, you can check the Protect Container From Accidental Deletion check box. This check box protects against an administrator deleting the OU. To delete the OU, you must go into the advanced view of the OU and uncheck the box.

Exercise 2.1 walks you through the process of creating several OUs for a multinational business. You'll be using this OU structure in later exercises within this chapter.

To perform the exercises included in this chapter, you must have administrative access to a Windows Server 2016 domain controller.

EXERCISE 2.1

Creating an OU Structure

1. Open Active Directory Users and Computers by clicking Start ➢ Administrative Tools ➢ Active Directory Users And Computers.

2. Right-click the name of the local domain and choose New ➢ Organizational Unit.

3. Type **North America** for the name of the first OU (see Figure 2.4). Uncheck the box Protect Container From Accidental Deletion and click OK to create this object.

FIGURE 2.4   New OU dialog box

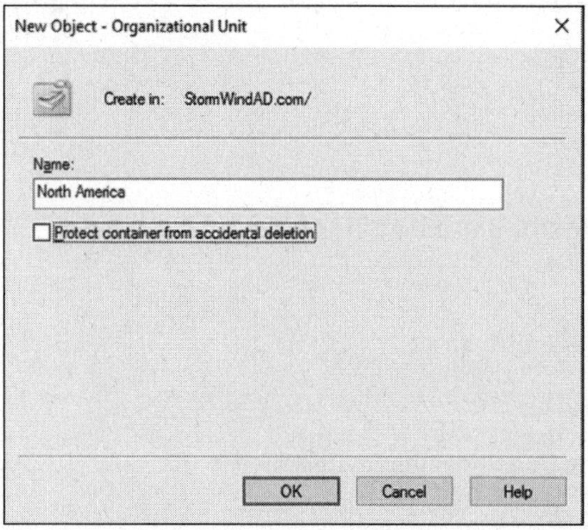

4. Create the following top-level OUs by right-clicking the name of the domain and choosing New ➢ Organizational Unit. Also make sure to uncheck Protect Container From Accidental Deletion for all OUs in these exercises because you'll be deleting some of these OUs in later ones.

    Africa

    Asia

    Europe

    South America

    Note that the order in which you create the OUs is not important. In this exercise, you are simply using a method that emphasizes the hierarchical relationship.

EXERCISE 2.1 *(continued)*

5. Create the following second-level OUs within the North America OU by right-clicking the North America OU and selecting New ➢ Organizational Unit:

    Austin

    Boston

    Canada

    Chicago

    Corporate

    Los Angeles

    Mexico

    New York

    San Francisco

6. Create the following OUs under the Asia OU:

    China

    India

    Malaysia

    Vietnam

7. Create the following OUs under the Europe OU:

    France

    Germany

    Spain

    UK

8. Create the following OUs under the South America OU:

    Argentina

    Brazil

    Chile

    Peru

9. Create the following third-level OUs under the India OU by right-clicking India within the Asia OU and selecting New ➢ Organizational Unit:

    Bombay

    New Delhi

10. Within the North America Corporate OU, create the following OUs:

Engineering

HR

Marketing

Research

Sales

11. When you have completed creating the OUs, close Active Directory.

Managing OUs

Managing network environments would still be challenging, even if things rarely changed. However, in the real world, business units, departments, and employee roles change frequently. As business and technical needs change, so should the structure of Active Directory.

Fortunately, changing the structure of OUs within a domain is a relatively simple process. In the following sections, you'll look at ways to delegate control of OUs and make other changes.

Moving, Deleting, and Renaming OUs

The process of moving, deleting, and renaming OUs is a simple one. Exercise 2.2 shows how you can easily modify and reorganize OUs to reflect changes in the business organization. The specific scenario covered in this exercise includes the following changes:

- The Research and Engineering departments have been combined to form a department known as Research and Development (RD).

- The Sales department has been moved from the Corporate headquarters office to the New York office.

- The Marketing department has been moved from the Corporate headquarters office to the Chicago office.

This exercise assumes you have already completed the steps in Exercise 2.1.

EXERCISE 2.2

Modifying OU Structure

1. Open Active Directory Users and Computers by clicking Start ➤ Administrative Tools ➤ Active Directory Users And Computers.

2. Right-click the Engineering OU (located within North America ➤ Corporate) and click Delete. When you are prompted for confirmation, click Yes. Note that if this OU contained objects, they would have all been automatically deleted as well.

3. Right-click the Research OU and select Rename. Type **RD** to change the name of the OU and press Enter.

4. Right-click the Sales OU and select Move. In the Move dialog box, expand the North America branch and click the New York OU. Click OK to move the OU.

5. You will use an alternate method to move the Marketing OU. Drag the Marketing OU and drop it onto the Chicago OU.

6. When you have finished, close the Active Directory Users and Computers administrative tool.

Administering Properties of OUs

Although OUs are primarily created for organizational purposes within the Active Directory environment, they have several settings that you can modify. To modify the properties of an OU using the Active Directory Users and Computers administrative tool, right-click the name of any OU and select Properties. When you do, the OU Properties dialog box appears. In the example shown in Figure 2.5, you'll see the options on the General tab.

FIGURE 2.5   The General tab of the OUs Properties dialog box

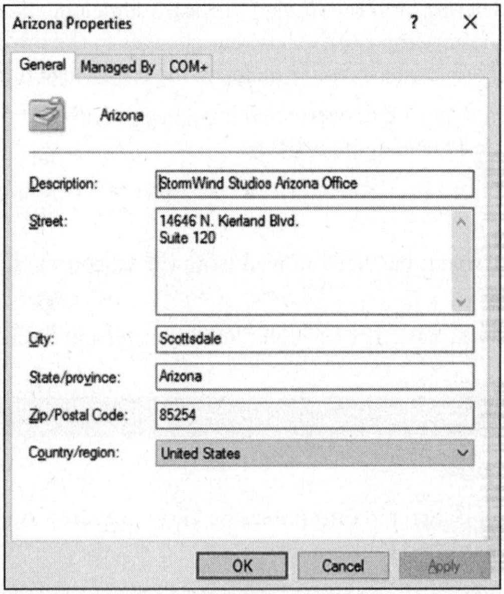

In any organization, it helps to know who is responsible for managing an OU. You can set this information on the Managed By tab (see Figure 2.6). The information specified on this tab is convenient because it is automatically pulled from the contact information on a user record. You should consider always having a contact for each OU within your organization so that other system administrators know whom to contact if they need to make any changes.

FIGURE 2.6   The Managed By tab of the OUs Properties dialog box

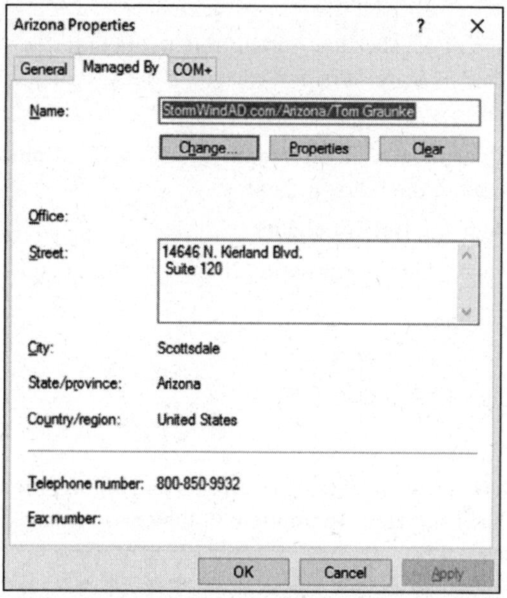

Delegating Control of OUs

In simple environments, one or a few system administrators may be responsible for managing all of the settings within Active Directory. For example, a single system administrator could manage all users within all OUs in the environment. In larger organizations, however, roles and responsibilities may be divided among many different individuals. A typical situation is one in which a system administrator is responsible for objects within only a few OUs in an Active Directory domain. Alternatively, one system administrator might manage User and Group objects while another is responsible for managing file and print services.

Fortunately, using the Active Directory Users and Computers tool, you can quickly and easily ensure that specific users receive only the permissions they need. In Exercise 2.3, you will use the Delegation of Control Wizard to assign permissions to individuals. To complete these steps successfully, first you must have created the objects in the previous exercises of this chapter.

Using the Delegation of Control Wizard

1. Open Active Directory Users and Computers by clicking Start ➤ Administrative Tools ➤ Active Directory Users And Computers.

2. Right-click the Corporate OU within the North America OU and select Delegate Control. This starts the Delegation of Control Wizard. Click Next to begin configuring security settings.

3. In the Users Or Groups page, click the Add button. In the Enter The Object Names To Select field, enter **Account Operators** and click the Check Names button. Click OK. Click Next to continue.

4. In the Tasks To Delegate page, select Delegate The Following Common Tasks and place a check mark next to the following items:

   Create, Delete, And Manage User Accounts

   Reset User Passwords And Force Password Change At Next Logon

   Read All User Information

   Create, Delete, And Manage Groups

   Modify The Membership Of A Group

5. Click Next to continue.

6. The Completing The Delegation Of Control Wizard page then provides a summary of the operations you have selected. To implement the changes, click Finish.

Although the common tasks available through the wizard are sufficient for many delegation operations, you may have cases in which you want more control. For example, you might want to give a particular system administrator permissions to modify only Computer objects. Exercise 2.4 uses the Delegation of Control Wizard to assign more granular permissions. To complete these steps successfully, you must have completed the previous exercises in this chapter.

Delegating Custom Tasks

1. Open Active Directory Users and Computers by clicking Start ➤ Administrative Tools ➤ Active Directory Users And Computers.

2. Right-click the Corporate OU within the North America OU and select Delegate Control. This starts the Delegation of Control Wizard. Click Next to begin making security settings.

3. In the Users Or Groups page, click the Add button. In the Enter The Object Names To Select field, enter **Server Operators** and click the Check Names button. Click OK and then click Next to continue.

4. In the Tasks To Delegate page, select the Create A Custom Task To Delegate radio button and click Next to continue.

5. In the Active Directory Object Type page, choose Only The Following Objects In The Folder and place a check mark next to the following items. (You will have to scroll down to see them all.)

   User Objects

   Computer Objects

   Contact Objects

   Group Objects

   Organizational Unit Objects

   Printer Objects

6. Click Next to continue.

7. In the Permissions page, place a check mark next to the General option and make sure the other options are not checked. Note that if the various objects within your Active Directory schema had property-specific settings, you would see those options here. Place a check mark next to the following items:

   Create All Child Objects

   Read All Properties

   Write All Properties

   This gives the members of the Server Operators group the ability to create new objects within the Corporate OU and the permissions to read and write all properties for these objects.

8. Click Next to continue.

9. The Completing The Delegation Of Control Wizard page provides a summary of the operations you have selected. To implement the changes, click Finish.

🌐 Real World Scenario

Delegation: Who's Responsible for What?

You're the IT director for a large, multinational organization. You've been with the company for quite a while, that is, since the environment had only a handful of offices and a few network and system administrators. Times have changed, however. Now system administrators must coordinate the efforts of hundreds of IT staffers in 14 countries.

For years now, a debate has been raging among IT administrators on the question of when to create a new child domain and when to make it just an OU. For example, let's say you have a remote office in Concord, New Hampshire. Do you give the remote office its own domain (as a child domain), or do you just make the Concord office an OU? Well, it really depends on who you want to manage the resources in Concord. Do you want to create domains or OUs based on location?

Fortunately, through the proper use of OUs and delegation, you are given a lot of flexibility in determining how to handle the administration. You can structure the administration in several ways. First, if you choose to create OUs based on a geographic business structure, you could delegate control of these OUs based on the job functions of various system administrators. For example, you could use one user account to administer the Concord OU. Within the Concord OU, this system administrator could delegate control of resources represented by the Printers and Scanners OUs.

Alternatively, the OU structure may create a functional representation of the business. For example, the Engineering OU might contain other OUs that are based on office locations such as New York and Paris. A system administrator of the Engineering domain could delegate permissions based on geography or job functions to the lower OUs. Regardless of whether you build a departmental, functional, or geographical OU model, keep in mind that each model excludes other models. This is one of the most important decisions you need to make. When you are making this decision or modifying previous decisions, your overriding concern is how it will affect the management and administration of the network. The good news is that, because Active Directory has so many features, the model you choose can be based on specific business requirements rather than imposed by architectural constraints.

Troubleshooting OUs

In general, you will find using OUs to be a relatively straightforward and painless process. With adequate planning, you'll be able to implement an intuitive and useful structure for OU objects.

The most common problems with OU configuration are related to the OU structure. When troubleshooting OUs, pay careful attention to the following factors:

Inheritance   By default, Group Policy and other settings are transferred automatically from parent OUs to child OUs and objects. Even if a specific OU is not given a set of permissions, objects within that OU might still get them from parent objects.

Delegation of Administration   If you allow the wrong user accounts or groups to perform specific tasks on OUs, you might be violating your company's security policy. Be sure to verify the delegations you have made at each OU level.

Organizational Issues   Sometimes, business practices do not easily map to the structure of Active Directory. A few misplaced OUs, user accounts, computer accounts, or groups can make administration difficult or inaccurate. In many cases, it might be beneficial to rearrange the OU structure to accommodate any changes in the business organization. In others, it might make more sense to change business processes.

If you regularly consider each of these issues when troubleshooting problems with OUs, you will be much less likely to make errors in the Active Directory configuration.

Creating and Managing Active Directory Objects

Now that you are familiar with the task of creating OUs, you should find creating and managing other Active Directory objects quite simple. The following sections will examine the details.

Overview of Active Directory Objects

When you install and configure a domain controller, Active Directory sets up an organizational structure for you, and you can create and manage several types of objects.

Active Directory Organization

When you are looking at your Active Directory structure, you will see objects that look like folders in File Explorer. These objects are containers, or *organizational units (OUs)*. The difference is that an OU is a container to which you can link a GPO. Normal containers cannot have a GPO linked to them. That's what makes an OU a special container.

By default, after you install and configure a domain controller, you will see the following organizational sections within the Active Directory Users and Computers tool (they look like folders):

Built-In   The *Built-In container* includes all of the standard groups that are installed by default when you promote a domain controller. You can use these groups to administer the servers in your environment. Examples include the Administrators group, Backup Operators group, and Print Operators group.

Computers   By default, the *Computers container* contains a list of the workstations in your domain. From here, you can manage all of the computers in your domain.

Domain Controllers   The *Domain Controllers OU* includes a list of all the domain controllers for the domain.

Foreign Security Principals   In environments that have more than one domain, you may need to grant permissions to users who reside in multiple domains. Generally, you manage this using Active Directory trees and forests. However, in some cases, you may want to provide resources to users who belong to domains that are not part of the forest.

Active Directory uses the concept of foreign security principals to allow permissions to be assigned to users who are not part of an Active Directory forest. This process is automatic and does not require the intervention of system administrators. You can then add the foreign security principals to domain local groups for which, in turn, you can grant permissions for resources within the domain. You can view a list of foreign security principals by using the Active Directory Users and Computers tool.

Foreign security principals containers are any objects to which security can be assigned and that are not part of the current domain. Security principals are Active Directory objects to which permissions can be applied, and they can be used to manage permissions in Active Directory.

Managed Service Accounts   The Managed Service Accounts container is a Windows Server 2016 container. Service accounts are accounts created to run specific services such as Exchange and SQL Server. Having a Managed Service Accounts container allows you to control the service accounts better and thus allows for better service account security. To create Managed Service Accounts, you must use the `New-ADServiceAccount` PowerShell command.

Users   The *Users container* includes all the security accounts that are part of the domain. When you first install the domain controller, there will be several groups in this container. For example, the Domain Admins group and the administrator account are created in this container.

You want to be sure to protect the administrator account. You should rename the admin account and make sure the password is complex. Protected admin accounts can make your network safer. Every hacker knows that there is an administrator account on the server by default. Be sure to make your network safer by protecting the admin account.

Active Directory Objects

You can create and manage several different types of Active Directory objects. The following are specific object types:

Computer   *Computer objects* represent workstations that are part of the Active Directory domain. All computers within a domain share the same security database, including user and group information. Computer objects are useful for managing security permissions and enforcing Group Policy restrictions.

Contact   *Contact objects* are usually used in OUs to specify the main administrative contact. Contacts are not security principals like users. They are used to specify information about individuals outside the organization.

Group   *Group objects* are logical collections of users primarily for assigning security permissions to resources. When managing users, you should place them into groups and then assign permissions to the group. This allows for flexible management without the need to set permissions for individual users.

InetOrgPerson   The *InetOrgPerson object* is an Active Directory object that defines attributes of users in Lightweight Directory Access Protocol (LDAP) and X.500 directories.

MSIMaging-PSPs   *MSIMaging-PSPs* is a container for all Enterprise Scan Post Scan Process objects.

MSMQ Queue Alias   An *MSMQ Queue Alias object* is an Active Directory object for the MSMQ-Custom-Recipient class type. The Microsoft Message Queuing (MSMQ) Queue Alias object associates an Active Directory path and a user-defined alias with a public, private, or direct single-element format name. This allows a queue alias to be used to reference a queue that might not be listed in Active Directory Domain Services (AD DS).

Organizational Unit   An *OU object* is created to build a hierarchy within the Active Directory domain. It is the smallest unit that can be used to create administrative groupings, and it can be used to assign group policies. Generally, the OU structure within a domain reflects a company's business organization.

Printer   *Printer objects* map to printers.

Shared Folder   *Shared Folder objects* map to server shares. They are used to organize the various file resources that may be available on file/print servers. Often, Shared Folder objects are used to give logical names to specific file collections. For example, system administrators might create separate shared folders for common applications, user data, and shared public files.

User   A *User object* is the fundamental security principal on which Active Directory is based. User accounts contain information about individuals as well as password and other permission information.

Creating Objects Using the Active Directory Users and Computers Tool

Exercise 2.5 walks you through the steps necessary to create various objects within an Active Directory domain. In this exercise, you create some basic Active Directory objects. To complete this exercise, you must have access to at least one Active Directory domain controller, and you should have also completed the previous exercises in this chapter.

EXERCISE 2.5

Creating Active Directory Objects

1. Open Active Directory Users and Computers by clicking Start ➢ Administrative Tools ➢ Active Directory Users And Computers.

2. Expand the current domain to list the objects currently contained within it. For this exercise, you will use the second- and third-level OUs contained within the North America top-level OU.

3. Right-click the Corporate OU and select New ➢ User. Fill in the following information:

    First Name: **Maria**

    Initial: **D**

    Last Name: **President**

    Full Name: (leave as default)

    User Logon Name: **mdpresident** (leave default domain)

    Click Next to continue.

4. Enter **P@ssw0rd** for the password for this user and then confirm it. Note that you can also make changes to password settings here. Click Next.

5. You will see a summary of the user information. Click Finish to create the new user.

6. Click the RD container and create another user in that container with the following information:

    First Name: **John**

    Initial: **Q**

    Last Name: **Adams**

    Full Name: (leave as default)

    User Logon Name: **jqadams** (leave default domain)

    Click Next to continue.

7. Assign the password **P@ssw0rd**. Click Next and then click Finish to create the user.

8. Right-click the RD OU and select New ➢ Contact. Use the following information to fill in the properties of the Contact object:

    First Name: **Jane**

    Initials: **R**

    Last Name: **Admin**

    Display Name: **jradmin**

    Click OK to create the new Contact object.

9. Right-click the RD OU and select New ➤ Shared Folder. Enter **Software** for the name and **\\server1\applications** for the network path (also known as the Universal Naming Convention [UNC] path). Note that you can create the object even though this resource (the physical server) does not exist. Click OK to create the Shared Folder object.

10. Right-click the HR OU and select New ➤ Group. Type **All Users** for the group name. Do not change the value in the Group Name (Pre–Windows 2000) field. For Group Scope, select Global, and for Group Type, select Security. To create the group, click OK.

11. Right-click the Sales OU and select New ➤ Computer. Type **Workstation1** for the name of the computer. Notice that the pre–Windows 2000 name is automatically populated and that, by default, the members of the Domain Admins group are the only ones who can add this computer to the domain. Place a check mark in the Assign This Computer Account As A Pre-Windows 2000 Computer box and then click OK to create the Computer object.

12. Close the Active Directory Users and Computers tool.

Configuring the User Principal Name

When you log into a domain, your logon name looks like an email address (for example, wpanek@willpanek.com). This is called your *user principal name (UPN)*. A UPN is the username followed by the @ sign and the domain name. At the time the user account is created, the UPN suffix is generated by default. The UPN is created as *userName@DomainName*, but an administrator can alter or change the default UPN. If your forest has multiple domains and you need to change the UPN to a different domain, you have that ability. To change the UPN suffix, in Active Directory Users and Computers, choose a user and go into their properties. Choose the Attribute Editor tab. Scroll down to the userPrincipalName attribute and make your changes. These changes then get replicated to the global catalog.

 If your organization has multiple forests set up by a trust, you can't change the UPN to a domain in the other forest. Global catalogs are used to log on users. Because UPNs get replicated to the local forest global catalog servers, you cannot log on to other forests using the UPN.

Using Templates

Now you are going to dive into user templates. *User templates* allow an Active Directory administrator to create a default account (for example, template_sales) and use that account to create all of the other users who match it (all the salespeople).

If you are creating multiple accounts, this can save you a lot of time and resources. For example, if you need to add 35 new salespeople to your company, you'll create one template for sales and use a copy of that template for all of the other new accounts. This saves you the trouble of filling out many of the same fields over and over again. When you copy a template, some of the information does *not* get copied over. This is because it is user-specific information. Here are some of the fields that do not get copied over from a template:

- Name
- Logon Name
- Password
- Email
- Phone Numbers
- Description
- Office
- Web Page

Many of the important fields such as Member Of (groups to which the user belongs), Profile Path, Department, and Company all get copied over. There is one important item that needs to be done when creating a template: the template account needs to be disabled after creation. You do not want anyone using this account to access your network. In Exercise 2.6, you will create a Sales template to use for your Sales department.

EXERCISE 2.6

Creating a User Template

1. Open Active Directory Users and Computers by clicking Start ➤ Administrative Tools ➤ Active Directory Users And Computers.

2. Expand the current domain to list the objects contained within it. For this exercise, you will use the Sales OU. Right-click the Sales OU and choose New ➤ User.

3. Use the following properties:

    First Name: **Sales**

    Last Name: **Template**

    Username: **sales_template**

    Password: **P@ssw0rd**

4. Click Next and then click Finish.

5. In the right window, double-click the Sales Template user to open the properties.

6. On the General tab, complete the following items:

    Description: **Template Account**

    Office: **Corporate**

Telephone: **999-999-9999**

Email: **Salet@abc.com**

Web: **www.abc.com**

7. Click the Profile tab. In the Profile Path field, type **\\ServerA\%username%**.

8. On the Members Of tab, click the Add button. At the Enter The Object Name To Select box, type **Administrator** and click the Check Names button. (Normally you would not add salespeople to the Administrators group, but you are doing so just for this exercise.) Click OK.

9. Click the Account tab. Scroll down in the Account Options box and check the Account Is Disabled check box.

10. Click OK in the user's Properties window to go back to the Sales OU.

11. Right-click the Sales Template account and choose Copy.

12. Enter the following information:

First Name: **Jenny**

Last Name: **Sales**

Username: **jsales**

Password: **P@ssw0rd**

Uncheck the Account Is Disabled check box.

13. In the right window, double-click the Jenny Sales user to open the properties.

14. Take a look at the Members Of tab, the General tab, and the Profile tab, and you will see that some of the fields are prefilled (including the Administrators group).

15. Close Jenny Sales Properties and exit Active Directory Users and Computers.

Importing Objects from a File

In Exercise 2.5, you created an account using the Active Directory Users and Computers tool. But what if you need to bulk import accounts? There are two main applications for doing bulk imports of accounts: the `ldifde.exe` utility and the `csvde.exe` utility. Both utilities import accounts from files.

The `ldifde` utility imports from line-delimited files. This utility allows an administrator to export and import data, thus allowing batch operations such as Add, Modify, and Delete to be performed in Active Directory. Windows Server 2016 includes `ldifde.exe` to help support batch operations.

The `csvde.exe` utility performs the same export functions as `ldifde.exe`, but `csvde.exe` uses a comma-separated value file format. The `csvde.exe` utility does not allow administrators to modify or delete objects. It only supports adding objects to Active Directory.

Active Directory Migration Tool

Another tool that administrators have used in the past is the *Active Directory Migration Tool (ADMT)*. ADMT allows an administrator to migrate users, groups, and computers from a previous version of the server to a current version of the server.

Administrators also used ADMT to migrate users, groups, and computers between Active Directory domains in different forests (interforest migration) and between Active Directory domains in the same forest (intraforest migration).

At the time this book was written, Microsoft had not yet released a new version of ADMT that is supported by Windows Server 2016. The reason I even mention it in this book is because Microsoft may be releasing a version of it soon and I wanted you to understand what it can do. Continue to check the Microsoft website to see whether a new version has been released.

Offline Domain Join of a Computer

Offline domain join gives administrators the ability to preprovision computer accounts in the domain to prepare operating systems for deployments. At startup, computers can then join the domain without the need to contact a domain controller. This helps reduce the time it takes to deploy computers in a datacenter.

Let's say your datacenter needs to have multiple virtual machines deployed. This is where offline domain join can be useful. Upon initial startup after the operating system is installed, offline domain join allows the virtual machines to join the domain automatically. No additional steps or restarts are needed.

The following are some of the benefits of using offline domain join:

- There is no additional network traffic for Active Directory state changes.
- There is no additional network traffic for computer state changes to the domain controller.
- Changes for both the Active Directory state and the computer state can be completed at a different times.

Managing Object Properties

Once you've created the necessary Active Directory objects, you'll probably need to make changes to their default properties. In addition to the settings you made when you were creating Active Directory objects, you can configure several more properties. You can also access object properties by right-clicking any object and selecting Properties from the pop-up menu.

Each object type contains a unique set of properties.

User Object Properties

The following list describes some of the properties of a User object (see Figure 2.7):

FIGURE 2.7 User Properties

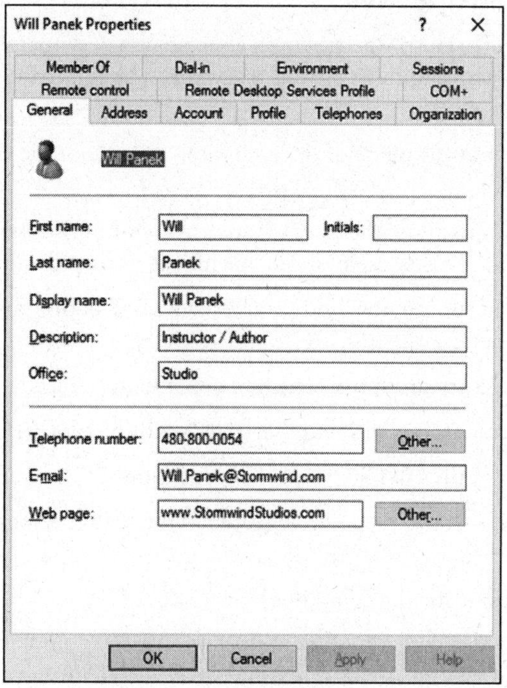

General   General account information about this user

Address   Physical location information about this user

Account   User logon name and other account restrictions, such as workstation restrictions and logon hours

Profile   Information about the user's roaming profile settings

Telephones   Telephone contact information for the user

Organization   The user's title, department, and company information

Member Of   Group membership information for the user

Dial-In   Remote Access Service (RAS) permissions for the user

Environment   Logon and other network settings for the user

Sessions   Session limits, including maximum session time and idle session settings

Remote Control   Remote control options for this user's session

Remote Desktop Services Profile   Information about the user's profile for use with Remote Desktop Services

Personal Virtual Desktop   Allows you to assign a user a specific virtual machine to use as a personal virtual desktop

COM+   Specifies a COM+ partition set for the user

Computer Object Properties

Computer objects have different properties than User objects. Computer objects refer to the systems that clients are operating to be part of a domain. The following list describes some Computer object properties:

General   Information about the name of the computer, the role of the computer, and its description

(You can enable an option to allow the Local System account of this machine to request services from other servers. This is useful if the machine is a trusted and secure computer.)

Operating System   The name, version, and service pack information for the operating system running on the computer

Member Of   Active Directory groups of which this Computer object is a member

Delegation   Allows you to set services that work on behalf of another user

Location   A description of the computer's physical location

Managed By   Information about the User or Contact object that is responsible for managing this computer

Dial-In   Sets dial-in options for the computer

Setting Properties for Active Directory Objects

Now that you have seen the various properties that can be set for the Active Directory objects, let's complete an exercise on how to configure some of these properties. Exercise 2.7 walks you through how to set various properties for Active Directory objects. To complete the steps in this exercise, first you must have completed Exercise 2.5.

Although it may seem a bit tedious, it's always a good idea to enter as much information as you know about Active Directory objects when you create them. Although the name Printer1 may be meaningful to you, users will appreciate the additional information, such as location, when they are searching for objects.

EXERCISE 2.7

Managing Object Properties

1. Open Active Directory Users and Computers by clicking Start ➢ Administrative Tools ➢ Active Directory Users And Computers.

2. Expand the name of the domain and select the RD container. Right-click the John Q. Adams user account and select Properties.

3. Here you will see the various Properties tabs for the User account. Make some configuration changes based on your personal preferences. Click OK to continue.

4. Select the HR OU. Right-click the All Users group and click Properties. In the All Users Properties dialog box, you will be able to modify the membership of the group.

   Click the Members tab and then click Add. Add the Maria D. President and John Q. Admin user accounts to the group. Click OK to save the settings and then OK to accept the group modifications.

5. Select the Sales OU. Right-click the Workstation1 Computer object. Notice that you can choose to disable the account or reset it (to allow another computer to join the domain under that same name). From the context menu, choose Properties. You'll see the properties for the Computer object.

   Examine the various options and make changes based on your personal preference. After you have examined the available options, click OK to continue.

6. Select the Corporate OU. Right-click the Maria D. President user account and choose Reset Password. You will be prompted to enter a new password, and then you'll be asked to confirm it. Note that you can also force the user to change this password upon the next logon, and you can also unlock the user's account from here. For this exercise, do not enter a new password; just click Cancel.

7. Close the Active Directory Users and Computers tool.

By now, you have probably noticed that Active Directory objects have a lot of common options. For example, Group and Computer objects both have a Managed By tab.

Windows Server 2016 allows you to manage many User objects at once. For instance, you can select several User objects by holding down the Shift or Ctrl key while selecting. You can then right-click any one of the selected objects and select Properties to display the properties that are available for multiple users. Notice that not every user property is available because some properties are unique to each user. You can configure the Description field for multiple object selections that include both users and nonusers, such as computers and groups.

 An important thing to think about when it comes to accounts is the difference between disabling an account and deleting an account. When you delete an account, the security ID (SID) gets deleted. Even if you later create an account with the same username, it will have a different SID number, and therefore it will be a different account. It is sometimes better to disable an account and place it into a nonactive OU called *Disabled*. This way, if you ever need to reaccess the account, you can do so.

Another object management task is the process of deprovisioning. *Deprovisioning* is the management of Active Directory objects in the container. When you remove an object from an Active Directory container, the deprovisioning process removes the object and synchronizes the container to stay current.

Understanding Groups

Now that you know how to create user accounts, it's time to learn how to create group accounts. As an instructor, I am always amazed when students (who work in the IT field) have no idea why they should use groups. This is something every organization should be using.

To illustrate their usefulness, let's say you have a Sales department user by the name of wpanek. Your organization has 100 resources shared on the network for users to access. Because wpanek is part of the Sales department, he has access to 50 of the resources. The Marketing department uses the other 50. If the organization is not using groups and wpanek moves from Sales to Marketing, how many changes do you have to make? The answer is 100. You have to move him out of the 50 resources he currently can use and place his account into the 50 new resources that he now needs.

Now let's say that you use groups. The Sales group has access to 50 resources, and the Marketing group has access to the other 50. If wpanek moves from Sales to Marketing, you need to make only two changes. You just have to take wpanek out of the Sales group and place him in the Marketing group. Once this is done, wpanek can access everything he needs to do his job.

Group Properties

Now that you understand why you should use groups, let's go over setting up groups and their properties (see Figure 2.8). When you are creating groups, it helps to understand some of the options that you need to use.

FIGURE 2.8   New Group dialog box

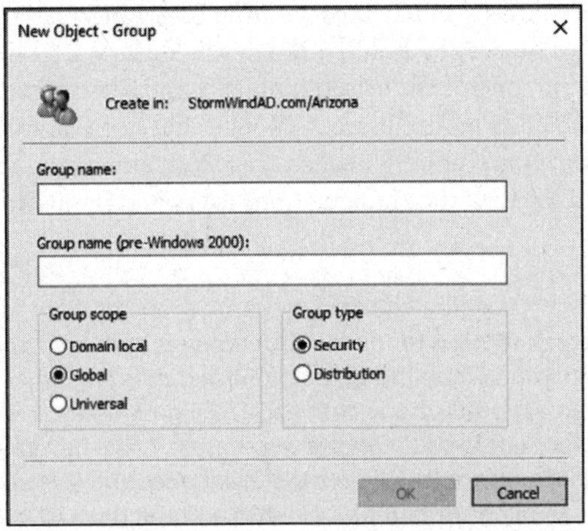

Group Type   You can choose from two group types: security groups and distribution groups.

Security Groups   These groups can have rights and permissions placed on them. For example, if you want to give a certain group of users access to a particular printer, but you want to control what they are allowed to do with this printer, you'd create a security group and then apply certain rights and permissions to this group.

Security groups can also receive emails. If someone sent an email to the group, all users within that group would receive it (as long as they have a mail system that allows for mail-enabled groups, like Exchange).

Distribution Groups   These groups are used for email *only* (as long as they have a mail system that allows for mail-enabled groups, like Exchange). You cannot place permissions and rights for objects on this group type.

Group Scope   When it comes to group scopes, you have three choices.

Domain Local Groups   Domain local groups are groups that remain in the domain in which they were created. You use these groups to grant permissions within a single domain. For example, if you create a domain local group named HPLaser, you cannot use that group in any other domain, and it has to reside in the domain in which you created it.

Global Groups   Global groups can contain other groups and accounts from the domain in which the group is created. In addition, you can give them permissions in any domain in the forest.

Universal Groups   Universal groups can include other groups and accounts from any domain in the domain tree or forest. You can give universal groups permissions in any domain in the domain tree or forest.

Creating Group Strategies

When you are creating a group strategy, think of this acronym that Microsoft likes to use in the exam: AGDLP (or AGLP). This acronym stands for a series of actions you should perform. Here is how it expands:

A   Accounts (Create your user accounts.)

G   Global groups (Put user accounts into global groups.)

DL   Domain local groups (Put global groups into domain local groups.)

P   Permissions (Assign permissions such as Deny or Apply on the domain local group.)

Another acronym that stands for a strategy you can use is AGUDLP (or AULP). Here is how it expands:

A   Accounts (Create your user accounts.)

G   Global groups (Put user accounts into global groups.)

U   Universal groups (Put the global groups into universal groups.)

DL   Domain local groups (Put universal groups into domain local groups.)

P   Permissions (Place permissions on the local group.)

Creating a Group

To create a new group, open the Active Directory Users and Computers snap-in. Click the OU where the group is going to reside. Right-click and choose New and then Group. After you create the group, just click the Members tab and choose Add. Add the users you want to reside in that group, and that's all there is to it.

Filtering and Advanced Active Directory Features

The Active Directory Users and Computers tool has a couple of other features that come in quite handy when you are managing many objects. You can access the Filter Options dialog box by clicking the View menu in the MMC and choosing Filter Options. You'll see a dialog box similar to the one shown in Figure 2.9. Here you can choose to filter objects by their specific types within the display. For example, if you are an administrator who works primarily with user accounts and groups, you can select those specific items by placing check marks in the list. In addition, you can create more complex filters by choosing Create Custom. Doing so provides you with an interface that looks similar to that of the Find command.

FIGURE 2.9   The Filter Options dialog box

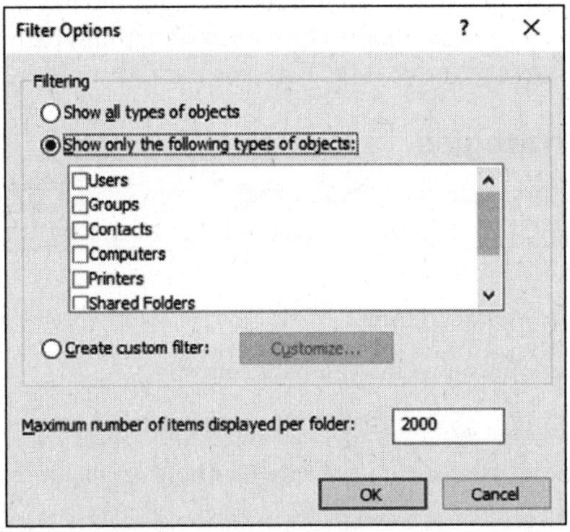

Another option in the Active Directory Users and Computers tool is to view advanced options. You can enable the advanced options by choosing Advanced Features in the View menu. This adds some top-level folders to the list under the name of the domain. Let's take a look at a couple of the new top-level folders.

The System folder (shown in Figure 2.10) provides additional features that you can configure to work with Active Directory. You can configure settings for the Distributed File

System (DFS), IP Security (IPSec) policies, the File Replication Service (FRS), and more. In addition to the System folder, you'll see the LostAndFound folder. This folder contains any files that may not have been replicated properly between domain controllers. You should check this folder periodically for any files so that you can decide whether you need to move them or copy them to other locations.

FIGURE 2.10 Advanced Features in the System folder of the Active Directory Users and Computers tool

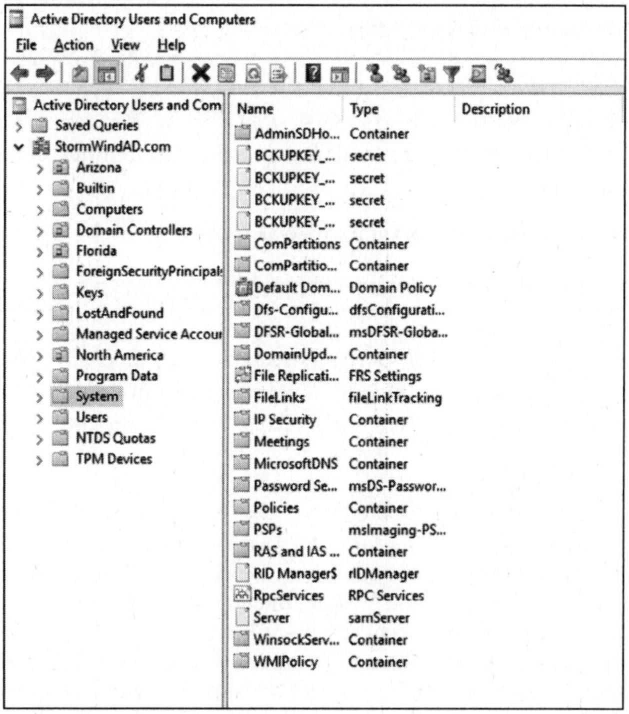

As you can see, managing Active Directory objects is generally a simple task. The Active Directory Users and Computers tool allows you to configure several objects. Let's move on to look at one more common administration function: moving objects.

Moving, Renaming, and Deleting Active Directory Objects

One of the extremely useful features of the Active Directory Users and Computers tool is its ability to move users and resources easily.

Exercise 2.8 walks you through the process of moving Active Directory objects. In this exercise, you will make several changes to the organization of Active Directory objects. To complete this exercise, first you must have completed Exercise 2.5.

EXERCISE 2.8

Moving Active Directory Objects

1. Open Active Directory Users and Computers by clicking Start ➢ Administrative Tools ➢ Active Directory Users And Computers.

2. Expand the name of the domain.

3. Select the Sales OU (under the New York OU), right-click Workstation1, and select Move. A dialog box appears. Select the RD OU and click OK to move the Computer object to that container.

4. Click the RD OU and verify that Workstation1 was moved.

5. Close the Active Directory Users and Computers tool.

In addition to moving objects within Active Directory, you can easily rename them by right-clicking an object and selecting Rename. Note that this option does not apply to all objects. You can remove objects from Active Directory by right-clicking them and choosing Delete.

Deleting an Active Directory object is an irreversible action. When an object is destroyed, any security permissions or other settings made for that object are removed as well. Because each object within Active Directory contains its own security identifier (SID), simply re-creating an object with the same name does not place any permissions on it. Before you delete an Active Directory object, be sure that you will never need it again. Windows Server 2016 has an Active Directory Recycle Bin to allow an administrator to retrieve a deleted object, but in case the Recycle Bin gets cleared, it's better to be safe than sorry. Also, the AD Recycle Bin is disabled by default, so it will be unavailable unless you turn that feature on. So, what is the moral of this story? Don't delete AD objects unless you are absolutely sure you want them gone.

Windows Server 2016 has a check box called Protect Container From Accidental Deletion for all OUs. If this check box is checked, to delete or move an OU, you must go into the Active Directory Users and Computers advanced options. Once you are in the advanced options, you can uncheck the box to move or delete the OU .

Resetting an Existing Computer Account

Every computer on the domain establishes a discrete channel of communication with the domain controller at logon time. The domain controller stores a randomly selected password (different from the user password) for authentication across the channel. The password is updated every 30 days.

Sometimes the computer's password and the domain controller's password don't match, and communication between the two machines fails. Without the ability to reset the computer account, you wouldn't be able to connect the machine to the domain. Fortunately, you can use the Active Directory Users and Computers tool to reestablish the connection.

Exercise 2.9 shows you how to reset an existing computer account. You should have completed the previous exercises in this chapter before you begin this exercise.

EXERCISE 2.9

Resetting an Existing Computer Account

1. Open Active Directory Users and Computers by clicking Start ➢ Administrative Tools ➢ Active Directory Users And Computers.

2. Expand the name of the domain.

3. Click the RD OU and then right-click the Workstation1 computer account.

4. Select Reset Account from the context menu. Click Yes to confirm your selection. Click OK at the success prompt.

5. When you reset the account, you break the connection between the computer and the domain. So, after performing this exercise, reconnect the computer to the domain if you want it to continue working on the network.

Throughout this book, I have tried to show you the PowerShell way of doing a task shown previously using an MMC snap-in. Well, this is going to be no different.

This example shows you how to reset the secure connection between the local computer and the domain to which it is joined using a PowerShell command. In this example, the domain controller that performs the operation is specified as StormDC1.StormWindAD.com. To execute this PowerShell command, you must run this command on the local computer:

```
Test-ComputerSecureChannel -Repair -Server StormDC1.StormWindAD.com
```

Understanding Dynamic Access Control

One of the advantages of Windows Server 2016 is the ability to apply data governance to your file server. This will help control who has access to information and auditing. You get these advantages through the use of *Dynamic Access Control (DAC)*. Dynamic Access Control allows you to identify data by using data classifications (both automatic and manual) and then control access to these files based on these classifications.

DAC also gives administrators the ability to control file access by using a central access policy. This central access policy will also allow an administrator to set up audit access to files for reporting and forensic investigation.

DAC allows an administrator to set up Active Directory Rights Management Service encryption for Microsoft Office documents. For example, you can set up encryption for any documents that contain financial information.

Dynamic Access Control gives an administrator the flexibility to configure file access and auditing to domain-based file servers. To do this, DAC controls claims in the authentication token, resource properties, and conditional expressions within permission and auditing entries.

Administrators have the ability to give users access to files and folders based on Active Directory attributes. For example, a user named Dana is given access to the file server share because in the user's Active Directory (department attribute) properties, the value contains the value Sales.

 For DAC to function properly, an administrator must enable Windows 7/8/10 computers and Windows Server 2012/2012 R2/2016 file servers to support claims and compound authentication.

Managing Security and Permissions

Now that you understand the basic issues, terms, and Active Directory objects that pertain to security, it's time to look at how you can apply this information to secure your network resources. The general practice for managing security is to assign users to groups and then grant permissions and logon parameters to the groups so that they can access certain resources.

For management ease and to implement a hierarchical structure, you can place groups within OUs. You can also assign Group Policy settings to all of the objects contained within an OU. By using this method, you can combine the benefits of a hierarchical structure (through OUs) with the use of security principals.

The primary tool you use to manage security permissions for users, groups, and computers is the Active Directory Users and Computers tool. Using this tool, you can create and manage Active Directory objects and organize them based on your business needs. Common tasks for many system administrators might include the following:

- Resetting a user's password (for example, in cases where they forget their password)

- Creating new user accounts (when, for instance, a new employee joins the company)

- Modifying group memberships based on changes in job requirements and functions

- Disabling user accounts (when, for example, users will be out of the office for long periods of time and will not require network resource access)

Once you've properly grouped your users, you need to set the actual permissions that affect the objects within Active Directory. The actual permissions that are available vary based on the type of object. Table 2.1 provides an example of some of the permissions that you can apply to various Active Directory objects and an explanation of what each permission does.

TABLE 2.1 Permissions of Active Directory objects

Permission	Explanation
Control Access	Changes security permissions on the object
Create Child	Creates objects within an OU (such as other OUs)
Delete Child	Deletes child objects within an OU
Delete Tree	Deletes an OU and the objects within it
List Contents	Views objects within an OU
List Object	Views a list of the objects within an OU
Read	Views properties of an object (such as a username)
Write	Modifies properties of an object

Using ACLs and ACEs

Each object in Active Directory has an *access control list*. The ACL is a list of user accounts and groups that are allowed to access the resource. For each ACL, there is an access control entry that defines what a user or a group can actually do with the resource. Deny permissions are always listed first. This means that if users have Deny permissions through user or group membership, they will not be allowed to access the object, even if they have explicit Allow permissions through other user or group permissions.

Real World Scenario

Using Groups Effectively

You are a new system administrator for a medium-sized organization, and your network spans a single campus environment. The previous administrator had migrated the network from Windows Server 2008 to Windows Server 2016 and everyone seems fine with the network and new workstations. As you familiarize yourself with the network, you realize that the previous administrator applied a very ad hoc approach. Many of the permissions to resources had been given to individual accounts on request. It seems that there was no particular strategy with regard to administration.

Management tells you that the company has acquired another company, ideally the first of several acquisitions. They tell you about these plans because they do not want any hiccups in the information system as necessary changes ensue.

You immediately realize that management practices of the past must be replaced with the best practices that have been developed for networks over the years. One of the fundamental practices that you need to establish for this environment is the use of groups to apply permissions and give privileges to users throughout the network.

It is quite simple to give permissions individually, and in some cases, it seems like overkill to create a group, give permissions to the group, and then add a user to the group. Using group-based permissions really pays off in the long run, however, regardless of how small your network is today.

One constant in the networking world is that networks grow. When they grow, it is much easier to add users to a well-thought-out system of groups and consistently applied policies and permissions than it is to patch these elements together for each individual user.

Don't get caught up in the "easy" way of dealing with each request as it comes down the pike. Take the time to figure out how the system will benefit from a more structured approach. Visualize your network as already large with numerous accounts, even if it is still small; this way, when it grows, you will be well positioned to manage the network as smoothly as possible.

Using Group Policy for Security

A very useful and powerful feature of Active Directory is a technology known as a *Group Policy*. Through the use of Group Policy settings, system administrators can assign thousands of different settings and options for users, groups, and OUs. Specifically, in relation to security, you can use many different options to control how important features such as password policies, user rights, and account lockout settings can be configured.

The general process for making these settings is to create a *Group Policy object (GPO)* with the settings you want and then link it to an OU or other Active Directory object.

Table 2.2 lists many Group Policy settings that are relevant to creating a secure Active Directory environment. Note that this list is not comprehensive—many other options are available through Windows Server 2016's administrative tools.

TABLE 2.2   Group Policy settings used for security purposes

Setting section	Setting name	Purpose
Account Policies ➢ Password Policy	Enforce Password History	Specifies how many passwords will be remembered. This option prevents users from reusing the same passwords whenever they're changed.
Account Policies ➢ Password Policy	Minimum Password Length	Prevents users from using short, weak passwords by specifying the minimum number of characters that the password must include.
Account Policies ➢ Account Lockout Policy	Account Lockout Threshold	Specifies how many bad password attempts can be entered before the account gets locked out.
Account Policies ➢ Account Lockout Policy	Account Lockout Duration	Specifies how long an account will remain locked out after too many bad password attempts have been entered. By setting this option to a reasonable value (such as 30 minutes), you can reduce administrative overhead while still maintaining fairly strong security.
Account Policies ➢ Account Lockout Policy	Reset Account Lockout Counter After	Specifies how long the Account Lockout Threshold counter will hold failed logon attempts before resetting to 0.
Local Policies ➢ Security Options	Accounts: Rename Administrator Account	Often, when trying to gain unauthorized access to a computer, individuals attempt to guess the administrator password. One method for increasing security is to rename this account so that no password allows entry using this logon.
Local Policies ➢ Security Options	Domain Controller: Allow Server Operators To Schedule Tasks	This option specifies whether members of the built-in Server Operators group are allowed to schedule tasks on the server.
Local Policies ➢ Security Options	Interactive Logon: Do Not Display Last User Name	Increases security by not displaying the name of the last user who logged on to the system.
Local Policies ➢ Security Options	Shutdown: Allow System To Be Shut Down Without Having To Log On	Allows system administrators to perform remote shutdown operations without logging on to the server.

You can use several different methods to configure Group Policy settings using the tools included with Windows Server 2016. Exercise 2.10 walks through the steps required to create a basic group policy for the purpose of enforcing security settings. To complete the steps of this exercise, you must have completed Exercise 2.1.

EXERCISE 2.10

Applying Security Policies by Using Group Policy

1.   Open the Group Policy Management Console tool.

2.   Expand Domains and then click the domain name.

3.   In the right pane, right-click the Default Domain Policy and choose Edit.

4.   In the Group Policy Management Editor window, expand Computer Configuration ➢ Policies ➢ Windows Settings ➢ Security Settings ➢ Account Policies ➢ Password Policy.

5.   In the right pane, double-click the Minimum Password Length setting.

6.   In the Security Policy Setting dialog box, make sure the box labeled Define This Policy Setting Option is checked. Increase the Password Must Be At Least value to eight characters.

7.   Click OK to return to the Group Policy Management Editor window.

8.   Expand User Configuration ➢ Policies ➢ Administrative Templates ➢ Control Panel. Double-click Prohibit Access To The Control Panel And PC settings, select Enabled, and then click OK.

9.   Close the Group Policy window.

Fine-Grained Password Policies

The Windows 2016 operating systems allow an organization to have different password and account lockout policies for different sets of users in a domain. In versions of Active Directory before 2008, an administrator could set up only one password policy and account lockout policy per domain.

The Default Domain policy for the domain is where these policy settings were configured. Because domains could have only one password and account lockout policy, organizations that wanted multiple password and account lockout settings had to either create a password filter or deploy multiple domains.

Fine-grained password policies allow you to specify multiple password policies within a single domain. Let's say you want administrators not to have to change their password as frequently as salespeople. Fine-grained password policies allow you to do just that.

Password Settings objects (PSOs) are created so that you can create fine-grained password policies. You create PSOs using the ADSI editor and then you can use those PSOs to create your fine-grained password policies.

Exercise 2.11 walks through the creation of a custom password policy using the ADSI Edit tool, and then you will link that policy to a group using Active Directory Users and Computers. Before completing this exercise, create a new global group named Passgroup in Active Directory Users and Computers.

 Administrators also have the ability to create fine-grained password policies using the Active Directory Administrative Center. I will show you how to create a new password policy in the section "Using the Active Directory Administrative Center" later in this chapter.

EXERCISE 2.11

Fine-Grained Password Policy

1. Open ADSI Edit by pressing the Windows key and choosing ADSI Edit.

2. Right-click ADSI Edit and then choose Connect To.

3. When the Connection Settings dialog box appears, click OK.

4. In the window on the left, expand Default Naming Context ➢ DC=yourdomainname,DC=com ➢ CN=System ➢ CN=Password Settings Container.

5. Right-click CN=Password Settings Container and choose New ➢ Object.

6. In the Select A Class box, choose msDS-PasswordSettings and click Next.

7. At the Common Name screen, type **CustomPolicy** and click Next.

8. At the Password Settings Precedence screen, enter **10** as the value. This works as a cost value. The lowest priority takes precedence.

9. At the Password Reversible Encryption Status For Users Accounts screen, set the value to False (recommended by Microsoft).

10. The Password History Length screen shows how many passwords are remembered before a password can be used again. You can set this for up to 1,024 remembered passwords. Set the value to **12**. Click Next.

11. At the Password Complexity screen, set the value to True.

12. The next screen will be the Minimum Password Length screen. Set the value to **8** and click Next.

13. At the Minimum Password Age screen, you must enter a value for the amount of time you want the password to be used at a minimum. Time is done in the I8 format, like so:

    −600000000 = 1 minute

    −36000000000 = 1 hour

    −864000000000 = 1 day

Enter **–8640000000000** (10 zeros) as your value for 10 days and click Next. You must put the – (minus) sign in the front of the value.

14. At the Maximum Password Age screen, set the value as **–51840000000000** (10 zeros). This value equals 60 days. Click Next.

15. At the Lockout Threshold screen, enter **3** and click Next.

16. At the Observation Window screen, enter **–3000000000** (5 minutes) and click Next.

17. At the Lockout Duration screen, enter **–18000000000** (30 minutes) and click Next.

18. Click Finished. If you received any errors, check all of your times to be sure the – (minus) sign appears in front of the number.

19. Close ADSI Edit.

20. Open the Active Directory Users and Computers snap-in.

21. On the View menu along the top, make sure Advanced Features is checked.

22. In the window on the left, expand Active Directory Users And Computers ➢ *yourdomain* ➢ System ➢ Password Settings Container.

23. In the details pane on the right side, right-click CustomPolicy and choose Properties.

24. Click the Attribute Editor tab.

25. Scroll down and select the msDS-PsoAppliesTo attribute. Click Edit.

26. In the Multi-valued Distinguished Name dialog box, click Add Windows Account.

27. Type in **Passgroup** (this is the group you created before the exercise) and click the Check Name button. Click OK.

28. Click OK twice more, and then you are finished. Close the Active Directory Users and Computers snap-in.

Publishing Active Directory Objects

One of the main goals of Active Directory is to make resources easy to find. Two of the most commonly used resources in a networked environment are server file shares and printers. These are so common, in fact, that most organizations have dedicated file and print servers. When it comes to managing these types of resources, Active Directory makes it easy to determine which files and printers are available to users.

With that being said, take a look at how Active Directory manages to publish shared folders and printers.

Making Active Directory Objects Available to Users

An important aspect of managing Active Directory objects is that a system administrator can control which objects users can see. The act of making an Active Directory object available is known as *publishing*. The two main types of publishable objects are Printer objects and Shared Folder objects.

The general process for creating server shares and shared printers has remained unchanged from previous versions of Windows: you create the various objects (a printer or a file system folder) and then enable them for sharing. To make these resources available via Active Directory, however, there's an additional step: you must publish the resources. Once an object has been published in Active Directory, clients will be able to use it.

When you publish objects in Active Directory, you should know the server name and share name of the resource. When system administrators use Active Directory objects, they can change the resource to which the object points, without having to reconfigure or even notify clients. For example, if you move a share from one server to another, all you need to do is to update the Shared Folder object's properties to point to the new location. Active Directory clients still refer to the resource with the same path and name that they used before.

Publishing Printers

Printers can be published easily within Active Directory. This makes them available to users in your domain.

Exercise 2.12 walks you through the steps you need to take to share and publish a Printer object by having you create and share a printer. To complete the printer installation, you need access to the Windows Server 2016 installation media (via the hard disk, a network share, or the DVD drive).

EXERCISE 2.12

Creating and Publishing a Printer

1. Click the Windows key on the keyboard and choose Control Panel.

2. Click Devices And Printers ➢ Add A Printer. This starts the Add Printer Wizard. Then click the Next button.

3. In the Choose A Local Or Network Printer page, select Add A Local Printer. This should automatically take you to the next page. If it does not, click Next.

4. On the Choose A Printer Port page, select Use An Existing Port. From the drop-down list beside that option, make sure LPT1: (Printer Port) is selected. Click Next.

5. On the Install The Printer Driver page, select Generic for the manufacturer. For the printer, highlight Generic/Text Only. Click Next.

6. On the Type A Printer Name page, type **Text Printer**. Uncheck the Set As The Default Printer box and then click Next.

7.   The Installing Printer screen appears. After the system is finished, the Printer Sharing page appears. Make sure the box labeled "Share this printer so that others on your network can find and use it" is selected, and accept the default share name of Text Printer.

8.   In the Location section, type **Building 203**, and in the Comment section, add the following comment: **This is a text-only Printer**. Click Next.

9.   On the You've Successfully Added Text Printer page, click Finish.

10. Next you need to verify that the printer will be listed in Active Directory. Right-click the Text Printer icon and select Printer Properties.

11. Select the Sharing tab and make sure that the List In The Directory box is checked. Note that you can also add additional printer drivers for other operating systems using this tab. Click OK to accept the settings.

Note that when you create and share a printer this way, an Active Directory Printer object is not displayed within the Active Directory Users and Computers tool. The printer is actually associated with the Computer object to which it is connected.

Publishing Shared Folders

Now that you've created and published a printer, you'll see how the same thing can be done to shared folders.

Exercise 2.13 walks through the steps required to create a folder, share it, and then publish it in Active Directory. This exercise assumes you are using the C: partition; however, you may want to change this based on your server configuration. This exercise assumes you have completed Exercise 2.5.

Creating and Publishing a Shared Folder

1.   Create a new folder in the root directory of your C: partition and name it **Test Share**. To do this, click the File Explorer link on the toolbar.

2.   Right-click the Test Share folder. Choose Share With ➤ Specific People.

3.   In the File Sharing dialog box, enter the names of users with whom you want to share this folder. In the upper box, enter **Everyone** and then click Add. Note that Everyone appears in the lower box. Click in the Permission Level column next to Everyone and choose Read/Write from the pop-up menu. Then click Share.

4.   You'll see a message that your folder has been shared. Click Done.

5.   Click the Windows key on the keyboard and choose Administrative Tools.

6. Open the Active Directory Users and Computers tool. Expand the current domain and right-click the RD OU. Select New > Shared Folder.

7. In the New Object - Shared Folder dialog box, type **Shared Folder Test** for the name of the folder. Then type the UNC path to the share (for example, **\\server1\Test Share**). Click OK to create the share.

Once you have created and published the Shared Folder object, clients can use the My Network Places icon to find it. The Shared Folder object will be organized based on the OU in which you created it. When you use publication, you can see how this makes it easy to manage shared folders.

Querying Active Directory

So far you've created several Active Directory resources. One of the main benefits of having all of your resource information in Active Directory is that you can easily find what you're looking for using the Find dialog box. Recall that I recommended that you always enter as much information as possible when creating Active Directory objects. This is where that extra effort begins to pay off.

Exercise 2.14 walks you through the steps to find specific objects in Active Directory. To complete this exercise, you must have completed Exercise 2.5.

EXERCISE 2.14

Finding Objects in Active Directory

1. Open Active Directory Users and Computers by clicking Start > Administrative Tools > Active Directory Users And Computers.

2. Right-click the name of the domain and select Find.

3. In the Find Users, Contacts, And Groups dialog box, select Users, Contacts, And Groups from the Find drop-down list. For the In setting, choose Entire Directory. This searches the entire Active Directory environment for the criteria you enter.

   Note that if this is a production domain and there are many objects, searching the whole directory may be a time-consuming and network-intensive operation.

4. In the Name field, type **admin** and then click Find Now to obtain the results of the search.

5. Now that you have found several results, you can narrow down the list. Click the Advanced tab of the Find Users, Contacts, And Groups dialog box.

   In the Field drop-down list, select User > Last Name. For Condition, select Starts With, and for Value, type **admin**. Click Add to add this condition to the search criteria. Click Find Now. Now only the users that have the last name Admin are shown.

6. When you have finished searching, close the Find Users, Contacts, And Groups dialog box and exit the Active Directory Users and Computers tool.

Using the many options available in the Find dialog box, you can usually narrow down the objects for which you are searching quickly and efficiently. Users and system administrators alike find this tool useful in environments of any size. Now that you have seen how to create objects in Active Directory, let's take a look at a new Windows Server 2016 feature called Active Directory Administrative Center.

Using the Active Directory Administrative Center

Windows Server 2016 has a feature called the *Active Directory Administrative Center*. This feature allows you to manage many Active Directory tasks from one central location (see Figure 2.11).

FIGURE 2.11   Administrative Center Overview screen

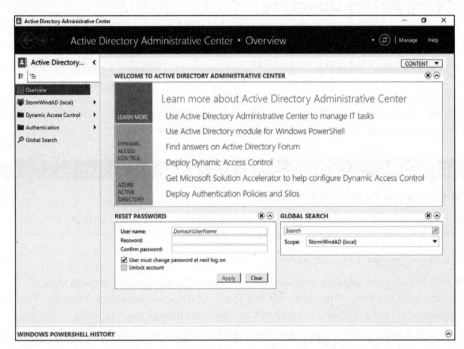

Using the Active Directory Administrative Center, here are some of the tasks that an administrator can perform:

- Reset passwords
- Create new objects
- Delete objects
- Move objects
- Perform global searches
- Configure properties for Active Directory objects

In Windows Server 2016, the Active Directory Administrative Center is just another tool in your Active Directory tool belt. It does not matter which way you create your Active Directory objects as long as you have a good understanding of how to create them.

One of the easy tasks that you can complete with the Active Directory Administrative center is the ability to create a Fine-Grained Password Policy.

Exercise 2.15 walks you through the steps to create a password policy for the IT Department. To complete this exercise, you must have a Global Security group called IT. If you do not have a group called IT, please create the IT group using Active Directory Users and Computers.

EXERCISE 2.15

Creating a PSO Using the Active Directory Administrative Center

1. Open the Active Directory Administrative Center by clicking Start ➢ Administrative Tools ➢ Active Directory Administrative Center.

2. Expand the domain, expand System, and then click Password Settings Container (see Figure 2.12).

FIGURE 2.12 Password Settings Container

EXERCISE 2.15 *(continued)*

3. In the right-hand side under Tasks, choose New ➤ Password Settings (see Figure 2.13).

FIGURE 2.13 New Password Settings

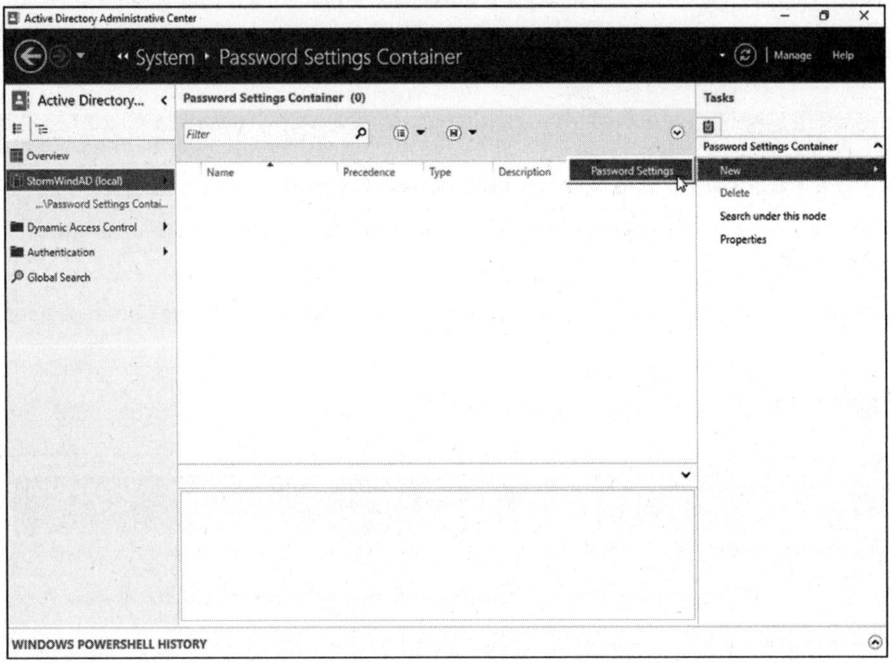

4. When the Password Settings dialog box appears, fill in the following settings (see Figure 2.14):
   - Name: **ITpso**
   - Precedence: **10**
   - Enforce Minimum Password Length: checked
   - Minimum Password Length (characters): **8**
   - Enforce Password History: checked
   - Number Of Passwords Remembered: **24**
   - Password Must Meet Complexity Requirements: checked
   - Protect From Accidental Deletion: checked

- Enforce Minimum Password Age: checked

- User Cannot Change The Password Within: **1** (for 1 day)

- Enforce Maximum Password Age: checked

- User Must Change The Password After: **60** (for 60 days)

- Enforce Account Lockout Policy: checked

- Number Of Failed Logon Attempts Allowed: **5**

- Reset Failed Logon Attempts Count After (min): **30**

- Account Will Be Locked Out : Until An Administrator Manually Unlocks The Account

- Protect From Accidental Deletion: checked

- Description: **IT Department Password Policy**

FIGURE 2.14   PSO settings

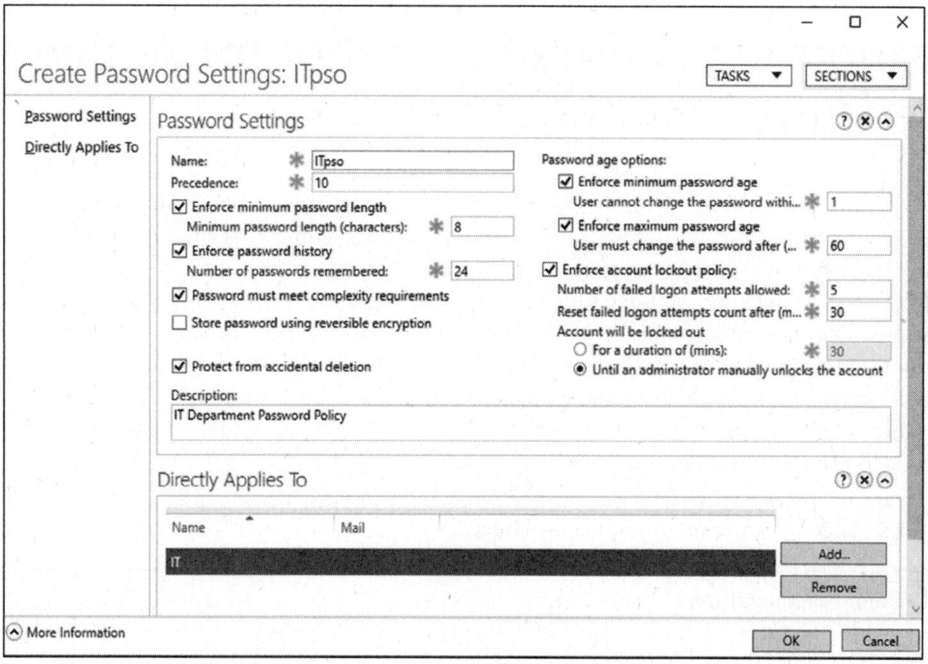

5.   Click the Add button.

6.   Type in **IT** and click the Check Names button (see Figure 2.15). Then click OK.

FIGURE 2.15   Select Users or Groups

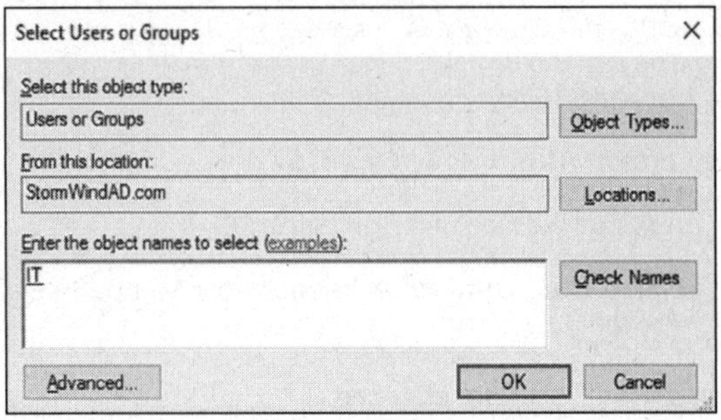

7.   Click OK to complete the PSO. Close the Active Directory Administrative Center.

Using the Command Prompt for Active Directory Configuration

Many IT administrators like to use command-line commands to configure and maintain their Active Directory environment. One advantage of using command-line commands is the ability to do multiple changes at once using batch files.

Another advantage of knowing how to manipulate Active Directory using the command prompt is working with Windows Server 2016 Server Core. Server Core is an installation of Windows Server 2016 that has no GUI windows. One of the ways to configure Server Core is to use commands in the command prompt window.

Table 2.3 shows you many of the command prompt commands and explains how each command affects Active Directory.

TABLE 2.3   Command prompt commands

Command	Explanation
Csvde	This command allows you to import and export data from Active Directory. The data gets stored in a comma-separated value (CSV) format.
Dcdiag	This troubleshooting command checks the state of your domain controllers in your forest and sends back a report of any problems.

Command	Explanation
Djoin	This command allows a computer account to join a domain, and it runs an offline domain join when a computer restarts.
Dsacls	This command allows you to see and change permissions in the access control list for objects in Active Directory Domain Services (AD DS).
Dsadd	This command allows you to add an object to the AD DS directory.
Dsamain	This command shows the Active Directory data stored in either a snapshot or a backup as if it were in a Lightweight Directory Access Protocol (LDAP) server.
Dsdbutil	This command provides database utilities for Active Directory Lightweight Directory Services (AD LDS).
Dsget	This command shows the properties of an object in the AD DS directory.
Dsmgmt	This command gives an administrator management utilities for AD LDS.
Dsmod	This command allows you to modify an AD DS object.
Dsmove	This command allows you to move an object in an Active Directory domain from its current OU to a new OU within the same forest.
Dsquery	This command allows you to query AD DS.
Dsrm	This command removes an object from the AD DS directory.
Ldifde	This command allows you to import and export data from Active Directory. The data is stored as LDAP Data Interchange Format (LDIF).
Ntdsutil	This is one of the most important commands for Active Directory. It allows you to do maintenance on the Active Directory database.
Repadmin	This command allows administrators to diagnose Active Directory replication problems between domain controllers.

PowerShell for Active Directory

Table 2.4 will show you just some of the available PowerShell commands for maintaining Active Directory. These PowerShell commands can help you do everything from unlocking disabled accounts to doing password resets.

To see a complete list of PowerShell commands for Active Directory, please visit Microsoft's website at:

https://technet.microsoft.com/en-us/library/ee617195.aspx

TABLE 2.4   PowerShell commands for Active Directory

Command	Explanation
Add-ADComputerServiceAccount	This command allows an administrator to add service accounts to Active Directory.
Add-ADGroupMember	This command allows you to add users to an Active Directory group.
Disable-ADAccount	Administrators can use this command to disable an Active Directory account.
Enable-ADAccount	Administrators can use this command to enable an Active Directory account.
Get-ADComputer	This command allows you to view one or more Active Directory computers.
Get-ADDomain	Administrators can use this command to view an Active Directory domain.
Get-ADFineGrainedPasswordPolicy	This command allows you to view the Active Directory fine-grained password policies.
Get-ADGroup	Administrators can use this command to view Active Directory groups.
Get-ADGroupMember	This command allows you to view the users in an Active Directory group.
Get-ADServiceAccount	Administrators can use this command to view the Active Directory service accounts.
Get-ADUser	This command allows you to view one or more Active Directory users.
New-ADComputer	Administrators can use this command to create a new Active Directory computer.
New-ADGroup	Administrators can use this command to create a new Active Directory group.

Command	Explanation
New-ADServiceAccount	This command is the *only* way that you can create a new Managed Service Account.
New-ADUser	Administrators can use this command to create a new Active Directory user.
Set-ADAccountPassword	This command allows you to modify the password of an Active Directory account.
Unlock-ADAccount	Administrators can use this command to unlock an Active Directory account.

Summary

This chapter covered the fundamentals of administering Active Directory. The most important part of administering Active Directory is learning about how to work with OUs. Therefore, you should be aware of the purpose of OUs; that is, they help you to organize and manage the directory. For instance, think of administrative control. If you wanted to delegate rights to another administrator (such as a sales manager), you could delegate that authority to that user within the Sales OU. As the system administrator, you would retain the rights to the castle.

You also looked at how to design an OU structure from an example. The example showed you how to design a proper OU layout. You can also create, organize, and reorganize OUs if need be.

In addition, you took a look at groups and group strategies. There are different types of groups (domain local, global, and universal groups), and you should know when each group is available and when to use each group.

Finally, this chapter covered how to use the Active Directory Users and Computers tool to manage Active Directory objects. If you're responsible for day-to-day system administration, there's a good chance that you are already familiar with this tool; if not, you should be after reading this chapter. Using this tool, you learned how to work with Active Directory objects such as User, Computer, and Group objects.

Exam Essentials

Understand the purpose of OUs.   OUs are used to create a hierarchical, logical organization for objects within an Active Directory domain.

Know the types of objects that can reside within OUs.   OUs can contain Active Directory User, Computer, Shared Folder, and other objects.

Understand how to use the Delegation of Control Wizard.   The Delegation of Control Wizard is used to assign specific permissions at the level of OUs.

Understand the concept of inheritance.   By default, child OUs inherit permissions and Group Policy assignments set for parent OUs. However, these settings can be overridden for more granular control of security.

Know groups and group strategies.   You can use three groups: domain local, global, and universal. Understand the group strategies and when they apply.

Understand how Active Directory objects work.   Active Directory objects represent some piece of information about components within a domain. The objects themselves have attributes that describe details about them.

Understand how Active Directory objects can be organized.   By using the Active Directory Users and Computers tool, you can create, move, rename, and delete various objects.

Understand how to import bulk users.   You can import multiple accounts by doing a bulk import. Bulk imports use files to import the data into Active Directory. Know the two utilities (`ldifde.exe` and `csvde.exe`) you need to perform the bulk imports and how to use them.

Learn how resources can be published.   A design goal for Active Directory was to make network resources easier for users to find. With that in mind, you should understand how using published printers and shared folders can simplify network resource management.

Review Questions

You can find the answers in the Appendix.

1. You are the administrator of an organization with a single Active Directory domain. A user who left the company returns after 16 weeks. The user tries to log on to their old computer and receives an error stating that authentication has failed. The user's account has been enabled. You need to ensure that the user is able to log on to the domain using that computer. What do you do?

   A. Reset the computer account in Active Directory. Disjoin the computer from the domain, and then rejoin the computer to the domain.

   B. Run the ADadd command to rejoin the computer account.

   C. Run the MMC utility on the user's computer, and add the Domain Computers snap-in.

   D. Re-create the user account and reconnect the user account to the computer account.

2. You are the administrator of an organization with a single Active Directory domain. One of your senior executives tries to log on to a machine and receives the error "This user account has expired. Ask your administrator to reactivate your account." You need to make sure that this doesn't happen again to this user. What do you do?

   A. Configure the domain policy to disable account lockouts.

   B. Configure the password policy to extend the maximum password age to 0.

   C. Modify the user's properties to set the Account Never Expires setting.

   D. Modify the user's properties to extend the maximum password age to 0.

3. You need to create a new user account using the command prompt. Which command would you use?

   A. dsmodify

   B. dscreate

   C. dsnew

   D. dsadd

4. Maria is a user who belongs to the Sales distribution global group. She is not able to access the laser printer that is shared on the network. The Sales global group has full access to the laser printer. How do you fix the problem?

   A. Change the group type to a security group.

   B. Add the Sales global group to the Administrators group.

   C. Add the Sales global group to the Printer Operators group.

   D. Change the Sales group to a local group.

5. You are a domain administrator for a large domain. Recently, you have been asked to make changes to some of the permissions related to OUs within the domain. To restrict security for the Texas OU further, you remove some permissions at that level. Later, a junior system administrator mentions that she is no longer able to make changes to objects within the

Austin OU (which is located within the Texas OU). Assuming that no other changes have been made to Active Directory permissions, which of the following characteristics of OUs might have caused the change in permissions?

A. Inheritance

B. Group Policy

C. Delegation

D. Object properties

6. Isabel, a system administrator, created a new Active Directory domain in an environment that already contains two trees. During the promotion of the domain controller, she chose to create a new Active Directory forest. Isabel is a member of the Enterprise Administrators group and has full permissions over all domains. During the organization's migration to Active Directory, many updates were made to the information stored within the domains. Recently, users and other system administrators have complained about not being able to find specific Active Directory objects in one or more domains (although the objects exist in others). To investigate the problem, Isabel wants to check for any objects that have not been properly replicated among domain controllers. If possible, she would like to restore these objects to their proper place within the relevant Active Directory domains.

Which two of the following actions should she perform to be able to view the relevant information? (Choose two.)

A. Change Active Directory permissions to allow object information to be viewed in all domains.

B. Select the Advanced Features item in the View menu.

C. Promote a member server in each domain to a domain controller.

D. Rebuild all domain controllers from the latest backups.

E. Examine the contents of the LostAndFound folder using the Active Directory Users and Computers tool.

7. You are a consultant hired to evaluate an organization's Active Directory domain. The domain contains more than 200,000 objects and hundreds of OUs. You begin examining the objects within the domain, but you find that the loading of the contents of specific OUs takes a long time. Furthermore, the list of objects can be large. You want to do the following:

▪ Use the built-in Active Directory administrative tools and avoid the use of third-party tools or utilities.

▪ Limit the list of objects within an OU to only the type of objects that you're examining (for example, only Computer objects).

▪ Prevent any changes to the Active Directory domain or any of the objects within it.

Which one of the following actions meets these requirements?

A. Use the Filter option in the Active Directory Users and Computers tool to restrict the display of objects.

B. Use the Delegation of Control Wizard to give yourself permissions over only a certain type of object.

   C. Implement a new naming convention for objects within an OU and then sort the results using this new naming convention.

   D. Use the Active Directory Domains and Trusts tool to view information from only selected domain controllers.

   E. Edit the domain Group Policy settings to allow yourself to view only the objects of interest.

8. You are the administrator for a small organization with four servers. You have one file server named StormSrvA that runs Windows Server 2016. You have a junior administrator who needs to do backups on this server. You need to ensure that the junior admin can use Windows Server Backup to create a complete backup of StormSrvA. What should you configure to allow the junior admin to do the backups?

   A. The local groups by using Computer Management

   B. A task by using Authorization Manager

   C. The User Rights Assignment by using the Local Group Policy Editor

   D. The Role Assignment by using Authorization Manager

9. Miguel is a junior-level system administrator, and he has basic knowledge about working with Active Directory. As his supervisor, you have asked Miguel to make several security-related changes to OUs within the company's Active Directory domain. You instruct Miguel to use the basic functionality provided in the Delegation of Control Wizard. Which of the following operations are represented as common tasks within the Delegation of Control Wizard? (Choose all that apply.)

   A. Reset passwords on user accounts.

   B. Manage Group Policy links.

   C. Modify the membership of a group.

   D. Create, delete, and manage groups.

10. You are the primary system administrator for a large Active Directory domain. Recently, you have hired another system administrator upon whom you intend to offload some of your responsibilities. This system administrator will be responsible for handling help desk calls and for basic user account management. You want to allow the new employee to have permissions to reset passwords for all users within a specific OU. However, for security reasons, it's important that the user not be able to make permissions changes for objects within other OUs in the domain. Which of the following is the best way to do this?

   A. Create a special administration account within the OU and grant it full permissions for all objects within Active Directory.

   B. Move the user's login account into the OU that the new employee is to administer.

   C. Move the user's login account to an OU that contains the OU (that is, the parent OU of the one that the new employee is to administer).

   D. Use the Delegation of Control Wizard to assign the necessary permissions on the OU that the new employee is to administer.

Chapter

3

Maintaining Active Directory

THE FOLLOWING 70-742 EXAM OBJECTIVES ARE COVERED IN THIS CHAPTER:

✓ **Maintain Active Directory**

- This objective may include but is not limited to: Back up Active Directory and SYSVOL; manage Active Directory offline; perform offline defragmentation of an Active Directory database; clean up metadata; configure Active Directory snapshots; perform object- and container-level recovery; perform Active Directory restore; configure and restore objects by using the Active Directory Recycle Bin; configure replication to Read-Only Domain Controllers (RODCs); configure Password Replication Policy (PRP) for RODC; monitor and manage replication; upgrade SYSVOL replication to Distributed File System Replication (DFSR).

✓ **Configure Active Directory in a complex enterprise environment**

- This objective may include but is not limited to: Configure a multi-domain and multi-forest Active Directory infrastructure; deploy Windows Server 2016 domain controllers within a pre-existing Active Directory environment; upgrade existing domains and forests; configure domain and forest functional levels; configure multiple user principal name (UPN) suffixes; configure external, forest, shortcut, and realm trusts; configure trust authentication; configure SID filtering; configure name suffix routing; configure sites and subnets; create and configure site links; manage site coverage; manage registration of SRV records; move domain controllers between sites; configure account policies.

Microsoft has designed Active Directory to be an enterprise-wide solution for managing network resources. In previous chapters, you saw how to create Active Directory objects based on an organization's logical design. Domain structure and organizational unit (OU) structure, for example, should be designed based primarily on an organization's business needs.

Now it's time to learn how Active Directory can map to an organization's *physical* requirements. Specifically, you must consider network connectivity between sites and the flow of information between domain controllers (DCs) under less-than-ideal conditions. These constraints determine how domain controllers can work together to ensure that the objects within Active Directory remain synchronized no matter how large and geographically dispersed the network.

Fortunately, through the use of the Active Directory Sites and Services administrative tool, you can quickly and easily create the various components of an Active Directory replication topology. Using this tool, you can create objects called *sites*, place servers in sites, and create connections between sites. Once you have configured Active Directory replication to fit your current network environment, you can sit back and allow Active Directory to make sure that information remains consistent across domain controllers.

This chapter covers the features of Active Directory, which allow system administrators to modify the behavior of replication based on their physical network design. Through the use of sites, system and network administrators will be able to leverage their network infrastructure best to support Windows Server 2016 and Active Directory.

So far, you have learned the steps necessary to install the Domain Name System (DNS) and to implement the first Active Directory domain. Although I briefly introduced multidomain Active Directory structures earlier, I focused on only a single domain and the objects within it.

Many businesses find that using a single domain provides an adequate solution to meet their business needs. By working with *trees* and *forests*, however, large organizations can use multiple domains to organize their environments better.

Overview of Network Planning

Before I discuss sites and replication, you need to understand some basic physical and network concepts.

The Three Types of Networks

When designing networks, system and network administrators use the following terms to define the types of connectivity between locations and servers:

Local Area Networks　A *local area network (LAN)* is usually characterized as a high-bandwidth network. Generally, an organization owns all of its LAN network hardware and software. Ethernet is by far the most common networking standard. Ethernet speeds are generally at least 10 Mbps and can scale to multiple gigabits per second. Currently, the standard for Ethernet is the 10 Gigabit Ethernet, which runs at 10 times the speed of Gigabit Ethernet (1 GB). Several LAN technologies, including routing and switching, are available to segment LANs and to reduce contention for network resources.

Wide Area Networks　The purpose of a *wide area network (WAN)* is similar to that of a LAN, that is, to connect network devices. Unlike LANs, however, WANs are usually leased from third-party telecommunications carriers and organizations known as *Internet service providers (ISPs)*. Although extremely high-speed WAN connections are available, they are generally costly for organizations to implement through a distributed environment. Therefore, WAN connections are characterized by lower-speed connections and, sometimes, nonpersistent connections.

The Internet　The *Internet* is a worldwide public network infrastructure based on the *Internet Protocol (IP)*. Access to the Internet is available through Internet service providers (ISPs). Because it is a public network, there is no single "owner" of the Internet. Instead, large network and telecommunications providers constantly upgrade the infrastructure of this network to meet growing demands.

Organizations use the Internet regularly to sell and market their products and services. For example, it's rare nowadays to see advertisements that don't direct you to one website or another. Through the use of technologies such as *virtual private networks (VPNs)*, organizations can use encryption and authentication technology to enable secure communications across the Internet.

Exploring Network Constraints

In an ideal situation, a high-speed network would connect all computers and networking devices. In such a situation, you would be able to ensure that any user of your network, regardless of location, would be able to access resources quickly and easily. When you are working in the real world, however, you have many other constraints to keep in mind, including network bandwidth and network cost.

Network Bandwidth

Network bandwidth generally refers to the amount of data that can pass through a specific connection in a given amount of time. For example, in a WAN situation, a T1 may have 1.544 Mbps (megabits per second), while a DSL might have a bandwidth of 56 Kbps or 57.6 Kbps (kilobits per second) or more. On the other hand, your LAN's Ethernet connection may have a bandwidth of 100 Mbps or 1000 Mbps. Different types of networks work at different speeds. Therefore, it's imperative that you always consider network bandwidth when thinking about how to deploy domain controllers in your environment.

Network Cost

Cost is perhaps the single largest factor in determining a network design. If cost were not a constraint, organizations would clearly elect to use high-bandwidth connections for all of their sites. Realistically, trade-offs in performance must be made for the sake of affordability. Some factors that can affect the cost of networking include the distance between networks and the types of technology available at locations throughout the world. In remote or less-developed locations, you may not even be able to get access through an ISP or telecom beyond a satellite connection or dial-up, and what is available can be quite costly. Network designers must keep these factors in mind, and they must often settle for less-than-ideal connectivity.

You have considered the monetary value of doing business. Now let's consider another aspect of cost. When designing and configuring networks, you can require certain devices to make data-transport decisions automatically based on an assigned network cost. These devices are commonly known as *routers*, and they use routing protocols to make routing decisions. One of the elements a router uses to configure a routing protocol is its ability to adjust the cost of a route. For example, a router may have multiple ways to connect to a remote site, and it may have multiple interfaces connected to it, each with different paths out of the network to which it is connected locally. When two or more routes are available, you can set up a routing protocol that states that the route with the lower cost is automatically used first.

Another cost is personnel. Do you have the personnel to do the job, or do you need to hire a consultant? Remember that even if you use individuals already on staff, they will be spending time on these projects. When your IT team is working on a project, this is a cost because they cannot also be working on day-to-day tasks.

All of these factors play an important role when you make your Active Directory implementation decisions.

Overview of Active Directory Replication and Sites

Now I need to address two topics that not only are covered heavily on the Microsoft exams but are two areas that all IT administrators should understand. Understanding Active Directory replication and sites can help you fine-tune a network to run at peak performance.

Replicating Active Directory

Regardless of the issues related to network design and technological constraints, network users have many different requirements and needs that must be addressed. First, network resources, such as files, printers, and shared directories, must be made available. Similarly, the resources stored within Active Directory, and its security information in particular, are required for many operations that occur within domains.

With these issues in mind, take a look at how you can configure Active Directory to reach connectivity goals using replication.

Active Directory was designed as a scalable, distributed database that contains information about an organization's network resources. In previous chapters, you saw how you can create and manage domains and how you can use domain controllers to store Active Directory databases.

Even in the simplest of network environments, you generally need more than one domain controller. The major reasons for this are *fault tolerance* (if one domain controller fails, others can still provide services as needed) and performance (the workload can be balanced between multiple domain controllers). Windows Server 2016 domain controllers have been designed to contain read-write copies as well as read-only copies of the Active Directory database. However, the domain controllers must also remain current when objects are created or modified on other domain controllers.

To keep information consistent between domain controllers, you use *Active Directory replication*. Replication is the process by which changes to the Active Directory database are transferred between domain controllers. The result is that all of the domain controllers within an Active Directory domain contain up-to-date information and achieve convergence. Keep in mind that domain controllers may be located very near to each other (for example, within the same server rack), or they may be located across the world from each other. Although the goals of replication are quite simple, the real-world constraints of network connections between servers cause many limitations that you must accommodate. If you have a domain controller on your local LAN, you may find that you have Gigabit Ethernet, which runs at 1000 Mbps between your server connections, whereas you may have a domain controller on the other side or a WAN where the network link runs at a fraction of a T1, 56 Kbps. Replication traffic must traverse each link to ensure convergence no matter what the speed or what bandwidth is available.

Throughout this chapter, you will study the technical details of Active Directory replication. You will also learn how to use the concept of sites and site links to map the logical structure of Active Directory to a physical network topology to help it work efficiently, no matter the type of link with which you are working.

Understanding Active Directory Site Concepts

One of the most important aspects of designing and implementing Active Directory is understanding how it allows you to separate the logical components of the directory service from the physical components.

The logical components—Active Directory domains, OUs, users, groups, and computers—map to the organizational and business requirements of a company.

The physical components, on the other hand, are designed based on the technical issues involved in keeping the network synchronized (that is, making sure that all parts of the network have the same up-to-date information). Active Directory uses the concept of sites to map to an organization's physical network. Stated simply, a *site* is a collection of well-connected subnets. The technical implications of sites are described later in this chapter.

It is important to understand that no specified relationship exists between Active Directory domains and Active Directory sites. An Active Directory site can contain many domains. Alternatively, a single Active Directory domain can span multiple sites. Figure 3.1 illustrates this very important characteristic of domains and sites.

FIGURE 3.1   Potential relationships between domains and sites

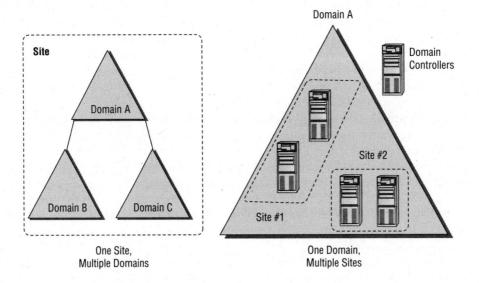

One Site,
Multiple Domains

One Domain,
Multiple Sites

There are two main reasons to use Active Directory sites: service requests and replication.

Service Requests

Clients often require the network services of a domain controller. One of the most common reasons for this is that they need the domain controller to perform network authentication. If your Active Directory network is set up with sites, clients can easily connect to the domain controller that is located closest to them. By doing this, they avoid many of the inefficiencies associated with connecting to distant domain controllers or to those that are located on the other side of a slow network connection. For example, by connecting to a local domain controller, you can avoid the problems associated with a saturated network link that might cause two domain controllers to be out of sync with each other.

Replication

As mentioned earlier, the purpose of Active Directory replication is to ensure that the information stored on all domain controllers within a domain remains synchronized. In environments with many domains and domain controllers, multiple communication paths usually connect them, which makes the synchronization process more complicated. A simple method of transferring updates and other changes to Active Directory involves all of the servers communicating directly with each other as soon as a change occurs; they can all update with the change and reach convergence again. This is not ideal, however, because it places high requirements on network bandwidth and is inefficient for many network environments that use slower and more costly WAN links, especially if all environments update at the same time. Such simultaneous updating could cause the network connection at the core of your network to become saturated and decrease the performance of the entire WAN.

Using sites, Active Directory can automatically determine the best methods for performing replication operations. Sites take into account an organization's network infrastructure, and Active Directory uses these sites to determine the most efficient method for synchronizing information between domain controllers. System administrators can make their physical network design map to Active Directory objects. Based on the creation and configuration of these objects, the Active Directory service can then manage replication traffic in an efficient way.

Whenever a change is made to the Active Directory database on a domain controller, the change is given an update sequence number. The domain controller can then propagate these changes to other domain controllers based on replication settings.

Windows Server 2016 uses a feature called *linked value replication* that is active only when the domain is in the Windows Server 2003, Windows Server 2008, Windows Server 2008 R2, Windows Server 2012, Windows Server 2012 R2, or Windows Server 2016 domain functional level. With linked value replication, only the group member is replicated. This greatly enhances replication efficiency and cuts down on network traffic utilization. Linked value replication is automatically enabled in Windows Server 2003, Windows Server 2008/2008 R2, Windows Server 2012/2012 R2, and Windows Server 2016 functional-level domains.

Planning Your Sites

Much of the challenge of designing Active Directory is related to mapping a company's business processes to the structure of a hierarchical data store. So far, you've seen many of these requirements. What about the existing network infrastructure, however? Clearly, when you plan for and design the structure of Active Directory, you must take into account your LAN and WAN characteristics. Let's see some of the ways that you can use Active Directory sites to manage replication traffic.

Synchronizing Active Directory is extremely important. To keep security permissions and objects within the directory consistent throughout the organization, you must use replication. The Active Directory data store supports *multimaster replication*; that is, data can be modified at any domain controller within the domain because replication ensures that information remains consistent throughout the organization.

Ideally, every site within an organization has reliable, high-speed connections with the other sites. A much more realistic scenario, however, is one in which bandwidth is limited and connections are sometimes either sporadically available or completely unavailable.

Using sites, network and system administrators can define which domain controllers are located on which areas of the network. These settings can be based on the bandwidth available between the areas of the network. Additionally, these administrators can define *subnets*—logically partitioned areas of the network—between areas of the network. Subnets are designed by subdividing IP addresses into usable blocks for assignment, and they are also objects found within the Sites and Services Microsoft Management Console (MMC) in the Administrative Tools folder. Windows Server 2016 Active Directory services use this information to decide how and when to replicate data between domain controllers.

Directly replicating information between all domain controllers might be a viable solution for some companies. For others, however, this might result in a lot of traffic traveling over slow or undersized network links. One way to synchronize data efficiently between sites that have slow connections is to use a *bridgehead server*. Bridgehead servers are designed to accept traffic between two remote sites and then to forward this information to the appropriate servers. Figure 3.2 provides an example of how a bridgehead server can reduce network bandwidth requirements and improve performance. Reduced network bandwidth requirements and improved performance can also be achieved by configuring replication to occur according to a predefined schedule if bandwidth usage statistics are available.

FIGURE 3.2   Using a bridgehead server

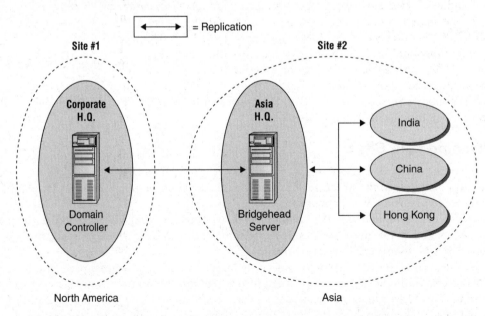

Bridgehead servers do not fit a normal hub-and-spoke WAN topology. Such a topology usually involves a core site (for example, company headquarters) with remote sites as links one off from the core. However, you can use a bridgehead server design to fit a distributed star, where you have a hub-and-spoke topology design with additional spokes coming out of the first set of spokes. Doing so would make some of your spoke sites into smaller core sites. It is at these sites that you would place your bridgehead servers. In Figure 3.2, you can see that your Asia headquarters site is also where you can connect to India, China, and Hong Kong, thus making the Asia headquarters the ideal site for the bridgehead server.

In addition to managing replication traffic, sites offer the advantage of allowing clients to access the nearest domain controller. This prevents problems with user authentication across slow network connections, and it can help find the shortest and fastest path to resources such as files and printers. Therefore, Microsoft recommends that you place at least one domain controller at each site that contains a slow link. Preferably, this domain controller also contains a copy of the global catalog so that logon attempts and resource search queries do not occur across slow links. The drawback, however, is that deploying more copies of the global catalog to servers increases replication traffic.

Through proper planning and deployment of sites, organizations can best use the capabilities of the network infrastructure while keeping Active Directory synchronized.

Understanding Distributed File System Replication

DFS Replication (DFSR) was created to replace the File Replication Service (FRS) that was introduced in the Windows 2000 Server operating systems. DFSR is a state-based, multimaster replication engine that supports replication scheduling and bandwidth throttling. DFSR has the ability to detect insertions, removals, and rearrangements of data in files. This allows DFS Replication to replicate only the changed file blocks when files are updated.

The DFS Replication component uses many different processes to keep data synchronized on multiple servers. To understand the DFSR process, it is helpful to understand some of the following concepts:

- DFSR is a multitasker replication engine, and changes that occur on one of the members are then replicated to all of the other members of the replication group.

- DFSR uses the update sequence number (USN) journal to detect changes on the volume, and then DFSR replicates the changes only after the file is closed.

- Before sending or receiving a file, DFSR uses a staging folder to stage the file.

- When a file is changed, DFSR replicates only the changed blocks and not the entire file. The RDC protocol is what helps determine the blocks that have changed in the file.

- One of the advantages of DFSR is that it is self-healing and can automatically recover from USN journal wraps, USN journal loss, or loss of the DFS Replication database.

- Windows Server 2016 DFSR includes the ability to add a failover cluster as a member of a replication group.

- Windows Server 2016 DFSR allows for read-only replicated folders on a particular member in which users cannot add or change files.

- In Windows Server 2016, it is possible to make changes to the SYSVOL folder of an RODC.

The Dfsrdiag.exe command-line tool includes three Windows Server 2016 command-line switches that provide enhanced diagnostic capabilities for DFSR:

Dfsrdiag.exe ReplState   When you use the ReplState switch, a summary of the replication status across all connections on the specified replication group member is provided. The ReplState switch takes a snapshot of the internal state of the DFSR service, and the updates that are currently being processed (downloaded or served) by the service are shown in a list.

Dfsrdiag.exe IdRecord   When replicating a file or folder, the DFSR service creates an ID record, and an administrator can use this ID record to determine whether a file has replicated properly to a specific member. The IdRecord switch returns the DFSR ID record for the file or folder that you specify by using its path or its unique identifier (UID).

Dfsrdiag.exe FileHash   The FileHash switch, when used against a particular file, will compute and display the hash value that is generated by the DFSR service. An administrator can then look at the hash values to compare two files. If the hash values for the two files are the same, then the two files are the same.

Implementing Sites and Subnets

Now that you have a good idea of the goals of replication, take a look at the following quick overview of the various Active Directory objects that are related to physical network topology.

The basic objects that are used for managing replication include the following:

Subnets   A *subnet* is a partition of a network. As I started to discuss earlier, subnets are logical IP blocks usually connected to other IP blocks through the use of routers and other network devices. All of the computers that are located on a given subnet are generally well connected with each other.

It is extremely important to understand the concepts of TCP/IP and the routing of network information when you are designing the topology for Active Directory replication.

Sites   An Active Directory site is a logical object that can contain servers and other objects related to Active Directory replication. Specifically, a *site* is a grouping of related subnets. Sites are created to match the physical network structure of an organization. Sites are primarily used for slow WAN links. If your network is well connected (using fiber optics, Category 6 Ethernet, and so on), then sites are not needed.

Site Links   A *site link* is created to define the types of connections that are available between the components of a site. Site links can reflect a relative cost for a network connection and can also reflect the bandwidth that is available for communications.

All of these components work together to determine how information is used to replicate data between domain controllers. Figure 3.3 provides an example of the physical components of Active Directory.

FIGURE 3.3   Active Directory replication objects

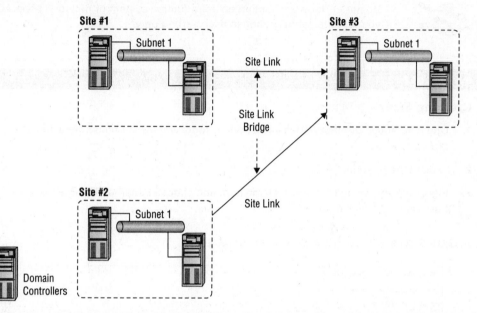

Many issues are related to configuring and managing sites, and all of them are covered in this chapter. Overall, using sites allows you to control the behavior of Active Directory replication between domain controllers. With this background and goal in mind, let's look at how you can implement sites to control Active Directory replication so that it is efficient and in sync.

If you do not have replication set up properly, after a while you will experience problems with your domain controllers. An example of a common replication problem is event log event ID 1311, which states that the Windows NT Directory Services (NTDS) Knowledge Consistency Checker (KCC) has found (and reported) a problem with Active Directory replication. This error message states that the replication configuration information in Active Directory does not accurately reflect the physical topology of the network. This error is commonly found on ailing networks that have replication problems for one reason or another.

Creating Sites

The primary method for creating and managing Active Directory replication components is to utilize the Active Directory Sites and Services tool or the MMC found within the `Administrative Tools` folder. Using this administrative component, you can graphically create and manage sites in much the same way that you create and manage OUs.

Exercise 3.1 walks you through the process of creating Active Directory sites. For you to complete this exercise, the local machine must be a domain controller. Also, this exercise assumes that you have not yet changed the default domain site configuration.

> Do not perform any testing on a production system or network. Make sure you test site configuration in a lab setting only.

EXERCISE 3.1

Creating Sites

1. Open the Active Directory Sites and Services tool from the Administrative Tools program group.

2. Expand the Sites folder.

3. Right-click the Default-First-Site-Name item and choose Rename. Rename the site CorporateHQ (see Figure 3.4).

FIGURE 3.4 Renaming the site to CorporateHQ

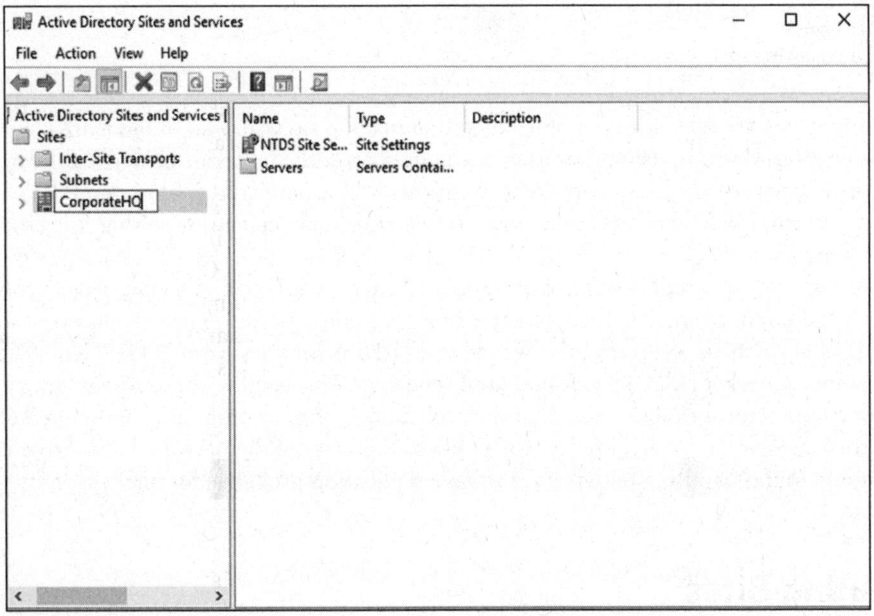

Active Directory Sites and Services		— □ ×
File Action View Help		

Active Directory Sites and Services [	Name	Type	Description
Sites	NTDS Site Se...	Site Settings	
> Inter-Site Transports	Servers	Servers Contai...	
> Subnets			
> CorporateHQ			

4. Create a new site by right-clicking the Sites object and selecting New Site.

5. In the New Object – Site dialog box, type **Farmington** for the site name. Click the DEFAULTIPSITELINK item, and an information screen pops up. Then click OK to create the site. Note that you cannot include spaces or other special characters in the name of a site.

6. Notice that the Farmington site is now listed under the Sites object.

7. Create another new site and name it **Portsmouth**. Again, choose the DEFAULTIPSITELINK item. Notice that the new site is listed under the Sites object.

8. When you have finished, close the Active Directory Sites and Services tool.

Creating Subnets

Once you have created the sites that map to your network topology, it's time to define the subnets that define the site boundaries.

Subnets are based on TCP/IPv4 or TCP/IPv6 address information. For example, the IPv4 address may be 10.10.0.0, and the subnet mask may be 255.255.0.0. This information specifies that all of the TCP/IP addresses that begin with the first two octets are part of the same TCP/IP subnet. All of the following TCP/IP addresses would be within this subnet:

- 10.10.1.5
- 10.10.100.17
- 10.10.110.120

The Active Directory Sites and Services tool expresses these subnets in a somewhat different notation. It uses the provided subnet address and appends a slash followed by the number of bits in the subnet mask. In the example in the previous paragraph, the subnet would be defined as 10.1.0.0/16.

Remember that sites typically represent distinct physical locations, and they almost always have their own subnets. The only way for a domain controller in one site to reach a DC in another site is to add subnet information about the remote site. Generally, information regarding the definition of subnets for a specific network environment will be available from a network designer. Exercise 3.2 walks you through the steps that you need to take to create subnets and assign subnets to sites. To complete the steps in this exercise, you must have completed Exercise 3.1.

EXERCISE 3.2

Creating Subnets

1. Open the Active Directory Sites and Services tool from the Administrative Tools program group.

2. Expand the Sites folder. Right-click the Subnets folder and select New Subnet.

3. In the New Object – Subnet dialog box, you are prompted for information about the IPv4 or IPv6 details for the new subnet. For the prefix, type **10.10.1.0/24** (you are staying with the more commonly used IPv4). This actually calculates out to 10.10.1.0 with the mask of 255.255.255.0. Click the Farmington site and then click OK to create the subnet.

4. In the Active Directory Sites and Services tool, right-click the newly created 10.10.1.0/24 subnet object and select Properties.

5. On the subnet's Properties dialog box, type **Farmington 100 MB LAN** for the description. Click OK to continue.

6. Create a new subnet using the following information:

   Address: **160.25.0.0/16**

   Site: **Portsmouth**

   Description: **Portsmouth 100Mbit LAN**

7. Finally, create another subnet using the following information:

   Address: **176.33.0.0/16**

   Site: **CorporateHQ**

   Description: **Corporate 100Mbit switched LAN**

8. When finished, close the Active Directory Sites and Services tool.

So far, you have created the basic components that govern Active Directory sites and subnets. You also linked these two components by defining which subnets belong in which sites. These two steps—creating sites and creating subnets—form the basis of mapping the physical network infrastructure of an organization to Active Directory. Now look at the various settings that you can make for sites.

Configuring Sites

Once you have created Active Directory sites and have defined which subnets they contain, it's time to make some additional configuration settings for the site structure. Specifically, you'll need to assign servers to specific sites and configure the site-licensing options. By placing servers in sites, you tell Active Directory replication services how to replicate information for various types of servers. Later in this chapter, you'll examine the details of working with replication within and between sites.

In Exercise 3.3, you will add servers to sites and configure CorpDC1 options. To complete the steps in this exercise, you must have completed Exercise 3.1 and Exercise 3.2.

EXERCISE 3.3

Configuring Sites

1. Open the Active Directory Sites and Services tool from the Administrative Tools program group.

2. Expand the Sites folder and click and expand the Farmington site.

3. Right-click the Servers container in the Farmington site and select New ➤ Server. Type **FarmingtonDC1** for the name of the server and then click OK.

4. Create a new Server object within the CorporateHQ site and name it **CorpDC1**. Note that this object also includes the name of the local domain controller.

5. Create two new Server objects within the Portsmouth site and name them **PortsmouthDC1** and **PortsmouthDC2**.

6. Right-click the CorpDC1 server object and select Properties. On the General tab of the CorpDC1 Properties box, select SMTP in the Transports Available For Inter-site Data Transfer box and click Add to make this server a preferred IP bridgehead server. Click OK to accept the settings.

7. When you have finished, close the Active Directory Sites and Services tool.

With the configuration of the basic settings for sites out of the way, it's time to focus on the real details of the site topology—creating site links and site link bridges.

Configuring Replication

Sites are generally used to define groups of computers that are located within a single geographic location. In most organizations, machines that are located in close physical proximity (for example, within a single building or branch office) are well connected. A typical example is a LAN in a branch office of a company. All of the computers may be connected using Ethernet, and routing and switching technology may be in place to reduce network congestion.

Often, however, domain controllers are located across various states, countries, and even continents. In such a situation, network connectivity is usually much slower, less reliable, and more costly than that for the equivalent LAN. Therefore, Active Directory replication must accommodate this situation accordingly. When managing replication traffic within Active Directory sites, you need to be aware of two types of synchronization:

Intrasite   *Intrasite replication* refers to the synchronization of Active Directory information between domain controllers that are located in the same site. In accordance with the concept of sites, these machines are usually well connected by a high-speed LAN.

Intersite   *Intersite replication* occurs between domain controllers in different sites. Usually, this means there is a WAN or other type of low-speed network connection between the various machines. Intersite replication is optimized for minimizing the amount of network traffic that occurs between sites.

In the following sections, you'll look at ways to configure both intrasite and intersite replication. Additionally, you'll see features of Active Directory replication architecture that you can use to accommodate the needs of almost any environment.

Intrasite Replication

Intrasite replication is generally a simple process. One domain controller contacts the others in the same site when changes to its copy of Active Directory are made. It compares the update sequence numbers in its own copy of Active Directory with those of the other domain controllers; then the most current information is chosen by the DC in question, and all domain controllers within the site use this information to make the necessary updates to their database.

Because you can assume that the domain controllers within an Active Directory site are well connected, you can pay less attention to exactly when and how replication takes place. Communications between domain controllers occur using the *Remote Procedure Call (RPC) protocol*. This protocol is optimized for transmitting and synchronizing information on fast and reliable network connections. The RPC protocol provides for fast replication at the expense of network bandwidth, which is usually readily available because most LANs today are running on Fast Ethernet (100 Mbps) at a minimum.

Intersite Replication

Intersite replication is optimized for low-bandwidth situations and network connections that have less reliability. Intersite replication offers several features that are tailored toward these types of connections. To begin with, two different protocols may be used to transfer information between sites:

RPC over IP   When connectivity is fairly reliable, IP is a good choice. IP-based communications require you to have a live connection between two or more domain controllers in different sites and let you transfer Active Directory information. RPC over IP was originally designed for slower WANs in which packet loss and corruption may often occur.

Simple Mail Transfer Protocol   *Simple Mail Transfer Protocol (SMTP)* is perhaps best known as the protocol that is used to send and receive email messages on the Internet. SMTP was designed to use a store-and-forward mechanism through which a server receives a copy of a message, records it to disk, and then attempts to forward it to another email server. If the destination server is unavailable, it holds the message and attempts to resend it at periodic intervals.

This type of communication is extremely useful for situations in which network connections are unreliable or not always available. For example, if a branch office in Peru were connected to the corporate office through a dial-up connection that is available only during certain hours, SMTP would be a good choice for communication with that branch.

SMTP is an inherently insecure network protocol. Therefore, if you would like to ensure that you transfer replication traffic securely and you use SMTP for Active Directory replication, you must take advantage of Windows Server 2016's Certificate Services functionality.

Other intersite replication characteristics are designed to address low-bandwidth situations and less-reliable network connections. These features give you a high degree of flexibility in controlling replication configuration. They include the following:

- Compression of Active Directory information. This compression is helpful because changes between domain controllers in remote sites may include a large amount of information and also because network bandwidth tends to be less available and more costly.

- Site links and site link bridges help determine intersite replication topology.

- Replication can occur based on a schedule defined by system administrators.

You can configure intersite replication by using the Active Directory Sites and Services tool. Select the name of the site for which you want to configure settings. Then right-click the NTDS Site Settings object in the right window pane and select Properties. By clicking the Change Schedule button in the NTDS Site Settings Properties dialog box, you'll be able to configure how often replication occurs between sites (see Figure 3.5).

FIGURE 3.5   Configuring intersite replication schedules

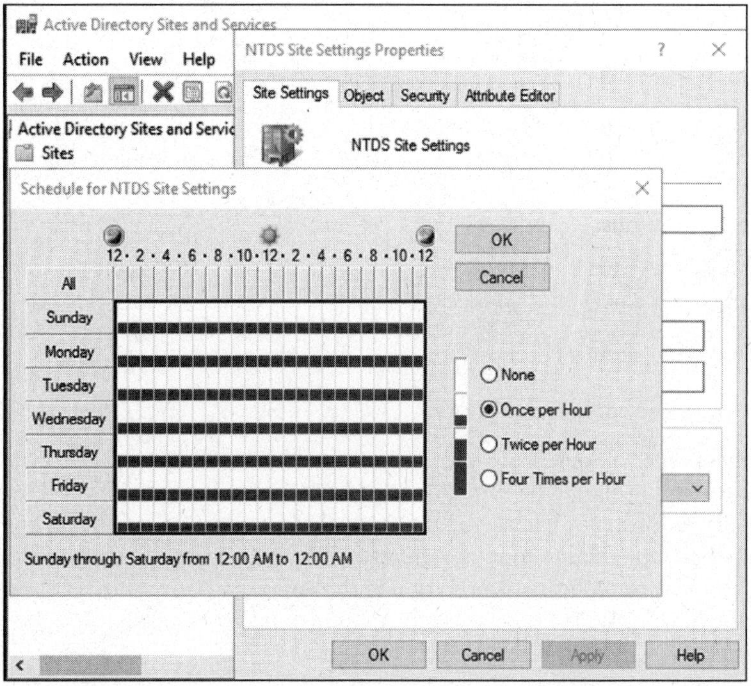

NOTE   You will see how to set the replication schedule in Exercise 3.4.

In the following sections, you will see how to configure site links and site link bridges as well as how to manage connection objects and bridgehead servers.

Creating Site Links and Site Link Bridges

The overall topology of intersite replication is based on the use of site links and site link bridges. *Site links* are logical connections that define a path between two Active Directory sites. Site links can include several descriptive elements that define their network characteristics. *Site link bridges* are used to connect site links so that the relationship can be transitive. Figure 3.6 provides an example of site links and site link bridges.

FIGURE 3.6   An example of site links and site link bridges

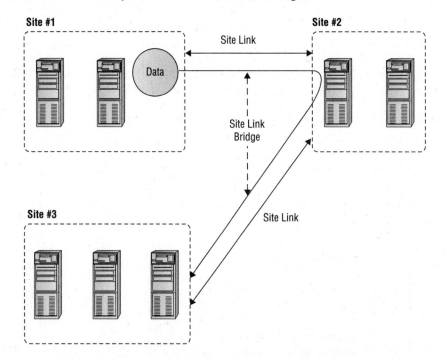

Both of these types of logical connections are used by Active Directory services to determine how information should be synchronized between domain controllers in remote sites. The Knowledge Consistency Checker (KCC) uses this information, which forms a replication topology based on the site topology created. The KCC service is responsible for determining the best way to replicate information within sites.

When creating site links for your environment, you'll need to consider the following factors:

Transporting Information   You can choose to use either RPC over IP or SMTP for transferring information over a site link. You will need to determine which is best based on your network infrastructure and the reliability of connections between sites.

Assigning a Cost Value   You can create multiple site links between sites and assign site links a cost value based on the type of connection. The system administrator determines the cost value, and the relative costs of site links are then used (by the system) to determine the optimal path for replication. The lower the cost, the more likely the link is to be used for replication.

For example, a company may primarily use a T1 link between branch offices, but it may also use a slower and circuit-switched dial-up ISDN connection for redundancy (in case the T1 fails). In this example, a system administrator may assign a cost of 25 to the T1 line and a cost of 100 to the ISDN line. This ensures that the more reliable and higher-bandwidth T1 connection is used whenever it's available but that the ISDN line is also available.

Determining a Replication Schedule   Once you've determined how and through which connections replication will take place, it's time to determine when information should be replicated. Replication requires network resources and occupies bandwidth. Therefore, you need to balance the need for consistent directory information with the need to conserve bandwidth. For example, if you determine that it's reasonable to have a lag time of six hours between when an update is made at one site and when it is replicated to all others, you might schedule replication to occur once in the morning, once during the lunch hour, and more frequently after normal work hours.

Based on these factors, you should be able to devise a strategy that allows you to configure site links.

Exercise 3.4 walks you through the process of creating site links and site link bridges. To complete the steps in this exercise, you must have completed Exercises 3.1, 3.2, and 3.3.

EXERCISE 3.4

Creating Site Links and Site Link Bridges

1. Open the Active Directory Sites and Services tool from the Administrative Tools program group.

2. Expand the Sites, Inter-site Transports, and IP objects. Right-click the DEFAULTIPSITELINK item in the right pane and select Rename. Rename the object **CorporateWAN**.

3. Right-click the CorporateWAN link and select Properties. In the General tab of the CorporateWAN Properties dialog box, type **T1 Connecting Corporate and Portsmouth Offices** for the description. Remove the Farmington site from the link by highlighting Farmington in the Sites In This Site Link box and clicking Remove. For the Cost value, type **50** and specify that replication should occur every **60** minutes. To create the site link, click OK.

4. Right-click the IP folder and select New Site Link. In the New Object – Site Link dialog box, name the link **CorporateDialup**. Add the Farmington and CorporateHQ sites to the site link and then click OK.

5. Right-click the CorporateDialup link and select Properties. In the General tab of the CorporateDialup Properties dialog box, type **ISDN Dialup between Corporate and Farmington** for the description. Set the Cost value to **100** and specify that replication should occur every **120** minutes. To specify that replication should occur only during certain times of the day, click the Change Schedule button.

6. In the Schedule For Corporate Dialup dialog box, highlight the area between 8:00 a.m. and 6:00 p.m. for the days Monday through Friday and click the Replication Not Available option. This will ensure that replication traffic is minimized during normal work hours.

7. Click OK to accept the new schedule and then click OK again to create the site link.

8. Right-click the IP object and select New Site Link Bridge. In the New Object – Site Link Bridge dialog box, name the site link bridge **CorporateBridge**. Note that the CorporateDialup and CorporateWAN site links are already added to the site link bridge. Because there must be at least two site links in each bridge, you will not be able to remove these links. Click OK to create the site link bridge.

9. When finished, close the Active Directory Sites and Services tool.

Creating Connection Objects

Generally, it is a good practice to allow Active Directory's replication mechanisms to schedule and manage replication functions automatically. In some cases, however, you may want to have additional control over replication. Perhaps you want to replicate certain changes on demand (for example, when you create new accounts). Or you may want to specify a custom schedule for certain servers.

Connection objects provide you with a way to set up these different types of replication schedules. You can create connection objects with the Active Directory Sites and Services tool by expanding a server object, right-clicking the NTDS Settings object, and selecting New Active Directory Domain Services Connection.

Within the properties of the connection object, which you can see in the right pane of the Active Directory Sites and Services tool, you can specify the type of transport to use for replication (RPC over IP or SMTP), the schedule for replication, and the domain controllers that participate in the replication. Additionally, you can right-click the connection object and select Replicate Now.

Moving Server Objects Between Sites

Using the Active Directory Sites and Services tool, you can easily move servers between sites. To do this, simply right-click the name of a domain controller and select Move. You can then select the site to which you want to move the domain controller object.

Figure 3.7 shows the Move Server dialog box. After the server is moved, all replication topology settings are updated automatically. If you want to choose custom replication settings, you'll need to create connection objects manually (as described earlier).

FIGURE 3.7 Choosing a new site for a specific server

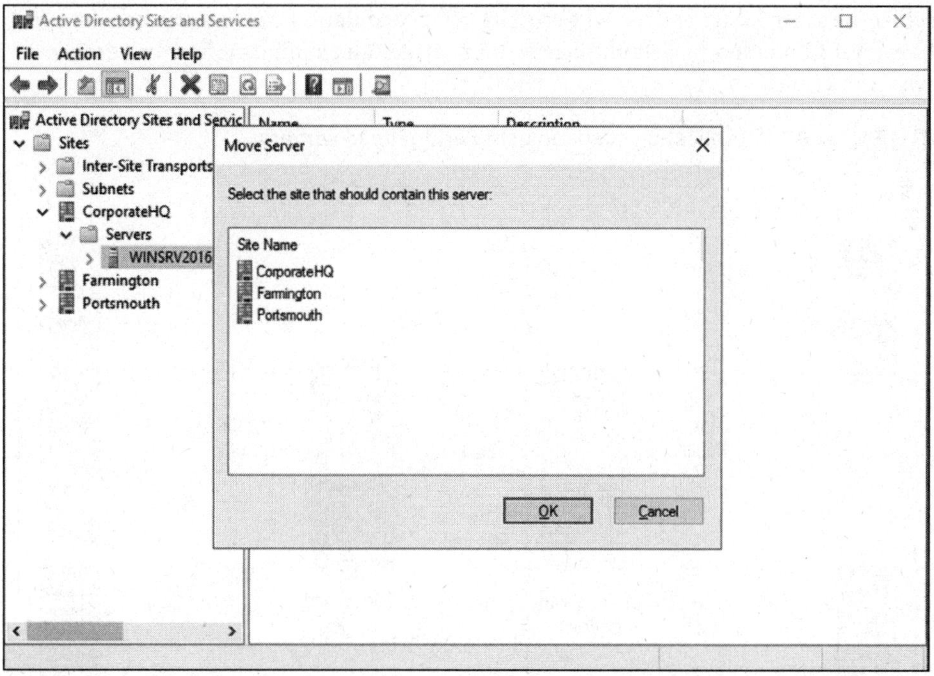

In Exercise 3.5, you move a server object between sites. To complete the steps in this exercise, you must have completed the previous exercises in this chapter.

EXERCISE 3.5

Moving Server Objects Between Sites

1. Open the Active Directory Sites and Services administrative tool.

2. Right-click the server named PortsmouthDC1 and select Move.

3. In the Move Server dialog box, select the Farmington site and then click OK. This moves this server to the Farmington site.

4. To move the server back, right-click PortsmouthDC1 (now located in the Farmington site) and then click Move. Select Portsmouth for the destination site.

5. When finished, close the Active Directory Sites and Services administrative tool.

Creating Bridgehead Servers

By default, all of the servers in one site communicate with all of the servers in another site. You can, however, further control replication between sites by using bridgehead servers. As mentioned earlier in the chapter, using bridgehead servers helps minimize replication traffic, especially in larger distributed star network topologies, and it allows you to dedicate machines that are better connected to receive replicated data. Data is replicated between sites every 180 minutes by default. Figure 3.8 provides an example of how bridgehead servers work.

FIGURE 3.8   A replication scenario using bridgehead servers

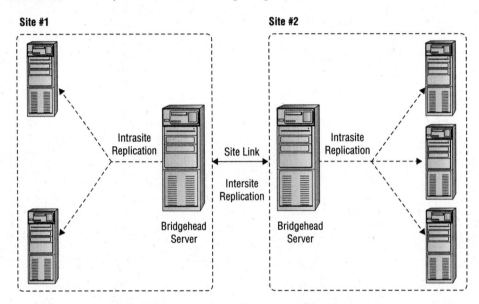

You can use a bridgehead server to specify which domain controllers are preferred for transferring replication information between sites. Different bridgehead servers can be selected for RPC over IP and SMTP replication, thus allowing you to balance the load. To create a bridgehead server for a site, simply right-click a domain controller and select Properties, which brings up the bridgehead server's Properties dialog box. To make the server a bridgehead server, just select one or both replication types (called *transports*) from the left side of the dialog box and click the Add button to add them to the right side of the dialog box.

RODCs and Replication

I have talked quite a bit about read-only domain controllers (RODCs) throughout the book. It's important that you understand that since RODCs don't actually commit changes against the Active Directory Domain Services (AD DS) database within your environment, then replication to and from your primary domain controller (PDC) and your RODCs can occur only one way. This is referred to as *unidirectional replication*. Any writable domain controller that serves as a replication partner to one of your RODCs will never pull changes from that RODC by design. This helps ensure that no malicious or corrupt changes that are made from an RODC are replicated throughout your entire forest. The RODC performs normal inbound replication for AD DS and Sysvol changes. Any other shares on an RODC that you configure to replicate using DFS Replication would still use bidirectional replication.

RODCs come with additional configuration settings like the *Password Replication Policy (PRP)*. The PRP is used to determine which user's credentials can be cached locally on a specific RODC. By default, an RODC will not cache an Active Directory user's credentials. That would defeat the purpose of an RODC. When a user wants to authenticate to an RODC, the authentication request is forwarded to a writable domain controller for authentication. If the request succeeds, it is then passed back to the RODC, and then that user will be able to log in to the domain.

Nonetheless, it is possible to allow certain user credentials to be cached on an RODC by configuring the PRP. Once a user has been added to the Allowed RODC Password Replication group, then that user's credentials will be cached, and that RODC would be able to authenticate that user locally again in the future. Because the RODC maintains only a subset of user credentials, if the RODC is compromised or stolen, only the user accounts that had been cached on the RODC must have their passwords changed. To configure an RODC PRP, open the properties of an RODC computer object in Active Directory and select the Password Replication Policy tab.

Configuring Server Topology

When you are using environments that require multiple sites, you must carefully consider where you place your servers. In doing so, you can greatly improve performance and end user experience by reducing the time they must spend performing common operations, such as authentication or searching Active Directory for resources.

There are two main issues to consider when you are designing a distributed Active Directory environment. The first is how you should place domain controllers within the network environment. The second is how to manage the use of global catalog servers. Finding the right balance between servers, server resources, and performance can be considered an art form for network and system administrators. In the following sections, you'll look at some of the important considerations that you must take into account when you design a replication server topology.

Placing Domain Controllers

Microsoft highly recommends that you have at least two domain controllers in each domain of your Active Directory environment. As mentioned earlier in this chapter, using additional domain controllers provides the following benefits:

- Increased network performance:
  - The servers can balance the burden of serving client requests.
  - Clients can connect to the server closest to them instead of performing authentication and security operations across a slow WAN link.

- Fault tolerance (In case one domain controller fails, the other still contains a valid and usable copy of the Active Directory database.)

- In Windows Server 2016, RODCs help increase security when users connect to a domain controller in an unsecured remote location.

Placing Global Catalog Servers

A *global catalog (GC)* server is a domain controller that contains a copy of all of the objects contained in the forest-wide domain controllers that compose the Active Directory database. Making a domain controller a GC server is simple, and you can change this setting quite easily. That brings us to the harder part—determining which domain controllers should also be GC servers.

Where you place domain controllers and GC servers and how many you deploy are important network planning decisions. Generally, you want to make GC servers available in every site that has a slow link. This means the most logical places to put GC servers are in every site and close to the WAN link for the best possible connectivity. However, having too many GC servers is a bad thing. The main issue is associated with replication traffic—you must keep each GC server within your environment synchronized with the other servers. In a very dynamic environment, using additional GC servers causes a considerable increase in network traffic. Therefore, you will want to find a good balance between replication burdens and GC query performance in your own large multidomain environment.

To create a GC server, simply expand the Server object in the Active Directory Sites and Services tool, right-click NTDS Settings, and select Properties to bring up the NTDS Settings Properties dialog box (see Figure 3.9). To configure a server as a GC server, simply place a check mark in the Global Catalog box.

FIGURE 3.9   Enabling the global catalog on an Active Directory domain controller

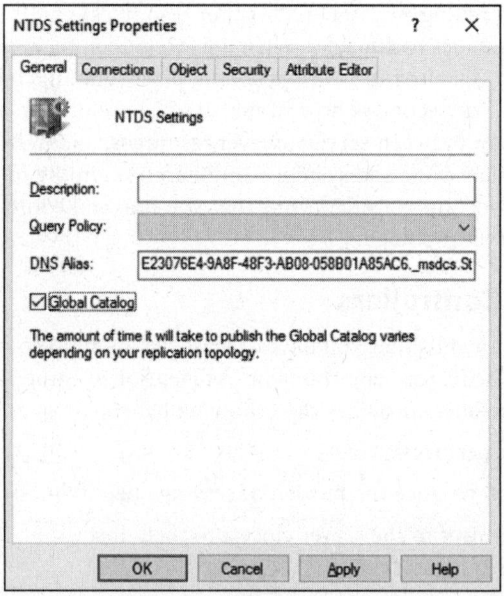

Accommodating a Changing Environment

You're a system administrator for a medium-sized business that consists of many offices located throughout the world. Some of these offices are well connected because they use high-speed, reliable links, while others are not so fortunate. Overall, things are going well until your CEO announces that the organization will be merging with another large company and that the business will be restructured. The restructuring will involve opening new offices, closing old ones, and transferring employees to different locations. Additionally, changes in the IT budget will affect the types of links that exist between offices. Your job as the system administrator is to ensure that the network environment and, specifically, Active Directory keep pace with the changes and ultimately outperform them.

An important skill for any technical professional is the ability to adapt quickly and efficiently to a changing organization. When a business grows, restructures, or forms relationships with other businesses, often many IT-related changes must also occur. You may have to create new network links, for example.

Fortunately, Active Directory was designed with these kinds of challenges in mind. For example, you can use the Active Directory Sites and Services administrative tool to reflect physical network changes in Active Directory topology. If a site that previously had 64 Kbps of bandwidth is upgraded to a T1 connection, you can change those characteristics for the site link objects. Conversely, if a site that was previously well connected is reduced to a slow, unreliable link, you can reconfigure the sites, change the site link transport mechanisms (perhaps from IP to SMTP to accommodate a nonpersistent link), and create connection objects (which would allow you to schedule replication traffic to occur during the least busy hours).

Suppose further that many of your operations move overseas to a European division. This might call for designating specific domain controllers as preferred bridgehead servers to reduce the amount of replication traffic over costly and slow overseas links.

Sweeping organizational changes inevitably require you to move servers between sites. For example, an office may close and its domain controllers may move to another region of the world. Again, you can accommodate this change by using Active Directory administrative tools. You may change your OU structure to reflect new logical and business-oriented changes, and you can move server objects between sites to reflect physical network changes.

Rarely can the job of mapping a physical infrastructure to Active Directory be "complete." In most environments, it's safe to assume that you will always need to make changes based on business needs. Overall, however, you should feel comfortable that the physical components of Active Directory are at your side to help you accommodate these changes.

Using Universal Group Membership Caching

To understand how Universal Group Membership Caching (UGMC) works, you must first understand how authentication works. When a user tries to authenticate with a domain controller, the first action that takes place is that the domain controller checks with the global catalog to see to which domain the user belongs.

If the domain controller (the one to which the user is trying to authenticate) is not a GC, then the domain controller sends a request to the GC to verify the user's domain. The GC responds with the user's information, and the domain controller authenticates the user (if the user belongs to the same domain as the domain controller).

There are two ways to speed up the authentication process. First, you can make all of the domain controller's global catalogs. But then you end up with a lot of GC replication traffic. This becomes even more of an issue if you have multiple sites. Now replication traffic can be too large for your site link connections.

Thus, if you have a slower site link connection or multiple domains, you can use Universal Group Membership Caching. If you are using UGMC, after a domain controller communicates with the global catalog, the domain controller will then cache the user's credentials for eight hours by default. Now if the user logs off the domain and then logs back into the domain, the domain controller will use the cached credentials and not ask the global catalog. The downside to using UGMC is that it is for authentication only. Global catalogs help speed up Active Directory searches, and they work with Directory Service–enabled applications (applications that have to work with Active Directory) such as Exchange and SQL.

Domain Controller Cloning

Throughout the book, I have talked about why so many organizations are switching to virtualization in their server rooms. Virtualization allows an administrator to take one physical server and turn it into multiple virtual servers by using Windows Server 2016.

In Windows Server 2016, administrators can now easily and safely create replica domain controllers by copying an existing virtual domain controller. Before Windows Server 2012, an administrator would have to deploy a server image that they prepared by using sysprep.exe. After going through the process of using sysprep.exe, the administrator would have to promote this server to a domain controller and then complete additional configuration requirements for deploying each replica domain controller.

Domain controller cloning allows an administrator to deploy rapidly a large number of domain controllers. To set up domain controller cloning, you must be a member of the Domain Admins group or have the equivalent permissions. The administrator must then run Windows PowerShell from an elevated command prompt.

Only Windows Server 2012 or Windows Server 2016 domain controllers that are hosted on a VM-compatible hypervisor can be used as a source for cloning. You should also make sure that the domain controller that you choose to clone is in a healthy state (use computer management to see the computer's state).

The following example is used to create a clone domain controller named TestClone with a static IP address of 10.0.0.5 and a subnet mask of 255.255.0.0. This command also configures the DNS Server and WINS server configurations.

```
New-ADDCCloneConfigFile -CloneComputerName "TestClone" -Static -IPv4Address
"10.0.0.5" -IPv4DNSResolver "10.0.0.1" -IPv4SubnetMask "255.255.0.0" -
PreferredWinsServer "10.0.0.1" -AlternateWinsServer "10.0.0.2"
```

 When you are ready to clone a domain controller, I recommend you visit Microsoft's TechNet site for all of the PowerShell commands needed to complete this entire process.

Configuring DNS SRV Records

When setting up Active Directory, there are a few DNS Service (SRV) records that are needed. SRV records show that a machine is running a specific service. There are a few services that are needed for the network to properly function. DNS must have service records for the domain controllers, global catalogs, PDC emulator, and the Kerberos KDC service.

The easiest way to configure the SRV records is to have these machines all be DNS clients. DNS clients will send their client information to the DNS server by default. But if the servers are not DNS clients or for some reason they do not register with DNS, you may need to manually create these SRV records. To manually create the SRV records, complete the following steps:

1. Open the DNS management tool by clicking Start ➢ Administrative Tools ➢ DNS.

2. Expand the Forward Lookup Zone and expand your zone name.

3. Right click _TCP and choose Other New Record.

4. Choose SRV record.

5. Enter the SRV record information.

Monitoring and Troubleshooting Active Directory Replication

For the most part, domain controllers handle the replication processes automatically. However, system administrators still need to monitor the performance of Active Directory replication because failed network links and incorrect configurations can sometimes prevent the synchronization of information between domain controllers.

You can monitor the behavior of Active Directory replication and troubleshoot the process if problems occur.

About System Monitor

The Windows Server 2016 System Monitor administrative tool was designed so that you can monitor many performance statistics associated with using Active Directory. Included within the various performance statistics that you can monitor are counters related to Active Directory replication.

Troubleshooting Replication

A common symptom of replication problems is that information is not updated on some or all domain controllers. For example, a system administrator creates a user account on one domain controller, but the changes are not propagated to other domain controllers. In most environments, this is a potentially serious problem because it affects network security and can prevent authorized users from accessing the resources they require.

You can take several steps to troubleshoot Active Directory replication. These steps are discussed in the following sections.

Verifying Network Connectivity

For replication to work properly in distributed environments, you must have network connectivity. Although ideally all domain controllers would be connected by high-speed LAN links, this is rarely the case for larger organizations. In the real world, dial-up connections and slow connections are common. If you have verified that your replication topology is set up properly, you should confirm that your servers are able to communicate. Problems such as a failed dial-up connection attempt can prevent important Active Directory information from being replicated.

Verifying Router and Firewall Configurations

Firewalls are used to restrict the types of traffic that can be transferred between networks. They are mainly used to increase security by preventing unauthorized users from transferring information. In some cases, company firewalls may block the types of network access that must be available for Active Directory replication to occur. For example, if a specific router or firewall prevents data from being transferred using SMTP, replication that uses this protocol will fail.

Examining the Event Logs

Whenever an error in the replication configuration occurs, the computer writes events to the Directory Service and File Replication Service event logs. By using the Event Viewer administrative tool, you can quickly and easily view the details associated with any problems in replication. For example, if one domain controller is unable to communicate with another to transfer changes, a log entry is created.

Verifying That Information Is Synchronized

It's often easy to forget to perform manual checks regarding the replication of Active Directory information. One of the reasons for this is that Active Directory domain controllers have their own read-write copies of the Active Directory database. Therefore, if connectivity does not exist, you will not encounter failures while creating new objects.

It is important to verify periodically that objects have been synchronized between domain controllers. This process might be as simple as logging on to a different domain controller and looking at the objects within a specific OU. This manual check, although it might be tedious, can prevent inconsistencies in the information stored on domain controllers, which, over time, can become an administration and security nightmare.

Verifying Authentication Scenarios

A common replication configuration issue occurs when clients are forced to authenticate across slow network connections. The primary symptom of the problem is that users complain about the amount of time it takes them to log on to Active Directory (especially during a period when there's a high volume of authentications, such as at the beginning of the workday).

Usually, you can alleviate this problem by using additional domain controllers or reconfiguring the site topology. A good way to test this is to consider the possible scenarios for the various clients that you support. Often, walking through a configuration, such as "A client in Domain1 is trying to authenticate using a domain controller in Domain2, which is located across a slow WAN connection," can be helpful in pinpointing potential problem areas.

Verifying the Replication Topology

The Active Directory Sites and Services tool allows you to verify that a replication topology is logically consistent. You can quickly and easily perform this task by right-clicking NTDS Settings within a Server object and choosing All Tasks ➢ Check Replication. If any errors are present, a dialog box alerts you to the problem.

Another way to verify replication is by using the command-line utility Repadmin. Table 3.1 shows some of the Repadmin commands.

TABLE 3.1   Repadmin commands

Command	Description
Repadmin Bridgeheads	Lists the bridgehead servers for a specified site.
Repadmin dsaguid	Returns a server name when given a GUID.
Repadmin failcache	Shows a list of failed replication events.
Repadmin istg	Returns the server name of the Inter-Site Topology Generator (ISTG) server for a specified site. The ISTG manages the inbound replication connection objects for the bridgehead servers in a site.

TABLE 3.1   Repadmin commands *(continued)*

Command	Description
Repadmin kcc	Forces the Knowledge Consistency Checker (KCC) to recalculate replication topology for a specified domain controller. The KCC modifies data in the local directory in response to system-wide changes.
Repadmin latency	Shows the amount of time between replications.
Repadmin queue	Shows tasks waiting in the replication queue.
Repadmin querysites	Uses routing information to determine the cost of a route from a specified site to another specified site or to other sites.
Repadmin replicate	Starts a replication event for the specified directory partition between domain controllers.
Repadmin replsummary	Displays the replication state and relative health of a forest.
Repadmin showrepl	Displays replication partners for each directory partition on a specified domain controller.

Reasons for Creating Multiple Domains

Before you look at the steps that you must take to create multiple domains, become familiar with the reasons an organization might want to create them.

In general, you should always try to reflect your organization's structure within a single domain. By using organizational units (OUs) and other objects, you can usually create an accurate and efficient structure within one domain. Creating and managing a single domain is usually much simpler than managing a more complex environment consisting of multiple domains.

That being said, you should familiarize yourself with some real benefits and reasons for creating multiple domains and some drawbacks of using them.

Reasons for Using Multiple Domains

You might need to implement multiple domains for several reasons. These reasons include the following considerations:

Scalability   Although Microsoft has designed Active Directory to accommodate millions of objects, this may not be practical for your current environment. Supporting thousands of users within a single domain requires more disk space, greater central processing unit (CPU) usage, and additional network burdens on your domain controllers (computers containing Active Directory security information). To determine the size of the Active Directory domain your network can support, you need to plan, design, test, and analyze within your own environment.

Reducing Replication Traffic   All of the domain controllers in a domain must keep an up-to-date copy of the entire Active Directory database. For small to medium-sized domains, this is generally not a problem. Windows Server 2016 and Active Directory manage all of the details of transferring the database behind the scenes. Other business and technical limitations might, however, affect Active Directory's ability to perform adequate replication. For example, if you have two sites that are connected by a slow network link (or a sporadic link or no link at all), replication is not practical. In this case, you would probably want to create separate domains to isolate replication traffic. Sporadic coverage across the wide area network (WAN) link would come from circuit-switching technologies such as Integrated Services Digital Network (ISDN) technologies. If you didn't have a link at all, then you would have a service provider outage or some other type of disruption. Separate domains mean separate replication traffic, but the amount of administrative overhead is increased significantly.

Because it's common to have WAN links in your business environment, you will always need to consider how your users authenticate to a domain controller (DC). DCs at a remote site are commonly used to authenticate users locally to their local area network (LAN). The most common design involves putting a DC at each remote site to keep authentication traffic from traversing the WAN. If it is the other way around, the authentication traffic may cause users problems if WAN utilization is high or if the link is broken and no other way to the central site is available. The design you are apt to see most often is one in which each server replicates its database of information to each other's server so that the network and its systems converge.

However, it's important to realize that the presence of slow WAN links alone is *not* a good reason to break an organization into multiple domains. The most common solution is to set up site links with the Sites and Services Microsoft Management Console (MMC). When you use this MMC, you can manage replication traffic and fine-tune independently of the domain architecture.

You would want to use a multidomain architecture, such as when two companies merge through an acquisition, for the following reasons:

Meeting Business Needs   Several business needs might justify the creation of multiple domains. Business needs can be broken down even further into organizational and political needs.

One of the organizational reasons for using multiple domains is to avoid potential problems associated with the Domain Administrator account. At least one user needs to have permissions at this level. If your organization is unable or unwilling to trust a single person to have this level of control over all business units, then multiple domains may be the best answer. Because each domain maintains its own security database, you can keep permissions and resources isolated. Through the use of trusts, however, you can still share resources.

A political need for separate domains might arise if you had two companies that merged with two separate but equal management staffs and two sets of officers. In such a situation, you might need to have Active Directory split into two separate databases to keep the security of the two groups separate. Some such organizations may need to keep the internal groups separate by law. A multidomain architecture provides exactly this type of pristinely separate environment.

Many Levels of Hierarchy   Larger organizations tend to have complex internal and external business structures that dictate the need for many different levels of organization. For example, two companies might merge and need to keep two sets of officers who are managed under two different logical groupings. In the, "Administer Active Directory" chapter, I showed you that you can use OUs to help group different branches of the company so that you can assign permissions, delegations, or whatever else you can think of without affecting anyone else. Managing data becomes much easier when you're using OUs, and if you design them correctly, OUs will help you control your network right from one console. You may need only one level of management—your company may be small enough to warrant the use of the default OU structure you see when Active Directory is first installed. If, however, you find that you need many levels of OUs to manage resources (or if large numbers of objects exist within each OU), it might make sense to create additional domains. Each domain would contain its own OU hierarchy and serve as the root of a new set of objects.

Decentralized Administration   Two main models of administration are commonly used: a centralized administration model and a decentralized administration model. In the centralized administration model, a single IT organization is responsible for managing all of the users, computers, and security permissions for the entire organization. In the decentralized administration model, each department or business unit might have its own IT department. In both cases, the needs of the administration model can play a significant role in whether you decide to use multiple domains.

Consider, for example, a multinational company that has a separate IT department for offices in each country. Each IT department is responsible for supporting only the users and computers within its own region. Because the administration model is largely decentralized, creating a separate domain for each of these major business units might make sense from a security and maintenance standpoint.

Multiple DNS or Domain Names   Another reason you may need to use a multidomain architecture is if you want or plan to use multiple DNS names within your organization. If you use multiple DNS names or domain names, you must create multiple Active Directory domains. Each AD domain can have only one *fully qualified domain name (FQDN)*. An FQDN is the full name of a system that consists of a local host, a second-level domain name, and a top-level domain (TLD). For example, corp.WillPanek.com is an FQDN, .com is the TLD, www is the host, and WillPanek is the second-level domain name.

Legality   One final reason you may need to use a multidomain architecture is legality within your organization. Some corporations have to follow state or federal regulations and laws. For this reason, they may need to have multiple domains.

Drawbacks of Multiple Domains

Although there are many reasons why it makes sense to have multiple domains, there are also reasons why you should not break an organizational structure into multiple domains, many of which are related to maintenance and administration. Here are some of the drawbacks to using multiple domains:

Administrative Inconsistency   One of the fundamental responsibilities of most system administrators is implementing and managing security. When you are implementing Group Policy and security settings in multiple domains, you want to be careful to ensure that the settings are consistent. In Windows Server 2016, security policies can be different between and within the same domains. If this is what the organization intended, then it is not a problem. However, if an organization wants to make the same settings apply to all users, then each domain requires a separate GPO with similar security settings.

Increased Management Challenges   Managing servers, users, and computers can become a considerable challenge when you are also managing multiple domains because many more administrative units are required. In general, you need to manage all user, group, and computer settings separately for the objects within each domain. The hierarchical structure provided by OUs, on the other hand, provides a much simpler and easier way to manage permissions.

Decreased Flexibility   Creating a domain involves the *promotion* of a DC to the new domain. Although the process is quite simple, it is much more difficult to rearrange the domain topology within an Active Directory environment than it is simply to reorganize OUs. When planning domains, you should ensure that the domain structure will not change often, if at all.

Now that you have examined the pros and cons related to creating multiple domains, it is time to see how to create trees and forests.

Creating Domain Trees and Forests

So far, this chapter has covered some important reasons for using multiple domains in a single network environment. Now it's time to look at how to create multidomain structures such as domain trees and domain forests.

Regardless of the number of domains you have in your environment, you always have a tree and a forest. This might surprise those of you who generally think of domain trees and forests as belonging only to Active Directory environments that consist of multiple domains. However, recall that when you install the first domain in an Active Directory environment, that domain automatically creates a new forest and a new tree.

In the following sections, you will learn how to plan trees and forests and how to promote domain controllers to establish a tree and forest environment.

Planning Trees and Forests

You have already seen several reasons why you might want to have multiple domains within a single company. What you haven't yet seen is how multiple domains can be related to each other and how their relationships can translate into domain forests and trees.

A fundamental commonality between the various domains that exist in trees and forests is that they all share the same Active Directory global catalog (GC). This means that if you modify the Active Directory schema, these changes must be propagated to all of the domain controllers in all of the domains. This is an important point because adding and modifying the structure of information in the GC can have widespread effects on replication and network traffic. Also, you need to ensure that any system you use in the GC role can handle it—you might need to size up the system's hardware requirements. This is especially true if there are multiple domains.

Every domain within an Active Directory configuration has its own unique name. For example, even though you might have a sales domain in two different trees, the complete names for each domain will be different (such as `sales.WillPanek1.com` and `sales.WillPanek2.com`).

In the following sections, you'll look at how you can organize multiple Active Directory domains based on business requirements.

Using a Single Tree

The concept of domain trees was created to preserve the relationship between multiple domains that share a common contiguous namespace. For example, you might have the following DNS domains (based on Internet names):

- `mycompany.com`
- `sales.mycompany.com`
- `engineering.mycompany.com`
- `europe.sales.mycompany.com`

Note that all of these domains fit within a single contiguous namespace. That is, they are all direct or indirect children of the `mycompany.com` domain. In this case, `mycompany.com` is called the *root domain*. All of the direct children (such as `sales.mycompany.com` and `engineering.mycompany.com`) are called *child domains*. Finally, *parent domains* are the domains that are directly above one domain. For example, `sales.mycompany.com` is the parent domain of `europe.sales.mycompany.com`. Figure 3.10 provides an example of a domain tree.

To establish a domain tree, you must first create the root domain for the tree. Then you can add child domains off this root. These child domains can then serve as parents for further subdomains. Each domain must have at least one domain controller, and domain controllers can participate in only one domain at a time. However, you can move a domain controller from one domain to another. To do this, you must first demote a domain controller to a member server and then promote it to a domain controller in another domain.

FIGURE 3.10   A domain tree

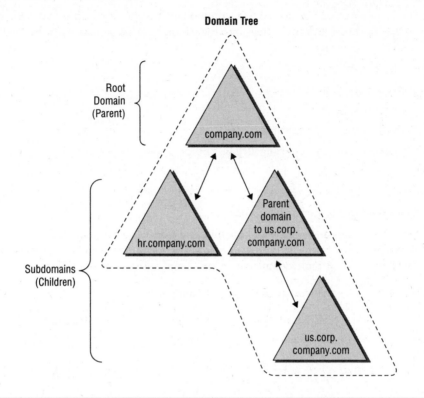

Domains are designed to be logical boundaries. The domains within a tree are, by default, automatically bound together using a two-way transitive trust relationship, which allows resources to be shared among domains through the use of the appropriate user and group assignments. Because trust relationships are transitive, all of the domains within the tree trust each other. Note, however, that a trust by itself does not automatically grant any security permissions to users or objects between domains. Trusts are designed only to *allow* resources to be shared; you must still go through the process of sharing and managing them. Enterprise administrators must explicitly assign security settings to resources before users can access resources between domains.

Using a single tree makes sense when your organization maintains only a single contiguous namespace. Regardless of the number of domains that exist within this environment and how different their security settings are from each other, they are related by a common name. Although domain trees make sense for many organizations, in some cases the network namespace may be considerably more complicated. You'll look at how forests address these situations next.

Using a Forest

Active Directory forests are designed to accommodate multiple noncontiguous namespaces. That is, they can combine domain trees into logical units. An example might be the following tree and domain structure:

- Tree: `Organization1.com`
  - `Sales.Organization1.com`
  - `Marketing.Organization1.com`
  - `Engineering.Organization1.com`
  - `NorthAmerica.Engineering.Organization1.com`
- Tree: `Organization2.com`
  - `Sales.Organization2.com`
  - `Engineering.Organization2.com.`

Figure 3.11 provides an example of how multiple trees can fit into a single forest. Such a situation might occur in the acquisition and merger of companies or if a company is logically divided into two or more completely separate and autonomous business units.

FIGURE 3.11   A single forest consisting of multiple trees

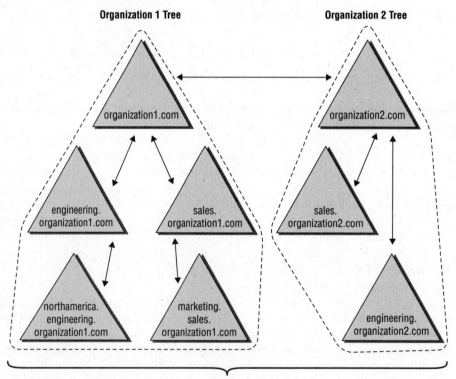

All of the trees within a forest are related through a single forest root domain. This is the first domain that was created in the Active Directory environment. The root domain in each tree creates a transitive trust with the forest root domain. The result is a configuration in which all of the trees within a domain and all of the domains within each tree trust each other. Again, as with domain trees, the presence of a trust relationship does not automatically signify that users have permissions to access resources across domains. It allows only objects and resources to be shared. Authorized network administrators must set up specific permissions.

All of the domains within a single Active Directory forest have the following features in common:

Schema   The *schema* is the Active Directory structure that defines how the information within the data store is structured. For the information stored on various domain controllers to remain compatible, all of the domain controllers within the entire Active Directory environment must share the same schema. For example, if you add a field for an employee benefit plan number, all domain controllers throughout the environment need to recognize this information before you can share information among them.

Global Catalog   One of the problems associated with working in large network environments is that sharing information across multiple domains can be costly in terms of network and server resources. Fortunately, Active Directory uses the global catalog (GC), which serves as a repository for information about a subset of all objects within *all* Active Directory domains in a forest. System administrators can determine what types of information should be added to the defaults in the GC. Generally, they decide to store commonly used information, such as a list of all of the printers, users, groups, and computers. In addition, they can configure specific domain controllers to carry a copy of the GC. Now if you have a question about where to find all of the color printers in the company, for example, all you need to do is to contact the nearest GC server.

Configuration Information   Some roles and functions must be managed for the entire forest. When you are dealing with multiple domains, this means that you must configure certain domain controllers to perform functions for the entire Active Directory environment. I will discuss some specifics of this later in this chapter.

The main purpose of allowing multiple domains to exist together is to allow them to share information and other resources. Now that you've seen the basics of domain trees and forests, take a look at how domains are actually created.

The Promotion Process

A domain tree is created when a new domain is added as the child of an existing domain. This relationship is established during the promotion of a Windows Server 2016 computer to a domain controller. Although the underlying relationships can be quite complicated in larger organizations, the Server Manager's Active Directory Installation Wizard makes it easy to create forests and trees.

Using the Active Directory Installation Wizard, you can quickly and easily create new domains by promoting a Windows Server 2016 stand-alone server or a member server to a domain controller. When you install a new domain controller, you can choose to make it part of an existing domain, or you can choose to make it the first domain controller in a new domain. In the following sections and exercises, you'll become familiar with the exact steps you need to take to create a domain tree and a domain forest when you promote a server to a domain controller.

Creating a Domain Tree

In previous chapters, you learned how to promote the first domain controller in the first domain in a forest, also known as the root. If you don't promote any other domain controllers, then that domain controller simply controls that one domain and only one tree is created. To create a new domain tree, you need to promote a Windows Server 2016 computer to a domain controller. In the Active Directory Installation Wizard, you select the option that makes this domain controller the first machine in a new domain that is a child of an existing domain. As a result, you will have a domain tree that contains two domains—a parent and a child, or two trees if you don't create a child domain.

Before you can create a new child domain, you need the following information:

- The name of the parent domain
- The name of the child domain (the one you are planning to install)
- The file system locations for the Active Directory database, logs, and shared system volume
- DNS configuration information
- The NetBIOS name for the new server
- A domain administrator username and password

Exercise 3.6 walks you through the process of creating a new child domain using Server Manager. This exercise assumes you have already created the parent domain and you are using a server in the domain that is not a domain controller.

EXERCISE 3.6

Creating a New Subdomain

1. Open Server Manager.

2. Click item 2, Add Roles And Features.

3. Make sure that the Role-Based Or Feature-Based Installation button is selected and click Next.

4. At the Select Destination screen, click Next.

5. At the Select Server Roles screen, check the Active Directory Domain Services check box. A box will appear stating that you need to install additional roles. Click the Add Features button. Then click Next.

6. At the Add Roles And Features Wizard screen, click Next.

7. At the Confirmation screen, click the Install button.

8. When the installation is complete, click the Close button.

9. Close Server Manager and restart the machine.

10. Log in and restart Server Manager.

11. In the Roles And Server Groups area, click the AD DS link.

12. In the Servers section, click the More link next to Configuration Required For Active Directory Domain Services.

13. At the All Servers Task Details screen, click the Promote This Server To A Domain Controller link.

14. At the Deployment Configuration screen, click the radio button Add A New Domain To An Existing Forest. In the Select Domain Type drop-down, chose Child Domain and then choose your parent domain. In the New Domain Name box, type in the name of your new domain. I used NewHampshire. Click the Next button.

15. At the Domain Controller Options screen, I set the following options:

    Domain Functional Level: Windows Server 2016

    Domain Name System (DNS) Server: Checked

    Global Catalog (GC): Checked

    Site Name: CorporateHQ

    Password: **P@ssw0rd**

    Click Next.

16. At the DNS screen, click Next.

17. At the Additional Options screen, accept the default NetBIOS domain name and click Next.

18. At the Paths screen, accept the default file locations and click Next.

19. At the Review Options screen, verify your settings and click Next.

20. At the Prerequisites Check screen, click the Install button (as long as there are no errors).

21. After the installation completes, the machine will automatically reboot. Log in as the administrator.

22. Close Server Manager.

Joining a New Domain Tree to a Forest

A *forest* is one or more trees that do not share a contiguous namespace. For example, you could join the `organization1.com` and `organization2.com` domains together to create a single Active Directory environment.

Any two trees can be joined together to create a forest, as long as the second tree is installed after the first and the trees have noncontiguous namespaces. (If the namespaces were contiguous, you would actually need to create a new domain for an existing tree.) The process of creating a new tree to form or add to a forest is as simple as promoting a server to a domain controller for a new domain that does *not* share a namespace with an existing Active Directory domain.

 The command-line tool adprep.exe is used to prepare a Microsoft Windows 2003, 2008, or 2008 R2 forest or a Windows 2003, 2008, or 2008 R2 domain for the installation of Windows Server 2016 domain controllers.

To add a new domain to an existing forest, you must already have at least one other domain, which is the root domain. Keep in mind that the entire forest structure is destroyed if the original root domain is ever removed entirely. Therefore, you should have at least two domain controllers in the Active Directory root domain; the second serves as a backup in case you have a problem with the first, and it can also serve as a backup solution for disaster recovery and fault tolerance purposes. Such a setup provides additional protection for the entire forest in case one of the domain controllers fails.

Adding Additional Domain Controllers

In addition to the operations you've already performed, you can use the Active Directory Installation Wizard to create additional domain controllers for any of your domains. There are two main reasons to create additional domain controllers:

Fault Tolerance and Reliability   You should always consider the theory of *disaster recovery (DR)* and have a plan, sometimes referred to as a *disaster recovery plan (DRP)*. If you're part of one of those organizations that rely upon their network directory services infrastructures, you need Active Directory to provide security and resources for all users.

For this reason, downtime and data loss are very costly. Through the use of multiple domain controllers, you can ensure that if one of the servers goes down, another one is available to perform the necessary tasks, such as user authentication and resource browsing. Additionally, data loss (perhaps from hard disk drive failure) will not result in the loss or unavailability of network security information because you can easily recover Active Directory information from the remaining, still-functional domain controller.

Performance   The burden of processing login requests and serving as a repository for security permissions and other information can be quite extensive, especially in larger businesses. By using multiple domain controllers, you can distribute this load across multiple systems. Additionally, by strategically placing domain controllers, you can greatly increase response times for common network operations, such as authentication and browsing for resources.

As a rule of thumb, you should always plan and design your infrastructure to have at least two domain controllers per domain. For many organizations, this provides a good balance between the cost of servers and the level of reliability and performance. For larger or more distributed organizations, however, additional domain controllers greatly improve performance.

Demoting a Domain Controller

In addition to being able to promote member servers to domain controllers, the Active Directory Installation Wizard can do the exact opposite, that is, demote domain controllers.

You might choose to demote a domain controller for a couple of reasons. First, if you have determined that the role of a server should change (for example, from a domain controller to a member or stand-alone server that you might make into a web server), you can easily demote it to make this happen. Another common reason to demote a domain controller is if you want to move the machine from one domain to another. You cannot do this in a single step: First you need to demote the existing domain controller to remove it from the current domain and then promote it into a new domain. The result is that the server is now a domain controller for a different domain.

To demote a domain controller, you simply access the Active Directory Installation Wizard. The wizard automatically notices that the local server is a domain controller, and it asks you to verify each step you take, as with most things you do in Windows. You are prompted to decide whether you really want to remove this machine from the current domain. Note that if the local server is a global catalog server, you will be warned that at least one copy of the GC must remain available so that you can perform logon authentication.

By default, at the end of the demotion process, the server is joined as a member server to the domain for which it was previously a domain controller. If you demote the last domain controller in the domain, the server becomes a stand-alone server.

Planning for Domain Controller Placement

You are the senior system administrator for a medium-sized Active Directory environment. Currently the environment consists of only one Active Directory domain. Your company's network is spread out over 40 different sites throughout North America. Recently, you've received complaints from users and other system administrators about the performance of Active Directory–related operations. For example, users report that it takes several minutes to log on to their machines between 9 a.m. and 10 a.m., when activity is at its highest. Simultaneously, system administrators complain that updating user information within the OUs for which they are responsible can take longer than expected.

Fortunately, Active Directory's distributed domain controller architecture allows you to optimize performance for this type of situation without making dramatic changes to your environment. You decide that the quickest and easiest solution is to deploy additional domain controllers throughout the organization. The domain controllers are generally placed within areas of the network that are connected by slow or unreliable links. For example, a small branch office in Des Moines, Iowa, receives its own domain controller. The process is quite simple: You install a new Windows Server 2016 computer and then run the Active Directory Installation Wizard in Server Manager to make the new machine a domain controller for an existing domain. Once the initial directory services data is copied to the new server, it is ready to service requests and updates of your domain information.

Note that there are potential drawbacks to this solution; for instance, you have to manage additional domain controllers and the network traffic generated from communications between the domain controllers. It's important that you monitor your network links to ensure that you've reached a good balance between replication traffic and overall Active Directory performance. In later chapters, you'll see how you can configure Active Directory sites to map Active Directory operations better to your physical network structure.

Removing a domain from your environment is not an operation that you should take lightly. Before you plan to remove a domain, make a list of all of the resources that depend on the domain and the reasons why the domain was originally created. If you are sure that your organization no longer requires the domain, then you can safely continue. If you are not sure, think again, because the process cannot be reversed and you could lose critical information!

Managing Multiple Domains

You can easily manage most of the operations that must occur *between* domains by using the Active Directory Domains and Trusts administrative tool. On the other hand, if you want to configure settings *within* a domain, you should use the Active Directory Users and Computers tool. In the following sections, you'll look at ways to perform two common domain management functions with the tools just mentioned: managing *single-master operations* and managing *trusts*. You'll also look at ways to manage UPN suffixes in order to simplify user accounts, and you'll examine GC servers in more detail.

Managing Single-Master Operations

For the most part, Active Directory functions in what is known as *multimaster* replication. That is, every domain controller within the environment contains a copy of the Active Directory database that is both readable and writable. This works well for most types of information. For example, if you want to modify the password of a user, you can easily do this on *any* of the domain controllers within a domain. The change is then automatically propagated to the other domain controllers.

However, some functions are not managed in a multimaster fashion. These operations are known as *operations masters*. You must perform single-master operations on specially designated domain controllers within the Active Directory forest. There are five main single-master functions: two that apply to an entire Active Directory forest and three that apply to each domain.

 To see what domain controllers hold which operation master roles, type **Netdom Query FSMO** at a command prompt or in a PowerShell window.

Forest Operations Masters

You use the Active Directory Domains and Trusts tool to configure forest-wide roles. The following single-master operations apply to the entire forest:

Schema Master   Earlier you learned that all of the domain controllers within a single Active Directory environment share the same schema. This ensures information consistency. However, developers and system administrators can modify the Active Directory schema by adding custom information. A trivial example might involve adding a field to employee information that specifies a user's favorite color.

When you need to make these types of changes, you must perform them on the domain controller that serves as the *Schema Master* for the environment. The Schema Master is then responsible for propagating all of the changes to all the other domain controllers within the forest.

Domain Naming Master   The purpose of the *Domain Naming Master* is to keep track of all the domains within an Active Directory forest. You access this domain controller whenever you need to add/remove new domains to a tree or forest.

Domain Operations Masters

You use the Active Directory Users and Computers snap-in to administer roles within a domain. Within each domain, at least one domain controller must fulfill each of the following roles:

Relative ID (RID) Master   Every security object within Active Directory must be assigned a unique identifier so that it is distinguishable from other objects. For example, if you have two OUs named IT that reside in different domains, you must have some way to distinguish easily between them. Furthermore, if you delete one of the IT OUs and then later re-create it, the system must be able to determine that it is not the same object as the other IT OU. The unique identifier for each object is made up of a domain identifier and a relative identifier (RID). RIDs are always unique within an Active Directory domain and are used for managing security information and authenticating users. The *RID Master* is responsible for creating these values within a domain whenever new Active Directory objects are created.

PDC Emulator Master   Within a domain, the *PDC Emulator Master* (also referred to as the PDC Emulator) is responsible for maintaining backward compatibility with Windows 95, 98, and NT clients. The PDC Emulator Master is also responsible for processing password changes between a domain user account and all of the domain controllers throughout the domain.

The PDC Emulator Master is also the default time server for all of the domain controllers in the domain. This is why it's a good practice to make sure that your PDC emulator has the proper time. It's the system that all others will rely on for time accuracy.

The PDC Emulator Master serves as the default domain controller to process authentication requests if another domain controller is unable to do so. The PDC Emulator Master also receives preferential treatment whenever domain security changes are made. PDC emulators are also the preferred point of contact for many services and applications that run on the domain.

Infrastructure Master   Whenever a user is added to or removed from a group, all of the other domain controllers should be made aware of this change. The role of the domain controller that acts as an *Infrastructure Master* is to ensure that group membership information stays synchronized within an Active Directory domain.

> **NOTE**   Unless there is only one domain controller, you should not place the Infrastructure Master on a global catalog server. If the Infrastructure Master and global catalog are on the same domain controller, the Infrastructure Master will not function.

Another service that a server can control for the network is the Windows Time service. The Windows Time service uses a suite of algorithms in the Network Time Protocol (NTP). This helps ensure that the time on all computers throughout a network is as accurate as possible. All client computers within a Windows Server 2016 domain are synchronized with the time of an authoritative computer.

Assigning Single-Master Roles

Now that you are familiar with the different types of single-master operations, take a look at Exercise 3.7. This exercise shows you how to assign these roles to servers within the Active Directory environment. In this exercise, you will assign single-master operations roles to various domain controllers within the environment. To complete the steps in this exercise, you need one Active Directory domain controller.

EXERCISE 3.7

Assigning Single-Master Operations

1. Open the Active Directory Domains and Trusts administrative tool.

2. Right-click Active Directory Domains And Trusts and choose Operations Masters.

3. In the Operations Masters dialog box, note that you can change the operations master by clicking the Change button. If you want to move this assignment to another computer, first you need to connect to that computer and then make the change. Click Close to continue without making any changes.

4. Close the Active Directory Domains and Trusts administrative tool.

5. Open the Active Directory Users and Computers administrative tool.

6. Right-click the name of a domain and select Operations Masters. This brings up the RID tab of the Operations Masters dialog box.

    Notice that you can change the computer that is assigned to the role. To change the role, first you need to connect to the appropriate domain controller. Notice that the PDC and Infrastructure roles have similar tabs. Click Close to continue without making any changes.

7. When you have finished, close the Active Directory Users and Computers tool.

Remember that you manage single-master operations with three different tools. You use the Active Directory Domains and Trusts tool to configure the Domain Name Master role, while you use the Active Directory Users and Computers snap-in to administer roles within a domain. Although this might not seem intuitive at first, it can help you remember which roles apply to domains and which apply to the whole forest. The third tool, the Schema Master role, is a bit different than these other two. To change the Schema Master role, you must install the Active Directory Schema MMS snap-in and change it there.

Seizing Roles

Changing roles from one domain controller to another is really simple. An administrator goes into Active Directory or PowerShell and changes an FSMO role from one machine to another. The problem happens when a machine with one of the roles crashes and goes down. You can't just switch the role from a machine that is not working.

So, what is an administrator to do? Well, at that point, what you need to do is seize control of the role. You do this through the use of PowerShell. Let's look at how to seize a role using PowerShell.

You may be familiar with seizing FSMO roles from previous versions of Windows Server. In previous versions, you would use the ntdsutil.exe command-line utility, but in Windows Server 2016 it needs to be done in PowerShell.

Normally, I would show you how to seize control of an FSMO role using an exercise, but since you probably don't have dozens of Microsoft Windows Server 2016 domain controllers just lying around, I will show you how to seize control through a step-by-step process.

To show you how to set up a step-by-step process, you first have to know what FSMO roles are assigned to what FSMO numbers. The following roles each have a corresponding number:

FSMO role	Number
PDCEmulator	0
RIDMaster	1
InfrastructureMaster	2
SchemaMaster	3
DomainNamingMaster	4

Now that you know the role and the number associated to it, you just need to know the PowerShell commands to seize control of the role. The following is an example of how to use PowerShell commands to seize control of one of the FSMO roles.

I am using the -Identity switch to specify the target domain controller (I am calling my target domain controller DC1) and the -OperationMasterRole to specify which role to transfer. I've also used the -Force command because my current FSMO holder is offline. I will be moving all of the roles to the target domain controller, DC1.

1. On a domain controller, log in as an administrator and start PowerShell with elevated privileges.

2. In PowerShell, type the following command:

```
Move-ADDirectoryServerOperationMasterRole -Identity DC1 -OperationMasterRole
0,1,2,3,4 -Force
```

3. Either type **Y** on each role move prompt or type **A** to accept all prompts.

4. After a few minutes, all of the FSMO roles should be successfully moved.

Finally, I want to show you a couple of useful PowerShell commands so that you can view which domain controller owns which FSMO role.

```
Get-ADForest DomainName | FT SchemaMaster,DomainNamingMaster
Get-ADDomain DomainName | FT PDCEmulator,RIDMaster,InfrastructureMaster
```

Managing Trusts

Trust relationships make it easier to share security information and network resources between domains. As was already mentioned, standard transitive two-way trusts are automatically created between the domains in a tree and between each of the trees in a forest. Figure 3.12 shows an example of the default trust relationships in an Active Directory forest.

FIGURE 3.12   Default trusts in an Active Directory forest

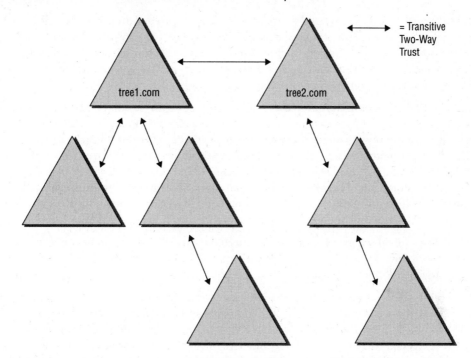

When configuring trusts, you need to consider two main characteristics:

Transitive Trusts   By default, Active Directory trusts are *transitive trusts*. The simplest way to understand transitive relationships is through this example: If Domain A trusts Domain B and Domain B trusts Domain C, then Domain A implicitly trusts Domain C. If you need to apply a tighter level of security, trusts can be configured as intransitive.

One-Way vs. Two-Way   Trusts can be configured as one-way or two-way relationships. The default operation is to create *two-way trusts* or *bidirectional trusts*. This makes it easier to manage trust relationships by reducing the trusts you must create. In some cases, however, you might decide against two-way trusts. In one-way relationships, the trusting domain allows resources to be shared with the trusted domain but not the other way around.

When domains are added together to form trees and forests, an automatic transitive two-way trust is created between them. Although the default trust relationships work well for most organizations, there are some reasons you might want to manage trusts manually:

▪ You may want to remove trusts between domains if you are absolutely sure you do not want resources to be shared between domains.

▪ Because of security concerns, you may need to keep resources isolated.

In addition to the default trust types, you can configure the following types of special trusts:

External Trusts   You use *external trusts* to provide access to resources on a Windows NT 4 domain or forest that cannot use a forest trust. Windows NT 4 domains cannot benefit from the other trust types that are used in Windows Server 2016. Thus, in some cases, external trusts could be your only option. External trusts are always nontransitive, but they can be established in a one-way or two-way configuration.

Default SID Filtering on External Trusts   When you set up an external trust, remember that it is possible for hackers to compromise a domain controller in a trusted domain. If this trust is compromised, a hacker can use the security identifier (SID) history attribute to associate SIDs with new user accounts, granting themselves unauthorized rights (this is called an *elevation-of-privileges attack*). To help prevent this type of attack, Windows Server 2016 automatically enables SID filter quarantining on all external trusts. SID filtering allows the domain controllers in the trusting domain (the domain with the resources) to remove all SID history attributes that are not members of the trusted domain.

Realm Trusts   *Realm trusts* are similar to external trusts. You use them to connect to a non-Windows domain that uses Kerberos authentication. Realm trusts can be transitive or nontransitive, one-way or two-way.

Cross-Forest Trusts   *Cross-forest trusts* are used to share resources between forests. They have been used since Windows Server 2000 domains and cannot be nontransitive, but you can establish them in a one-way or a two-way configuration. Authentication requests in either forest can reach the other forest in a two-way cross-forest trust. If you want one forest to trust another forest, you must set it (at a minimum) to at least the forest function level of Windows Server 2003.

Selective Authentication vs. Forest-Wide Authentication   Forest-wide authentication on a forest trust means that users of the trusted forest can access all of the resources of the trusting forest. Selective authentication means that users cannot authenticate to a domain controller or resource server in the trusting forest unless they are explicitly allowed to do so. Exercise 3.8 will show you the steps necessary to change forest-wide authentication to selective authentication.

Shortcut Trusts   In some cases, you may actually want to create direct trusts between two domains that implicitly trust each other. Such a trust is sometimes referred to as a *shortcut trust*, and it can improve the speed at which resources are accessed across many different domains. Let's say you have a forest, as shown in Figure 3.13.

FIGURE 3.13   Example of a forest

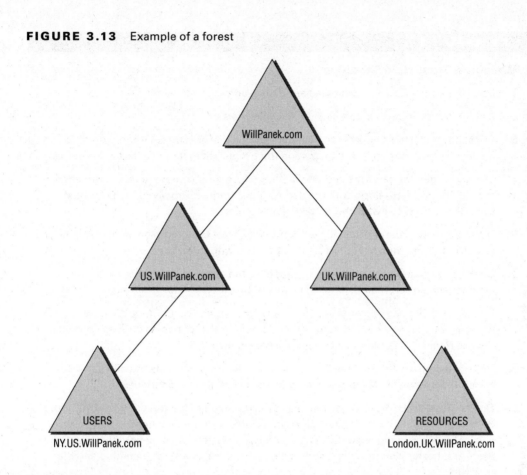

Users in the NY.us.WillPanek.com domain can access resources in the London.uk.WillPanek.com domain, but the users have to authenticate using the parent domains to gain access (NY.us.WillPanek.com to us.WillPanek.com to WillPanek.com to uk.WillPanek.com to finally reach London.uk.WillPanek.com). This process can be slow. An administrator can set up a one-way trust from London.uk.WillPanek.com (trusting domain) to NY.us.WillPanek.com (trusted domain) so that the users can access the resources directly.

> **NOTE**   Perhaps the most important aspect to remember regarding trusts is that creating them only *allows* you to share resources between domains. The trust does not grant any permissions between domains by itself. Once a trust has been established, however, system administrators can easily assign the necessary permissions.

Exercise 3.8 walks you through the steps necessary to manage trusts. In this exercise, you will see how to assign trust relationships between domains. To complete the steps in this exercise, you must have domain administrator access permissions.

EXERCISE 3.8

Managing Trust Relationships

1. Open the Active Directory Domains and Trusts administrative tool.

2. Right-click the name of a domain and select Properties.

3. Select the Trusts tab. You will see a list of the trusts that are currently configured. To modify the trust properties for an existing trust, highlight that trust and click Properties.

4. The Properties window for the trust displays information about the trust's direction, transitivity, and type along with the names of the domains involved in the relationship. Click Cancel to exit without making any changes.

5. To create a new trust relationship, click the New Trust button on the Trusts tab. The New Trust Wizard appears. Click Next to proceed with the wizard.

6. On the Trust Name page, you are prompted for the name of the domain with which the trust should be created. Enter the name of the domain and click Next.

7. On the Trust Type page, you would normally choose the Trust With A Windows Domain option if you know that the other domain uses a Windows domain controller. Choose Realm Trust. Click Next when you have finished.

8. On the Transitivity Of Trust page, you choose whether the trust is transitive or non-transitive. Choose the Nontransitive option and click Next to continue.

9. On the Direction Of Trust page, you select the direction of the trust. If you want both domains to trust each other, you select the Two-Way option. Otherwise, you select either One-Way: Incoming or One-Way: Outgoing, depending on where the affected users are located. For the sake of this exercise, choose One-Way: Incoming and then click Next.

10. On the Trust Password page, you need to specify a password that should be used to administer the trust. Type **P@ssw0rd** and confirm it. Note that if there is an existing trust relationship between the domains, the passwords must match. Click Next to continue.

11. Now you see the Trust Selections Complete page that recaps the selections you have made. Because this is an exercise, you don't actually want to establish this trust. Click Cancel to cancel the wizard without saving the changes.

12. Exit the trust properties for the domain by clicking Cancel.

To Enable Selective Authentication

1. In the console tree, right-click the name of a domain and select Properties.

2. Select the Trusts tab. Under either Domains Trusted By This Domain (Outgoing Trusts) or Domains That Trust This Domain (Incoming Trusts), click the forest trust that you want to administer and then click Properties.

3. On the Authentication tab, click Selective Authentication and then click OK.

Managing UPN Suffixes

User principal name (UPN) suffixes are the part of a user's name that appears after the @ symbol. For example, the UPN suffix of wpanek@WillPanek.com would be WillPanek.com. By default, the UPN suffix is determined by the name of the domain in which the user is created. In this example, the user wpanek was created in the domain WillPanek.com, so the two pieces of the UPN logically fit together. However, you might find it useful to provide an alternative UPN suffix to consolidate the UPNs forest-wide.

For instance, if you manage a forest that consists of WillPanek.com and WillPanek2.com, you might want all of your users to adopt the more generally applicable WillPanek.com UPN suffix. By adding additional UPN suffixes to the forest, you can easily choose the appropriate suffix when it comes time to create new users. Exercise 3.9 shows you how to add additional suffixes to a forest.

EXERCISE 3.9

Adding a UPN Suffix

1. Open the Active Directory Domains and Trusts administrative tool.

2. Right-click Active Directory Domains And Trusts in the left side of the window and select Properties.

3. On the UPN Suffixes tab of the Active Directory Domains And Trusts Properties dialog box, enter an alternative UPN suffix in the Alternative UPN Suffixes field. Click the Add button to add the suffix to the list.

4. To remove a UPN suffix, select its name in the list and click the Remove button.

Name Suffix Routing

Name Suffix Routing is a mechanism that is used to manage how authentication requests are routed across Active Directory forests that are joined together by forest trusts. To simplify the administration of authentication requests, when you create a forest trust, all unique name suffixes are routed by default. A *unique name suffix* is a name suffix within a forest, such as a user principal name (UPN) suffix, service principal name (SPN) suffix, or Domain Name System forest, or a domain tree name that is not subordinate to any other name suffix. Name Suffix Routing is managed from the Active Directory Domains and Trusts Administrative Console.

Managing Global Catalog Servers

One of the best features of a distributed directory service like Active Directory is that you can store different pieces of information in different places within an organization. For example, a domain in Japan might store a list of users who operate within a company's

Asian operations business unit, while one in New York would contain a list of users who operate within its North American operations business unit. This architecture allows system administrators to place the most frequently accessed information on domain controllers in different domains, thereby reducing disk space requirements and replication traffic.

However, you may encounter a problem when you deal with information that is segmented into multiple domains. The issue involves querying information stored within Active Directory. For example, what would happen if a user wanted a list of all the printers available in all domains within the Active Directory forest? In this case, the search would normally require information from at least one domain controller in each of the domains within the environment. Some of these domain controllers may be located across slow WAN links or may have unreliable connections. The result would include an extremely long wait while retrieving the results of the query, that is, if any results came up without the query timing out.

Fortunately, Active Directory has a mechanism that speeds up such searches. You can configure any number of domain controllers to host a copy of the GC. The GC contains all of the schema information and a subset of the attributes for all domains within the Active Directory environment. Although a default set of information is normally included with the GC, system administrators can choose to add additional information to this data store if it is needed. To help reduce replication traffic and to keep the GC's database small, only a limited subset of each object's attributes is replicated. This is called the *partial attribute set (PAS)*. You can change the PAS by modifying the schema and marking attributes for replication to the GC.

Servers that contain a copy of the GC are known as *GC servers*. Now whenever a user executes a query that requires information from multiple domains, they need only contact the nearest GC server for this information. Similarly, when users must authenticate across domains, they do not have to wait for a response from a domain controller that may be located across the world. The result is that the overall performance of Active Directory queries improves.

Exercise 3.10 walks you through the steps that you need to take to configure a domain controller as a GC server. Generally, GC servers are useful only in environments that use multiple Active Directory domains.

EXERCISE 3.10

Managing GC Servers

1. Open the Active Directory Sites and Services administrative tool.

2. Find the name of the local domain controller within the list of objects, typically under Default First Site Name ➤ Servers, and expand this object. Right-click NTDS Settings, and select Properties.

3. In the NTDS Settings Properties dialog box, type **Primary GC Server for Domain** in the Description field. Note that there is a check box that determines whether this computer contains a copy of the global catalog. If the box is checked, then this

domain controller contains a subset of information from all other domains within the Active Directory environment. Select the Global Catalog check box and then click OK to continue.

4. When you have finished, close the Active Directory Sites and Services administrative tool.

Managing Universal Group Membership Caching

Many networks run into problems with available network bandwidth and server hardware limitations. For this reason, it may not be wise to install a GC in smaller branch offices. Windows Server 2016 can help these smaller sites by deploying domain controllers that use *Universal Group Membership Caching (UGMC)*.

Once enabled, Universal Group Membership Caching stores information locally when a user attempts to log on for the first time. With the use of a GC, the domain controller retains the universal group membership for that logged-on user.

The next time that user attempts to log on, the authenticating domain controller running Windows Server 2016 will obtain the universal group membership information from its local cache without the need to contact a GC. By default, the universal group membership information is retained on the domain controller for eight hours.

There are several advantages of using Universal Group Membership Caching:

Faster Logon Times Because the domain controller does not need to contact a global catalog, logon authentication is faster.

Reduced Network Bandwidth The domain controller does not have to handle object replication for all of the objects located in the forest.

Ability to Use Existing Hardware There is no need to upgrade hardware to support a GC.

Exercise 3.11 shows you the steps necessary to configure Universal Group Membership Caching.

EXERCISE 3.11

Managing Universal Group Membership Caching

1. Open the Active Directory Sites and Services administrative tool.

2. Click Sites and then click CorporateHQ. In the right pane, right-click NTDS Settings and choose Properties.

3. In the NTDS Site Settings Properties dialog box, check the box Enable Universal Group Membership Caching and then click OK to continue.

4. When you have finished, close the Active Directory Sites and Services administrative tool.

Upgrading Existing Domains and Forests

Now that you have a new operating system to which you can upgrade, it's important that you take some time to learn about the different ways you can get your infrastructure up-to-date. There are quite a few upgrade paths to consider. Table 3.2 illustrates the most commonly used in-place upgrade paths for upgrading your domain controllers from Windows Server 2008 to Windows Server 2016. The in-place upgrades hold true only for 64-bit versions of Server 2008 to Server 2016. You cannot in-place upgrade domain controllers that run either Windows Server 2003 or a 32-bit version of Windows Server 2008. If your current environmental configurations fall outside of the possibility of an in-place upgrade, then you will need to install new domain controllers on the most up-to-date Windows Server OS and then delete the old ones.

TABLE 3.2   Supported domain controller in-place upgrade paths

If you are running these editions...	You can upgrade to these editions...
Windows Server 2008 Standard with SP2 or Windows Server 2008 Enterprise with SP2	Windows Server 2016 Standard or Windows Server 2016 Datacenter
Windows Server 2008 Datacenter with SP2	Windows Server 2016 Datacenter
Windows Web Server 2008	Windows Server 2016 Standard
Windows Server 2008 R2 Standard with SP1 or Windows Server 2008 R2 Enterprise with SP1	Windows Server 2016 Standard or Windows Server 2016 Datacenter
Windows Server 2008 R2 Datacenter with SP1	Windows Server 2016 Datacenter
Windows Web Server 2008 R2	Windows Server 2016 Standard
Windows Server 2012/2012 R2 Standard	Windows Server 2016 Standard
Windows Server 2012/2012 R2 Datacenter	Windows Server 2016 Datacenter

When preparing for your domain controller upgrade, make sure you make a full backup of your Active Directory environment prior to performing the task. If you have never actually performed a full backup and restore of your Active Directory environment, then I recommend doing so by following the instructions later in this chapter. You never know if a backup actually works until you perform the restore, and you should never make infrastructure changes without a backup of your current configuration.

Maintain Active Directory

If you have deployed Active Directory in your network environment, your users now depend on it to function properly in order to do their jobs. From network authentications to file access to print and web services, Active Directory has become a mission-critical component of your business. Therefore, the importance of backing up the Active Directory data store should be evident.

As I discussed in earlier chapters, it is important to have multiple domain controllers available to provide backup in case of a problem. The same goes for Active Directory itself—it too should be backed up by being saved. This way, if a massive disaster occurs in which you need to restore your directory services, you will have that option available to you.

Backups are just good common sense, but here are several specific reasons to back up data:

Protect Against Hardware Failures Computer hardware devices have finite lifetimes, and all hardware eventually fails. MBTF is the average time a device will function before it actually fails. There is also a rating derived from benchmark testing of hard disk devices that tells you when you may be at risk for an unavoidable disaster. Some types of failures, such as corrupted hard disk drives, can result in significant data loss.

Protect Against Accidental Deletion or Modification of Data Although the threat of hardware failures is very real, in most environments, mistakes in modifying or deleting data are much more common. For example, suppose a system administrator accidentally deletes all of the objects within a specific OU. Clearly, it's very important to be able to retrieve this information from a backup.

Keep Historical Information Users and system administrators sometimes modify files and then later find out that they require access to an older version of the file. Or a file is accidentally deleted and a user does not discover that fact until much later. By keeping multiple backups over time, you can recover information from prior backups when necessary.

Protect Against Malicious Deletion or Modification of Data Even in the most secure environments, it is conceivable that unauthorized users (or authorized ones with malicious intent!) could delete or modify information. In such cases, the loss of data might require valid backups from which to restore critical information.

Windows Server 2016 includes a Backup utility that is designed to back up operating system files and the Active Directory data store. It allows for basic backup functionality, such as scheduling backup jobs and selecting which files to back up. Figure 3.14 shows the main screen of the Windows Server 2016 Backup utility.

In the following sections, we'll look at the details of using the Windows Server 2016 Backup utility and how you can restore Active Directory when problems do occur.

FIGURE 3.14   The main screen of the Windows Server 2016 Backup utility

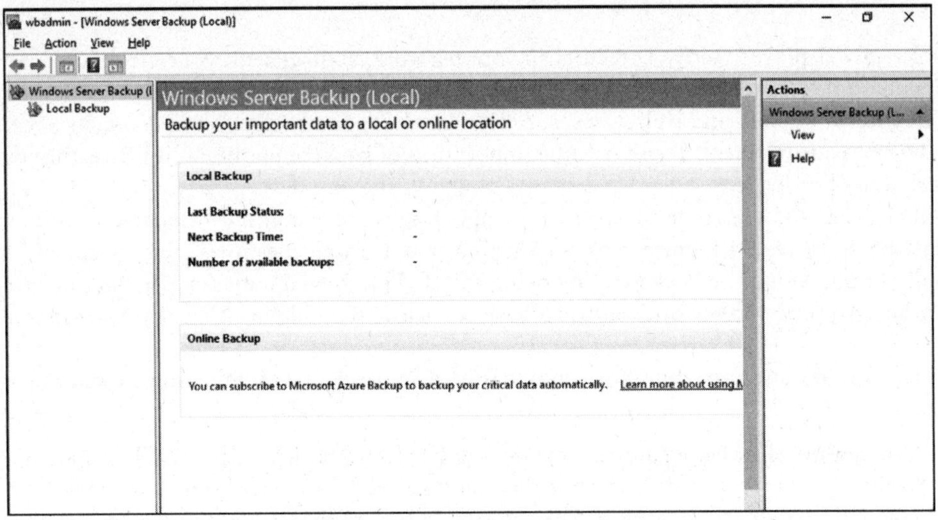

Overview of the Windows Server 2016 Backup Utility

Although the general purpose behind performing backup operations—protecting information—is straightforward, system administrators must consider many options when determining the optimal backup-and-recovery scenario for their environment. Factors include what to back up, how often to back up, and when the backups should be performed.

In the following sections, you'll see how the Windows Server 2016 Backup utility makes it easy to implement a backup plan for many network environments.

> Although the Windows Server 2016 Backup utility provides the basic functionality required to back up your files, you may want to investigate third-party products that provide additional functionality. These applications can provide options for specific types of backups (such as those for Exchange Server and SQL Server) as well as disaster recovery options, networking functionality, centralized management, and support for more advanced hardware.

Backup Types

One of the most important issues you will have to deal with when you are performing backups is keeping track of which files you have backed up and which files you need to back up. Whenever a backup of a file is made, the archive bit for the file is set. You can view the attributes of system files by right-clicking them and selecting Properties. By clicking the

Advanced button in the Properties dialog box, you will access the Advanced Attributes dialog box. Here you will see the option Folder Is Ready For Archiving. Figure 3.15 shows an example of the attributes for a folder.

FIGURE 3.15   Viewing the Archive attributes for a folder

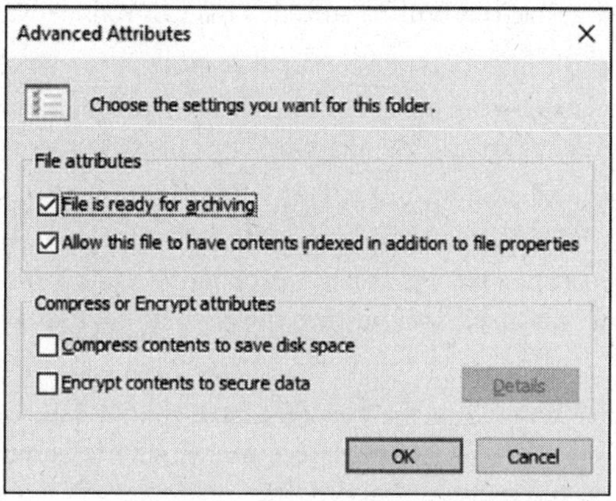

Although it is possible to back up all of the files in the file system during each backup operation, it's sometimes more convenient to back up only selected files (such as those that have changed since the last backup operation). When performing backups, you can back up to removable media (DVD) or to a network location.

It is recommended by Microsoft to do a backup to a network location. The reason for this is that if your company suffers from a disaster (fire, hurricane, and so forth), your data can all still be lost—including the backup. If you back up to a removable media source, a copy of the backup can be taken offsite. This protects against a major disaster.

> **NOTE**   Although Windows Server 2016 does not support all of these backup types, it's very important that you understand the most common backup types. Most Administrators use third-party software for their backups. That's why it's important to know all of the different types.

Several types of backups can be performed:

Normal   Normal backups (also referred to as *system* or *full backups*) back up all of the selected files and then mark them as backed up. This option is usually used when a full system backup is made. Windows Server 2016 supports this backup.

Copy   *Copy backups* back up all of the selected files but do not mark them as backed up. This is useful when you want to make additional backups of files for moving files offsite or you want to make multiple copies of the same data for archival purposes.

Incremental   *Incremental backups* copy any selected files that are marked as ready for backup (typically because they have not been backed up or they have been changed since the last backup) and then mark the files as backed up. When the next incremental backup is run, only the files that are not marked as having been backed up are stored. Incremental backups are used in conjunction with normal (full) backups.

The most common backup process is to make a full backup and then make subsequent incremental backups. The benefit to this method is that only files that have changed since the last full or incremental backup will be stored. This can reduce backup times and disk or tape storage space requirements.

When recovering information from this type of backup method, a system administrator must first restore the full backup and then restore each of the incremental backups.

Differential *Differential backups* are similar in purpose to incremental backups with one important exception: Differential backups copy all of the files that are marked for backup but do not mark the files as backed up. When restoring files in a situation that uses normal and differential backups, you need only restore the normal backup and the latest differential backup.

Daily *Daily backups* back up all of the files that have changed during a single day. This operation uses the file time/date stamps to determine which files should be backed up and does not mark the files as having been backed up.

Backing Up System State Data

When you are planning to back up and restore Active Directory, be aware that the most important component is known as the *System State data*. System State data includes the components upon which the Windows Server 2016 operating system relies for normal operations. The Windows Server 2016 Backup utility offers you the ability to back up the System State data to another type of media (such as a hard disk or network share). Specifically, it will back up the following components for a Windows Server 2016 domain controller:

Active Directory The *Active Directory data store* is at the heart of Active Directory. It contains all of the information necessary to create and manage network resources, such as users and computers. In most environments that use Active Directory, users and system administrators rely on the proper functioning of these services in order to do their jobs.

Boot Files *Boot files* are the files required for booting the Windows Server 2016 operating system and can be used in the case of boot file corruption.

COM+ Class Registration Database The *COM+ Class Registration database* is a listing of all of the COM+ Class registrations stored on the computer. Applications that run on a Windows Server 2016 computer might require the registration of various share code components. As part of the System State backup process, Windows Server 2016 stores all of the information related to Component Object Model+ (COM+) components so that it can be quickly and easily restored.

Registry The Windows Server 2016 *Registry* is a central repository of information related to the operating system configuration (such as desktop and network settings), user settings, and application settings. Therefore, the Registry is absolutely vital to the proper functioning of Windows Server 2016.

Sysvol Directory The *Sysvol directory* includes data and files that are shared between the domain controllers within an Active Directory domain. Many operating system services rely on this information in order to function properly.

Bare Metal Backups and Restores

One of the options you have in Windows Server 2016 is to do a *Bare Metal Restore (BMR)*. This is a restore of a machine after the machine has been completely wiped out and formatted. This type of restore is done usually after a catastrophic machine failure or crash.

Windows Server 2016 gives you the ability to backup all of the files needed for a Bare Metal Restore by choosing the Bare Metal Recovery checkbox (see Figure 3.16).

FIGURE 3.16 Bare Metal Recovery option

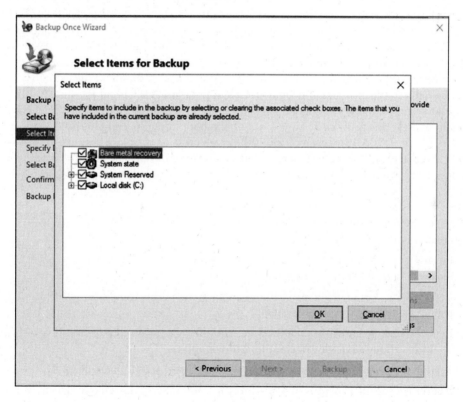

When you choose the Bare Metal Restore option in Windows Server 2016, all of the sub-options (System State, System Reserved, and Local Disk) automatically get checked.

When preparing your network for a Bare Metal Backup, you want to make sure that you have everything you need on hand to complete this type of restore. You may want to keep a copy of the server software, server drivers, and so forth on hand and ready to go, just in case you have to do a full restore.

Scheduling Backups

In addition to specifying which files to back up, you can schedule backup jobs to occur at specific times. Planning *when* to perform backups is just as important as deciding *what* to back up. Performing backup operations can reduce overall system performance; therefore, you should plan to back up information during times of minimal activity on your servers.

To add a backup operation to the schedule, you can simply click the Add button on the Specify Backup Time window.

Restoring System State Data

In some cases, the Active Directory data store or other System State data may become corrupt or unavailable. This could be due to many different reasons. A hard disk failure might, for example, result in the loss of data. Or the accidental deletion of an OU and all of its objects might require a restore operation to be performed.

The actual steps involved in restoring System State data are based on the details of what has caused the data loss and what effect this data loss has had on the system. In the best-case scenario, the System State data is corrupt or inaccurate but the operating system can still boot. If this is the case, all you must do is boot into a special *Directory Services Restore Mode (DSRM)* and then restore the System State data from a backup. This process will replace the current System State data with that from the backup. Therefore, any changes that have been made since the last backup will be completely lost and must be redone.

In a worst-case scenario, all of the information on a server has been lost or a hardware failure is preventing the machine from properly booting. If this is the case, here are several steps that you must take in order to recover System State data:

1. Fix any hardware problem that might prevent the computer from booting (for example, replace any failed hard disks).

2. Reinstall the Windows Server 2016 operating system. This should be performed like a regular installation on a new system.

3. Reinstall any device drivers that may be required by your backup device. If you backed up information to the file system, this will not apply.

4. Restore the System State data using the Windows Server 2016 Backup utility.

I'll cover the technical details of performing restores later in this section. For now, however, you should understand the importance of backing up information and, whenever possible, testing the validity of backups.

Backing Up and Restoring Group Policy Objects

Group Policy Objects (GPOs) are a major part of Active Directory. When you back up Active Directory, GPOs can also get backed up. You also have the ability to back up GPOs through the Group Policy Management Console (GPMC). This gives you the ability to back up and restore individual GPOs.

To back up all GPOs, open the GPMC and right-click the Group Policy Objects container. You will see the option Back Up All. After you choose this option, a wizard will start, asking you for the backup location. Choose a location and click Backup.

To back up an individual GPO, right-click the GPO (in the Group Policy Objects container) and choose Backup. Again, after you choose this option, a wizard will start, asking you for the backup location. Choose a location and click Backup.

To restore a GPO, it's the same process as above except, instead of choosing Backup, you will choose either Manage Backups (to restore all GPOs) or Restore (for an individual GPO).

Setting Up an Active Directory Backup

The Windows Server 2016 Backup utility makes it easy to back up the System data (including Active Directory) as part of a normal backup operation. We've already covered the ideas behind the different backup types and why and when they are used.

Exercise 3.12 walks you through the process of backing up the domain controller. In order to complete this exercise, the local machine must be a domain controller, and you must have a DVD burner or network location to back up the System State.

    The Windows Server 2016 Backup utility is not installed by default. If you have already installed the Windows Server 2016 Backup utility, skip to step 9.

EXERCISE 3.12

Backing Up Active Directory

1. To install the Windows Server 2016 Backup utility, click the Start Key ➤ Server Manager.

2. In the center console, click the link for Add Roles And Features.

3. At the Select Installation Type screen, choose role-based or feature-based installation and click Next.

4. The Select Destination Server screen appears. Choose Select A Server From The Server Pool, and choose your server under Server Pool. Click Next.

5. Click Next at the Select Server Roles screen.

6. At the Select Features screen, scroll down and check the box next to Windows Server Backup. Click Next.

7. At the Confirmation screen, click the checkbox to Restart the destination server automatically. This will bring up a dialog box. Click Yes, and then click the Install button.

8. Click the Close button when finished. Close Server Manager.

9. Open Windows Backup by clicking the Windows Key ➤ Administrative Tools ➤ Windows Server Backup.

10. On the left-hand side, click Local Backup. Then, under Actions, click Backup Once.

11. When the Backup Once Wizard appears, click Different Options and click Next.

12. At the Select Backup Configuration screen, choose Custom and click Next.

13. Click the Add Items button. Choose System State and click OK. Click Next.

14. At the Specify Destination Type, choose Remote Shared Folder. Click Next.

15. Put in the shared path you want to use and click Next.

16. At the Confirmation screen, click the Backup button.

17. Once the backup is complete, close the Windows Server Backup utility.

Restoring Active Directory

Active Directory has been designed with fault tolerance in mind. For example, it is highly recommended by Microsoft that each domain have at least two domain controllers. Each of these domain controllers contains a copy of the Active Directory data store. Should one of the domain controllers fail, the available one can take over the failed server's functionality. When the failed server is repaired, it can then be promoted to a domain controller in the existing environment. This process effectively restores the failed domain controller without incurring any downtime for end users because all of the Active Directory data is replicated to the repaired server in the next scheduled replication.

In some cases, you might need to restore Active Directory from a backup. For example, suppose a system administrator accidentally deletes several hundred users from the domain and does not realize it until the change has been propagated to all of the other domain controllers. Manually re-creating the accounts is not an option because the objects' security identifiers will be different (and all permissions must be reset). Clearly, a method for restoring from backup is the best solution. You can elect to make the Active Directory restore authoritative or nonauthoritative, as described in the following sections.

Overview of Authoritative Restore

Restoring Active Directory and other System State data is an important process should system files or the Active Directory data store become corrupt or otherwise unavailable. Fortunately, the Windows Server 2016 Backup utility allows you to restore data easily from a backup, should the need arise.

I mentioned earlier that in the case of the accidental deletion of information from Active Directory, you might need to restore the Active Directory from a recent backup. But what happens if there is more than one domain controller in the environment? Even if you did perform a restore, the information on this domain controller would be seen as outdated and it would be overwritten by the data from another domain controller. This data from the older domain controller is exactly the information you want to replace. The domain controller that was reloaded using a backup would have an older time stamp, and the other domain controllers would re-delete the information from the backup.

Fortunately, Windows Server 2016 and Active Directory allow you to perform what is called an *authoritative restore*. The authoritative restore process specifies a domain controller as having the authoritative (or master) copy of the Active Directory data store. When other domain controllers communicate with this domain controller, their information will be overwritten with Active Directory data stored on the local machine.

Now that you have an idea of how an authoritative restore is supposed to work, let's move on to looking at the details of performing the process.

Performing an Authoritative Restore

When you are restoring Active Directory information on a Windows Server 2016 domain controller, make sure that Active Directory services are not running. This is because the restore of System State data requires full access to system files and the Active Directory data store. If you attempt to restore System State data while the domain controller is active, you will see an error message.

In general, restoring data and operating system files is a straightforward process. It is important to note that restoring a System State backup will replace the existing Registry, Sysvol, and Active Directory files, so that any changes you made since the last backup will be lost.

In addition to restoring the entire Active Directory database, you can also restore only specific subtrees within Active Directory using the restoresubtree command in the ntdsutil utility. This allows you to restore specific information, and it is useful in case of accidental deletion of isolated material.

Following the authoritative restore process, Active Directory should be updated to the time of the last backup. Furthermore, all of the other domain controllers for this domain will have their Active Directory information overwritten by the results of the restore operation. The result is an Active Directory environment that has been recovered from media.

Overview of Nonauthoritative Restore

Now that you understand why you would use an authoritative restore and how it is performed, it's an easy conceptual jump to understand a *nonauthoritative restore*. Remember that by making a restore authoritative, you are simply telling other domain controllers in the domain to recognize the restored machine as the newest copy of Active Directory for replication purposes. If you only have one domain controller, the authoritative restore process becomes moot; you can simply skip the steps required to make the restore authoritative and begin using the domain controller immediately after the normal restore is complete.

If you have more than one domain controller in the domain and you need to perform a nonauthoritative restore, simply allow the domain controller to receive Active Directory database information from other domain controllers in the domain using normal replication methods.

Active Directory Recycle Bin

The Active Directory Recycle Bin is a great feature that allows an administrator to restore an Active Directory object that has been deleted.

Let's say that you have a junior administrator who has been making changes to Active Directory for hours. The junior admin then deletes an OU from Active Directory. You would then have to reload the OU from a tape backup, or even worse, you may have to reload the entire Active Directory (depending on your backup software), thus losing the hours of work the junior admin has completed.

The problem here is that when you delete a security object from Active Directory, the object's Security ID (SID) gets removed. All users' rights and permissions are associated with the users' SID number and not their account name. This is where the AD Recycle Bin can help.

The *Active Directory Recycle Bin* allows you to preserve and restore accidentally deleted Active Directory objects without the need of using a backup.

The Active Directory Recycle Bin works for both the Active Directory Domain Services (AD DS) and the Active Directory Lightweight Directory Services (AD LDS) environments.

By enabling (disabled by default) the Active Directory Recycle Bin, any deleted Active Directory objects are preserved and Active Directory objects can be restored, in their entirety, to the same condition that they were in immediately before deletion. This means that all group memberships and access rights that the object had before deletion will remain intact.

To enable the Active Directory Recycle Bin, you must do the following (you must be a member of the Schema Admins group):

- Run the adprep /forestprep command to prepare the forest on the server that holds the schema master to update the schema.

- Run the adprep /domainprep /gpprep command to prepare the domain on the server that holds the infrastructure operations master role.

- If a read-only domain controller (RODC) is present in your environment, you must also run the adprep /rodcprep command.

- Make sure that all domain controllers in your Active Directory forest are running Windows Server 2016, Windows Server 2012 / 2012 R2, or Windows Server 2008 R2.

- Make sure that the forest functional level is set to Windows Server 2016, Windows Server 2012 / 2012 R2, or Windows Server 2008 R2.

Restartable Active Directory

Administrators have the ability to stop and restart Active Directory in the Windows Server 2016 operating system without the need to reboot the entire system. Administrators can perform these actions either by using the Microsoft Management Console (MMC) snap-ins or the command line.

With *Restartable Active Directory Services*, an administrator has the ability to stop Active Directory Services so that updates and other tasks can be applied to a domain controller. One task that an administrator can perform while Active Directory is stopped is an offline defragmentation of the database.

One of the advantages of a Restartable Active Directory is that other services running on the same server do not depend on Active Directory to continue to function properly while Active Directory is stopped. An administrator has the ability to stop and restart the Active Directory Domain Services in the Local Services MMC snap-in.

Offline Maintenance

As you learned in the preceding section, there are times when you have to be offline to do maintenance. For example, you need to perform authoritative and nonauthoritative restores while the domain controller is offline. The main utility we use for offline maintenance is ntdsutil.

Ntdsutil.exe

The primary method by which system administrators can do offline maintenance is through the ntdsutil command-line tool. You can launch this tool by simply entering ntdsutil at a command prompt. For the commands to work properly, you must start the command prompt with elevated privileges. The **ntdsutil** command is both interactive and context sensitive. That is, once you launch the utility, you'll see an ntdsutil command prompt. At this prompt, you can enter various commands that set your context within the application. For example, if you enter **domain management**, you'll be able to enter domain-related commands. Several operations also require you to connect to a domain, a domain controller, or an Active Directory object before you perform a command.

Table 3.3 provides a list of some of the domain-management commands supported by the ntdsutil tool. You can access this functionality by typing the command at an elevated command prompt. Once you are in the ntdsutil prompt, you can use the question mark to see all of the commands available.

TABLE 3.3   Ntdsutil offline maintenance commands

Ntdsutil **Domain Management Command**	**Purpose**
Help or ?	Displays information about the commands that are available within the Domain Management menu of the ntdsutil utility.
Activate instance %s	Sets NTDS or a specific AD LDS instance as the active instance.

TABLE 3.3   Ntdsutil offline maintenance commands *(continued)*

Ntdsutil **Domain Management Command**	**Purpose**
Authoritative restore	Sets the domain controller for the authoritative restore of the Active Directory database.
Change service account	This allows an administrator to change the AD LDS service account to username and password. You can use a "NULL" for a blank password, and you can use * to prompt the user to enter a password.
configurable settings	Allows an administrator to manage configurable settings.
DS behavior	Allows an administrator to view and modify AD DS or AD LDS behavior.
files	This command allows an administrator to manage the AD DS or AD LDS database files.
Group Membership Evaluation	Allows an administrator to evaluate the security IDs (SIDs) in a token for a given user or group.
LDAP policies	Administrators can manage the Lightweight Directory Access Protocol (LDAP) protocol policies.
metadata cleanup	Removes metadata from decommissioned domain controllers.
security account management	This command allows an administrator to manage SIDs.
Set DSRM Password	Resets the Directory Service Restore mode administrator account password.

Active Directory Database Mounting Tool

One issue that an administrator may run into when trying to restore Active Directory is the need to restore several backups to compare the Active Directory data that each backup contains. Windows Server 2016 has a utility called the Active Directory database mounting tool (Dsamain.exe), which can resolve this issue.

The `Dsamain.exe` tool can help the recovery processes by giving you a way to compare data as it exists in snapshots (taken at different times) so that you have the ability to decide which Active Directory database to restore.

Creating snapshots on a regular basis will allow you to have enough data so that you can keep accurate records of how the Active Directory database changes over time. The `ntdsutil` utility allows you to take snapshots by using the `ntdsutil snapshot` operation.

> You are not required to run the `ntdsutil snapshot` operation to use `Dsamain.exe`. You have the ability to use a backup of the Active Directory database.

You must be a member of the Domain Admins group or the Enterprise Admins group to view any snapshots taken due to the fact that these snapshots contain sensitive Active Directory data.

Compact the Directory Database File (Offline Defragmentation)

One task that all of us have been doing for years is the process of defragging the operating systems that we run. We have used the defragmentation utility since Windows NT. Defragging a system helps return free space from data to the hard drive.

You can also use the defragmentation process to compact the Active Directory database while it's offline. Offline defragmentation helps return free disk space and check Active Directory database integrity.

To perform an offline defragmentation, you would use the `ntdsutil` command. When you perform a defragmentation of the Active Directory database, a new compacted version of the database is created. This new database file can be created on the same machine (if space permits) or on a network location. After the new file is created, copy the compacted `Ntds.dit` file back to the original location.

It is a good practice, if space allows, to maintain a copy of the older, original database file. You can either rename the older database file and keep it in its current location or copy the older database file to an alternate location.

Monitoring Replication

At times you may need to keep an eye on how your replication traffic is working on your domain controllers. We are going to examine the replication utility that you can use to help determine if there are problems on your domain.

Repadmin Utility

The `Repadmin` utility is included when you install Windows Server 2016. This command-line tool helps administrators diagnose replication problems between Windows domain controllers.

Repadmin allows administrators to view the replication topology of each domain controller as seen from the domain controller's perspective. Administrators can also use Repadmin to create the replication topology manually. By manually creating the replication topology, administrators can force replication events between domain controllers and view the replication metadata vectors.

To access the Repadmin utility, open a command prompt using an elevated privilege (Run ➤ CMD). At the command prompt, type **Repadmin.exe**, and all of the available options will appear.

Using the ADSI Editor

Another utility (explained earlier in the chapter) that allows you to manage objects and attributes in Active Directory is the Active Directory Service Interfaces Editor (ADSI Edit). Earlier we used ADSI Edit (Adsiedit.msc) to create multiple password policies to allow for fine-grained password policies. ADSI Edit allows you to view every object and attribute in an Active Directory forest.

One advantage to using the Adsiedit.msc MMC snap-in is that this tool allows you to query, view, create, and edit attributes that are not exposed through other Active Directory Microsoft Management Console (MMC) snap-ins.

ADSI Edit allows you to administer an AD LDS instance. To do this, you must first connect and bind to the instance. After you connect and bind to the instance, you can administer the containers and objects within the instance by browsing to the containers or objects and then right-clicking them. To complete this task, you must be a member of the Administrators group for the AD LDS instance.

Wbadmin Command-Line Utility

The wbadmin command allows you to back up and restore your operating system, volumes, files, folders, and applications from a command prompt.

You must be a member of the Administrators group to configure a backup schedule. You must be a member of the Backup Operators or the Administrators group (or you must have been delegated the appropriate permissions) to perform all other tasks using the wbadmin command.

To use the wbadmin command, you must run wbadmin from an elevated command prompt (to open an elevated command prompt, click Start, right-click Command Prompt, and then click Run As Administrator). Table 3.4 shows some of the wbadmin commands.

TABLE 3.4 Wbadmin commands

Command	Description
Wbadmin enable backup	Configures and enables a daily backup schedule.
Wbadmin disable backup	Disables your daily backups.

Command	Description
Wbadmin start backup	Runs a one-time backup.
Wbadmin stop job	Stops the currently running backup or recovery operation.
Wbadmin get items	Lists the items included in a specific backup.
Wbadmin start recovery	Runs a recovery of the volumes, applications, files, or folders specified.
Wbadmin get status	Shows the status of the currently running backup or recovery operation.
Wbadmin start systemstaterecovery	Runs a system state recovery.
Wbadmin start systemstatebackup	Runs a system state backup.
Wbadmin start sysrecovery	Runs a recovery of the full system state.

Summary

In this chapter, I discussed the purpose of Active Directory replication. As you have learned, replication is used to keep domain controllers synchronized, and it is important in Active Directory environments of all sizes. Replication is the process by which changes to the Active Directory database are transferred between domain controllers.

This chapter also covered the concepts of sites, site boundaries, and subnets. In addition to learning how to configure them, you learned that subnets define physical portions of your network environment and that sites are defined as collections of well-connected IP subnets. Site boundaries are defined by the subnet or subnets that you include in your site configuration.

I also covered the basics of replication and the differences between intrasite and intersite replication. Additionally, I covered the purpose and use of bridgehead servers in depth. Although replication is a behind-the-scenes type of task, the optimal configuration of sites in distributed network environments results in better use of bandwidth and faster response by network resources. For these reasons, you should be sure you thoroughly understand the concepts related to managing replication for Active Directory.

I covered the placement of domain controllers and global catalog servers in the network and how, when placed properly, they can increase the performance of Active Directory operations.

I also showed how to monitor and troubleshoot replication. The Windows Server 2016 System Monitor administrative tool was designed so that you can monitor many performance statistics associated with using Active Directory.

The chapter also covered the basics of linking multiple domains in trees and forests. You now know why you would want to plan for them and the benefits and drawbacks of using only one domain or of having a multidomain environment. For example, you might decide to have multiple domains if you have an acquisitions-and-mergers situation where you need to keep multiple administrators. In addition, by using multiple domains, organizations can retain separate security databases; however, in such cases, they are also able to share resources between domains.

You can use multiple domains to provide two major benefits for the network directory services—security and availability. These benefits are made possible through Active Directory and the administrative tools that can be used to access it.

System administrators can simplify operations while still ensuring that only authorized users have access to their data. Multiple domains can interact to form Active Directory trees and forests, and you can use the Active Directory Installation Wizard to create new Active Directory trees and forests.

Exam Essentials

Understand the reasons for using multiple domains.   There are seven primary reasons for using multiple domains: They provide additional scalability, they reduce replication traffic, they help with political and organizational issues, they provide many levels of hierarchy, they allow for decentralized administration, they preserve legality, and they allow for multiple DNS or domain names.

Understand the drawbacks of using multiple domains.   With multiple domains, maintaining administrative consistency is more difficult. The number of administrative units multiplies as well, which makes it difficult to keep track of network resources. Finally, it is much more difficult to rearrange the domain topology within an Active Directory environment than it is simply to reorganize OUs.

Know how to create a domain tree.   To create a new domain tree, you need to promote a Windows Server 2016 computer to a domain controller, select the option that makes this domain controller the first machine in a new domain, and make that domain the first domain of a new tree. The result is a new domain tree.

Know how to join a domain tree to a forest.   Creating a new tree to form or add to a forest is as simple as promoting a server to a domain controller for a new domain that does *not* share a namespace with an existing Active Directory domain. To add a domain to an existing forest, you must already have at least one other domain. This domain serves as the root domain for the entire forest.

Understand how to manage single-master operations.   Single-master operations must be performed on specially designated machines within the Active Directory forest. There are five main single-master functions: two that apply to an entire Active Directory forest

(Schema Master and Domain Naming Master) and three that apply to each domain (RID Master, PDC Emulator Master, and Infrastructure Master).

Understand how to manage trusts.   When configuring trusts, you'll need to consider two main characteristics: transitivity and direction. The simplest way to understand transitive relationships is through this example: If Domain A trusts Domain B and Domain B trusts Domain C, then Domain A implicitly trusts Domain C. Trusts can be configured as nontransitive so that this type of behavior does not occur. In one-way relationships, the trusting domain allows resources to be shared with the trusted domain. In two-way relationships, both domains trust each other equally. Special trusts include external trusts, realm trusts, cross-forest trusts, and shortcut trusts.

Understand how to manage UPN suffixes.   By default, the name of the domain in which the user is created determines the UPN suffix. By adding additional UPN suffixes to the forest, you can easily choose more manageable suffixes when it comes time to create new users.

Understand how to manage global catalog servers.   You can configure any number of domain controllers to host a copy of the global catalog (GC). The GC contains all of the schema information and a subset of the attributes for all domains within the Active Directory environment. Servers that contain a copy of the GC are known as GC servers. Whenever a user executes a query that requires information from multiple domains, they need only contact the nearest GC server for this information. Similarly, when users must authenticate across domains, they will not have to wait for a response from a domain controller that may be located across the world. The result is increased overall performance of Active Directory queries.

Understand universal group membership caching.   You can enable a domain controller as a Universal Group Membership Caching server. The Universal Group Membership Caching machine will then send a request for the logon authentication of a user to the GC server. The GC will then send the information back to the Universal Group Membership Caching server to be cached locally for eight hours (by default). The user can then authenticate without the need to contact the GC again.

Understand the purpose of Active Directory replication.   Replication is used to keep domain controllers synchronized, and it is important in Active Directory environments of all sizes. Replication is the process by which changes to the Active Directory database are transferred between domain controllers.

Understand the concept of sites, site boundaries, and subnets.   Subnets define physical portions of your network environment. Sites are defined as collections of well-connected IP subnets. Site boundaries are defined by the subnet or subnets that you include in your site configuration.

Understand the differences between intrasite and intersite replication.   Intrasite replication is designed to synchronize Active Directory information to machines that are located in the same site. Intersite replication is used to synchronize information for domain controllers that are located in different sites.

Understand the purpose of bridgehead servers.   Bridgehead servers are designed to accept traffic between two remote sites and then to forward this information to the appropriate servers. One way to efficiently synchronize data between sites that are connected with slow connections is to use a bridgehead server.

Implement site links, site link bridges, and connection objects.   You can use all three of these object types to finely control the behavior of Active Directory replication and to manage replication traffic. Site links are created to define the types of connections that are available between the components of a site. Site links can reflect a relative cost for a network connection and can reflect the bandwidth that is available for communications. You can use site link bridges to connect site links so that the relationship can be transitive. Connection objects provide you with a way to set up special types of replication schedules such as immediate replication on demand or specifying a custom schedule for certain servers.

Configure replication schedules and site link costs.   You can create multiple site links between sites, and you can assign site links a cost value based on the type of connection. The system administrator determines the cost value, and the relative costs of site links are then used to determine the optimal path for replication. The lower the cost, the more likely the link is to be used for replication. Once you've determined how and through which connections replication will take place, it's time to determine *when* information should be replicated. Replication requires network resources and occupies bandwidth. Therefore, you need to balance the need for consistent directory information with the need to conserve bandwidth.

Determine where to place domain controllers and global catalog servers based on a set of requirements.   Where you place domain controllers and global catalog servers can positively affect the performance of Active Directory operations. However, to optimize performance, you need to know the best places to put these servers in a network environment that consists of multiple sites.

Monitor and troubleshoot replication.   The Windows Server 2016 System Monitor administrative tool is designed so that you can monitor many performance statistics associated with using Active Directory. In addition to this monitoring, you should always verify basic network connectivity and router and firewall connections and also examine the event logs.

Understand the various backup types available with the Windows Server 2016 Backup utility.   The Windows Server 2016 Backup utility can perform full and incremental backup operations. Some third-party backup utilities also support differential and daily backups. You can use each of these operations as part of an efficient backup strategy.

Know how to restore Active Directory.   Restoring the Active Directory database is considerably different from other restore operations. To restore some of or the entire Active Directory database, you must first boot the machine into Directory Services Restore mode.

Understand the importance of an authoritative restore process.   You use an authoritative restore when you want to restore earlier information from an Active Directory backup and you want the older information to be propagated to other domain controllers in the environment.

Understand offline maintenance using `ntdsutil`.   The ntdsutil command-line tool is a primary method by which system administrators perform offline maintenance. Understand how to launch this tool by entering **ntdsutil** at a command prompt.

Review Questions

You can find the answers in the Appendix.

1. You need to deactivate the UGMC option on some of your domain controllers. At which level in Active Directory would you deactivate UGMC?

   A. Server

   B. Site

   C. Domain

   D. Forest

2. You work for an organization with a single domain forest. Your company has one main location and two branch locations. All locations are configured as Active Directory sites, and all sites are connected with the DEFAULTIPSITELINK object. Your connections are running slower than company policy allows. You want to decrease the replication latency between all domain controllers in the various sites. What should you do?

   A. Decrease the replication interval for the DEFAULTIPSITELINK object.

   B. Decrease the replication interval for the site.

   C. Decrease the replication schedule for the site.

   D. Decrease the replication schedule for all domain controllers.

3. You need to enable three of your domain controllers as global catalog servers. Where would you configure the domain controllers as global catalogs?

   A. Forest, NTDS settings

   B. Domain, NTDS settings

   C. Site, NTDS settings

   D. Server, NTDS settings

4. Daniel is responsible for managing Active Directory replication traffic for a medium-sized organization that has deployed a single Active Directory domain. Currently, the environment is configured with two sites and the default settings for replication. Each site consists of 15 domain controllers. Recently, network administrators have complained that Active Directory traffic is using a large amount of available network bandwidth between the two sites. Daniel has been asked to meet the following requirements:

   - Reduce the amount of network traffic between domain controllers in the two sites.

   - Minimize the amount of change to the current site topology.

   - Require no changes to the existing physical network infrastructure.

Daniel decides that it would be most efficient to configure specific domain controllers in each site that will receive the majority of replication traffic from the other site. Which of the following solutions meets the requirements?

A. Create additional sites that are designed only for replication traffic and move the existing domain controllers to these sites.

B. Create multiple site links between the two sites.

C. Create a site link bridge between the two sites.

D. Configure one server at each site to act as a preferred bridgehead server.

5. Which of the following does not need to be created manually when you are setting up a replication scenario involving three domains and three sites?

A. Sites

B. Site links

C. Connection objects

D. Subnets

6. Which of the following services of Active Directory is responsible for maintaining the replication topology?

A. File Replication Service

B. Knowledge Consistency Checker

C. Windows Internet Name Service

D. Domain Name System

7. A system administrator for an Active Directory environment that consists of three sites wants to configure site links to be transitive. Which of the following Active Directory objects are responsible for representing a transitive relationship between sites?

A. Additional sites

B. Additional site links

C. Bridgehead servers

D. Site link bridges

8. You have configured your Active Directory environment with multiple sites and have placed the appropriate resources in each of the sites. You are now trying to choose a protocol for the transfer of replication information between two sites. The connection between the two sites has the following characteristics:

- The link is generally unavailable during certain parts of the day because of an unreliable network provider.

- The replication transmission must be attempted whether the link is available or not. If the link was unavailable during a scheduled replication, the information should automatically be received after the link becomes available again.

- Replication traffic must be able to travel over a standard Internet connection.

Which of the following protocols meets these requirements?

A. IP

B. SMTP

C. RPC

D. DHCP

9. A system administrator suspects that there is an error in the replication configuration. How can the system administrator look for specific error messages related to replication?

A. By using the Active Directory Sites and Services administrative tool

B. By using the Computer Management tool

C. By going to Event Viewer ➤ System Log

D. By going to Event Viewer ➤ Directory Service Log

10. Christina is responsible for managing Active Directory replication traffic for a medium-sized organization. Currently, the environment is configured with a single site and the default settings for replication. The site contains more than 50 domain controllers, and the system administrators are often making changes to the Active Directory database. Recently, network administrators have complained that Active Directory traffic is consuming a large amount of network bandwidth between portions of the network that are connected by slow links. Ordinarily, the amount of replication traffic is reasonable, but recently users have complained about slow network performance during certain hours of the day.

Christina has been asked to alleviate the problem while meeting the following requirements:

- Be able to control exactly when replication occurs.

- Be able to base Active Directory replication on the physical network infrastructure.

- Perform the changes without creating or removing any domain controllers.

Which two of the following steps can Christina take to meet these requirements? (Choose two.)

A. Create and define connection objects that specify the hours during which replication will occur.

B. Create multiple site links.

C. Create a site link bridge.

D. Create new Active Directory sites that reflect the physical network topology.

E. Configure one server at each of the new sites to act as a bridgehead server.

Chapter

4

Implementing GPOs

THE FOLLOWING 70-742 EXAM OBJECTIVES ARE COVERED IN THIS CHAPTER:

✓ **Create and manage Group Policy Objects (GPOs)**

- This objective may include but is not limited to: Configure a central store; manage starter GPOs; configure GPO links; configure multiple local Group Policies; back up, import, copy, and restore GPOs; create and configure a migration table; reset default GPOs; delegate Group Policy management; detect health issues using the Group Policy Infrastructure Status dashboard

✓ **Configure Group Policy processing**

- This objective may include but is not limited to: Configure processing order and precedence; configure blocking of inheritance; configure enforced policies; configure security filtering and Windows Management Instrumentation (WMI) filtering; configure loopback processing; configure and manage slow-link processing and Group Policy caching; configure client-side extension (CSE) behavior; force a Group Policy update

✓ **Configure Group Policy settings**

- This objective may include but is not limited to: Configure software installation; configure folder redirection; configure scripts; configure administrative templates; import security templates; import a custom administrative template file; configure property filters for administrative templates

✓ **Configure Group Policy preferences**

- This objective may include but is not limited to: Configure printer preferences; define network drive mappings; configure power options; configure custom registry settings; configure Control Panel settings; configure Internet Explorer settings; configure file and folder deployment; configure shortcut deployment; configure item-level targeting

For many years, making changes to computer or user environments was a time-consuming process. If you wanted to install a service pack or a piece of software, unless you had a third-party utility, you had to use the *sneakernet* (that is, you had to walk from one computer to another with a disk containing the software).

Installing any type of software or company-wide security change was one of the biggest challenges faced by system administrators. It was difficult enough just to deploy and manage workstations throughout the environment. Combine this with the fact that users were generally able to make system configuration changes to their own machines; it quickly became a management nightmare!

For example, imagine that a user noticed that they did not have enough disk space to copy a large file. Instead of seeking assistance from the IT help desk, they may have decided to do a little cleanup on their own. Unfortunately, this cleanup operation may have resulted in deleting critical system files! Or, consider the case of users who changed system settings "just to see what they did." Relatively minor changes, such as modifying TCP/IP bindings or Desktop settings, could cause hours of support headaches. Now multiply these (or other common) problems by hundreds (or even thousands) of end users. Clearly, system administrators needed to have a secure way to limit the options available to users of client operating systems.

How do you prevent problems such as these from occurring in a Windows Server 2016 environment? Fortunately, there's a readily available solution delivered with the base operating system that's easy to implement. Two of the most important system administration features in Windows Server 2016 and Active Directory are *Group Policy* and *Security Policy*. By using *Group Policy Objects (GPOs)*, administrators can quickly and easily define restrictions on common actions and then apply them at the site, domain, or organizational unit (OU) level. In this chapter, you will see how group and security policies work, and then you will look at how to implement them within an Active Directory environment.

Introducing Group Policy

One of the strengths of Windows-based operating systems is their flexibility. End users and system administrators can configure many different options to suit the network environment and their personal tastes. However, this flexibility comes at a price—generally, end users on a network should not change many of these options. For example, TCP/IP configuration and security policies should remain consistent for all client computers. In fact, end users really don't need to be able to change these types of settings in the first place because many of them do not understand the purpose of these settings.

Windows Server 2016 *group policies* are designed to provide system administrators with the ability to customize end-user settings and to place restrictions on the types of actions that users can perform. Group policies can be easily created by system administrators and then later applied to one or more users or computers within the environment. Although they ultimately do affect Registry settings, it is much easier to configure and apply settings through the use of Group Policy than it is to make changes to the Registry manually. To make management easy, Microsoft has set up Windows Server 2008, Windows Server 2008 R2, Windows Server 2012, Windows Server 2012 R2, and Windows Server 2016 so that Group Policy settings are all managed from within the Microsoft Management Console (MMC) in the Group Policy Management Console (GPMC).

Group policies have several potential uses. I'll cover the use of group policies for software deployment, and I'll also focus on the technical background of group policies and how they apply to general configuration management.

Let's begin by looking at how group policies function.

Understanding Group Policy Settings

Group Policy settings are based on *Group Policy administrative templates*. These templates provide a list of user-friendly configuration options and specify the system settings to which they apply. For example, an option for a user or computer that reads Require A Specific Desktop Wallpaper Setting would map to a key in the Registry that maintains this value. When the option is set, the appropriate change is made in the Registry of the affected users and computers.

By default, Windows Server 2016 comes with several administrative template files that you can use to manage common settings. Additionally, system administrators and application developers can create their own administrative template files to set options for specific functionality.

Most Group Policy items have three different settings options (see Figure 4.1):

Enabled   Specifies that a setting for this GPO has been configured. Some settings require values or options to be set.

Disabled   Specifies that this option is disabled for client computers. Note that disabling an option *is* a setting. That is, it specifies that the system administrator wants to disallow certain functionality.

Not Configured   Specifies that these settings have been neither enabled nor disabled. Not Configured is the default option for most settings. It simply states that this group policy will not specify an option and that other policy settings may take precedence.

FIGURE 4.1   Group Policy configuration settings

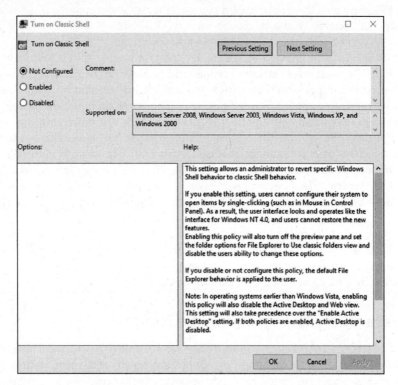

The specific options available (and their effects) will depend on the setting. Often, you will need additional information. For example, when setting the Account Lockout policy, you must specify how many bad login attempts may be made before the account is locked out. With this in mind, let's look at the types of user and computer settings that can be managed.

Group Policy settings can apply to two types of Active Directory objects: User objects and Computer objects. Because both users and computers can be placed into groups and organized within OUs, this type of configuration simplifies the management of hundreds, or even thousands, of computers.

The main options you can configure within user and computer group policies are as follows:

Software Settings   The *Software Settings* options apply to specific applications and software that might be installed on the computer. System administrators can use these settings to make new applications available to end users and to control the default configuration for these applications.

Windows Settings   The *Windows Settings* options allow system administrators to customize the behavior of the Windows operating system. The specific options that are available here are divided into two types: user and computer. User-specific settings let you configure Internet Explorer (including the default home page and other settings). Computer settings include security options, such as Account Policy and Event Log options.

Administrative Templates   *Administrative templates* are used to configure user and computer settings further. In addition to the default options available, system administrators can create their own administrative templates with custom options.

Group Policy Preferences   The Windows Server 2016 operating system includes *Group Policy preferences (GPPs)*, which give you more than 20 Group Policy extensions. These extensions, in turn, give you a vast range of configurable settings within a Group Policy Object. Included in the new Group Policy preference extensions are settings for folder options, mapped drives, printers, the Registry, local users and groups, scheduled tasks, services, and the Start menu.

Besides providing easier management, Group Policy preferences give an administrator the ability to deploy settings for client computers without restricting the users from changing the settings. This gives an administrator the flexibility needed to decide which settings to enforce and which not to enforce.

Figure 4.2 shows some of the options you can configure with Group Policy.

FIGURE 4.2   Group Policy options

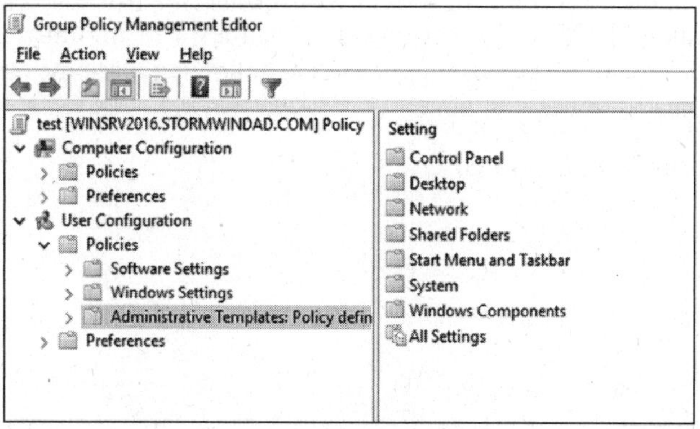

ADMX Central Store   Another consideration in GPO settings is whether to set up an *ADMX Central Store*. GPO administrative template files are saved as ADMX (.admx) files and AMXL (.amxl) for the supported languages. To get the most benefit out of using administrative templates, you should create an ADMX Central Store.

You create the Central Store in the SYSVOL folder on a domain controller. The Central Store is a repository for all of your administrative templates, and the Group Policy tools check it. The Group Policy tools then use any ADMX files that they find in the Central Store. These files then replicate to all domain controllers in the domain.

If you want your clients to be able to edit domain-based GPOs by using the ADMX files that are stored in the ADMX Central Store, you must be using Windows Vista, Windows 7,

Windows 8, Windows 10, Server 2008, Server 2008 R2, Server 2012, Windows Server 2012 R2, or Server 2016.

Security Template   *Security templates* are used to configure security settings through a GPO. Some of the security settings that can be configured are settings for account policies, local policies, event logs, restricted groups, system services, and the Registry.

Starter GPOs   *Starter Group Policy Objects* give administrators the ability to store a collection of administrative template policy settings in a single object. Administrators then have the ability to import and export starter GPOs to distribute the GPOs easily to other environments. When a GPO is created from a starter GPO, as with any template, the new GPO receives the settings and values that were defined from the administrative template policy in the starter GPO.

Group Policy settings do not take effect immediately. You must run the gpupdate command at the command prompt or wait for the regular update cycle in order for the policy changes to take effect.

The Security Settings Section of the GPO

One of the most important sections of a GPO is the Security Settings section. The Security Settings section, under the Windows Settings section, allows an administrator to secure many aspects of the computer and user policies. The following are some of the configurable options for the Security Settings section:

Computer Section Only of the GPO

- Account Policies
- Local Policies
- Event Policies
- Restricted Groups
- System Services
- Registry
- File System
- Wired Network
- Windows Firewall with Advanced Security
- Network List Manager Policies
- Wireless Networks
- Network Access Protection
- Application Control Policies

- IP Security Policies
- Advanced Audit Policy Configuration

Computer and User Sections of the GPO

- Public Key Policies
- Software Restriction Policy

Restricted Groups

The *Restricted Groups* settings allow you to control group membership by using a GPO. The group membership I am referring to is the normal Active Directory groups (domain local, global, and universal). The settings offer two configurable properties: Members and Members Of.

 The users on the Members list do not belong to the restricted group. The users on the Members Of list do belong to the restricted group. When you configure a Restricted Group policy, members of the restricted group that are not on the Members list are removed. Users who are on the Members list who are not currently a member of the restricted group are added.

Software Restriction Policy

Software restriction policies allow administrators to identify software and to control its ability to run on the user's local computer, organizational unit, domain, or site. This prevents users from installing unauthorized software. Software Restriction Policy is discussed in greater detail later in this chapter in the section "Implementing Software Deployment."

Client-Side Extensions

In Windows Server, group policies are designed using both server-side and client-side extensions (CSEs). The server-side elements include a user interface for creating each Group Policy Object (GPO). When a Windows client system logs into the Active Directory network, the client-side extensions (normally a series of DLL files) receive their GPOs and the GPOs make changes to the Windows client systems.

 Within GPOs, there are computer policies that exist for each CSE. The policies normally include a maximum of three options: Allow Processing Across A Slow Network Connection, Do Not Apply During Periodic Background Processing, and Process Even If The Group Policy Objects Have Not Changed.

Group Policy Objects

So far, I have discussed what group policies are designed to do. Now it's time to drill down to determine exactly how you can set up and configure them.

 To make them easier to manage, group policies may be placed in items called *Group Policy Objects (GPOs)*. GPOs act as containers for the settings made within Group Policy files, which simplifies the management of settings. For example, as a system administrator, you might have different policies for users and computers in different departments. Based on these requirements, you could create a GPO for members of the Sales department and another for members of the Engineering department. Then you could apply the GPOs to the OU for each department. Another important concept you need to understand is that Group Policy settings are hierarchical; that is, system administrators can apply Group Policy settings at four different levels. These levels determine the GPO processing priority.

Local   Every Windows operating system computer has one Group Policy Object that is stored locally. This GPO functions for both the computer and user Group Policy processing.

Sites   At the highest level, system administrators can configure GPOs to apply to entire sites within an Active Directory environment. These settings apply to all of the domains and servers that are part of a site. Group Policy settings managed at the site level may apply to more than one domain within the same forest. Therefore, they are useful when you want to make settings that apply to all of the domains within an Active Directory tree or forest.

Domains   Domains are the third level to which system administrators can assign GPOs. GPO settings placed at the domain level will apply to all of the User and Computer objects within the domain. Usually, system administrators make master settings at the domain level.

Organizational Units (OUs)   The most granular level of settings for GPOs is the OU level. By configuring Group Policy options for OUs, system administrators can take advantage of the hierarchical structure of Active Directory. If the OU structure is planned well, you will find it easy to make logical GPO assignments for various business units at the OU level.

Based on the business need and the organization of the Active Directory environment, system administrators might decide to set up Group Policy settings at any of these four levels. Because the settings are cumulative by default, a User object might receive policy settings from the site level, from the domain level, and from the OUs in which it is contained.

You can also apply Group Policy settings to the local computer (in which case Active Directory is not used at all), but this limits the manageability of the Group Policy settings.

Group Policy Inheritance

In most cases, Group Policy settings are cumulative. For example, a GPO at the domain level might specify that all users within the domain must change their password every 60 days, and a GPO at the OU level might specify the default desktop background for all users and computers within that OU. In this case, both settings apply, so users within the OU are forced to change their password every 60 days and have the default Desktop setting.

What happens if there's a conflict in the settings? For example, suppose you create a scenario where a GPO at the site level specifies that users are to use red wallpaper and another GPO at the OU level specifies that they must use green wallpaper. The users at the OU layer would have green wallpaper by default. Although hypothetical, this raises an important point about *inheritance*. By default, the settings at the most specific level (in this case, the OU that contains the User object) override those at more general levels. As a friend of mine from Microsoft always says, "Last one to apply wins."

Although the default behavior is for settings to be cumulative and inherited, system administrators can modify this behavior. They can set two main options at the various levels to which GPOs might apply.

Block Policy Inheritance   The *Block Policy Inheritance* option specifies that Group Policy settings for an object are not inherited from its parents. You might use this, for example, when a child OU requires completely different settings from a parent OU. Note, however, that you should manage blocking policy inheritance carefully because this option allows other system administrators to override the settings made at higher levels.

Force Policy Inheritance   The *Enforced option* (sometimes referred as *No Override*) can be placed on a parent object, and it ensures that all lower-level objects inherit these settings. In some cases, system administrators want to ensure that Group Policy inheritance is not blocked at other levels. For example, suppose it is corporate policy that all network accounts are locked out after five incorrect password attempts. In this case, you would not want lower-level system administrators to override the option with other settings.

System administrators generally use this option when they want to enforce a specific setting globally. For example, if a password expiration policy should apply to all users and computers within a domain, a GPO with the *Force Policy Inheritance* option enabled could be created at the domain level.

You must consider one final case: If a conflict exists between the computer and user settings, the user settings take effect. If, for instance, a system administrator applies a default desktop setting for the Computer policy and a different default desktop setting for the User policy, the one they specify in the User policy takes effect. This is because the user settings are more specific, and they allow system administrators to make changes for individual users regardless of the computer they're using.

Planning a Group Policy Strategy

Through the use of Group Policy settings, system administrators can control many different aspects of their network environment. As you'll see throughout this chapter, system administrators can use GPOs to configure user settings and computer configurations. Windows Server 2016 includes many different administrative tools for performing these tasks. However, it's important to keep in mind that, as with many aspects of using Active Directory, a successful Group Policy strategy involves planning.

Because there are thousands of possible Group Policy settings and many different ways to implement them, you should start by determining the business and technical needs of your organization. For example, you should first group your users based on their work functions. You might find, for example, that users in remote branch offices require particular network configuration options. In that case, you might implement Group Policy settings best at the site level. In another instance, you might find that certain departments have varying requirements for disk quota settings. In this case, it would probably make the most sense to apply GPOs to the appropriate department OUs within the domain.

The overall goal should be to reduce complexity (for example, by reducing the overall number of GPOs and GPO links) while still meeting the needs of your users. By taking into account the various needs of your users and the parts of your organization, you can often determine a logical and efficient method of creating and applying GPOs. Although it's rare that you'll come across a right or wrong method of implementing Group Policy settings, you will usually encounter some that are either better or worse than others.

By implementing a logical and consistent set of policies, you'll also be well prepared to troubleshoot any problems that might come up or to adapt to your organization's changing requirements. Later in this chapter, you'll learn about some specific methods for determining effective Group Policy settings before you apply them.

Implementing Group Policy

Now that I've covered the basic layout and structure of group policies and how they work, let's look at how you can implement them in an Active Directory environment. In the following sections, you'll start by creating GPOs. Then you'll apply these GPOs to specific Active Directory objects, and you'll take a look at how to use administrative templates.

Creating GPOs

In Windows Server 2000 and Windows Server 2003, you could create GPOs from many different locations. For example, you could use Active Directory Users and Computers to create GPOs on your OUs along with other GPO tools. In Windows Server 2016, things are simpler. You can create GPOs for OUs in only one location: the Group Policy Management Console (GPMC). You have your choice of three applications for setting up policies on your Windows Server 2016 computers.

Local Computer Policy Tool   This administrative tool allows you to quickly access the Group Policy settings that are available for the local computer. These options apply to the local machine and to users who access it. You must be a member of the local Administrators group to access and make changes to these settings.

Administrators may need the ability to work on Multiple Local Group Policy Objects (MLGPOs) at the same time. To do this, you would complete the following steps. (You can't configure MLGPOs on domain controllers.)

1. Open the MMC by typing **MMC** in the Run command box.

2. Click File and then click Add/Remove Snap-in.

3. From the available snap-ins list, choose Group Policy Object Editor and click Add.

4. In the Select Group Policy Object dialog box, click the Browse button.

5. Click the Users tab in the Browse For The Group Policy Object dialog box.

6. Click the user or group for which you want to create or edit a local Group Policy and click OK.

7. Click Finish and then click OK.

8. Configure the multiple policy settings.

Group Policy Management Console   You must use the GPMC to manage Group Policy deployment. The GPMC provides a single solution for managing all Group Policy–related tasks, and it is also best suited to handle enterprise-level tasks, such as forest-related work.

The GPMC allows administrators to manage Group Policy and GPOs all from one easy-to-use console whether their enterprise solution spans multiple domains and sites within one or more forests or is local to one site. The GPMC adds flexibility, manageability, and functionality. Using this console, you can also perform other functions, such as backup and restore, importing, and copying.

Auditpol.exe   Auditpol.exe is a command-line utility that works with Windows Vista, Windows 7, Windows 8, Windows 10, Windows Server 2008, Windows Server 2008 R2, Windows Server 2012, Windows Server 2012 R2, and Windows Server 2016. An administrator has the ability to display information about policies and also to perform some functions to manipulate audit policies. Table 4.1 shows some of the switches available for auditpol.exe.

TABLE 4.1   Auditpol.exe switches

Switch	Description
/?	This is the Auditpol.exe help command.
/get	This allows you to display the current audit policy.
/set	This allows you to set a policy.
/list	This displays selectable policy elements.
/backup	This allows you to save the audit policy to a file.
/restore	This restores a policy from a previous backup.
/clear	This clears the audit policy.
/remove	This removes all per-user audit policy settings and disables all system audit policy settings.
/ResourceSACL	This configures the Global Resource SACL.

You should be careful when making Group Policy settings because certain options might prevent the proper use of systems on your network. Always test Group Policy settings on a small group of users before you deploy them throughout your organization. You'll probably find that some settings need to be changed to be effective.

Exercise 4.1 walks you through the process of installing the Group Policy Management MMC snap-in for editing Group Policy settings and creating a GPO.

EXERCISE 4.1

Creating a Group Policy Object Using the GPMC

1. Click the Windows button and choose Administrative Tools ➢ Group Policy Management. The Group Policy Management tool opens.

2. Expand the Forest, Domains, *your domain name,* and North America containers. Right-click the Corporate OU and then choose Create A GPO In This Domain, And Link It Here.

3. When the New GPO dialog box appears, type **Warning Box** in the Name field. Click OK.

4. The New GPO will be listed on the right side of the Group Policy Management window. Right-click the GPO and choose Edit.

5. In the Group Policy Management Editor, expand the following: Computer Configuration ➢ Policies ➢ Windows Settings ➢ Security Settings ➢ Local Policies ➢ Security Options. On the right side, scroll down and double-click Interactive Logon: Message Text For Users Attempting To Log On.

6. Click the box Define This Policy Setting In The Template. In the text box, type **Unauthorized use of this machine is prohibited** and then click OK. Close the GPO and return to the GPMC main screen.

7. Under the domain name (in the GPMC), right-click Group Policy Objects and choose New.

8. When the New GPO dialog box appears, type **Unlinked Test GPO** in the Name field. Click OK.

9. On the right side, the new GPO will appear. Right-click Unlinked Test GPO and choose Edit.

10. Under the User Configuration section, click Policies ➢ Administrative Templates ➢ Desktop. On the right side, double-click Hide And Disable All Items On The Desktop and then click Enabled. Click OK and then close the GPMC.

Note that Group Policy changes may not take effect until the next user logs in (some settings may even require that the machine be rebooted). That is, users who are currently working on the system will not see the effects of the changes until they log off and log in again. GPOs are reapplied every 90 minutes with a 30-minute offset. In other words, users who are logged in will have their policies reapplied every 60 to 120 minutes. Not all settings are reapplied (for example, software settings and password policies).

Linking Existing GPOs to Active Directory

Creating a GPO is the first step in assigning group policies. The second step is to link the GPO to a specific Active Directory object. As mentioned earlier in this chapter, GPOs can be linked to sites, domains, and OUs.

Exercise 4.2 walks you through the steps that you must take to assign an existing GPO to an OU within the local domain. In this exercise, you will link the Test Domain Policy GPO to an OU. To complete the steps in this exercise, you must have completed Exercise 4.1.

EXERCISE 4.2

Linking Existing GPOs to Active Directory

1. Open the Group Policy Management Console.

2. Expand the Forest and Domain containers and right-click the Africa OU.

3. Choose Link An Existing GPO.

4. The Select GPO dialog box appears. Click Unlinked Test GPO and click OK.

5. Close the Group Policy Management Console.

Note that the GPMC tool offers a lot of flexibility in assigning GPOs. You can create new GPOs, add multiple GPOs, edit them directly, change priority settings, remove links, and delete GPOs all from within this interface. In general, creating new GPOs using the GPMC tool is the quickest and easiest way to create the settings you need.

To test the Group Policy settings, you can simply create a user account within the Africa OU that you used in Exercise 4.2. Then, using another computer that is a member of the same domain, you can log on as the newly created user.

Forcing a GPO to Update

There will be times when you need a GPO to get processed immediately. If you are testing a GPO, you will not want to wait for the GPO to process in its own time or you may not want to have to log off the domain and log back onto the domain just to get the GPO processed.

Windows Server 2016 has changed how GPOs get processed. In a Windows Server 2016 domain, when a user logs onto the domain, the latest version of the Group Policy gets downloaded from the domain controller, and it writes that policy to the local store.

If you have your GPOs set up and running in synchronous mode, then the next time the computer restarts, it will use the most recently downloaded GPO from the local store and not download the GPO from the domain. This is a new feature in Windows Server 2016, and it helps to reduce the time it takes to log onto the domain because the GPO policy doesn't need to be downloaded each time.

So, now that you understand how GPOs get processed in Windows Server 2016, let's look at a few different ways that you can force a GPO to get processed immediately.

Forcing the GPO from the Server

Windows Server 2016 has an MMC called Group Policy Management Console (GPMC), and by using this MMC, you can remotely refresh an organizational unit (OU) and force the GPO on all users and computers within that OU. The GPMC remote refresh automatically updates all settings, including security settings, which are configured in the GPO that is linked to the OU. In the OU's context menu, you can choose to refresh remotely the OU and the GPOs associated with that OU. When you remotely refresh an OU, the following steps occur:

1. Windows Server 2016 does an Active Directory query, and that query returns a list of all users and computers that belong to the OU.

2. Windows Management Instrumentation (WMI) queries all users and computers that are currently logged into the domain and creates a list that will be used.

3. Using the list that was created in step 2, a remote scheduled task is created, and a GPUpdate.exe /force is executed on all of the users and computers that are logged into the domain. The remote scheduled task is then scheduled to execute with a 10-minute random delay to help decrease the load on network traffic.

 When you are using the GPMC to force a GPO update, you do not have the ability to change the 10-minute random delay, but if you force the GPO through the use of PowerShell, you have the ability to set the delay.

Another way that you can force a GPO to update immediately is to use Windows PowerShell. By using the PowerShell command Invoke-GPUpdate cmdlet, you cannot only force the GPO but also set the parameters to be more granular.

Forcing the GPO from the Client

As an administrator, you have the ability also to force a GPO onto a client machine on which you may be working. The GPUpdate.exe command allows you to run a GPO on a client machine. The GPUpdate command will run on all Windows client machines from

Windows Vista to Windows Server 2016. Table 4.2 shows some of the GPUpdate switches you can use.

TABLE 4.2 GPUpdate.exe switches

Switch	Description
/target:{Computer | User}	Updates only the User or Computer policy settings for the computer or user specified.
/force	Forces the GPO to reapply all policy settings. By default, only policy settings that have changed are applied.
/wait: <VALUE>	Determines the number of seconds that the system will wait after a policy is processed before returning to the command prompt.
/logoff	The domain user account will automatically log off the computer after the Group Policy settings are updated.
/boot	The computer will automatically restart after the Group Policy settings are applied.
/sync	This switch forces the next available foreground policy application to be done synchronously. Foreground policies are applied when the computer boots up and the user logs in.
/?	Displays help at the command prompt.

Managing Group Policy

Now that you have implemented GPOs and applied them to sites, domains, and OUs within Active Directory, it's time to look at some ways to manage them. In the following sections, you'll look at how multiple GPOs can interact with one another and ways that you can provide security for GPO management. Using these features is an important part of working with Active Directory, and if you properly plan Group Policy, you can greatly reduce the time the help desk spends troubleshooting common problems.

Managing GPOs

One of the benefits of GPOs is that they're modular and can apply to many different objects and levels within Active Directory. This can also be one of the drawbacks of GPOs if they're not managed properly. A common administrative function related to using GPOs is finding all of the Active Directory links for each of these objects. You can do this when you are viewing the Linked Group Policy Objects tab of the site, domain, or OU in the GPMC (shown in Figure 4.3).

FIGURE 4.3   Viewing GPO links to an Active Directory OU

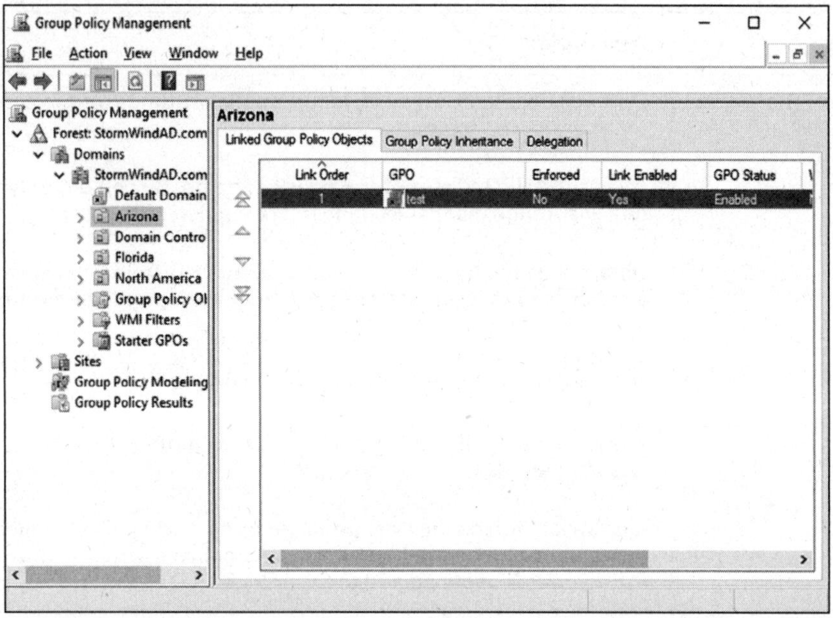

In addition to the common action of delegating permissions on OUs, you can set permissions regarding the modification of GPOs. The best way to accomplish this is to add users to the Group Policy Creator/Owners built-in security group. The members of this group are able to modify security policy.

Windows Management Instrumentation

Windows Management Instrumentation (WMI) scripts are used to gather information or to help GPOs deploy better. The best way to explain this is to give an example. Let's say you wanted to deploy Microsoft Office 2016 to everyone in the company. You would first set up a GPO to deploy the Office package (explained later in the section "Deploying Software Through a GPO").

You can then place a WMI script on the GPO stating that only computers with 10 GB of hard disk space actually deploy Office. Now if a computer has 10 GB of free space, the Office GPO would get installed. If the computer does not have the 10 GB of hard disk space, the GPO will not deploy. You can use WMI scripts to check for computer information such as MAC addresses. WMI is a powerful tool because if you know how to write scripts, the possibilities are endless. The following script is a sample of a WMI script that is checking for at least 10 GB of free space on the C: partition/volume:

```
Select * from Win32_LogicalDisk where FreeSpace > 10737418240 AND Caption = "C:"
```

Security Filtering of a Group Policy

Another method of securing access to GPOs is to set permissions on the GPOs themselves. You can do this by opening the GPMC, selecting the GPO, and clicking the Advanced button in the Delegation tab. The Unlinked Test GPO Security Settings dialog box appears (see Figure 4.4).

FIGURE 4.4   A GPO's Security Settings dialog box

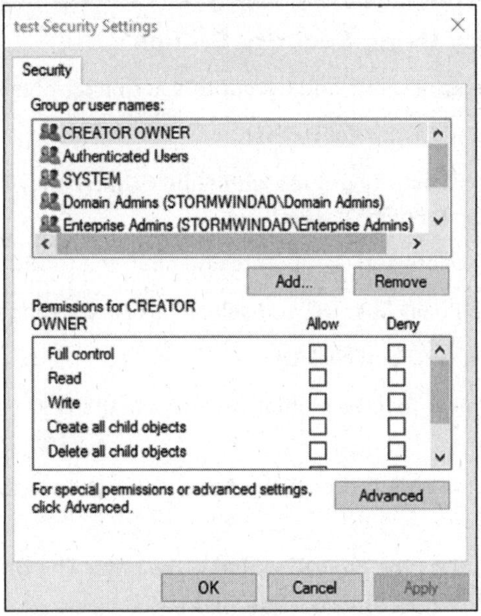

The following permissions options are available:

- Full Control
- Read
- Write
- Create All Child Objects
- Delete All Child Objects
- Apply Group Policy

You might have to scroll the Permissions window to see the Apply Group Policy item. Of these, the Apply Group Policy setting is particularly important because you use it to filter the scope of the GPO. *Filtering* is the process by which selected security groups are included or excluded from the effects of the GPOs. To specify that the settings should apply to a GPO, you should select the Allow check box for both the Apply Group Policy setting and the Read setting. These settings will be applied only if the security group is also contained within a site, domain, or OU to which the GPO is linked. To disable GPO access for a group, choose Deny for both of these settings. Finally, if you do not want to specify either Allow or Deny, leave both boxes blank. This is effectively the same as having no setting.

In Exercise 4.3, you will filter Group Policy using security groups. To complete the steps in this exercise, you must have completed Exercises 4.1 and 4.2.

EXERCISE 4.3

Filtering Group Policy Using Security Groups

1. Open the Active Directory Users and Computers administrative tool.

2. Create a new OU called **Group Policy Test**.

3. Create two new global security groups within the Group Policy Test OU and name them **PolicyEnabled** and **PolicyDisabled**.

4. Exit Active Directory Users and Computers and open the GPMC.

5. Right-click the Group Policy Test OU and select Link An Existing GPO.

6. Choose Unlinked Test GPO and click OK.

7. Expand the Group Policy Test OU so that you can see the GPO (Unlinked Test GPO) underneath the OU.

8. Click the Delegation tab and then click the Advanced button in the lower-right corner of the window.

9. Click the Add button and type **PolicyEnabled** in the Enter The Object Names To Select field. Click the Check Names button. Then click OK.

10. Add a group named **PolicyDisabled** in the same way.

11. Highlight the PolicyEnabled group and select Allow for the Read and Apply Group Policy permissions. This ensures that users in the PolicyEnabled group will be affected by this policy.

12. Highlight the PolicyDisabled group and select Deny for the Read and Apply Group Policy permissions. This ensures that users in the PolicyDisabled group will not be affected by this policy.

13. Click OK. You will see a message stating that you are choosing to use the Deny permission and that the Deny permission takes precedence over the Allow entries. Click the Yes button to continue.

14. When you have finished, close the GPMC tool.

Delegating Administrative Control of GPOs

So far, you have learned about how to use Group Policy to manage user and computer settings. What you haven't done yet is to determine who can modify GPOs. It's important to establish the appropriate security on GPOs themselves for two reasons:

- If the security settings aren't set properly, users and system administrators can easily override them. This defeats the purpose of having the GPOs in the first place.

- Having many different system administrators creating and modifying GPOs can become extremely difficult to manage. When problems arise, the hierarchical nature of GPO inheritance can make it difficult to pinpoint the problem.

Fortunately, through the use of delegation, determining security permissions for GPOs is a simple task. Exercise 4.4 walks you through the steps that you must take to grant the appropriate permissions to a user account. Specifically, the process involves delegating the ability to manage Group Policy links on an Active Directory object (such as an OU). To complete this exercise, you must have completed Exercises 4.1 and 4.2.

EXERCISE 4.4

Delegating Administrative Control of Group Policy

1. Open the Active Directory Users and Computers tool.

2. Expand the local domain and create a user named **Policy Admin** within the Group Policy Test OU.

3. Exit Active Directory Users and Computers and open the GPMC.

4. Click the Group Policy Test OU and select the Delegation tab.

5. Click the Add button. In the field Enter The Object Name To Select, type **Policy Admin** and click the Check Names button.

6. The Add Group Or User dialog box appears. In the Permissions drop-down list, make sure that the item labeled Edit Settings, Delete, Modify Security is chosen. Click OK.

7. At this point you should be looking at the Group Policy Test Delegation window. Click the Advanced button in the lower-right corner.

8. Highlight the Policy Admin account and check the Allow Full Control box. This user now has full control of these OUs and all child OUs and GPOs for these OUs. Click OK.

   If you just want to give this user individual rights, then, in the Properties window (step 8), click the Advanced button and then the Effective Permissions tab. This is where you can also choose a user and give them only the rights that you want them to have.

9. When you have finished, close the GPMC tool.

Understanding Delegation

Although I have talked about delegation throughout the book, it's important to discuss it again in the context of OUs, Group Policy, and Active Directory.

Once configured, Active Directory administrative delegation allows an administrator to delegate tasks (usually administration related) to specific user accounts or groups. What this means is that if you don't manage it all, the user accounts (or groups) you choose will be able to manage their portions of the tree.

It's important to be aware of the benefits of Active Directory Delegation (AD Delegation). *AD Delegation* will help you manage the assignment of administrative control over objects in Active Directory, such as users, groups, computers, printers, domains, and sites. AD Delegation is used to create more administrators, which essentially saves time.

For example, let's say you have a company whose IT department is small and situated in a central location. The central location connects three other smaller remote sites. These sites do not each warrant a full-time IT person, but the manager on staff (for example) at each remote site can become an administrator for their portion of the tree. If that manager administers the user accounts for the staff at the remote site, this reduces the burden on the system administrator of doing trivial administrative work, such as unlocking user accounts or changing passwords, and thus it reduces costs.

Controlling Inheritance and Filtering Group Policy

Controlling inheritance is an important function when you are managing GPOs. Earlier in this chapter, you learned that, by default, GPO settings flow from higher-level Active Directory objects to lower-level ones. For example, the effective set of Group Policy settings for a user might be based on GPOs assigned at the site level, at the domain level, and in the OU hierarchy. In general, this is probably the behavior you would want.

In some cases, however, you might want to block Group Policy inheritance. You can accomplish this easily by selecting the object to which a GPO has been linked. Right-click the object and choose Block Inheritance. By enabling this option, you are effectively specifying that this object starts with a clean slate; that is, no other Group Policy settings will apply to the contents of this Active Directory site, domain, or OU.

System administrators can also force inheritance. By setting the Enforced option, they can prevent other system administrators from making changes to default policies. You can set the Enforced option by right-clicking the GPO and choosing the Enforced item (see Figure 4.5).

FIGURE 4.5   Setting the Enforced GPO option

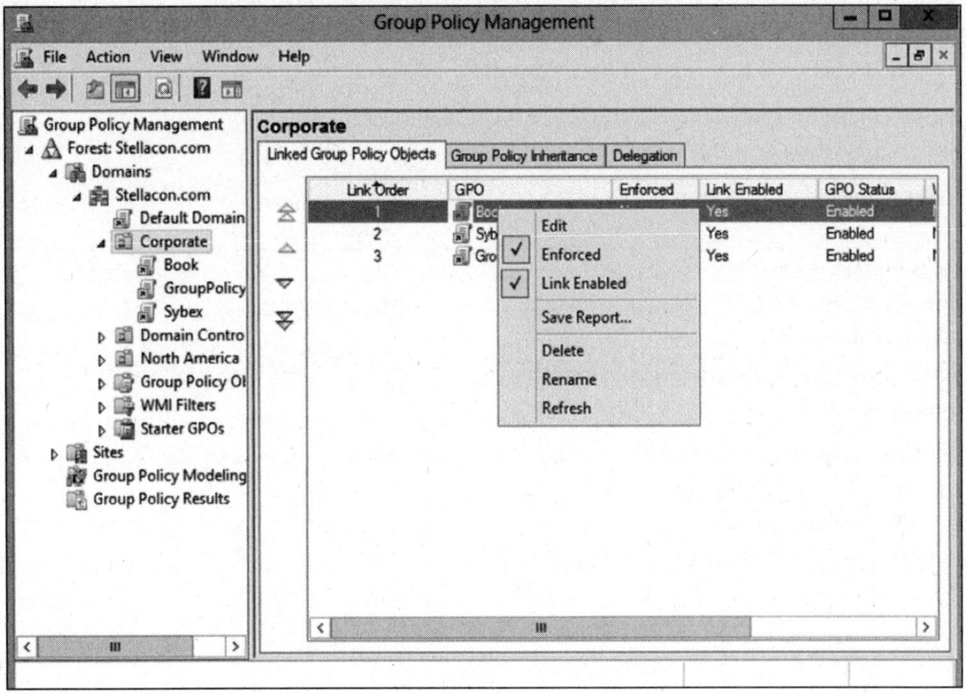

Assigning Script Policies

System administrators might want to make several changes and implement certain settings that would apply while the computer is starting up or the user is logging on. Perhaps the most common operation that logon scripts perform is mapping network drives. Although users can manually map network drives, providing this functionality within login scripts ensures that mappings stay consistent and that users only need to remember the drive letters for their resources.

Script policies are specific options that are part of Group Policy settings for users and computers. These settings direct the operating system to the specific files that should be processed during the startup/shutdown or logon/logoff processes. You can create the scripts by using the *Windows Script Host (WSH)* or with standard batch file commands. WSH allows developers and system administrators to create scripts quickly and easily using Visual Basic Scripting Edition (VBScript) or JScript (Microsoft's implementation of JavaScript). Additionally, WSH can be expanded to accommodate other common scripting languages.

To set script policy options, you simply edit the Group Policy settings. As shown in Figure 4.6, there are two main areas for setting script policy settings.

Startup/Shutdown Scripts   These settings are located within the Computer Configuration ➢ Windows Settings ➢ Scripts (Startup/Shutdown) object.

Logon/Logoff Scripts   These settings are located within the User Configuration ➢ Windows Settings ➢ Scripts (Logon/Logoff) object.

FIGURE 4.6   Viewing Startup/Shutdown script policy settings

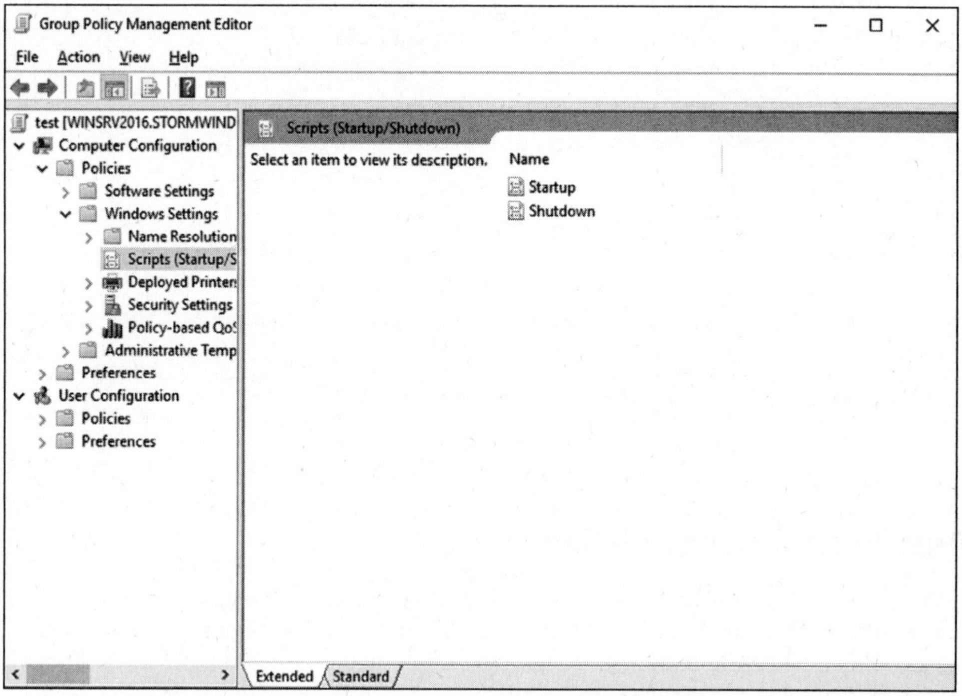

To assign scripts, simply double-click the setting and its Properties dialog box appears. For instance, if you double-click the Startup setting, the Startup Properties dialog box appears (see Figure 4.7). To add a script filename, click the Add button. When you do, you will be asked to provide the name of the script file (such as MapNetworkDrives.vbs or ResetEnvironment.bat).

Note that you can change the order in which the scripts are run by using the Up and Down buttons. The Show Files button opens the directory folder in which you should store the Logon script files. To ensure that the files are replicated to all domain controllers, you should be sure you place the files within the SYSVOL share.

FIGURE 4.7   Setting scripting options

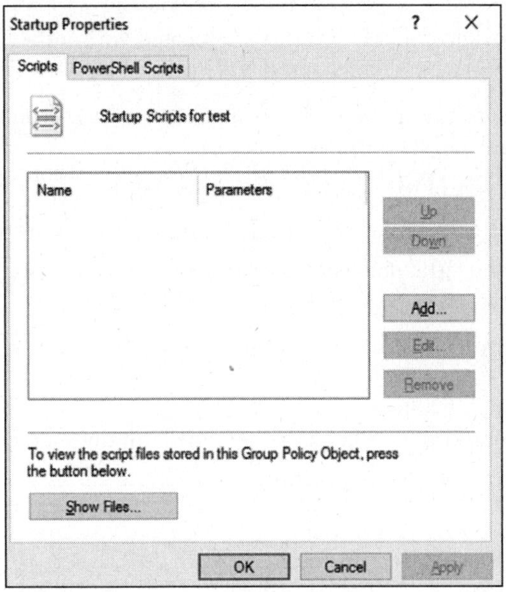

Understanding the Loopback Policy

There may be times when the user settings of a Group Policy Object should be applied to a computer based on its location instead of the User object. Usually, the user Group Policy processing dictates that the GPOs be applied in order during computer startup based on the computers located in their organizational unit. User GPOs, on the other hand, are applied in order during logon, regardless of the computer to which they log on.

In some situations, this processing order may not be appropriate. A good example is a kiosk machine. You would not want applications that have been assigned or published to a user to be installed when the user is logged on to the kiosk machine. *Loopback Policy* allows two ways to retrieve the list of GPOs for any user when they are using a specific computer in an OU.

Merge Mode   The GPOs for the computer are added to the end of the GPOs for the user. Because of this, the computer's GPOs have higher precedence than the user's GPOs.

Replace Mode   In Replace mode, the user's GPOs are not used. Only the GPOs of the Computer object are used.

Managing Network Configuration

Group policies are also useful in network configuration. Although administrators can handle network settings at the protocol level using many different methods, such as Dynamic Host Configuration Protocol (DHCP), Group Policy allows them to set which functions and operations are available to users and computers.

Figure 4.8 shows some of the features that are available for managing Group Policy settings. The paths to these settings are as follows:

Computer Network Options These settings are located within the Computer Configuration ➢ Administrative Templates ➢ Network ➢ Network Connections folder.

User Network Options These settings are located within User Configuration ➢ Administrative Templates ➢ Network.

Here are some examples of the types of settings available:

▪ The ability to allow or disallow the modification of network settings.

In many environments, the improper changing of network configurations and protocol settings is a common cause of help desk calls.

▪ The ability to allow or disallow the creation of Remote Access Service (RAS) connections.

FIGURE 4.8 Viewing Group Policy User network configuration options

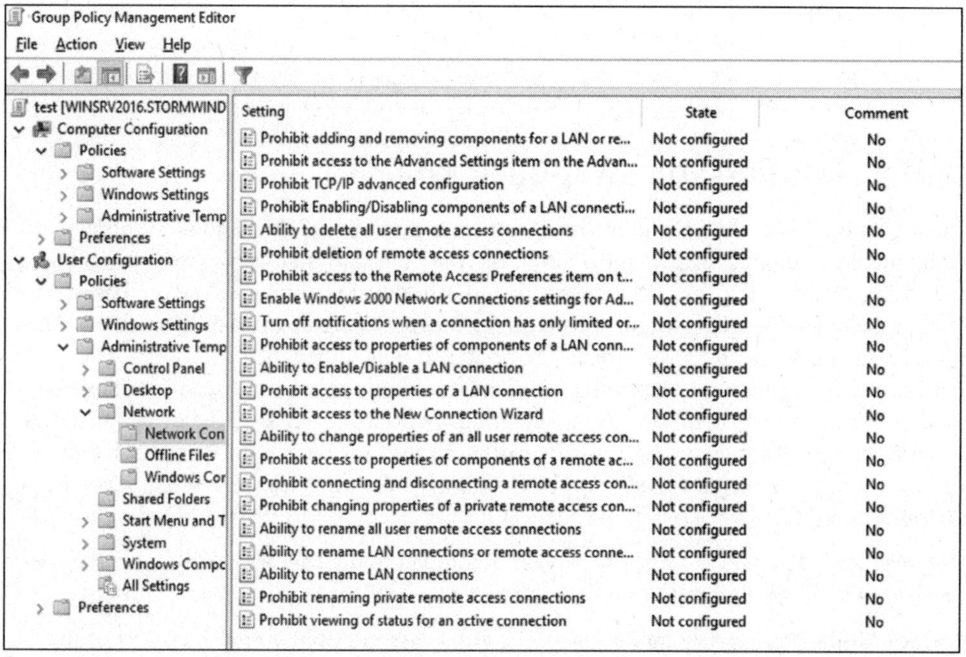

This option is useful, especially in larger networked environments, because the use of modems and other WAN devices can pose a security threat to the network.

▪ The ability to set offline files and folders options.

This is especially useful for keeping files synchronized for traveling users, and it is commonly configured for laptops.

Each setting includes detailed instructions in the description area of the GPO Editor window. By using these configuration options, system administrators can maintain consistency for users and computers and avoid many of the most common troubleshooting calls.

Configuring Network Settings

In Windows Server 2016, you can set a lot of user and network settings by using GPOs. Some of the different settings that can be configured are configure printer preferences, defining network drive mappings, configuring power options, setting custom registry settings, munipulating Control Panel settings, configuring Internet Explorer settings, settings for file and folder deployment, setting up shortcut deployments and configuring item-level targeting.

To configure any of these settings, open the Group Policy Management Console and choose the GPO you want to edit. Once you start editing, you can configure any of these network settings.

Automatically Enrolling User and Computer Certificates in Group Policy

You can also use Group Policy to enroll user and computer certificates automatically, making the entire certificate process transparent to your end users. Before proceeding, you should understand what certificates are and why they are an important part of network security.

Think of a digital certificate as a carrying case for a public key. A certificate contains the public key and a set of attributes, including the key holder's name and email address. These attributes specify something about the holder: their identity, what they're allowed to do with the certificate, and so on. The attributes and the public key are bound together because the certificate is digitally signed by the entity that issued it. Anyone who wants to verify the certificate's contents can verify the issuer's signature.

Certificates are one part of what security experts call a *public-key infrastructure (PKI)*. A PKI has several different components that you can mix and match to achieve the desired results. Microsoft's PKI implementation offers the following functions:

Certificate Authorities   CAs issue certificates, revoke certificates they've issued, and publish certificates for their clients. Big CAs like Thawte and VeriSign do this for millions of users. If you want, you can also set up your own CA for each department or workgroup in your organization. Each CA is responsible for choosing which attributes it will include in a certificate and what mechanism it will use to verify those attributes before it issues the certificate.

Certificate Publishers   They make certificates publicly available, inside or outside an organization. This allows widespread availability of the critical material needed to support the entire PKI.

PKI-Savvy Applications   These allow you and your users to do useful things with certificates, such as encrypt email or network connections. Ideally, the user shouldn't have to know (or even be aware of) what the application is doing—everything should work seamlessly and automatically. The best-known examples of PKI-savvy applications are web browsers such as Internet Explorer and Firefox and email applications such as Outlook.

Certificate Templates   These act like rubber stamps. By specifying a particular template as the model you want to use for a newly issued certificate, you're actually telling the CA which optional attributes to add to the certificate as well as implicitly telling it how to fill some of the mandatory attributes. Templates greatly simplify the process of issuing certificates because they keep you from having to memorize the names of all of the attributes you may potentially want to put in a certificate.

Learn More About PKI

When discussing certificates, it's also important to mention PKI and its definition. The exam doesn't go deeply into PKI, but I recommend you do some extra research on your own because it is an important technology and shouldn't be overlooked. PKI is actually a simple concept with a lot of moving parts. When broken down to its bare essentials, PKI is nothing more than a server and workstations utilizing a software service to add security to your infrastructure. When you use PKI, you are adding a layer of protection. The auto-enrollment Settings policy determines whether users and/or computers are automatically enrolled for the appropriate certificates when necessary. By default, this policy is enabled if a certificate server is installed, but you can make changes to the settings, as shown in Exercise 4.5.

In Exercise 4.5, you will learn how to configure automatic certificate enrollment in Group Policy. You must have first completed the other exercises in this chapter in order to proceed with Exercise 4.5.

EXERCISE 4.5

Configuring Automatic Certificate Enrollment in Group Policy

1. Open the Group Policy Management Console tool.

2. Right-click the North America OU that you created in the previous exercises in this book.

3. Choose Create A GPO In This Domain And Link It Here and name it **Test CA**. Click OK.

4. Right-click the Test CA GPO and choose Edit.

5. Open Computer Configuration ➢ Policies ➢ Windows Settings ➢ Security Settings ➢ Public Key Policies.

6. Double-click Certificate Services Client – Auto-Enrollment in the right pane.

7. The Certificate Services Client – Auto-Enrollment Properties dialog box will appear.

8. For now, don't change anything. Just become familiar with the settings in this dialog box. Click OK to close it.

Redirecting Folders

Another set of Group Policy settings that you will learn about are the *folder redirection settings*. Group Policy provides a means for redirecting the Documents, Desktop, and Start Menu folders, as well as cached application data, to network locations. Folder redirection is particularly useful for the following reasons:

- When they are using roaming user profiles, a user's Documents folder is copied to the local machine each time they log on. This requires high bandwidth consumption and time if the Documents folder is large. If you redirect the Documents folder, it stays in the redirected location, and the user opens and saves files directly to that location.

- Documents are always available no matter where the user logs on.

- Data in the shared location can be backed up during the normal backup cycle without user intervention.

- Data can be redirected to a more robust server-side administered disk that is less prone to physical and user errors.

    When you decide to redirect folders, you have two options: basic and advanced.

- Basic redirection redirects everyone's folders to the same location (but each user gets their own folder within that location).

- Advanced redirection redirects folders to different locations based on group membership. For instance, you could configure the Engineers group to redirect their folders to //Engineering1/Documents/ and the Marketing group to //Marketing1/Documents/. Again, individual users still get their own folder within the redirected location.

    To configure folder redirection, follow the steps in Exercise 4.6. You must have completed the other exercises in this chapter to proceed with this exercise.

EXERCISE 4.6

Configuring Folder Redirection in Group Policy

1. Open the GPMC tool.

2. Open the North America OU and then edit the Test CA GPO.

3. Open User Configuration ➢ Policies ➢ Windows Settings ➢ Folder Redirection ➢ Documents.

4. Right-click Documents, and select Properties.

EXERCISE 4.6 *(continued)*

5. On the Target tab of the Documents Properties dialog box, choose the Basic – Redirect Everyone's Folder To The Same Location selection from the Settings drop-down list.

6. Leave the default option for the Target Folder Location drop-down list and specify a network path in the Root Path field.

7. Click the Settings tab. All of the default settings are self-explanatory and should typically be left at the default setting. Click OK when you have finished.

Folder Redirection Facts

Try not to mix up the concepts of *folder redirection* and *offline folders*, especially in a world with ever-increasing numbers of mobile users. Folder redirection and offline folders are different features.

Windows Server 2016 folder redirection works as follows: The system uses a pointer that moves the folders you want to a location you specify. Users do not see any of this—it is transparent to them. One problem with folder redirection is that it does not work for mobile users (users who will be offline and who will not have access to files they may need).

Offline folders, however, are copies of folders that were local to you. Files are now available locally to you on the system you have with you. They are also located back on the server where they are stored. The next time you log in, the folders are synchronized so that both folders contain the latest data. This is a perfect feature for mobile users, whereas folder redirection provides no benefit for the mobile user.

Managing GPOs with Windows PowerShell Group Policy Cmdlets

As stated earlier in this book, *Windows PowerShell* is a Windows command-line shell and scripting language. Windows PowerShell can also help an administrator automate many of the same tasks that you perform using the Group Policy Management Console.

Windows Server 2016 helps you perform many of the Group Policy tasks by providing more than 25 cmdlets. Each of these cmdlets is a simple, single-function command-line tool.

The Windows PowerShell Group Policy cmdlets can help you perform some of the following tasks for domain-based Group Policy Objects:

▪ Maintain, create, remove, back up, and import GPOs

▪ Create, update, and remove GPO links to Active Directory containers

- Set Active Directory OUs and domain permissions and inheritance flags
- Configure Group Policy registry settings
- Create and edit Starter GPOs

The requirement for Windows PowerShell Group Policy cmdlets is Windows Server 2016 on either a domain controller or a member server that has the GPMC installed. Windows 7, Windows 8, and Windows 10 also have the ability to use Windows PowerShell Group Policy cmdlets if they have Remote Server Administration Tools (RSAT) installed. RSAT includes the GPMC and its cmdlets. PowerShell is also a requirement.

Item-Level Targeting

Administrators have the ability to apply individual preference items only to selected users or computers using a GPO feature called item-level targeting. *Item-level targeting* allows an administrator to select specific items that the GPO will look at and then apply that GPO only to the specific users or computers. Administrators have the ability to include multiple preference items, and each item can be customized for specific users or computers to use.

The target item has a value that belongs to it, and the value can be either true or false. Administrators can get even more granular by using the operation command of AND or OR while building this GPO, and this will allow an administrator to combine the targeted items with the preceding one. Once all of the conditions are executed, if the final value is false, then the GPO is not applied. If the final value is true, the GPO is applied to the users or computers that were previously determined. Administrators have the ability to item-level target the following items:

- Battery Present Targeting
- Computer Name Targeting
- CPU Speed Targeting
- Date Match Targeting
- Disk Space Targeting
- Domain Targeting
- Environment Variable Targeting
- File Match Targeting
- IP Address Range Targeting
- Language Targeting
- LDAP Query Targeting
- MAC Address Range Targeting
- MSI Query Targeting
- Network Connection Targeting
- Operating System Targeting

- Organizational Unit Targeting
- PCMCIA Present Targeting
- Portable Computer Targeting
- Processing Mode Targeting
- RAM Targeting
- Registry Match Targeting
- Security Group Targeting
- Site Targeting
- Terminal Session Targeting
- Time Range Targeting
- User Targeting
- WMI Query Targeting

Administrators can easily set up item-level targeting by following these steps:

1. Open the Group Policy Management Console. Select the GPO that will contain the new preferences by right-clicking the GPO and then choose Edit.

2. In the console tree under Computer Configuration or User Configuration, expand the Preferences folder and then browse to the preference extension.

3. Double-click the node for the preference extension and then right-click the preference item and click Properties.

4. In the Properties dialog box, click the Common tab.

5. Select Item-Level Targeting and then click Targeting.

6. Click New Item. If you are configuring multiple targeted items, on the Item Option menu, click the logical operation (AND or OR). Then click OK when finished.

7. Click the OK button on the Properties dialog box, and you are all set.

Back Up, Restore, Import, Copy, and Migration Tables

One of the biggest advantages of using the Group Policy Management Console is that it is a one-stop shopping utility. You can do everything you need to do for GPOs in one location. The GPMC not only allows you to create and link a GPO but also lets you back up, restore, import, copy, and use migration tables.

Backing Up a GPO

Since this book is about Windows Server 2016 and everything you should do to set up the server properly, then you most likely already understand what backups can do for you.

The reason we back up data as an administrator is in the event of a crash or major error that requires us to reload data to the server. Backups should be done daily on all data that is important to your organization. Backups can be done either by using Windows Server 2016's backup utility, or you can purchase third party software/hardware to back up your data.

I am an IT Director, and data recoverability is one of the most critical items that I deal with on a daily basis. I use a third-party hardware device from a company called Unitrends. This is just one of many companies that helps protect an organization's data.

This hardware device does hourly backups for all of my servers. One of the nice features of the Unitrends box is that it backs up onto the hardware device and then sends my data up to the cloud automatically for an offsite backup. This way, if I need to recover just one piece of data, I can grab it off the hardware device. But if I have a major issue, such as a fire that destroys the entire server room, I have an offsite backup from which I can retrieve my data.

It's the same for GPOs. You need to make sure you back up your GPOs in the event of an issue that requires you to do a reload. To back up your GPOs manually, you can go into the GPMC MMC and, under Group Policy Objects, you can right click and choose Backup All or right click on the specific GPO and choose Backup.

Restoring a GPO

There may be times when you have to restore a GPO that was previously backed up. There are normally two reasons why you have to restore a GPO—you accidently deleted the GPO, or you need to restore the GPO to a previous state. (This normally happens if you make changes and it causes an issue.) Restoring a GPO is simple.

1. Open the Group Policy Management Console.

2. In the console tree, right-click Group Policy Objects and choose Manage Backups.

3. Choose the backup you want to restore and click the Restore button.

Importing or Copying GPOs

As an administrator, there may be times when you need to import or copy a GPO from one domain to another domain. Administrators do this so that the second domain has the same settings as the first domain.

An administrator can use the import or copy-to-transfer settings from one GPO to another GPO within the same domain, to a GPO in another domain in the same forest, or to a GPO in a domain in a different forest.

Importing or copying a GPO is an easy process. To do this, an administrator completes the following steps:

1. Open the Group Policy Management Console.

2. In the console tree, right-click Group Policy Objects and choose either Import Settings or Copy.

Migration Tables

One issue that we run into when copying or moving a GPO from one system to another is that when some GPOs are built, they are domain specific. This can be a problem when they are moved to a system in another domain. This is where migration tables can help you out.

Migration tables will tell you how domain specific settings should be treated when the GPO is moved from the domain in which it was created to another domain.

Migration tables are files that are used to map previous domain information (such as users and groups) to the new domain's object-specific data. Migration tables have mapping entries that map the old data to the new data.

Migration tables store their mapping data in an XML format, and the migration tables have their own extension name, .migtable. If you want to create your own migration table, you can use the *Migration Table Editor (MTE)*. The MTE is an easy-to-use utility for configuring or just viewing migration tables.

It does not matter if you decide to copy or import a GPO, migration tables apply to any of the settings within the GPO. However, if you copy a GPO instead of move it, you have the option of bringing the Discretionary Access Control List (DACL) option over with the copy.

If you are looking at using migration tables, there are three settings that can be used:

Do Not Use A Migration Table   If an administrator chooses this option, the GPO is copied over exactly as is. All security objects and UNC paths are copied over without any modification.

Use A Migration Table   If an administrator chooses this option, the GPO has all of the options that can be in the migration table mapped.

Use A Migration Table Exclusively   If an administrator chooses this option, all security principals and UNC path information in the GPO are chosen. If any of this information is not included in the migration table, the operation will fail.

To open the Migration Table Editor, perform the following steps:

1. Open the Group Policy Management Console.

2. In the console tree, right-click Group Policy Objects and choose Open Migration Table Editor.

Resetting the Default GPO

There may be a time when you need to reset the default GPO to its original settings. This is easy to do as long as you understand how to use the DCGPOFix command-line utility. This command-line utility is just what it spells—it fixes the domain controller's GPO. To use this command, you would use the following syntax:

```
DCGPOFix [/ignoreschema] [/target: {Domain | DC | Both}] [/?]
```

So, let's take a look at the switches in the previous command. The /ignoreschema switch ignores the current version of the Active Directory Schema. The reason you use this switch is because this command works only on the same schema version as the Windows version in which the command was shipped. By using this switch, you don't need to worry about what schema you have on the system.

The next switch is [/target: {Domain | DC | Both}]. This switch specifies the GPO you are going to restore. An administrator has the ability to restore the Default Domain Policy GPO, the Default Domain Controllers GPO, or both. The final switch, /?, displays the help for this command.

Deploying Software Through a GPO

It's difficult enough to manage applications on a stand-alone computer. It seems that the process of installing, configuring, and uninstalling applications is never finished. Add in the hassle of computer reboots and reinstalling corrupted applications, and the reduction in productivity can be substantial.

Software administrators who manage software in network environments have even more concerns.

- First, they must determine which applications specific users require.

- Then, IT departments must purchase the appropriate licenses for the software and acquire any necessary media.

- Next, the system administrators need to install the applications on users' machines. This process generally involves help desk staff visiting computers, or it requires end users to install the software themselves. Both processes entail several potential problems, including installation inconsistency and lost productivity from downtime experienced when applications were installed.

- Finally, software administrators still need to manage software updates and remove unused software.

One of the key design goals for Active Directory was to reduce some of the headaches involved in managing software and configurations in a networked environment. To that end, Windows Server 2016 offers several features that can make the task of deploying software easier and less error prone. Before you dive into the technical details, however, you need to examine the issues related to software deployment.

The Software Management Life Cycle

Although it may seem that the use of a new application requires only the installation of the necessary software, the overall process of managing applications involves many more steps. When managing software applications, there are three main phases to their life cycle, as follows:

Phase 1: Deploying Software   The first step in using applications is to install them on the appropriate client computers. Generally, some applications are deployed during the initial configuration of a PC, and others are deployed when they are requested. In the latter case, this often used to mean that system administrators and help desk staffs have to visit client computers and manually walk through the installation process. With Windows Server 2016 and GPOs, the entire process can be automated.

Before You Install, Stop

It is important to understand that just because you can easily deploy software, it does not necessarily mean you have the right to do so. Before you install software on client computers, you must make sure you have the appropriate licenses for the software. Furthermore, it's important to take the time to track application installations. As many system administrators have discovered, it's much more difficult to inventory software installations after they've been performed. Another issue you may encounter is that you lack available resources (for instance, your system does not meet the minimum hardware requirements) and that you face problems such as limited hard disk space or memory that may not be able to handle the applications that you want to load and use. You may also find that your user account does not have the permission to install software. It's important to consider not only how you will install software but also whether you can.

Phase 2: Maintaining Software   Once an application is installed and in use on client computers, you need to ensure that the software is maintained. You must keep programs up-to-date by applying changes due to bug fixes, enhancements, and other types of updates. This is normally done with service packs, hot fixes, and updates. As with the initial software deployment, software maintenance can be tedious. Some programs require older versions to be uninstalled before updates are added. Others allow for automatically upgrading over existing installations. Managing and deploying software updates can consume a significant amount of the IT staff's time.

Using Windows Update

Make sure that you learn about Windows Update, a service that allows you to connect to Microsoft's website and download what your system may need to bring it up to compliance. This tool is helpful if you are running a stand-alone system, but if you want to deploy software across the enterprise, the best way to accomplish this is first to test the updates you are downloading and make sure you can use them and that they are not bug ridden. Then you can use a tool such as the Windows Server Update Service (WSUS), which was formerly called the Software Update Services (SUS).

You can check for updates at Microsoft's website (http://update.microsoft.com). Microsoft likes to ask many types of questions about WSUS on its certification exams. WSUS is described in detail in other Sybex certification books.

Phase 3: Removing Software   The end of the life cycle for many software products involves the actual removal of unused programs. Removing software is necessary when applications become outdated or when users no longer require their functionality. One of the traditional problems with uninstalling applications is that many of the installed files may not be removed. Furthermore, the removal of shared components can sometimes cause other programs to stop functioning properly. Also, users often forget to uninstall applications that they no longer need, and these programs continue to occupy disk space and consume valuable system resources.

The Microsoft Windows Installer (MSI) manages each of these three phases of the software maintenance life cycle. Now that you have an overview of the process, let's move forward to look at the steps involved in deploying software using Group Policy.

 The *Microsoft Windows Installer* (sometimes referred to as Microsoft Installer or Windows Installer) is an application installation and configuration service. An instruction file (the Microsoft Installer package) contains information about what needs to be done to install a product. It's common to confuse the two.

The Windows Installer

If you've installed newer application programs (such as Microsoft Office 2016), you've probably noticed the updated setup and installation routines. Applications that comply with the updated standard use the *Windows Installer specification* and MSI software packages for deployment. Each package contains information about various setup options and the files required for installation. Although the benefits may not seem dramatic on the surface, there's a lot of new functionality under the hood.

The Windows Installer was created to solve many of the problems associated with traditional application development. It has several components, including the Installer service (which runs on Windows 2000, XP, Vista, Windows 7, Windows 8, Windows 10, Windows Server 2003, Windows Server 2008, Windows Server 2008 R2, Windows Server 2012, Windows Server 2012 R2, and Windows Server 2016 computers), the Installer program (msiexec.exe) that is responsible for executing the instructions in a *Windows Installer package*, and the specifications third-party developers use to create their own packages. Within each installation package file is a relational structure (similar to the structure of tables in databases) that records information about the programs contained within the package.

To appreciate the true value of the Windows Installer, you'll need to look at some of the problems with traditional software deployment mechanisms and then at how the Windows Installer addresses many of them.

Application Installation Issues

Before the Windows Installer, applications were installed using a setup program that managed the various operations required for a program to operate. These operations included copying files, changing registry settings, and managing any other operating system changes that might be required (such as starting or stopping services). However, this method had several problems:

- The setup process was not robust, and aborting the operation often left many unnecessary files in the file system.

- The process included uninstalling an application (this also often left many unnecessary files in the file system) and remnants in the Windows registry and operating system folders. Over time, these remnants would result in reduced overall system performance and wasted disk space.

- There was no standard method for applying upgrades to applications, and installing a new version often required users to uninstall the old application, reboot, and then install the new program.

- Conflicts between different versions of *dynamic link libraries (DLLs)*—shared program code used across different applications—could cause the installation or removal of one application to break the functionality of another.

Benefits of the Windows Installer

Because of the many problems associated with traditional software installation, Microsoft created the *Windows Installer.* This system provides for better manageability of the software installation process and allows system administrators more control over the deployment process. Specifically, the Windows Installer provides the following benefits:

Improved Software Removal   The process of removing software is an important one because remnants left behind during the uninstall process can eventually clutter up the registry and file system. During the installation process, the Windows Installer keeps track of all of the changes made by a setup package. When it comes time to remove an application, all of these changes can then be rolled back.

More Robust Installation Routines   If a typical setup program is aborted during the software installation process, the results are unpredictable. If the actual installation hasn't yet begun, then the installer generally removes any temporary files that may have been created. However, if the file copy routine starts before the system encounters an error, it is likely that the files will not be automatically removed from the operating system. In contrast, the Windows Installer allows you to roll back any changes when the application setup process is aborted.

Ability to Use Elevated Privileges   Installing applications usually requires the user to have Administrator permissions on the local computer because file system and registry changes are required. When installing software for network users, system administrators have two options. First, they can log off of the computer before installing the software and then log back on as a user who has Administrator permissions on the local computer. This method is tedious and time-consuming. The second option is to give users Administrator permissions temporarily on their own machines. This method could cause security problems and requires the attention of a system administrator.

Through the use of the Installer service, the Windows Installer is able to use temporarily elevated privileges to install applications. This allows users, regardless of their security settings, to execute the installation of authorized applications. This saves time and preserves security.

Support for Repairing Corrupted Applications   Regardless of how well a network environment is managed, critical files are sometimes lost or corrupted. Such problems can prevent applications from running properly and can cause crashes. Windows Installer packages provide you with the ability to verify the installation of an application and, if necessary, replace any missing or corrupted files. This support saves time and lessens end-user headaches associated with removing and reinstalling an entire application to replace just a few files.

Prevention of File Conflicts   Generally, different versions of the same files should be compatible with each other. In the real world, however, this isn't always the case. A classic problem in the Windows world is the case of one program replacing DLLs that are used by several other programs. Windows Installer accurately tracks which files are used by certain programs and ensures that any shared files are not improperly deleted or overwritten.

Automated Installations   A typical application setup process requires end users or system administrators to respond to several prompts. For example, a user may be able to choose the program group in which icons will be created and the file system location to which the program will be installed. Additionally, they may be required to choose which options are installed. Although this type of flexibility is useful, it can be tedious when you are rolling out multiple applications. By using features of the Windows Installer, however, users are able to specify setup options before the process begins. This allows system administrators to ensure consistency in installations, and it saves users time.

Advertising and On-Demand Installations   One of the most powerful features of the Windows Installer is its ability to perform on-demand software installations. Prior to the Windows Installer, application installation options were quite basic—either a program was installed or it was not. When setting up a computer, system administrators would be required to guess which applications the user might need and install all of them.

The Windows Installer supports a function known as advertising. *Advertising* makes applications appear to be available via the Start menu. However, the programs themselves may not actually be installed on the system. When a user attempts to access an advertised application, the Windows Installer automatically downloads the necessary files from a server and installs the program. The result is that applications are installed only when they are needed, and the process requires no intervention from the end user.

To anyone who has managed many software applications in a network environment, all of these features of the Windows Installer are likely welcome ones. They also make life easier for end users and application developers; they can focus on the "real work" that their jobs demand.

Windows Installer File Types

When performing software deployment with the Windows Installer in Windows Server 2016, you may encounter several different file types.

Microsoft Windows Installer Packages   To take full advantage of Windows Installer functionality, applications must include Microsoft Windows Installer packages. Third-party application vendors and software developers normally create these packages, and they include the information required to install and configure the application and any supporting files.

Microsoft Transformation Files   *Microsoft Transformation (MST) files* are useful when you are customizing the details of how applications are installed. When a system administrator chooses to assign or publish an application, they may want to specify additional options for the package. For example, if a system administrator wants to allow users to install only the Microsoft Word and Microsoft PowerPoint components of Office 2016, they could specify these options within a transformation file. Then, when users install the application, they will be provided only with the options related to these components.

Microsoft Patches   To maintain software, patches are often required. Patches may make Registry and/or file system changes. *Patch files (MSP)* are used for minor system changes and are subject to certain limitations. Specifically, a patch file cannot remove any installed program components and cannot delete or modify any shortcuts created by the user.

Initialization Files   To provide support for publishing non–Windows Installer applications, *initialization files* can be used. These files provide links to a standard executable file that is used to install an application. An example might be \\server1\software\program1\ setup.exe. These files can then be published and advertised, and users can access the *Add Or Remove Programs* icon to install them over the network.

Application Assignment Scripts   *Application assignment scripts (AAS)* store information regarding assigning programs and any settings that the system administrator makes. These files are created when Group Policy is used to create software package assignments for users and computers.

Each of these types of files provides functionality that allows the system administrator to customize software deployment. Windows Installer packages have special properties that you can view by right-clicking the file in File Explorer and choosing Properties (see Figure 4.9).

FIGURE 4.9   Viewing the properties of an MSI package file

Deploying Applications

The functionality provided by Windows Installer offers many advantages to end users who install their own software. However, that is just the beginning in a networked environment. As you'll see later in this chapter, the various features of Windows Installer and compatible packages allow system administrators to determine central applications that users will be able to install.

There are two main methods of making programs available to end users using Active Directory: assigning and publishing. Both assigning and publishing applications greatly ease the process of deploying and managing applications in a network environment.

In the following sections, you'll look at how the processes of assigning and publishing applications can make life easier for IT staff and users alike. The various settings for assigned and published applications are managed through the use of GPOs.

Assigning Applications

Software applications can be assigned to users and computers. *Assigning* a software package makes the program available for automatic installation. The applications advertise their availability to the affected users or computers by placing icons within the Programs folder of the Start menu for Windows 8 (and before) and Windows Server 2012/2012 R2, and within the Apps area on Windows 10 and Windows Server 2016.

When applications are assigned to a user, programs will be advertised to the user regardless of which computer they are using. That is, icons for the advertised program will appear regardless of whether the program is installed on that computer. If the user clicks an icon for a program that has not yet been installed on the local computer, the application will automatically be accessed from a server and it will be installed.

When an application is assigned to a computer, the program is made available to any users of the computer. For example, all users who log on to a computer that has been assigned Microsoft Office 2016 will have access to the components of the application. If the user did not previously install Microsoft Office 2016, they will be prompted for any required setup information when the program first runs.

Generally, applications that are required by the vast majority of users should be assigned to computers. This reduces the amount of network bandwidth required to install applications on demand and improves the end-user experience by preventing the delay involved when installing an application the first time it is accessed. Any applications that may be used by only a few users (or those with specific job tasks) should be assigned to users.

Publishing Applications

When applications are *published*, they are advertised, but no icons are automatically created. Instead, the applications are made available for installation using the Programs and Features icon in Control Panel.

Implementing Software Deployment

So far, you have become familiar with the issues related to software deployment and management from a theoretical level. Now it's time to drill down into the actual steps required to deploy software using the features of Active Directory and the GPMC. In the following sections, you will walk through the steps required to create an application distribution share point, to publish and assign applications, to update previously installed applications, to verify the installation of applications, and to update Windows operating systems.

Preparing for Software Deployment

Before you can install applications on client computers, you must make sure that the necessary files are available to end users. In many network environments, system administrators create shares on file servers that include the installation files for many applications. Based on security permissions, either end users or system administrators can then connect to these shares from a client computer and install the needed software. The efficient organization of these shares can save the help desk from having to carry around a library of DVDs, and it allows you to install applications easily on many computers at once.

One of the problems in network environments is that users frequently install applications whether or not they really need them. They may stumble upon applications that are stored on common file servers and install them out of curiosity. These actions can often decrease productivity and may violate software licensing agreements. You can help avoid this by placing all of your application installation files in hidden shares (for example, software$).

Exercise 4.7 walks you through the process of creating a software distribution share point. In this exercise, you will prepare for software deployment by creating a directory share and placing certain types of files in this directory. To complete the steps in this exercise, you must have access to the Microsoft Office 2013 or Microsoft Office 2016 installation files (via DVD or through a network share) and have 2,000 MB of free disk space. For this exercise, I used Microsoft Office 2016.

EXERCISE 4.7

Creating a Software Deployment Share

1. Using File Explorer, create a folder called **Software** that you can use with application sharing. Be sure that the volume on which you create this folder has at least 2,000 MB of available disk space.

2. Create a folder called `Office 2016` within the `Software` folder.

3. Copy all of the installation files for Microsoft Office 2016 from the DVD or network share containing the files to the `Office 2016` folder you created in step 2. If you prefer, you can use switches to install all of the Office 2016 installation files.

4. Right-click the `Software` folder (created in step 1) and select Share. In the Choose People On Your Network To Share With dialog box, type **Everyone**, and click the Add button. Next click the Share button. When you see a message that the sharing process is complete, click Done.

Software Restriction Policies

One of the biggest problems that we face as IT managers is users downloading and installing software. Many software packages don't cause any issues and are completely safe. Unfortunately, many software packages do have viruses and can cause problems. This is where software restriction policies can help. Software restriction policies help to identify software and to control its ability to run on a local computer, organizational unit, domain, or site.

Software restriction policies give administrators the ability to regulate unknown or untrusted software. Software restriction policies allow you to protect your computers from unwanted software by identifying and also specifying what software packages are allowed to be installed.

When configuring software restriction policies, an administrator is able to define a default security level of Unrestricted (software is allowed) or Disallowed (software is not allowed to run) for a GPO. Administrators can make exceptions to this default security level. They can create software restriction policy rules for specific software.

To create a software policy using the Group Policy Management Console, create a new GPO. In the GPO, expand the Windows Settings for either the user or computer configuration section, expand Security, right-click Software Restriction Policy, and choose New Software Restriction Policy. Set the policy for the level of security that you need.

Using AppLocker

AppLocker is a feature in Windows 7, Windows 8, Windows 10, Windows Server 2012/2012 R2, and Windows Server 2016. It is the replacement for software restriction policies. *AppLocker* allows you to configure a Denied list and an Accepted list for applications. Applications that are configured on the Denied list will not run on the system, whereas applications on the Accepted list will operate properly.

The new capabilities and extensions of the AppLocker feature help reduce administrative overhead and help administrators control how users can access and use files, such as EXE files, scripts, Windows Installer files (MSI and MSP files), and DLLs.

Group Policy Slow Link Detection

When setting up GPOs, most of us assume that the connection speeds between servers and clients are going to be fast. In today's world, it is unlikely to see slow connections between locations, but they are still out there. Sometimes connection speeds can cause issues with the deployment of GPOs, specifically ones that are deploying software.

A setting in the Computer and User section of the GPO called *Group Policy Slow Link Detection* defines a slow connection for the purposes of applying and updating GPOs. If the data transfer rate from the domain controller providing the GPO to the computer is slower than what you have specified in this setting, the connection is considered to be a slow connection. If a connection is considered slow, the system response will vary depending on the policy. For example, if a GPO is going to deploy software and the connection is considered slow, the software may not be installed on the client computer. If you configure this option as 0, all connections are considered fast connections.

Publishing and Assigning Applications

As mentioned earlier, system administrators can make software packages available to users by using publishing and assigning operations. Both of these operations allow system administrators to leverage the power of Active Directory and, specifically, GPOs to determine which applications are available to users. Additionally, OUs can provide the organization that can help group users based on their job functions and software requirements.

The general process involves creating a GPO that includes software deployment settings for users and computers and then linking this GPO to Active Directory objects.

Exercise 4.8 walks you through the steps required to publish and assign applications. In this exercise, you will create applications and assign them to specific Active Directory objects using GPOs. To complete the steps in this exercise, you must have completed Exercise 4.7.

EXERCISE 4.8

Publishing and Assigning Applications Using Group Policy

1. Open the Active Directory Users and Computers tool from the Administrative Tools program group (using the Windows key).

2. Expand the domain and create a new top-level OU called **Software**.

3. Within the Software OU, create a user named **Jane User** with a login name of **juser** (choose the defaults for all other options).

4. Exit Active Directory Users and Computers and open the Group Policy Management Console.

5. Right-click the Software OU and choose Create A GPO In This Domain And Link It Here.

6. For the name of the new GPO, type **Software Deployment**.

7. To edit the Software Deployment GPO, right-click it and choose Edit. Expand the Computer Configuration ➢ Policies ➢ Software Settings object.

8. Right-click the Software Installation item and select New ➢ Package.

9. Navigate to the Software share you created in Exercise 4.7.

10. Within the Software share, double-click the Office 2016 folder and select the appropriate MSI file depending on the version of Office 2016 you have. Office 2016 Professional is being used in this example, so you'll see that the OFFICEMUI.MSI file is chosen. Click Open.

11. In the Deploy Software dialog box, choose Advanced. (Note that the Published option is unavailable because applications cannot be published to computers.) Click OK to return to the Deploy Software dialog box.

12. To examine the deployment options of this package, click the Deployment tab. Accept the default settings by clicking OK.

13. Within the Group Policy Object Editor, expand the User Configuration ➢ Software Settings object.

EXERCISE 4.8 *(continued)*

14. Right-click the Software Installation item and select New ➢ Package.

15. Navigate to the Software share you created in Exercise 4.7.

16. Within the Software share, double-click the Office 2016 folder and select the appropriate MSI file. Click Open.

17. For the Software Deployment option, select Published in the Deploy Software dialog box and click OK.

18. Close the GPMC.

The overall process involved with deploying software using Active Directory is quite simple. However, you shouldn't let the intuitive graphical interface fool you—there's a lot of power under the hood of these software deployment features! Once you've properly assigned and published applications, it's time to see the effects of your work.

Applying Software Updates

The steps described in the previous section work only when you are installing a new application. However, software companies often release updates that you need to install on top of existing applications. These updates usually consist of bug fixes or other changes that are required to keep the software up-to-date. You can apply software updates in Active Directory by using the Upgrades tab of the software package Properties dialog box found in the Group Policy Object Editor.

In Exercise 4.9, you will apply a software update to an existing application. You should add the upgrade package to the GPO in the same way you added the original application in steps 8 through 12 of Exercise 4.8. You should also have completed Exercise 4.8 before attempting this exercise.

EXERCISE 4.9

Applying Software Updates

1. Open the Group Policy Management Console from the Administrative Tools program group.

2. Click the Software OU, right-click the Software Deployment GPO, and choose Edit.

3. Expand the Computer Configuration ➢ Policies ➢ Software Settings ➢ Software Installation object.

4. Right-click the software package and select Properties from the context menu to bring up the Properties dialog box.

5. Select the Upgrades tab and click the Add button.

6. Click the Current Group Policy Object (GPO) radio button in the Choose A Package From section of the dialog box or click the Browse button to select the GPO to which you want to apply the upgrade. Consult your application's documentation to see whether you should choose the Uninstall The Existing Package, Then Install The Upgrade Package radio button or the Package Can Upgrade Over The Existing Package radio button.

7. Click Cancel to close the Add Upgrade Package dialog box.

8. Click Cancel and exit the GPMC.

You should understand that not all upgrades make sense in all situations. For instance, if the Panek 2015 files are incompatible with the Panek 2018 application, then your Panek 2015 users might not want you to perform the upgrade without taking additional steps to ensure that they can continue to use their files. In addition, users might have some choice about which version they use when it doesn't affect the support of the network.

Regardless of the underlying reason for allowing this flexibility, you should be aware that there are two basic types of upgrades that are available for administrators to provide to the users:

Mandatory Upgrade   Forces everyone who currently has an existing version of the program to upgrade according to the GPO. Users who have never installed the program for whatever reason will be able to install only the new, upgraded version.

Nonmandatory Upgrade   Allows users to choose whether they would like to upgrade. This upgrade type also allows users who do not have their application installed to choose which version they would like to use.

Verifying Software Installation

To ensure that the software installation settings you make in a GPO have taken place, you can log into the domain from a Windows 10, Windows 8, or Windows 7 computer that is within the OU to which the software settings apply. When you log in, you will notice two changes. First, the application is installed on the computer (if it was not installed already). To access the application, a user needs to click one of the icons within the Program group of the Start menu. Note also that applications are available to any of the users who log on to this machine. Second, the settings apply to any computers that are contained within the OU and to any users who log on to these computers.

If you publish an application to users, the change may not be as evident, but it is equally useful. When you log on to a Windows 7, Windows 8, or Windows 10 computer that is a member of the domain, and when you use a user account from the OU where you published the application, you will be able to install any of the published applications automatically. On a Windows 10, Windows 8, or Windows 7 computer, you can do this by accessing the Programs icon in Control Panel. By clicking Add New Programs, you access a display of the applications available for installation. By clicking the Add button in the Add New Programs section of the Programs dialog box, you will automatically begin the installation of the published application.

Configuring Automatic Updates in Group Policy

So far you've seen the advantages of deploying application software in a group policy. Group policies also provide a way to install operating system updates across the network for Windows 10, Windows 7, Windows 8, Windows Server 2008/2008 R2, Windows Server 2012/2012 R2, and Windows Server 2016 machines using Windows Update in conjunction with Windows Server Update Service (WSUS). WSUS is the newer version of SUS, and it is used on a Windows Server 2016 system to update systems. As you may remember, WSUS and SUS are patch-management tools that help you deploy updates to your systems in a controlled manner.

Windows Update is available through the Microsoft website, and it is used to provide the most current files for Windows operating systems. Examples of updates include security fixes, critical updates, updated help files, and updated drivers. You can access Windows Update by clicking the Windows Update icon in the system tray.

WSUS is used to leverage the features of Windows Update within a corporate environment by downloading Windows updates to a corporate server, which in turn provides the updates to the internal corporate clients. This allows administrators to test and have full control over what updates are deployed within the corporate environment.

Within an enterprise network that is using Active Directory, you would typically see automatic updates configured through Group Policy. Group policies are used to manage configuration and security settings via Active Directory. Group Policy is also used to specify what server a client will use for automatic updates.

If the WSUS client were part of an enterprise network that is using Active Directory, you would configure the client via a group policy.

Configuring Software Deployment Settings

In addition to the basic operations of assigning and publishing applications, you can use several other options to specify the details of how software is deployed. In the following sections, you will examine the various options that are available and their effects on the software installation process.

The Software Installation Properties Dialog Box

The most important software deployment settings are contained in the Software Installation Properties dialog box, which you can access by right-clicking the Software Installation item and selecting Properties from the context menu. The following sections describe the features contained on the various tabs of the dialog box.

Managing Package Defaults

On the Deployment tab of the Software Installation Properties dialog box, you'll be able to specify some defaults for any packages that you create within this GPO. Figure 4.10 shows the Deployment options for managing software installation settings.

FIGURE 4.10   Deployment tab of the Software Installation Properties dialog box

The following options are used for managing software installation settings:

Default Package Location   This setting specifies the default file system or network location for software installation packages. This is useful if you are already using a specific share on a file server for hosting the necessary installation files.

New Packages   These settings specify the default type of package assignment that will be used when you add a new package to either the user or computer settings. If you'll be assigning or publishing multiple packages, you may find it useful to set a default here. Selecting the Advanced option (see Figure 4.11) enables Group Policy to display the package's Properties dialog box each time a new package is added.

FIGURE 4.11   Advanced Deployment dialog box

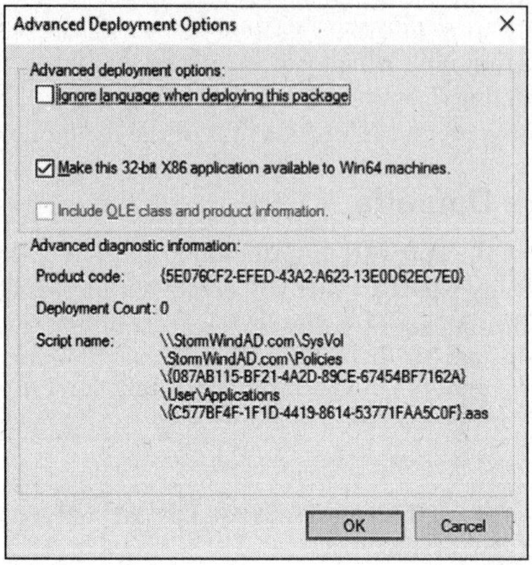

Installation User Interface Options   When installing an application, system administrators may or may not want end users to see all of the advanced installation options. If Basic is chosen, the user will be able to configure only the minimal settings (such as the installation location). If Maximum is chosen, all of the available installation options will be displayed. The specific installation options available will depend on the package itself.

Uninstall Applications When They Fall Out Of The Scope Of Management   So far, you have seen how applications can be assigned and published to users or computers. But what happens when effective GPOs change? For example, suppose User A is currently located within the Sales OU. A GPO that assigns the Microsoft Office 2013 suite of applications is linked to the Sales OU. You decide to move User A to the Engineering OU, which has no software deployment settings. Should the application be uninstalled or should it remain?

If the Uninstall Applications When They Fall Out Of The Scope of Management option is checked, applications will be removed if they are not specifically assigned or published within GPOs. In this example, this means Office 2013 would be uninstalled for User A. If this box is left unchecked, however, the application will remain installed.

Managing File Extension Mappings

One of the potential problems associated with using many different file types is that it's difficult to keep track of which applications work with which files. For example, if you received a file with the filename extension .abc, you would have no idea which application you would need to view it.

Fortunately, through software deployment settings, system administrators can specify mappings for specific *filename extensions*. For example, you could specify that whenever users attempt to access a file with the extension .vsd, the operating system should attempt to open the file using Visio diagramming software. If Visio is not installed on the user's machine, the computer can automatically download and install it (assuming that the application has been properly advertised).

This method allows users to have applications automatically installed when they are needed. The following is an example of a sequence of events that might occur:

1. A user receives an email message that contains a PDF (.pdf) file attachment.

2. The computer realizes that the PDF file does not have the appropriate viewing application for this type of file installed. However, it also realizes that a filename extension mapping is available within the Active Directory software deployment settings.

3. The client computer automatically requests the PDF software package from the server, and it uses the Microsoft Windows Installer to install the application automatically.

4. The computer opens the attachment for the user.

Notice that all of these steps were carried out without any further interaction with the user.

You can manage filename extension mappings by right-clicking the Software Installation item, selecting Properties, and then clicking the File Extensions tab.

Creating Application Categories

In many network environments, the list of supported applications can include hundreds of items. For users who are looking for only one specific program, searching through a list of all of these programs can be difficult and time-consuming.

Fortunately, methods for categorizing the applications are available on your network. You can easily manage the application categories for users and computers by right-clicking the Software Installation item, selecting Properties, and then clicking the Categories tab.

Figure 4.12 shows you the categories tab of the Software Installation package. When creating categories, it is a good idea to use category names that are meaningful to users because it will make it easier for them to find the programs they're seeking.

FIGURE 4.12 The Categories tab of the Software Installation Properties dialog box

Once the software installation categories have been created, you can view them by clicking the Programs or Programs And Features icon in Control Panel. When you click Add New Programs, you'll see that several options appear in the Category drop-down list. Now when you select the properties for a package, you will be able to assign the application to one or more of the categories.

Removing Programs

As discussed in the beginning of the chapter, an important phase in the software management life cycle is the removal of applications. Fortunately, if you use the GPMC and the Windows Installer packages, the process is simple. To remove an application, you can right-click the package within the Group Policy settings and select All Tasks ➤ Remove. This brings up a removal text box (see Figure 4.13).

FIGURE 4.13   Removing a software package

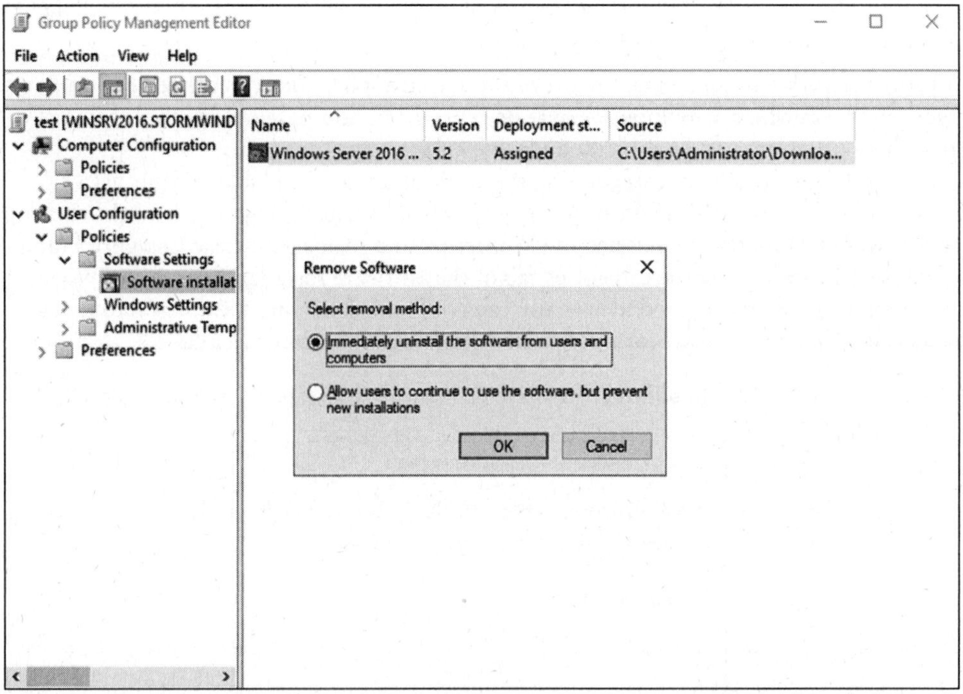

When choosing to remove a software package from a GPO, you have two options, shown here:

Immediately Uninstall The Software From Users And Computers   System administrators can choose this option to ensure that an application is no longer available to users who are affected by the GPO. When this option is selected, the program will be uninstalled automatically from users and/or computers that have the package. This option might be useful, for example, if the license for a certain application has expired or if a program is no longer on the approved applications list.

Allow Users To Continue To Use The Software, But Prevent New Installations   This option prevents users from making new installations of a package, but it does not remove the software if it has already been installed for users. This is a good option if the company has run out of additional licenses for the software but the existing licenses are still valid.

If you no longer require the ability to install or repair an application, you can delete it from your software distribution share point by deleting the appropriate Windows Installer package files. This will free up additional disk space for newer applications.

Microsoft Windows Installer Settings

Several options influence the behavior of the Windows Installer; you can set them within a GPO. You can access these options by navigating to User Configuration ➤ Administrative Templates ➤ Windows Components ➤ Windows Installer.

The options are as follows:

Always Install With Elevated Privileges   This policy allows users to install applications that require elevated privileges. For example, if a user does not have the permissions necessary to modify the Registry but the installation program must make Registry changes, this policy will allow the process to succeed.

Prevent Removable Media Source For Any Install   This option disallows the installation of software using removable media (such as a CD-ROM or DVD-ROM). It is useful for ensuring that users install only approved applications.

Prohibit Rollback   When this option is enabled, the Windows Installer does not store the system state information that is required to roll back the installation of an application. System administrators may choose this option to reduce the amount of temporary disk space required during installation and to increase the performance of the installation operation. However, the drawback is that the system cannot roll back to its original state if the installation fails and the application needs to be removed.

Specify The Order In Which Windows Installer Searches   This setting specifies the order in which the Windows Installer will search for installation files. The options include n (for network shares), m (for searching removal media), and u (for searching the Internet for installation files).

With these options, system administrators can control how the Windows Installer operates for specific users who are affected by the GPO.

Troubleshooting Group Policies

Because of the wide variety of configurations that are possible when you are establishing GPOs, you should be aware of some common troubleshooting methods. These methods will help isolate problems in policy settings or GPO links.

One possible problem with GPO configuration is that logons and system startups may take a long time. This occurs especially in large environments when the Group Policy settings must be transmitted over the network and, in many cases, slow WAN links. In general, the number of GPOs should be limited because of the processing overhead and network requirements during logon. By default, GPOs are processed in a synchronous manner. This means that the processing of one GPO must be completed before another one is applied (as opposed to asynchronous processing, where they can all execute at the same time).

When a group policy gets processed on a Windows-based operating system, client-side extensions are the mechanisms that interpret the stored policy and then make the appropriate changes to the operating system environment. When an administrator is troubleshooting a given extension's application of policy, the administrator can view the configuration parameters for that extension in the operating system's Registry. To view the extension in the Registry, you would view the following key:

```
HKEY_LOCAL_MACHINE\Software\Microsoft\Windows \CurrentVersion\Group Policy
```

The most common issue associated with Group Policy is the unexpected setting of Group Policy options. In Windows Server 2000, administrators spent countless hours analyzing inheritance hierarchy and individual settings to determine why a particular user or computer was having policy problems. For instance, say a user named wpanek complains that the Run option is missing from his Start menu. The wpanek user account is stored in the New Hampshire OU, and you've applied group policies at the OU, domain, and site levels. To determine the source of the problem, you would have to sift through each GPO manually to find the Start menu policy as well as to figure out the applicable inheritance settings.

Windows Server 2016 has a handy feature called *Resultant Set of Policy (RSoP)* that displays the exact settings that actually apply to individual users, computers, OUs, domains, and sites after inheritance and filtering have taken effect. In the example just described, you could run RSoP on the wpanek account and view a single set of Group Policy settings that represent the settings that apply to that account. In addition, each setting's Properties dialog box displays the GPO from which the setting is derived as well as the order of priority, the filter status, and other useful information, as you will see a bit later.

RSoP actually runs in two modes:

Logging Mode   *Logging* mode displays the actual settings that apply to users and computers, as shown in the example in the preceding paragraph.

Planning Mode   *Planning* mode can be applied to users, computers, OUs, domains, and sites, and you use it before you apply any settings. As its name implies, planning mode is used to plan GPOs.

Additionally, you can run the command-line utility gpresult.exe to get a quick snapshot of the Group Policy settings that apply to a user and/or computer. Let's take a closer look at the two modes and the gpresult.exe command.

RSoP in Logging Mode

RSoP in logging mode can query policy settings only for users and computers. The easiest way to access RSoP in logging mode is through the Active Directory Users and Computers tool, although you can run it as a stand-alone MMC snap-in if you want.

To analyze the policy settings for wpanek from the earlier example, you would right-click the user icon in Active Directory Users and Computers and select All Tasks ➢ Resultant Set of Policy (Logging). The Group Policy Results Wizard appears. The wizard walks you through the steps necessary to view the RSoP for wpanek.

The Computer Selection page, shown in Figure 4.14, requires you to select a computer for which to display settings. Remember that a GPO contains both user and computer settings, so you must choose a computer to which the user is logged on in order to continue with the wizard. If the user has never logged on to a computer, then you must run RSoP in planning mode because there is no logged policy information yet for that user.

FIGURE 4.14   The Computer Selection page of the Group Policy Results Wizard

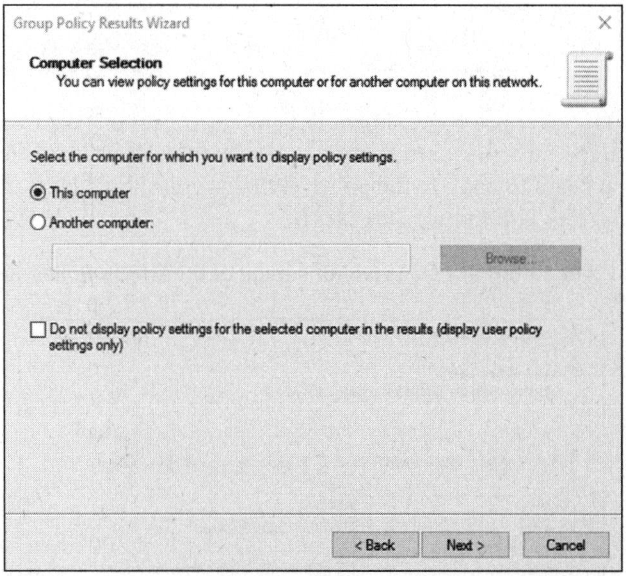

The User Selection page, shown in Figure 4.15, requires you to select a user account to analyze. Because I selected a user from the Active Directory Users and Computers tool, the username is filled in automatically. This page is most useful if you are running RSoP in MMC mode and don't have the luxury of selecting a user contextually.

FIGURE 4.15 The User Selection page of the Group Policy Results Wizard

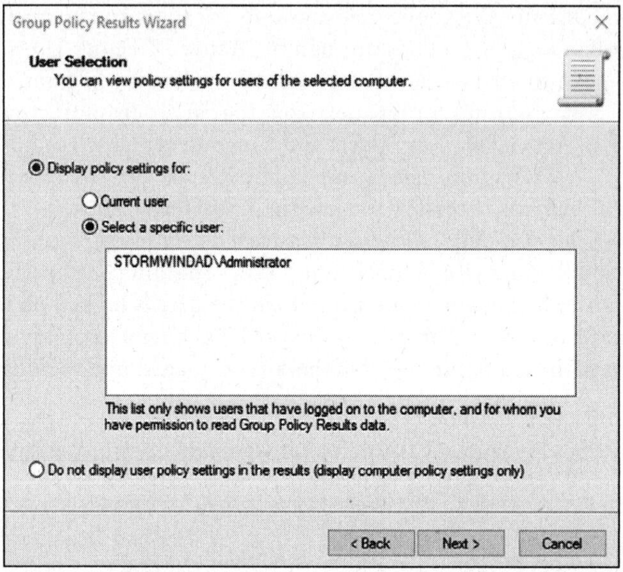

The Summary Of Selections page, shown in Figure 4.16, summarizes your choices and provides an option for gathering extended error information. If you need to make any changes before you begin to analyze the policy settings, you should click the Back button on the Summary screen. Otherwise, click Next.

FIGURE 4.16 The Summary Of Selections page of the Group Policy Results Wizard

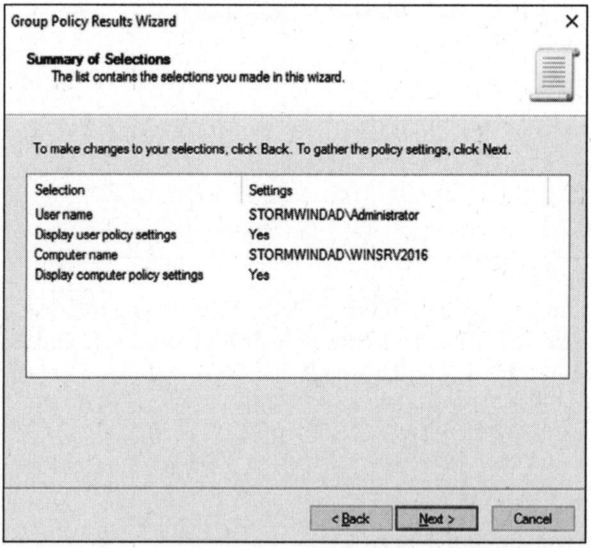

After the wizard completes, you will see the window shown in Figure 4.17. This window displays only the policy settings that apply to the user and computer that you selected in the wizard. You can see these users and computers at the topmost level of the tree.

FIGURE 4.17   The User Selection page for the administrator on computer WinSRV2016

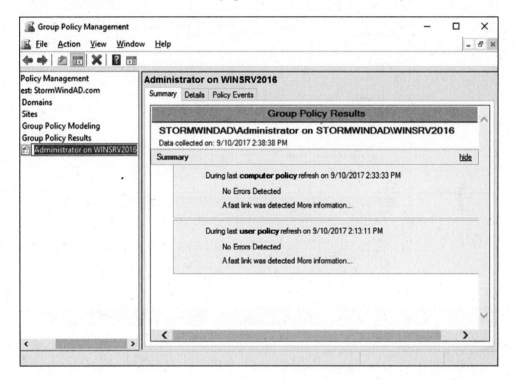

Any warnings or errors appear as a yellow triangle or red X over the applicable icon at the level where the warning or error occurred. To view more information about the warning or error, right-click the icon and select Properties.

You cannot make changes to any of the individual settings because RSoP is a diagnostic tool and not an editor, but you can get more information about settings by clicking a setting and selecting Properties from the context menu.

The Details tab of the user's Properties window, shown in Figure 4.18, displays the actual setting that applies to the user in question based on GPO inheritance.

RSoP in Planning Mode

Running RSoP in planning mode isn't much different from running RSoP in logging mode, but the RSoP Wizard asks for a bit more information than you saw earlier.

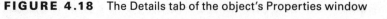

FIGURE 4.18   The Details tab of the object's Properties window

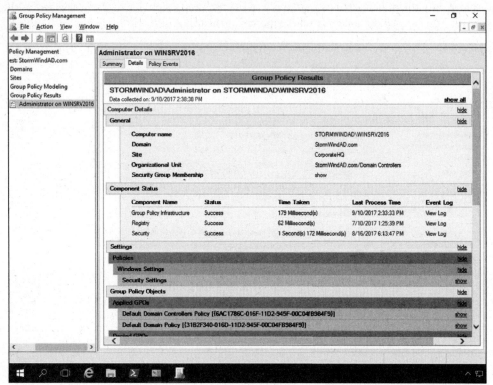

In the former example, wpanek couldn't see the Run option in the Start menu because his user account is affected by the New Hampshire GPO in the San Jose OU. As an administrator, you could plan to move his user account to the North America OU. Before doing so, you could verify his new policy settings by running RSoP in planning mode. Run the RSoP on the user wpanek under the scenario that you've already moved him from the San Jose OU to the North America OU. At this point, you haven't actually moved the user, but you can see what his settings would be if you did.

Using the *gpresult.exe* Command

The command-line utility gpresult.exe is included as part of the RSoP tool. Running the command by itself without any switches returns the following Group Policy information about the local user and computer:

- The name of the domain controller from which the local machine retrieved the policy information
- The date and time at which the policies were applied

- Which policies were applied
- Which policies were filtered out
- Group membership

You can use the switches shown in Table 4.3 to get information for remote users and computers and to enable other options.

TABLE 4.3 gpresult switches

Switch	Description
/S *systemname*	Generates RSoP information for a remote computer name.
/USER *username*	Generates RSoP information for a remote username.
/x /h filename	Generates a report in either XML (/x) or HTML (/h) format. The filename and location is specified by the *filename* parameter.
/V	Specifies verbose mode, which displays more verbose information such as user rights information.
/Z	Specifies an even greater level of verbose information.
/SCOPE MACHINE	Displays maximum information about the computer policies applied to this system.
/SCOPE USER	Displays maximum information about the user policies applied to this system.
>*textfile.txt*	Writes the output to a text file.

Table 4.3 is not a complete list. To see a complete list of the gpresult.exe command, visit Microsoft at www.microsoft.com.

For example, to obtain information about user wpanek in a system called WILLPANEK, you would use the command gpresult/S WILLPANEK/USERwpanek.

Through the use of these techniques, you should be able to track down even the most elusive Group Policy problems. Remember, however, that good troubleshooting skills do not replace planning adequately and maintaining GPO settings!

Using the Group Policy Infrastructure Status Dashboard

In Windows Server 2016, the Group Policy Management MMC also allows you to see the Active Directory Domain Services Infrastructure status. To see the Group Policy Infrastructure Status Dashboard, open the Group Policy Management Console. Click on a GPO and then click the Status Tab. You would then click the Detect Now button to see the Infrastructure Dashboard (see Figure 4.19).

FIGURE 4.19   The Infrastructure Dashboard

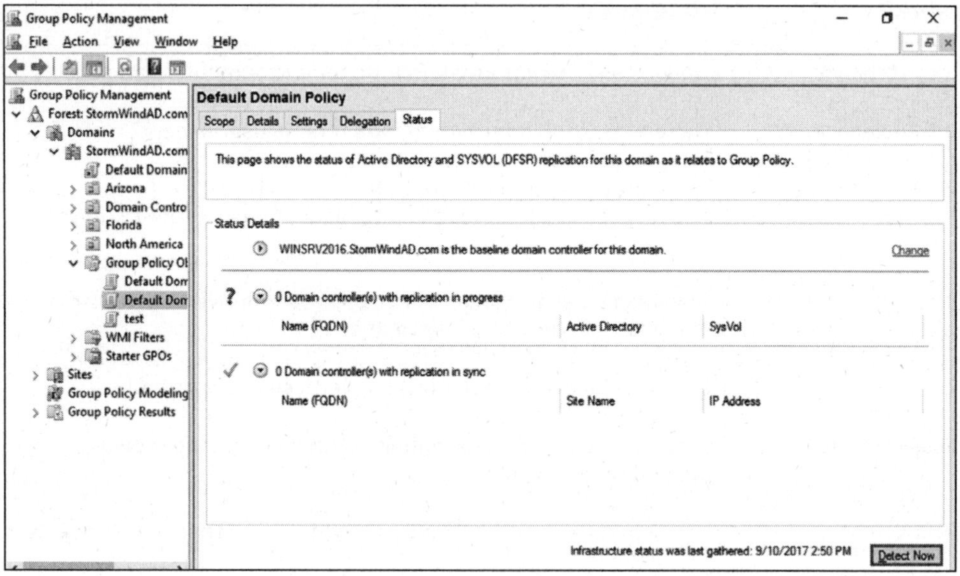

Summary

In this chapter, you examined Active Directory's solution to a common headache for many systems administrators: policy settings. Specifically, I discussed topics that covered Group Policy.

I covered the fundamentals of Group Policy including its fundamental purpose. You can use Group Policy to enforce granular permissions for users in an Active Directory environment. Group policies can restrict and modify the actions allowed for users and computers within the Active Directory environment.

Certain Group Policy settings may apply to users, computers, or both. Computer settings affect all users who access the machines to which the policy applies. User settings affect users regardless of the machines to which they log on.

You learned that you can link Group Policy Objects to Active Directory sites, domains, or OUs. This link determines to which objects the policies apply. GPO links can interact through inheritance and filtering to result in an effective set of policies.

The chapter covered inheritance and how GPOs filter down. I showed you how to use the Enforced option on a GPO issued from a parent and how to block a GPO from a child.

You can also use administrative templates to simplify the creation of GPOs. There are some basic default templates that come with Windows Server 2016.

In addition, administrators can delegate control over GPOs in order to distribute administrative responsibilities. Delegation is an important concept because it allows for distributed administration.

You can also deploy software using GPOs. This feature can save time and increase productivity throughout the entire software management life cycle by automating software installation and removal on client computers. The Windows Installer offers a more robust method for managing installation and removal, and applications that support it can take advantage of new Active Directory features. Make sure you are comfortable using the Windows Installer.

You learned about publishing applications via Active Directory and the difference between publishing and assigning applications. You can assign some applications to users and computers so that they are always available. You can also publish them to users so that the user can install them with minimal effort when required.

You also learned how to prepare for software deployment. Before your users can take advantage of automated software installation, you must set up an installation share and provide the appropriate permissions.

The final portion of the chapter covered the Resultant Set of Policy (RSoP) tool, which you can use in logging mode or planning mode to determine exactly which set of policies applies to users, computers, OUs, domains, and sites.

Exam Essentials

Understand the purpose of Group Policy.   System administrators use Group Policy to enforce granular permissions for users in an Active Directory environment.

Understand user and computer settings.   Certain Group Policy settings may apply to users, computers, or both. Computer settings affect all users that access the machines to which the policy applies. User settings affect users, regardless of which machines they log on to.

Know the interactions between Group Policy Objects and Active Directory.   GPOs can be linked to Active Directory objects. This link determines to which objects the policies apply.

Understand filtering and inheritance interactions between GPOs.   For ease of administration, GPOs can interact via inheritance and filtering. It is important to understand these interactions when you are implementing and troubleshooting Group Policy.

Know how Group Policy settings can affect script policies and network settings.   You can use special sets of GPOs to manage network configuration settings.

Understand how delegation of administration can be used in an Active Directory environment.   Delegation is an important concept because it allows for distributed administration.

Know how to use the Resultant Set of Policy (RSoP) tool to troubleshoot and plan Group Policy.   Windows Server 2016 includes the RSoP feature, which you can run in logging mode or planning mode to determine exactly which set of policies applies to users, computers, OUs, domains, and sites.

Identify common problems with the software life cycle.   IT professionals face many challenges with client applications, including development, deployment, maintenance, and troubleshooting.

Understand the benefits of the Windows Installer.   Using the Windows Installer is an updated way to install applications on Windows-based machines. It offers a more robust method for making the system changes required by applications, and it allows for a cleaner uninstall. Windows Installer–based applications can also take advantage of new Active Directory features.

Understand the difference between publishing and assigning applications.   Some applications can be assigned to users and computers so that they are always available. Applications can be published to users so that the user may install the application with a minimal amount of effort when it is required.

Know how to prepare for software deployment.   Before your users can take advantage of automated software installation, you must set up an installation share and provide the appropriate permissions.

Know how to configure application settings using Active Directory and Group Policy.   Using standard Windows Server 2016 administrative tools, you can create an application policy that meets your requirements. You can use automatic, on-demand installation of applications as well as many other features.

Create application categories to simplify the list of published applications.   It's important to group applications by functionality or the users to whom they apply, especially in organizations that support a large number of programs.

Review Questions

You can find the answers in the Appendix.

1. The process of assigning permissions to set Group Policy for objects within an OU is known as _____.

   A. Promotion

   B. Inheritance

   C. Delegation

   D. Filtering

2. Which of the following statements is true regarding the actions that occur when a software package is removed from a GPO that is linked to an OU?

   A. The application will be automatically uninstalled for all users within the OU.

   B. Current application installations will be unaffected by the change.

   C. The system administrator may determine the effect.

   D. The current user may determine the effect.

3. You are the network administrator for your organization. You are working on creating a new GPO for the sales OU. You want the GPO to take effect immediately. Which command would you use?

   A. GPForce

   B. GPUpdate

   C. GPResult

   D. GPExecute

4. You are the network administrator for your organization. You are working on creating a new GPO for the Marketing OU. You want the GPO to take effect immediately, and you need to use Windows PowerShell. Which PowerShell cmdlet command would you use?

   A. Invoke-GPUpdate

   B. Invoke-GPForce

   C. Invoke-GPResult

   D. Invoke-GPExecute

5. You are the network administrator, and you have decided to set up a GPO with item-level targeting. Which of the following is *not* an option for item-level targeting?

   A. Battery Present Targeting

   B. Computer Name Targeting

   C. CPU Speed Targeting

   D. DVD Present Targeting

6. You are the network administrator for a large organization that uses Windows Server 2012 R2 domain controllers and DNS servers. All of your client machines currently have the Windows XP operating system. You want to be able to have client computers edit the domain-based GPOs by using the ADMX files that are located in the ADMX Central Store. How do you accomplish this task? (Choose all that apply.)

   A. Upgrade your clients to Windows 8.

   B. Upgrade your clients to Windows 7.

   C. Add the client machines to the ADMX edit utility.

   D. In the ADMX store, choose the box Allow All Client Privileges.

7. You work for an organization with a single Windows Server 2016 Active Directory domain. The domain has OUs for Sales, Marketing, Admin, R&D, and Finance. You need the users in the Finance OU only to get Microsoft Office 2016 installed automatically onto their computers. You create a GPO named OfficeApp. What is the next step in getting all of the Finance users Office 2016?

   A. Edit the GPO, and assign the Office application to the user's account. Link the GPO to the Finance OU.

   B. Edit the GPO, and assign the Office application to the user's account. Link the GPO to the domain.

   C. Edit the GPO, and assign the Office application to the computer account. Link the GPO to the domain.

   D. Edit the GPO, and assign the Office application to the computer account. Link the GPO to the Finance OU.

8. You are hired as a consultant to the ABC Company. The owner of the company complains that she continues to have desktop wallpaper that she did not choose. When you speak with the IT team, you find out that a former employee created 20 GPOs and they have not been able to figure out which GPO is changing the owner's desktop wallpaper. How can you resolve this issue?

   A. Run the RSoP utility against all forest computer accounts.

   B. Run the RSoP utility against the owner's computer account.

   C. Run the RSoP utility against the owner's user account.

   D. Run the RSoP utility against all domain computer accounts.

9. You are the network administrator for a large organization that has multiple sites and multiple OUs. You have a site named SalesSite that is for the sales building across the street. In the domain, there is an OU for all salespeople called Sales. You set up a GPO for the Sales-Site, and you need to be sure that it applies to the Sales OU. The Sales OU GPOs cannot override the SalesSite GPO. What do you do?

   A. On the GPO, disable the Block Child Inheritance setting.

   B. On the GPO, set the Enforce setting.

   C. On the GPO, set the priorities to 1.

   D. On the Sales OU, set the Inherit Parent Policy settings.

10. You are the administrator for an organization that has multiple locations. You are running Windows Server 2012 R2, and you have only one domain with multiple OUs set up for each location. One of your locations, Boston, is connected to the main location by a 256 Kbps ISDN line. You configure a GPO to assign a sales application to all computers in the entire domain. You have to be sure that Boston users receive the GPO properly. What should you do?

A. Disable the Slow Link Detection setting in the GPO.

B. Link the GPO to the Boston OU.

C. Change the properties of the GPO to publish the application to the Boston OU.

D. Have the users in Boston run the GPResult/force command.

Chapter

5

Understanding Certificates

THE FOLLOWING 70-742 EXAM OBJECTIVES ARE COVERED IN THIS CHAPTER:

✓ **Install and configure AD CS**

- This objective may include but is not limited to: Install Active Directory Integrated Enterprise Certificate Authority (CA); install offline root and subordinate CAs; install standalone CAs; configure Certificate Revocation List (CRL) distribution points; install and configure Online Responder; implement administrative role separation; configure CA backup and recovery.

✓ **Manage certificates**

- This objective may include but is not limited to: Manage certificate templates; implement and manage certificate deployment, validation, and revocation; manage certificate renewal; manage certificate enrollment and renewal for computers and users using Group Policies; configure and manage key archival and recovery.

In this chapter, I will discuss certificate services and the importance of securing the corporate *public key infrastructure (PKI)* environment. The Windows 2016 PKI implementation resides in Active Directory Certificate Services (AD CS). PKI is the collection of technology, protocols, services, standards, and policies that control the issuing and management of public and private keys using digital certificates, which are the core of PKI. Encryption is used to protect data messages. While certificates provide a certain level of security, they are still vulnerable.

Features of Windows Server 2016 Certificate Services

Active Directory Certificate Services is a server role included in Windows Server 2016. AD CS allows administrators to customize, issue, and manage public key certificates. AD CS issues digital certificates for authentication, encryption and decryption, and signing.

The following are just some of the features regarding Active Directory Certificate Services (AD CS) in Windows Server 2016:

Server Core and Minimal Server Interface Support   You can install and deploy any of the six AD CS role services to any version of Windows Server 2016, including Server Core and Minimal Server Interface. The Minimal Server Interface looks and feels like a Server Core installation with most of the GUI management utilities intact. Windows Server 2016 Minimal Server Interface reduces the attack surface and lowers the footprint by removing components such as File Explorer and Internet Explorer and their supporting libraries.

Site-Aware Certificate Enrollment   Windows 8/8.1/10 and Windows Server 2016 computers default to using certificate authorities within their sites when requesting certificates. However, you must configure site information on the certificate authorities' objects within Active Directory for the site-awareness feature to be worthwhile. Once configured, computers running Windows 8/8.1/10 and Windows Server 2016 request certificates from a certificate authority running in the same site as the computer.

Automatic Certificate Renewal for Non-Domain-Joined Computers   Certificate Enrollment Web Services (CES) allows non-domain-joined computers and computers not directly connected to the corporate network to request and retrieve certificates.

AD CS in Windows Server 2016 includes the ability for these clients to renew certificates automatically for non-domain-joined computers.

Enforcement of Certificate Renewal with the Same Key   In earlier versions of Windows, clients that received certificates from templates that were configured for renewal with the same key had to renew their certificates using the same key, or renewal would fail.

With Windows 8/8.1/10 or Windows Server 2016, you can continue this behavior, or you can configure certificate templates to give higher priority to Trusted Platform Module (TPM)–based KSPs for generating keys. Moreover, using renewal with the same key, administrators can rest assured that the key remains on TPM after renewal.

This feature allows you to enforce renewal with the same key, which can reduce administrative costs (when keys are renewed automatically) and increase key security (when keys are stored using TPM-based KSPs).

Internationalized Domain Names (IDNs)   International languages often contain characters that cannot be represented using ASCII encoding, which limits the function of these languages when enrolling for a certificate. Windows Server 2016 now includes support for international domain names.

Default Security Increased on the Certificate Authority Role Service   Certificate authorities running on Windows Server 2016 include increased RPC (Remote Procedure Call) security. Increased RPC security on the CA requires that all clients must encrypt the RPC communication between themselves and the CA when requesting certificates.

Active Directory Certificate Services Roles

The Active Directory Certificate Services role provides six role services to issue and manage public key certificates in an enterprise environment. These roles are listed in Table 5.1 and described in the following sections.

TABLE 5.1   AD CS roles

Role Service	Description
Certificate Authority (CA)	The CA service includes root and subordinate CAs for issuing certificates to users, computers, and services. This role service also manages certificate validity.
Web Enrollment	This is a web-based interface to enable users to enroll, request, and retrieve certificates as well as retrieve certificate revocation lists from a CA using a web browser.
Online Responder	The Online Responder service retrieves revocation status requests for specific certificates and the status of these certificates, and it returns a signed response with the requested certificate status information.

TABLE 5.1   AD CS roles *(continued)*

Role Service	Description
Network Device Enrollment Service (NDES)	NDES enables routers and other non-domain-joined network devices to acquire certificates.
Certificate Enrollment Policy Web Server (CEP)	CEP enables users and computers to inquire about certificate enrollment policy information.
Certificate Enrollment Web Services (CES)	CES enables users and computers to enroll for certificates with the HTTPS protocol. CEP and CES can be used together to support certificate enrollment for non-domain-joined computers and computers not directly connected to the corporate network.

Planning the Certificate Authority Hierarchy

A *certification authority (CA)* is a trusted server designed to grant certificates to individuals, computers, or organizations to certify the identity and other attributes of the certificate subject.

A CA receives a certificate request, verifies the requester's identity data according to the policy of the CA, and uses its private key to apply its digital signature to the certificate. The CA issues the certificate to the subject of the certificate as a security credential within a PKI environment. A CA is also responsible for revoking certificates and publishing a *certificate revocation list (CRL)*.

A CA can be a third-party issuer, such as VeriSign, or you can create your own CA by installing Active Directory Certificate Services. Every CA also has a certificate confirming its identity, issued by another trusted CA or root CAs.

Cryptography

The Cryptography options for a certificate authority provide increased deployment flexibility to those with a more advanced understanding of cryptography. You can implement cryptographic options by using cryptographic service providers (CSPs) or key storage providers (KSPs).

CSPs are hardware and software components of Windows operating systems that provide generic cryptographic functions. CSPs can provide a variety of encryption and signature algorithms. Key storage providers can provide strong key protection on computers running Windows Server 2012/2016, Windows Server 2008/2008 R2, Windows Vista, Windows 7, Windows 8/8.1 or Windows 10. Figure 5.1 shows some of the Cryptography options in the AD CS installation.

FIGURE 5.1 Cryptography for CA screen

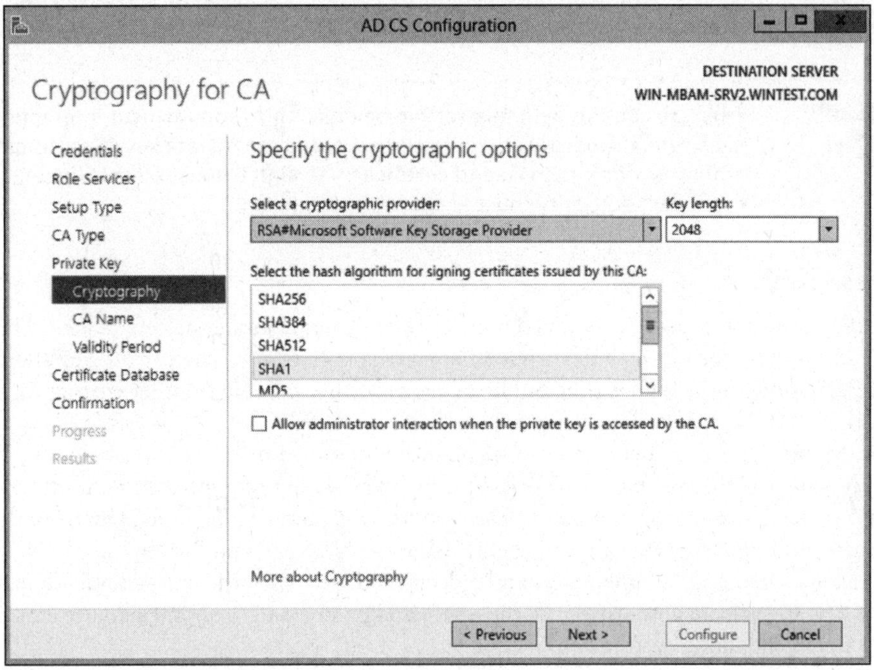

AD CS Configuration

Cryptography for CA

DESTINATION SERVER
WIN-MBAM-SRV2.WINTEST.COM

Credentials
Role Services
Setup Type
CA Type
Private Key
  Cryptography
  CA Name
  Validity Period
Certificate Database
Confirmation
Progress
Results

Specify the cryptographic options

Select a cryptographic provider:

RSA#Microsoft Software Key Storage Provider

Key length:

2048

Select the hash algorithm for signing certificates issued by this CA:

SHA256
SHA384
SHA512
SHA1
MD5

☐ Allow administrator interaction when the private key is accessed by the CA.

More about Cryptography

< Previous   Next >   Configure   Cancel

Here are the options:

Select a Cryptographic Provider   Windows Server 2016 provides many CSPs and KSPs, and you can install additional CSPs or KSPs provided by third parties. In Windows Server 2016, the algorithm name is listed in the provider list. All providers with a number sign (#) in the name are cryptography next-generation (CNG) providers. CNG providers can support multiple asymmetric algorithms. CSPs implement only a single algorithm.

Key Length   Each CSP and KSP supports different character lengths for cryptographic keys. Configuring a longer key length hardens against an attack by a hacker to decrypt the key and also degrades the performance of cryptographic operations.

Select The Hash Algorithm For Signing Certificates Used By This CA   The CA uses hash algorithms to sign CA certificates and issues certificates to ensure that an external identity has not tampered with a certificate. Each CSP can support different hash algorithms.

Make sure that your applications, your devices, and all operating systems that may request certificates from this certificate authority support the selected hash algorithm.

Allow Administrator Interaction When The Private Key Is Accessed By The CA   Use this option to help secure the CA and its private key by requiring an administrator to enter a password before every cryptographic operation.

> Exercise caution with this setting because this requires user interaction each time the certificate authority accesses the private key. A certificate authority signs each issued certificate. To sign the issued certificate, the certificate authority must access the private key.

Private Key

A certificate authority uses its assigned certificate to generate and issue certificates. The certificate used by the CA includes a public key and a private key. The private key should be available only to the owner. The public key is publicly available to other entities on the network.

For example, a user's public key can be published within a certificate in a folder so that it is accessible to other people in the organization. The sender of a message can retrieve the user's certificate from Active Directory Domain Services, obtain the public key from the certificate, and then encrypt the message by using the recipient's public key.

Data encrypted with a public key can be decrypted only with the mathematically paired private key. Certificate authorities use their private key to create a digital signature in the certificate when issuing certificates.

Enterprise Certificate Authorities

Enterprise certificate authorities (CAs) publish certificates and CRLs to Active Directory. Enterprise CAs access domain data stored in Active Directory. Enterprise CAs engage certificate templates when issuing certificates. The enterprise CA uses default configuration data in the certificate template to create a certificate with the appropriate attributes for that certificate type.

If you want to enable automatic certificate approval and automatic user certificate enrollment, use enterprise CAs to issue certificates. These features are available only when the CA infrastructure is integrated with Active Directory. Additionally, only enterprise CAs can issue certificates that enable smart card logon because this process requires the CA to map the user account in Active Directory to the smart card certificates.

A *root CA*, sometimes called a *root authority*, is the most trusted CA type in an organization's PKI. The root CA is the only CA that signs its own certificate. The physical security and the certificate issuance policy of a root CA should be tightly reinforced. If the root CA is compromised or if it issues a certificate to an unauthorized identity, any certificate-based security in your organization is compromised by the exposed private key. The best practice is to deploy a second PKI tier to issue certificates from other CAs, called *subordinate CAs* (see Figure 5.2).

FIGURE 5.2 Two-tier PKI hierarchy model

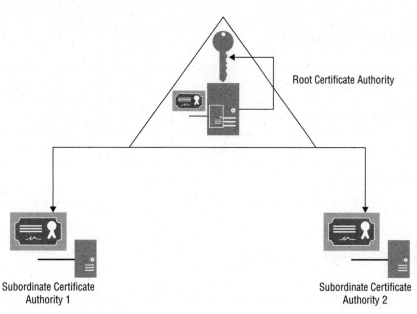

Root Certificate Authority

Subordinate Certificate
Authority 1

Subordinate Certificate
Authority 2

A *subordinate CA* is one that has received its signing certificate by a root CA, third-party CA, or stand-alone CA in your organization. Subordinate CAs normally issue certificates for specific purposes, such as secure email, SSL, Wireless 801.x security, or smart card authentication. Subordinate CAs can also issue certificates to other, more subordinate CAs. A root CA, the subordinate CAs certified by the root, and subordinate CAs certified by other subordinate CAs form a certification hierarchy.

Stand-alone certificate authorities are not integrated into Active Directory and do not support certificate templates. If you deploy stand-alone CAs, you must include all the information about the requested certificate type in the certificate request. By default, all submitted certificate requests to a stand-alone CA are placed in a pending queue, awaiting a CA administrator's approval. Stand-alone CAs can issue certificates automatically upon request, but this is not recommended because the requests are not authenticated.

Because stand-alone CAs are not Active Directory integrated, a stand-alone CA would seem like a less appropriate choice for an enterprise. However, stand-alone root CAs offer a layer of protection when a powered-down stand-alone CA is less likely to be compromised and does not have a footprint in Active Directory. More organizations are deploying *offline stand-alone root CAs* that are brought online only temporarily for re-issuing signing certificates to subordinate CAs. Some organizations permanently keep the offline stand-alone root CA disconnected from the network and distribute signing certificates only via removable media such as CDs, DVDs, or USB flash drives. Offline root CAs have the following characteristics:

- Deployed as a stand-alone root CA
- Deployed on a non-domain-joined server to avoid being offline or powered down for long periods without requiring computer password synchronizations

⊕ **Real World Scenario**

Protect the Offline Root CA

Best practice strongly recommends you securely store and back up the offline standalone root CA. A large Medical center implemented their offline stand-alone root CA solution by installing their root CA on a laptop. They routinely kept the laptop in the datacenter until a new administrator discovered and returned laptop to the help desk for repurposing. Needless to say, the laptop was re-imaged, and the entire PKI infrastructure was wiped out. No one was aware until the subordinate CA's certificate had expired a year later and certificates could no longer be issued. You can avoid this catastrophic scenario by securely storing and backing up the offline stand-alone CA.

Two-Tier and Three-Tier Models

It's acceptable for a single enterprise to have multiple PKIs. Multiple PKIs result in one root CA for each PKI and possibly multiple subordinate CAs that chain to their respective roots.

Organizations also may choose a third-tier CA hierarchy model, which involves adding a CA policy server. CA policy servers are designed to implement specific certificate policies that can include certificate life cycle, encryption type, key length, and some approval workflow.

Validity Period

All certificates issued by a certification authority have a validity period. The *validity period* is a time range that specifies how long PKI clients can accept the certificate as an authoritative credential based on the identity stated in the subject of the certificate. This assertion presumes the certificate is not revoked before the validity period ends and the issuing CA remains trusted. The validity period limits the time in which an issued certificate is exposed to the possibility of being compromised.

All CAs have an expiration date based on its CA certificate's validity ending period. This rule affects the CA's ability to issue certificates and not the validity period of its CA certificate. Because of this rule, organizations must plan for the renewal of every certificate issued to a CA in the certification hierarchy to ensure the existing trust chains and to extend the lifetimes of CAs.

Active Directory Certificate Services enforces a rule that a CA never issues a certificate past the expiration date of its own certificate. Because of this behavior, when a CA's certificate reaches the end of its validity period, all certificates issued by the CA will also expire. Certificates issued by the now-expired CA will not be honored as valid security credentials.

Active Directory Certificate Services allows for the maximum validity periods shown in Table 5.2, which are based on the type of certificate. You configure these validity periods using certificate templates.

TABLE 5.2   AD CS maximum validity periods

Certificate Type	Maximum Validity Period
Root certificate authority	Determined during CA deployment
Subordinate CA Internet Protocol Security Enrollment agent Domain controller	Up to five years, but never more than the root CA's or the issuing CA's validity period
All other certificates	One year, but never more than the root CA's or issuing CA's validity period

Certificate Validation

PKI trust requires a certificate to be validated for both its expiration and its overall chain of trust. When a certificate user leaves the company, you will want to make sure that no one can use that certificate for authentication and revoke the certificate. Revocation checking is one of the key components of PKI.

Certificate revocation uses certificate revocation lists. CRLs contain a list of certificates that are no longer valid, and the CRL can become large. To solve this, you can access a delta CRL that contains changes or new revocations. So when discussing CRLs, there are two main types:

Base CRLs   A Base CRL is a CRL that contains all non-expired revoked certificates.

Delta CRLs   A Delta CRL is a CRL that contains all non-expired certificates that have been revoked since the last base CRL was published.

CRLs are accessed through *CRL distribution points (CDPs)*, which are part of a CA role in Windows Server 2016. HTTP, FTP, LDAP, or file-based addresses may be used as URLs. Only newly issued certificates will recognize new changes in the CRL URL; old certificates will use the old URL for revocation list operations.

When setting up the CRL, you can set a time interval for how often the servers check the CRL. This is referred to as the CRL publication interval or Delta CRL publication interval. So if you want to have your certificate servers check the CRL more or less frequently, set the publication interval.

Online Responders

When a new certificate is issued, the computer queries the issuing CA to find out whether the certificate has been revoked. Traditionally, certificate revocation checking can be done by retrieving certificate revocation lists that are published in Lightweight Directory Access Protocol (LDAP) or Hypertext Transfer Protocol (HTTP) or by using a newer HTTP method named the Online Certificate Status Protocol (OCSP).

OCSP is a lightweight HTTP protocol that responds faster and more efficiently than downloading a traditional CRL. An *online responder* is a trusted server that receives and responds to individual client requests for the status of a certificate. An OCSP responder retrieves CRLs and provides digitally signed real-time certificate revocation status responses to clients based on a given certificate authority's CRL. The amount of data retrieved per request remains constant regardless of the number of revoked certificates.

Online responders process certificate status requests more efficiently than direct access to CRLs in several scenarios (http://technet.microsoft.com/en-us/library/cc725958.aspx):

- When clients have slow VPN connections or do not have the high-speed connections required to download large CRLs

- When network utilization peaks because revocation-checking activity is high, such as when large numbers of users log on or send signed email simultaneously

- When revocation data for certificates is needed from a non-Microsoft certification authority

- When revocation data is needed to verify individual certificate status requests rather than all revoked or suspended certificates

Installing AD CS

Server Manager provides a graphical user interface to install Active Directory Certificate Services on local and remote computers running Windows Server 2016. The Remote Server Administration Tools for Windows Server 2016 also includes Server Manager, which allows you to run Server Manager on a computer running Windows 8/8.1. In Exercise 5.1, you'll install an AD CS role on the local computer using Server Manager.

EXERCISE 5.1

Installing AD CS Through Server Manager

1. Start Server Manager.

2. Click Manage and click Add Roles And Features.

3. The Add Roles And Features Wizard shows the Before You Begin screen. Click Next.

4. Click Role-Based Or Feature-Based Installation on the Select Installation Type screen. Click Next.

5. Click the server on which you want to install Active Directory Certificate Services from the Server Pool list on the Select Destination Server screen. Click Next.

6. Select the Active Directory Certificate Services check box on the Select Server Roles screen.

   Server Manager prompts you to add more features associated with this role, such as management tools. Leave the default selections. Click Add Features to close the dialog. Click Next on the Select Server Roles screen.

7. Click Next on the Select Features screen.

8. Server Manager displays the Active Directory Certificate Services screen. This screen provides a simple role introduction and noteworthy information, such as that the name of the certificate authority cannot be changed. Click Next.

9. From the Select Role Services screen, select the check boxes next to the AD CS role services you want to install on the computer. Click Next.

10. Read the Confirm Installation Selections screen. This screen provides a list of roles, role services, and features that the current installation prepares on the computer. Click Install to start the installation.

Installation Using Windows PowerShell

A major benefit gained from basing Windows Server 2016's Server Manager on Windows PowerShell is consistency of installation. Server Manager relies on its Windows PowerShell foundation as the underlying engine responsible for installing any of the Active Directory Certificate Services role services. However, you cannot use Server Manager to install roles and features on a Windows Server 2016 core installation.

The Server Manager module for Windows PowerShell provides cmdlets to install, view, and remove features and roles included in Windows Server 2016. You can use these cmdlets on any installation of Windows Server 2016 because it provides Windows PowerShell in all installation types. Also, these cmdlets can install, view, and uninstall Active Directory Certificate Services role services from remote computers running Windows Server 2016.

To view the installation state of Active Directory Certificate Services using Windows PowerShell, follow these steps:

1. Open an elevated Windows PowerShell console. (On Server Core installations, type **PowerShell** in the command console.)

2. In the Windows PowerShell console, type the following command and press Enter:

   ```
   Get-WindowsFeature *adcs-cert*
   ```

The Windows PowerShell cmdlet outputs three columns of information: Display Name, Name, and Install State. The Display Name column is a user-friendly name that describes the feature or service role's use. The Name column represents the name of the component. You use this name with the `Install-WindowsFeature` and `Remove-WindowsFeature` cmdlets. Use the Install State column to determine the installation state of the role or service role.

Typically, the Install State column shows one of three install states: Removed, Available, and Installed. The Removed install state designates that its associated role or feature is not included in the current installation of Windows. You cannot install the associated role or feature without the installation media or Internet connectivity to Windows Update if the feature or role is removed. The Available installation state indicates that the role or feature is staged in the current installation of Windows; however, it is currently not installed. The Installed installation state indicates that the role or feature is installed on the current installation of the computer and is ready, or it has been deployed or configured.

The Active Directory Certificate Services entry from the cmdlet's output represents the parent role. Six child role services appear underneath the parent role. A lowercase *x* appears between the opening and closing square brackets in the parent role if any of the six child role services are installed. The cmdlet also places a lowercase *x* between the opening and closing square brackets for any installed child role service. You should interpret entries without a lowercase *x* between the opening and closing square brackets as not installed. Check the install state to determine whether the role or role service is staged on your installation of Windows.

To install Active Directory Certificate Services using Windows PowerShell, follow these steps:

1. Open an elevated Windows PowerShell console.

2. Use the `Get-WindowsFeature` cmdlet to ensure that the Active Directory Certificate Services role's installation state is Available.

3. In the Windows PowerShell console, type the following command and press Enter:

   ```
   Install-WindowsFeature adcs-cert-authority -IncludeManagementTools
   ```

4. Use the `Get-WindowsFeature` cmdlet to verify the installation.

The preceding command instructs the Server Manager module of Windows PowerShell to take the staged binaries for the Certificate Authority role service and install them to the current computer.

It's important to remember the `-IncludeManagementTools` argument when installing a feature using Windows PowerShell. The Server Manager module for Windows PowerShell does not install a feature or role management tool by default. The `Install-WindowsFeature` cmdlet does not install the role management tool without this argument. The Server Manager GUI automatically selects installing the role management tool for you, and it gives you a choice of not to install it before completing the installation.

You can install any of the other child role services using the `Install-WindowsFeature` cmdlet simply by replacing the `adcs-cert-authority` argument with the associated name of the child role service. The following example installs the Active Directory Certificate Services Web Enrollment role service:

```
Install-WindowsFeature adcs-web-enrollment -IncludeManagementTools
```

> **NOTE** The role and feature installation experience is consistent on Windows Server 2016 using the Server Manager module for Windows PowerShell. You can use the same syntax to install a feature or role listed using `Get-WindowsFeature`.

Configuring Active Directory Certificate Services

You begin the Active Directory Certificate Services deployment by starting the AD CS Configuration Wizard (Exercise 5.2). To start the wizard, click the Configure Active Directory Certificate Services On The Destination Server link shown in the Action Flag dialog. The wizard shows the current destination for the role deployment in the Destination Server portion of the screen.

EXERCISE 5.2

Configuring AD CS Through Server Manager

1. After the AD CS installation is successful, click the Configure Active Directory Certificate Services On The Destination Server link.

2. The Credentials screen of the AD CS Configuration Wizard displays the required credentials to perform specific AD CS role services deployment. The wizard shows your current credentials in the Credentials portion of the screen. Click Change if your current credentials do not match the credentials needed for the current role service deployment. Otherwise, continue by clicking Next.

3. Select the check boxes for the Certification Authority and Online Responder role services.

4. The Setup Type screen of the AD CS Configuration Wizard shows the two types of certificate authorities you can configure with Active Directory Certificate Services: enterprise or stand-alone. An enterprise certificate authority must run on domain-joined computers and typically remains online to issue certificates or certificate policies. Select Enterprise and click Next.

5. In the Setup Type dialog box, select Enterprise CA and click Next.

6. In the CA Type dialog box, click Root CA and click Next.

EXERCISE 5.2 *(continued)*

7. In the Private Key dialog box, verify that Create A New Private Key is selected and click Next.

8. Select the RSA# Microsoft Software Key Storage Provider.

9. Windows Server 2012 includes a number of CSPs and KSPs, and you can install additional CSPs or KSPs provided by third parties. In Windows Server 2016, the provider list includes the name of the algorithm. All providers with a number sign (#) in the name are CNG providers. CNG providers can support multiple asymmetric algorithms. CSPs implement only a single algorithm.

10. Select a key length of 2048.

11. Each CSP and KSP supports different character lengths for cryptographic keys. Configuring a longer key length can enhance security by making it more difficult for a hacker or disgruntled employee to decrypt the key, but it can also slow down the performance of cryptographic operations.

12. Select the SHA1 hash algorithm and click Next.

13. Enter a name for the root CA server and click Next.

14. In the Certificate Request dialog box, verify that Save A Certificate Request To File On The Target Machine is selected and click Next.

15. In the CA Database dialog box, verify the location for the log files in the Certificate Database Log Location box and click Next.

16. In the Confirmation dialog box, click Configure.

17. In the Results dialog box, click Close.

The CA uses hash algorithms to sign CA certificates and issues certificates to ensure that an external identity has not tampered with a certificate. Each CSP can support different hash algorithms. Make sure your applications, devices, and all operating systems that may request certificates from this certificate authority support the selected hash algorithm.

Use the Create A New Private Key option when creating or reinstalling a certificate authority.

Certificate Authority Name

Names for CAs cannot exceed 64 characters in length. You can create a name by using any Unicode character, but you might want the ANSI character set if interoperability is a concern.

In Active Directory Domain Services (AD DS), the name you specify when you configure a server as a CA (Figure 5.3) becomes the common name of the CA, and this name is reflected in every certificate the CA issues. Because of this behavior, it is important that you do not use the fully qualified domain name (FQDN) for the common name of the CA. Hackers can acquire a copy of a certificate and use the FQDN of the CA to compromise security.

FIGURE 5.3   Specifying the name of the CA

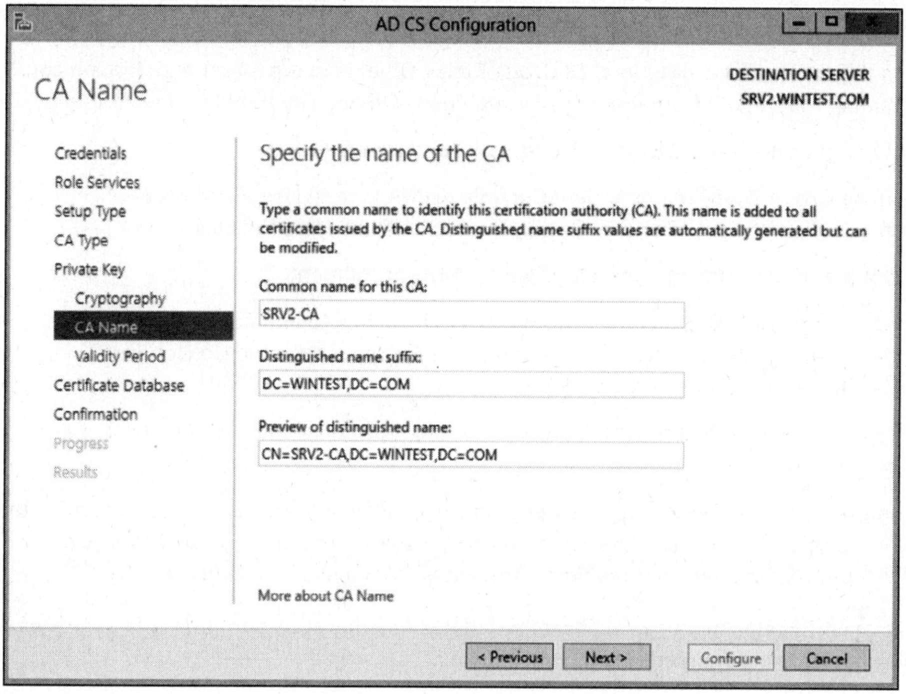

The CA name does not have to be the computer's name. Changing the name after installing Active Directory Certificate Services (AD CS) will invalidate every certificate issued by the CA.

Group Policy Certificate Auto-Enrollment

Many certificates can be distributed without the client interaction. These can include most types of certificates issued to computers and services as well as many certificates issued to users.

To enroll clients automatically for certificates in a domain environment, you must do the following:

- Configure a certificate template with auto-enroll permissions
- Configure an auto-enrollment policy for the domain

Membership in Domain Admins or Enterprise Admins, or equivalent, is the minimum required to complete this procedure. In Exercise 5.3 we are going to configure a group policy to support the auto-enrollment feature.

EXERCISE 5.3

Configure an Auto-Enrollment Group Policy for a Domain

1. On a domain controller running Windows Server 2016, click Start ➢ Administrative Tools ➢ Group Policy Management.

2. In the console tree, double-click Group Policy Objects in the forest and domain containing the Default Domain Policy Group Policy Object (GPO) that you want to edit.

3. Right-click the Default Domain Policy GPO and click Edit.

4. In the Group Policy Management Console (GPMC), go to User Configuration ➢ Windows Settings ➢ Security Settings and click Public Key Policies.

5. Double-click Certificate Services Client – Auto-Enrollment.

6. Select the Enroll Certificates Automatically check box to enable auto-enrollment. If you want to block auto-enrollment from occurring, select the Do Not Enroll Certificates Automatically check box.

7. If you are enabling certificate auto-enrollment, you can select the following check boxes:

"Renew expired certificates, update pending certificates, and remove revoked certificates enables auto-enrollment for certificate renewal, issuance of pending certificate requests, and the automatic removal of revoked certificates from a user's certificate store."

"Update certificates that use certificate templates enables auto-enrollment for issuance of certificates that supersede issued certificates."

8. Click OK to accept your changes.

Key-Based Renewal for Non-Domain-Joined Computers

Windows Server 2016 combines automatic certificate renewal with AD CS Certificate Enrollment Web Services to enable non-domain-joined computers to renew their certificates automatically before they expire like Internet-facing web servers.

Many organizations and service providers maintain servers that require SSL certificates. These servers are not typically joined to the same domain as an issuing certificate authority, and they do not have identity records or accounts in the organization's Active Directory. This means they cannot benefit from today's automatic certificate renewal, which is based on secured certificate templates in Active Directory. As a result, these organizations manage and renew SSL certificates manually, a time-intensive and error-prone process. Neglecting to renew a single SSL certificate can cause a massive and costly system outage.

Currently, Certificate Enrollment Web Services supports three types of server-side authentication modes:

- Windows integrated (Kerberos)
- Certificate-based
- Username and password

These authentication mode options, however, are not viable choices when the client is not joined to a domain and the enterprise certificate authority makes authorization decisions using templates that are based on the Active Directory group membership of the requestor.

Consider the following authentication options for automatic renewal:

Windows Integrated   This authentication option is not suitable for auto renewal because the two domains to which the certificate authority and the requesting server belong do not have a trust relationship between them or the requesting server is not joined to any domain.

Certificate-Based   The initially enrolled server certificate is not suitable for authentication because it contains no identity information within it that can be mapped to a directory account object.

Username And Password   Usernames and passwords can be cached within the system's identity vault and used for authentication to the enrollment server. However, passwords usually have shorter lifetimes than server SSL certificates. (Both default and recommended settings for passwords are shorter than the default and recommended certificate lifetime.) Thus, by the time renewal happens, the password will likely have changed.

Anonymous   This authentication option is not suitable since MS CEP and CES do not support this option, making automatic renewal impossible for these targeted server systems.

Enforcement of Certificate Renewal with Same Key

Windows 8/8.1/10 and Windows Server 2016 provide an efficient mechanism to increase the security of renewing hardware-based certificates. This is accomplished by enforcing the certificate renewal to occur for the same key. This guarantees the same assurance level for the key throughout its life cycle. Additionally, Windows Server 2016's Certificate Template Management Console supports CSP/KSP ordering that clients may choose for generating a private/public key pair. This way, you can give a higher priority to hardware-based keys (Trusted Platform Module or smart card) over software-based keys.

Cryptographic Service Provider/Key Service Provider Ordering

Another problem addressed in Windows Server 2016 is GUI support for CSP/KSP ordering. With increased interest in the deployment of Trusted Platform Module in enterprise scenarios, providing a mechanism for prioritizing TPM-based keys over other types of keys has become a "must-have" for certificate enrollment based on certificate templates. This is important from the client perspective when enrolling for a non-exportable key. You want to have assurance that the non-exportable keys are generated in the TPM and are not software based (assuming that no malware is involved and the user is not malicious).

Currently this prioritization is captured as an attribute of a certificate template object in Active Directory; however, a user interface does not exist for modifying such properties, and Microsoft does not support it. Windows Server 2016's Certificate Template Management Console fully supports CSP/KSP ordering.

Managing Certificate Authority: Certificate Templates Overview

Enterprise certificate authorities issue certificates from certificate templates, a preconfigured list of certificate settings. This allows administrators to enroll users and computers for certificates without the need to create complex certificate requests. Windows Server 2016 AD CS does include a minor user interface change and the Active Directory Certificate Services Administration module for Windows PowerShell. The new Compatibility tab in the Certificate Templates Management Console lets you identify incompatible certificate template settings between different versions of Windows-based certificate recipients and the certificate authority. The AD CS Administration module for Windows PowerShell lets you manage common AD CS management tasks using Windows PowerShell.

Certificate Template Compatibility

Multiple versions of certificate templates have been released for the family of Windows Server products. New certificate template versions include settings that control the features relevant to each new certificate authority. However, not all features are compatible with all certificate authorities and certificate requests. Therefore, it can be difficult to determine which certificate templates are compatible with different versions of certificate authorities and different Windows-based certificate requestors.

Version 2 certificate templates are customizable certificate templates that are supported with Windows Server 2008 Enterprise CAs or Windows Server 2003 Enterprise edition CAs. Version 2 certificate templates enable advanced CA features, such as key archiving and recovery and certificate auto-enrollment.

> To use version 2 templates, Active Directory must be upgraded to support Windows Server 2008 or Windows Server 2003 schema changes. Standard editions of Windows Server 2008 and Windows Server 2003 support only version 1 certificate templates, which are not customizable and do not support key archival or automatic enrollment.

Version 3 certificate templates were new to Windows Server 2008. Version 3 certificate templates function similarly to version 2 templates, and they support new Active Directory Certificate Services features available in Windows Server 2008. These features include CNG, which introduces support for Suite B cryptographic algorithms such as elliptic curve cryptography (ECC).

The Windows Server 2016 Certificate Template Management Console includes a new certificate template Compatibility tab that lets you select the Windows operating system of the certificate authority and the Windows operating system of the certificate recipient.

The Certificate Template Management Console determines incompatible settings between the selections and shows a list of template settings that the management console adds or removes from template selection.

You view the compatibility table from the Certificate Template Management Console. You can launch the Certificate Template Management Console by typing **certtmpl.msc** in the Run dialog or on the Start screen and pressing Enter.

Creating Certificate Templates

When creating a new certificate template, you copy an existing template similar to the configuration defaults needed for your particular application. It is best to review the default list of certificate templates and find the template that best matches your application's requirements.

The Request Handling tab (Figure 5.4) in the Certificate Templates Management console has the Renew With Same Key Certificate Template Configuration option. This certificate template option becomes visible in the user interface when you configure the Certification Authority and the Certificate Recipient options to Windows Server 2016 and Windows 8/8.1, Windows 10 respectively.

FIGURE 5.4   Request Handling tab of the Certificate Templates Management console

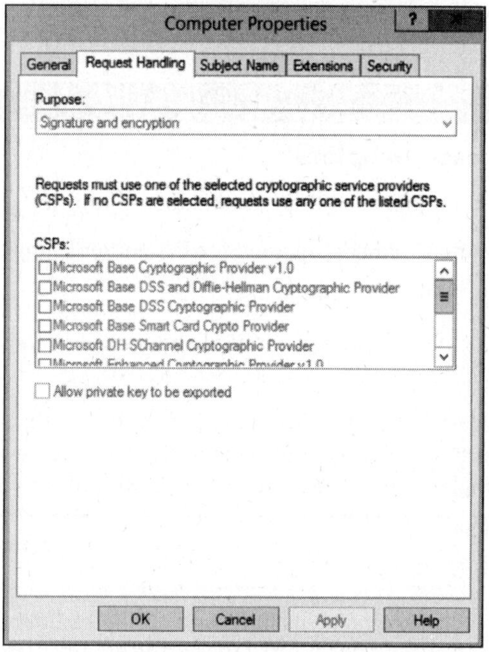

You will create an example certificate template in Exercise 5.4.

EXERCISE 5.4

Creating a Certificate Template

1. Start the Certificate Templates snap-in, read through the certificate templates titles, and choose the Computer Template.

2. In the details pane, right-click an existing certificate and click Duplicate Template.

3. Choose to duplicate the template as a Windows Server 2008–based template.

4. On the General tab, enter the template display name and the template name and click OK.

5. Define any additional attributes for the newly created certificate template.

Publishing the Certificate Template

After creating a certificate template and applying the proper security permissions, you will want to deploy the new certificate template by publishing to the Active Directory where it can be shared with other Enterprise CAs. The following exercise will take us through the steps to perform the task.

In Exercise 5.5, you will deploy a certificate template.

EXERCISE 5.5

Publishing a Certificate Template

1. In Server Manager, click Tools and then Certification Authority.

2. In the Certification Authority MMC, expand the CA Server Name.

3. Select the Certificate Templates container.

4. Right-click the Certificate Templates container and then click New Certificate Template To Issue.

5. In the Enable Certificate Templates dialog box, select the certificate template or templates that you want the CA server to issue and click OK. The newly selected certificate template or templates should appear in the details pane on the right.

If a certificate template is not displayed in the Enable Certificate Templates dialog box, the replication of the certificate template may not have finished on all domain controllers in the forest.

Certificate Revocation

Revocation renders a certificate invalid and lists the revoked certificate in the CRL. You can revoke a certificate in the Certificate Authority snap-in with the steps shown in Exercise 5.6.

Revoking a Certificate

1. Start the Certification Authority snap-in.

2. In the console tree, click the issuing certificate container.

3. In the right pane, select and right-click the target certificate.

4. Select All Tasks.

5. Select Revoke Certificate.

6. In the Certificate Revocation dialog box, you must select one of the following reason codes:

   Unspecified: Default reason code. This lacks information during future audits.

   Key Compromise: Select this when you think the key has been compromised.

   CA Compromise: Select this when you suspect the issuing CA of being compromised.

   Change of Affiliation: Select this when the person has exited the organization or changed roles.

   Superseded: Select this when issuing a new certificate to replace an existing certificate.

   Cease of Operation: Select this when the issuing device or server has been decommissioned.

   Certificate Hold: Select this to suspend an existing certificate temporarily.

7. Click OK.

Display the Current Site Name for Certificate Authorities

Enter the following command to display current site names for one or more certificate authorities:

```
Certutil -ping caDnsName, [caDnsName, ...]
```

The command utilizes the DsGetSiteName API on each named certificate authority. After determining the site for all the certificate authorities, certutil.exe uses the DsQuerySitesByCost API to obtain the client's site costs for all the name certificate authorities.

CA Policy Auditing

PKI auditing logging is not enabled on the Windows 2016 CA server by default. After the auditing is enabled, all the events will be logged in the Security log.

Exercise 5.7 covers the steps that the CA administrator must complete to enable auditing.

EXERCISE 5.7

Configuring CA Policy Auditing

1. Enable Object Access/Success Auditing in the CA machine's local security policy:

   a. Start `mmc.exe`.

   b. Add the snap-in Group Policy Object Editor and select the Local Computer GPO.

   c. Under the path `Computer Configuration\Windows Settings\ Security Settings\Local Policies\Audit Policy`, enable success auditing for Object Access.

2. Enable auditing on the CA:

   a. Start the CA Management snap-in.

   b. Open the CA Properties dialog.

   c. On the Auditing tab, check the Change CA Configuration and Change CA Security Settings options.

Backing Up the Certificate Authority Server

The AD CS certificate authority deployment creates a database. The CA records certificates issued by the CA, private keys archived by the CA, revoked certificates, and all certificate requests to the database regardless of issuance status.

Configure the database location on an NTFS partition on the server's disk drives to provide the best security possible for the database file. Specify the location for the database in the Certificate Database Location box. By default, the wizard configured the database location to `systemroot\system32\certlog`. The name of the database file uses the CA's name, with an `.edb` extension.

The certificate database uses a transaction log to ensure the integrity of the database. The CA records its transactions in its configured log files. The CA then commits each transaction from the log file into the database. The CA then updates the last committed transaction in the database, and the process continues.

The CA database logs are selected when restoring the CA from a backup. If a CA is restored from a backup that is one month old, then the CA database can be updated with more recent activity recorded in the log to restore the database to its most current state.

When you back up a CA, the existing certificate database logs are truncated in size because they are no longer needed to restore the certificate database to its most current state.

The recommended method to back up a CA is to leverage the native Backup utility (included with the operating system) to back up the entire server, including the system state, which contains the CA's data. However, the Certificate Authority snap-in can be used to back up and restore the CA, but this backup method is intended only in cases where you want to migrate CA data to different server hardware. The public key and private key are backed up or restored using the PKCS #12 PFX format.

The Backup Or Restore Wizard will ask you to supply a password when backing up the public and private keys and CA certificates. This password will be needed to restore the CA.

Start the Certificate Authority snap-in for Exercise 5.8, which explains how to back up a CA.

EXERCISE 5.8

Backing Up the Certificate Authority Server

1. Start the Certification Authority MMC.

2. In the left pane, right-click the name of the server; then choose All Tasks ➢ Back Up CA.

3. When the Certification Authority Backup Wizard appears, click Next.

4. At the Items To Back Up screen, click the Private Key And CA Certificate check box. Next to the Back Up To This Location field, click the Browse button. Choose a location for your backup and click OK. Click Next.

5. At the Select A Password screen, enter and confirm a password. For this exercise, enter **P@ssw0rd**. Click Next.

Configuring and Managing Key Archive and Recovery

The key archive stores a certificate's subject name, public key, private key, and supported cryptographic algorithms in its CA database. This procedure can be performed manually or automatically, depending on the configuration. If the certificate template requires key archiving, then the process requires no manual intervention. However, key archiving can also be performed manually if the private key is exported and then sent to an administrator for import into the CA database.

There is also a Key Recovery Agent template available in the standard templates within Active Directory Certificate Services. The Key Recovery Agent template enables Domain Admins and Enterprise Admins to export private keys. Additionally, you can add other accounts and groups to have the necessary permissions (Read and Enroll) through the Security tab of the template.

The Key Recovery Agent template also needs to be enabled, as with other certificate templates, through the Certification Authority tool by selecting Certificate Template To Issue. See "Publishing a Certificate Template" earlier in this chapter for more details on enabling a certificate template on a CA.

With the Key Recovery Agent template in place, the following process must take place for key archiving and recovery:

1. Request a key recovery agent certificate using the Certificates snap-in.

2. Issue the key recovery agent certificate using the Certification Authority tool.

3. Retrieve the enrolled certificate using the Certificates snap-in.

4. Configure the CA for key archiving and recovery.

The final step, configuring the CA for key archiving and recovery, takes place in the Properties dialog box of each CA that will need to archive and recover keys. Specifically, the Recovery Agents tab configures the behavior of the CA when a request includes key archiving.

Each Key Recovery Agent certificate should be added using the Add button on the Recovery Agents tab.

PowerShell for AD CS

Table 5.3 will show you just some of the available PowerShell commands for maintaining an Active Directory Certificate Server.

TABLE 5.3 PowerShell Commands for AD CS

Command	Description
Add-CAAuthorityInformationAccess	This command allows an administrator to configure the Authority Information Access (AIA) or Online Certificate Status Protocol (OCSP) URI on a CA.
Add-CACrlDistributionPoint	Administrators can use this command to add a certificate revocation list (CRL) distribution point.
Add-CATemplate	This command allows an administrator to add a certificate template to the CA.
Backup-CARoleService	This command can be used to back up the CA database and private key information.

Command	Description
Confirm-CAEndorsementKeyInfo	Administrators can use this command to check the endorsement certificate of a TPM on the local CA.
Get-CAAuthorityInformationAccess	This command allows an admin to view the Authority Information Access (AIA) and Online Certificate Status Protocol (OCSP) URI information set.
Get-CACrlDistributionPoint	Administrators can use this command to view all the locations set for the CRL distribution point (CDP).
Get-CATemplate	This command allows an admin to view the list of templates set on the CA for issuance of certificates.
Remove-CAAuthorityInformationAccess	Administrators can use this command to remove Authority Information Access (AIA) or Online Certificate Status Protocol (OCSP) URI from the CA.
Remove-CACrlDistributionPoint	This command allows an administrator to delete the URI for the certificate revocation list (CRL) distribution point (CDP) from the CA.
Remove-CATemplate	Administrators can use this command to delete the templates from the CA.
Restore-CARoleService	This command allows an administrator to restore the CA database and private key information.

Summary

In this chapter, I discussed the certificate authority role and some of the new features in Microsoft Windows Server 2016, including additional management options, new certificate templates, and better support for globalized organizations with limited IDN support. I also covered the details of the same-key certificate renewal requirement and the effects of the new increased default security settings on the CA role service.

I also showed you just some of the PowerShell commands that you can use to configure and modify the Active Directory Certificate Server.

Exam Essentials

Understand the concepts behind certificate authority.   Certificate authority servers manage certificates. Make sure you understand why companies use certificate servers and how they work.

Understand certificate enrollment.   You need to understand the many different ways to issue certificates to users and computers. You also need to understand the differences between installing certificates using GPOs, auto-enrollment, and web enrollment.

Review Questions

You can find the answers in the Appendix.

1. You are the network administrator for a large organization. You need to add a certificate template to the Certificate Authority. What PowerShell command would you use?

   A. Get-CSTemplate

   B. Add-CSTemplate

   C. Add-CATemplate

   D. New-Template

2. Channel Fishing Company wants to configure a CA server in the DMZ to issue certificates to remote users. How would you accomplish this? (Choose all that apply.)

   A. You should consider having the Certificate Enrollment Policy Web Server role included in the solution.

   B. You should consider having the online responder included in the solution.

   C. You should consider having the Network Device Enrollment Service included in the solution.

   D. You should consider having the web service included in the solution.

   E. You should consider having the Certificate Enrollment Web Service included in the solution.

   F. You should consider having the Web Enrollment service included in the solution.

3. The certificate revocation list (CRL) polling begins to consume bandwidth. What steps should you consider to reduce network traffic?

   A. You should consider implementing the Certificate Enrollment Policy Web Server role and Certificate Enrollment Web Services role.

   B. You should consider implementing an online responder.

   C. You should consider implementing an online issuing CA and a root CA.

   D. You should consider publishing more CRLs.

4. ABC Industries wants configuration modifications of the Certification Authority role service to be logged. How would you implement this? (Choose all that apply.)

   A. You should consider enabling auditing of system events.

   B. You should consider enabling logging.

   C. You should consider enabling auditing of object access.

   D. You should consider enabling auditing of privilege use.

   E. You should consider enabling auditing of process tracking.

5. You are the network administrator for an Active Directory forest named WillPanek.com. The forest contains a single domain. The domain contains a single Windows Server 2016 server named Server1. An administrator named John Smith plans to set up Server1 as a stand-alone certification authority (CA). You need John Smith to set up Server1 as a stand-alone CA. What group does John Smith need to be part of to configure Server1 as a stand-alone CA?

   A. Administrators group on Server1

   B. Domain Admins group in WillPanek.com

   C. Cert Publishers group on Server1

   D. Key Admins group in WillPanek.com

6. You are the network administrator for WillPanek.com. You set up an enterprise certification authority (CA) named ServerCA1. You are planning to issue certificates based on the User certificate template. You need to make sure that the issued certificates are valid for two years and that they also support auto-enrollment. What should you do first?

   A. Run the certutil.exe command and specify the resubmit parameter.

   B. Duplicate the User certificate template.

   C. Add a new certificate template for CA1 to issue.

   D. Modify the Request Handling settings for the CA.

7. You have set up an enterprise root certification authority (CA) named Server1. Computers on the network have successfully enrolled and received certificates that will expire in one year. The certificates are based on a template named CA_Template1. You need to ensure that new certificates based on CA_Template1 are valid for three years. What should you do to make sure that they are valid for three years?

   A. Modify the Validity period for the certificate template.

   B. Instruct users to request certificates by running the certreq.exe command.

   C. Instruct users to request certificates by using the Certificates console.

   D. Modify the Validity period for the root CA certificate.

8. You are the network administrator for a large company. You need to make sure that certificate clients check the CRL at least every 30 minutes to see whether a certificate has been revoked or not. Which of the following should you configure to accomplish this goal?

   A. Key recovery agent

   B. CRL publication interval

   C. Delta CRL publication interval

   D. Certificate templates.

9. You are the network admin for your company. You need to see all of the location sets for the CRL distribution point (CDP). What PowerShell command would you use?

A. View-CACrlDistributionPoint

B. See-CACrlDistributionPoint

C. Add-CACrlDistributionPoint

D. Get-CACrlDistributionPoint

10. You are the network admin for your company. You need to see the list of templates set on the CA for issuance of certificates. What PowerShell command would you use?

A. Get-CATemplate

B. View-CATemplate

C. Add-CATemplate

D. New-CATemplate

Configure Access and Information Protection Solutions

THE FOLLOWING 70-742 EXAM OBJECTIVES ARE COVERED IN THIS CHAPTER:

✓ **Install and configure Active Directory Federation Services (AD FS)**

   ■ This objective may include but is not limited to: Upgrade and migrate previous AD FS workloads to Windows Server 2016; implement claims-based authentication, including Relying Party Trusts; configure authentication policies; configure multi-factor authentication; implement and configure device registration; integrate AD FS with Microsoft Passport; configure for use with Microsoft Azure and Office 365; configure AD FS to enable authentication of users stored in LDAP directories.

✓ **Implement Web Application Proxy (WAP)**

   ■ This objective may include but is not limited to: Install and configure WAP; implement WAP in pass-through mode; implement WAP as AD FS proxy; integrate WAP with AD FS; configure AD FS requirements; publish web apps via WAP; publish Remote Desktop Gateway applications; configure HTTP to HTTPS redirects; configure internal and external Fully Qualified Domain Names (FQDNs).

✓ **Install and configure Active Directory Rights**

   ■ This objective may include but is not limited to: Install a licensor certificate AD RMS server; manage AD RMS Service Connection Point (SCP); manage AD RMS templates; configure Exclusion Policies; back upand restore AD RMS.

In this chapter, I will discuss Active Directory Federation Services and how to set up relying party trusts with certificates. I will also discuss rights management, which Microsoft created to further protect documents, email, and web pages from unauthorized copying, printing, forwarding, editing, deleting, and so forth.

Finally, I will talk about using the Web Application Proxy and how this can be setup in conjunction with AD FS for greater control of which applications get accessed through AD FS.

Implement Active Directory Federation Services

Active Directory Federation Services (AD FS) demands a great deal of preparation and planning to ensure a successful implementation. The type of certificate authority used to sign the AD FS server's certificate must be planned. The SSL encryption level must be negotiated with the partnering organization. For instance, how much Active Directory information should be shared with the partnering organization? What should the DNS structure look like to support federation communications? You must explore all of these questions before implementing AD FS. In the followings sections, I will discuss how to deploy AD FS and the configurations used to set up a federated partnership between businesses.

What Is a Claim?

A *claim* is an identifiable element (email address, username, password, and so on) that a trusted source asserts about an identity, such as, for example, the SID of a user or computer. An identity can contain more than one claim, and any combination of those claims can be used to authorize access to resources.

Windows Server 2016 extends the authorization identity beyond using the SID for identity and enables administrators to configure authorization based on claims published in Active Directory.

Today, the claims-based identity model brings us to cloud-based authentication. One analogy to the claim-based model is the old airport check-in procedure:

1. You first check in at the ticket counter.

2. You present a suitable form of ID (driver's license, passport, credit card, and so on). After verifying that your picture ID matches your face (authentication), the

agent pulls up your flight information and verifies that you've paid for a ticket (authorization).

3. You receive a boarding pass (token). The boarding pass lets the gate agents know your name and frequent flyer number (authentication and personalization), your flight number and seating priority (authorization), and more. The boarding pass has barcode information (certificate) with a boarding serial number proving that the boarding pass was issued by the airline and not a (self-signed) forgery.

Active Directory Federation Service is Microsoft's claims-based identity solution providing browser-based clients (internal or external to your network) with transparent access to one or more protected Internet-facing applications.

When an application is hosted in a different network than the user accounts, users are occasionally prompted for secondary credentials when they attempt to access the application. These secondary credentials represent the identity of the users in the domain where the application is hosted. The web server hosting the application usually requires these credentials to make the most proper authorization decision.

AD FS makes secondary accounts and their credentials unnecessary by providing trust relationships that send a user's digital identity and access rights to trusted partners. In a federated environment, each organization continues to manage its own identities, but each organization can also securely send and accept identities from other organizations. This seamless process is referred to as *single sign-on (SSO)*.

Windows Server 2016 AD FS federation servers can extract Windows authorization claims from a user's authorization token that is created when the user authenticates to the AD FS federation server. AD FS inserts these claims into its claim pipeline for processing. You can configure Windows authorization claims to pass through the pipeline as is, or you can configure AD FS to transform Windows authorization claims into a different or well-known claim type.

Claims Provider

A *claims provider* is a federation server that processes trusted identity claims requests. A federation server processes requests to issue, manage, and validate security tokens. Security tokens consist of a collection of identity claims, such as a user's name or role or an anonymous identifier. A federation server can issue tokens in several formats. In addition, a federation server can protect the contents of security tokens in transmission with an X.509 certificate.

For example, when a Stellacon Corporation user needs access to Fabrikam's web application, the Stellacon Corporation user must request claims from the Stellacon Corporation AD FS server claims provider. The claim is transformed into an encrypted security token, which is then sent to Fabrikam's AD FS server.

Relying Party

A *relying party* is a federation server that receives security tokens from a trusted federation partner claims provider. In turn, the relying party issues new security tokens that a local relying party application consumes. In the prior example, Fabrikam is the relying party that relies on the Stellacon's claims provider to validate the user's claim. By using a relying-party federation server in conjunction with a claims provider, organizations can offer web single sign-on to users from partner organizations. In this scenario, each organization manages its own identity stores.

Endpoints

Endpoints provide access to the federation server functionality of AD FS, such as token issuance, information card issuance, and the publishing of federation metadata. Based on the type of endpoint, you can enable or disable the endpoint or control whether the endpoint is published to AD FS proxies.

Table 6.1 describes the property fields that distinguish the various built-in endpoints that AD FS exposes. The table includes the types of endpoints and their methods of client authentication. Table 6.2 describes the AD FS security modes.

TABLE 6.1   AD FS Endpoints

Name	Description
WS-Trust 1.3	An endpoint built on a standard Simple Object Access Protocol (SOAP)–based protocol for issuing security tokens.
WS-Trust 2005	An endpoint built on a prestandard, SOAP-based protocol for issuing security tokens.
WS-Federation Passive/SAML Web SSO	An endpoint published to support protocols that redirect web browser clients to issue security tokens.
Federation Metadata	A standard-formatted endpoint for exchanging metadata about a claims provider or a relying party.
SAML Artifact Resolution	An endpoint built on a subset of the Security Assertion Markup Language (SAML) version 2.0 protocol that describes how a relying party can access a token directly from a claims provider.
WS-Trust WSDL	An endpoint that publishes WS-Trust Web Services Definition Language (WSDL) containing the metadata that the federation service must be able to accept from other federation servers.
SAML Token (Asymmetric)	The client accepts a SAML token with an asymmetric key.

TABLE 6.2 AD FS Security Modes

Name	Description
Transport	The client credentials are included at the transport layer. Confidentiality is preserved at the transport layer (Secure Sockets Layer [SSL]).
Mixed	The client credentials are included in the header of a SOAP message. Confidentiality is preserved at the transport layer (SSL).
Message	The client credentials are included in the header of a SOAP message. Confidentiality is preserved by encryption inside the SOAP message.

Claim Descriptions

Claim descriptions are claim types based on an entity's or user's attribute like a user's email address, common name or UPN. AD FS publishes these claims types in the federation metadata and most common claim descriptions are pre-configured in the AD FS Management snap-in.

The claim descriptions are published to federation metadata which is stored in the AD FS configuration database. The claim descriptions include a claim type URI, name, publishing state, and description.

Claim Rules

Claim rules define how AD FS processes a claim. The most common rule is using a user's email address as a valid claim. The email address claim is validated through the partner's Active Directory email attribute for the user's account. If there is a match, the claim is accepted as valid.

Claim rules can quickly evolve into more complex rules with more attributes such as a user's employee ID or department. The key goal of claim rules is to process the claim in a manner that validates the user's claim and to assemble a user's profile information based on a sufficient number of attributes to place the user into a role or group.

The Attribute Store

Attribute stores are the repositories containing claim values. AD FS natively supports Active Directory, by default, as an attribute store. SQL Server, AD LDS, and custom attribute stores are also supported.

AD FS Role Services

The AD FS server role includes federation, proxy, and web agent services. These services enable the following:

- Web SSO
- Federated web-based resources

- Customizing the access experience
- Managing authorization to access applications

Based on your organization's requirements, you can deploy servers running any one of the following AD FS role services:

Active Directory Federation Service   Microsoft federation solution for accepting and issuing claims based token for users to experience a single sign-on to a partnered web application.

Federation Service Proxy   The Federation Service Proxy forwards user claims over the internet or DMZ using WS-Federation Passive Requestor Profile (WS-F PRP) protocols to the internal ADFS farm. Only the user credential data is forwarded to the Federation Service. All other datagram packets are dropped.

Claims-Aware Agent   The claims-aware agent resides on a web server with a claims-aware application to enable the Microsoft ASP.NET application to accept AD FS security token claims.

Windows Token-Based Agent   The Windows token-based agent resides on a web server with a Windows NT token-based application to translate an AD FS security token to an impersonation-level Windows NT token-based authentication.

What's New for AD FS in Windows Server 2016?

The Active Directory Federation Services role in Windows Server 2016 introduces the following new features:

- HTTP.SYS
- Server Manager integration
- AD FS deployment cmdlets in the AD FS module for Windows PowerShell
- Interoperability with Windows authorization claims
- Web proxy service

HTTP.SYS

Prior AD FS versions relied on IIS components for the AD FS claim functions. Microsoft has improved the overall claims handling performance and SSO customization by building the AD FS 3.0 code on top of the standard kernel mode driver—HTTP.SYS. This approach also avoids the huge security "no-no" of hosting IIS on a domain controller.

The classic netsh HTTP command can be entered to query and configure HTTP.SYS. AD FS proxy server introduces interesting deployment nuisances and "gotchas" with HTTP.SYS, which I will discuss in the "Web Proxy Service" section.

Improved Installation Experience

The installation experience for Active Directory Federation Services 3.0 was cumbersome, requiring multiple hotfixes, as well as .NET Framework 3.5, Windows PowerShell, and the

Windows Identity Foundation SDK. Windows Server 2016's AD FS role includes all of the software you need to run AD FS for an improved installation experience.

Web Proxy Service

The kernel mode (HTTP.SYS) in Windows Server 2016 includes server name indication (SNI) support configuration. I strongly recommend verifying that your current load balancer/ reverse proxy firmware supports SNI. This prerequisite is a sore spot for most AD FS 3.0 upgrade projects in the field. Therefore, it's worthwhile checking the following:

- Your preferred load balancer/device needs to support SNI.

- Clients and user agents need to support SNI and should not become locked out of authentication.

- All SSL termination endpoints vulnerable to the recent heartbleed bug (http:// heartbleed.com) need to be patched, exposing OpenSSL libraries and certificates.

AD FS Dependency Changes in Windows Server 2016

Active Directory Federation Services was built on a claim-based identity framework called *Windows Identity Foundation (WIF)*. Prior to Windows Server 2016, WIF was distributed in a software development kit and the .NET runtime. WIF is currently integrated into version 4.5 of the .NET Framework, which ships with Windows Server 2016.

Windows Identity Foundation

WIF is a set of .NET Framework classes; it is a framework for implementing claims-based identity for applications. Any web application or web service that uses .NET Framework version 4.5 or newer can run WIF.

New Claims Model and Principal Object

Claims are at the core of .NET Framework 4.5. The base claim classes (`Claim`, `ClaimsIdentity`, `ClaimsPrincipal`, `ClaimTypes`, and `ClaimValueTypes`) all live directly in `mscorlib`. Interfaces are no longer necessary to plug claims in the .NET identity system. `WindowsPrincipal`, `GenericPrincipal`, and `RolePrincipal` now inherit from `ClaimsPrincipal`, `WindowsIdentity`, and `GenericIdentity`, and `FormsIdentity` now inherit from `ClaimsIdentity`. In short, every principal class will now serve claims. The integration classes and interfaces (`WindowsClaimsIdentity`, `WindowsClaimsPrincipal`, `IClaimsPrincipal`, and `IClaimsIdentity`) have thus been removed. The `ClaimsIdentity` object model also contains various improvements, which makes it easier to query the identity's claims collection.

As you climb further up "Mount Federation," you will realize that not all vendor SAML flavors are compatible, and configuration challenges can bring even the most seasoned system integrators to their knees. SAML deserves an entire book, so to avoid this chapter reaching encyclopedia size, I will touch on just a few pointers.

AD FS negotiates SAML authentication in order of security strength from the weakest to the strongest, as shown in Table 6.3. The default mode, Kerberos, is considered the strongest method. The authentication precedence can be tuned by executing the PowerShell command Set-AD FSProperties -AuthenticationContextOrder to select an order to meet your organization's security requirements.

TABLE 6.3 SAML-supported authentication methods

Authentication Method	Authentication Context Class URI
Username/password	urn:oasis:names:tc:SAML:3.0:ac:classes:Password
Password-protected transport	urn:oasis:names:tc:SAML:3.0:ac:classes:PasswordProtectedTransport
Transport Layer Security (TLS) Client	urn:oasis:names:tc:SAML:3.0:ac:classes:TLSClient
X.509 certificate	urn:oasis:names:tc:SAML:3.0:ac:classes:X509
Integrated Windows authentication	urn:federation:authentication:windows
Kerberos	urn:oasis:names:tc:SAML:3.0:classes:Kerberos

Active Directory Federation Services Installation

I will now describe how to install and deploy Active Directory Federation Services roles on computers running Windows Server 2016 (see Exercise 6.1). You will learn about the following:

- Deploying AD FS role services using Windows PowerShell
- Supporting upgrade scenarios for AD FS

EXERCISE 6.1

Installing the AD FS Role on a Computer Using Server Manager

1. Start Server Manager.

2. Click Manage and click Add Roles And Features. Click Next.

3. The Add Roles And Features Wizard shows the Before You Begin screen. Click Next.

4. Click Role-Based Or Feature-Based Installation on the Select Installation Type screen. Click Next.

5. Click the server on which you want to install Active Directory Federation Services from the Server Pool list on the Select Destination Server screen. Click Next.

6. Select the Active Directory Federation Services check box on the Select Server Roles screen. Server Manager will prompt you to add other features associated with this role, such as management tools. Leave the default selections. Click Add Features to close the dialog.

7. Click Next on the Select Server Roles screen.

8. Click Next on the Select Features screen.

9. Server Manager shows the Active Directory Federation Services screen. This screen displays simple role introduction and important AD FS configuration information. Click Next.

10. From the Select Server Roles screen, select the check box next to the AD FS role services to install on the computer. Click Next.

11. Server Manager prompts you to add other features associated with this role, such as management tools. Leave the default selections. Click Add Features to close the dialog.

12. Read the Confirm Installation Selections screen. This screen provides a list of roles, role services, and features that the current installation prepares on the computer. Click Install to begin the installation.

Role Installation Using Windows PowerShell

To view the installation state of AD FS using Windows PowerShell, open an elevated Windows PowerShell console, type the following command, and press Enter:

```
Get-WindowsFeature "adfs*","*fed*"
```

Upgrading to Windows AD FS 2016

Windows Server 2016's AD FS role supports upgrading version 3.0 of Active Directory Federation Services. You cannot upgrade versions of AD FS prior to version 3.0 using Windows Server 2016.

Table 6.4 represents the support upgrade matrix for the AD FS role in Windows Server 2016.

TABLE 6.4   Support upgrade matrix for the AD FS role in Windows Server 2016

AD FS and Operating System Version	Windows Server 2016 Upgrade Supported
AD FS 3.0 running on Windows Server 2008	Yes
AD FS 3.0 running on Windows Server 2008 R2	Yes

TABLE 6.4 Support upgrade matrix for the AD FS role in Windows Server 2016 *(continued)*

AD FS and Operating System Version	Windows Server 2016 Upgrade Supported
AD FS 3.0 Proxy running on Windows Server 2008	Yes
AD FS 3.0 Proxy running on Windows Server 2008 R2	Yes
AD FS 1.1 running on Windows Server 2008	No
AD FS 1.1 running on Windows Server 2008 R2	No
AD FS 1.1 Proxy running on Windows Server 2008	No
AD FS 1.1 Proxy running on Windows Server 2008 R2	No
AD FS 1.1 Web Agents on Windows Server 2008 or Windows Server 2008 R2	Yes

Configuring Active Directory Federation Services

Windows Server 2016 delineates role installation and role deployment. Role installations make staged role services and features available for deployment. Role deployment enables you to configure the role service, which enables the role service in your environment. AD FS in Windows Server 2016 uses the same deployment tools as AD FS 3.0. However, an entry point to start these tools is included in Server Manager. Server Manager indicates that one or more role services are eligible for deployment by showing an exclamation point inside a yellow triangle on the Action Flag notification. Click the action flag to show the role services you can deploy.

AD FS Graphical Deployment

The Run The AD FS Management snap-in link in Windows Server 2016 Server Manager is how you perform the initial configuration for the AD FS roles using the graphical interface. Alternatively, you can start the AD FS management console using the AD FS Management tile on the Start screen. The Start screen tile points to the Microsoft.IdentityServer.msc file located in the C:\windows\adfs folder.

To configure AD FS, select Start ➤ Run and type **FsConfigWizard.exe**; alternatively, click the FsConfigWizard.exe file located in the C:\windows\adfs folder.

Exercise 6.2 uses the AD FS Federation Server Configuration Wizard. To complete this exercise, you'll need an active SSL certificate assigned to the server and a managed service account for AD FS service.

EXERCISE 6.2

Configuring the AD FS Role on the Computer Using Server Manager

1. Select Create The First Federation Server In The Federation Server Farm.

2. Select the administrative account with permissions to configure the AD FS server and click Next.

3. Select the server certificate from the SSL certificate drop-down list.

4. Select the AD FS service name from the drop-down list.

5. Type **ADFS-Test** in the federation service's Display Name field and click Next.

6. Select Create A Database On This Server Using Windows Internal Database and click Next.

7. Click Next on the Review Options screen.

8. If the prerequisites check is successful, click Configure on the Prerequisite Check screen.

9. If the Result screen displays "This Server was successfully configured," you can click Close.

Deployment Using Windows PowerShell

Windows Server 2016 includes the Active Directory Federation Services module for Windows PowerShell when you install the AD FS role using Server Manager. The AD FS module for Windows PowerShell includes five new cmdlets to deploy the AD FS role:

- `Add-AdfsProxy`
- `Add-AdfsFarmNode`
- `Export-AdfsDeploymentSQLScript`
- `Install-AdfsStand-alone`
- `Install-AdfsFarm`

These AD FS cmdlets provide the same functionality as the command-line version of the AD FS Federation Server Configuration Wizard, `fsconfig .exe`. The AD FS role in Windows Server 2016 includes `fsconfig.exe` to remain compatible with previously authored deployment scripts. New deployments should take advantage of the deployment cmdlets included in the AD FS module for Windows PowerShell.

Add-AdfsProxy   Configures a server as a federation server proxy.

FederationServiceName   Specifies the name of the federation service for which a server proxies requests.

FederationServiceTrustCredentials   Specifies the credentials of the Active Directory identity that is authorized to register new federation server proxies. By default, this is the account under which the federation service runs or an account that is a member of the Administrators group on the federation server.

ForwardProxy   Specifies the DNS name and port of an HTTP proxy that this federation server proxy uses to obtain access to the federation service.

Add-AdfsFarmNode   Adds this computer to an existing federation server farm.

CertificateThumbprint   Specifies the value of the certificate thumbprint of the certificate that should be used in the SSL binding of the default website in IIS. This value should match the thumbprint of a valid certificate in the Local Computer certificate store.

OverwriteConfiguration   Must be used to remove an existing AD FS configuration database and overwrite it with a new database.

SQLConnectionString   Specifies the SQL Server database that will store the AD FS configuration settings. If not specified, AD FS uses Windows Internal Database to store configuration settings.

ServiceAccountCredential   Specifies the Active Directory account under which the AD FS service runs. All nodes in the farm must have the same service account.

PrimaryComputerName   Specifies the name of the primary federation server in the farm that this computer will join.

PrimaryComputerPort   Specifies the value of the HTTP port that this computer uses to connect with the primary computer in order to synchronize configuration settings. Specify a value for this parameter only if the HTTP port on the primary computer is not 80.

Active Directory Federation Services Certificates

There are three types of certificates used by an AD FS implementation:

- Service communications
- Token decrypting
- Token signing

The service communications certificate is required for communication with web clients over SSL and with web application proxy services using Windows Communication Foundation (WCF) components. This certificate is specified at configuration time for AD FS.

The token decrypting certificate is required to decrypt claims and tokens received by the federation service. The public key for the decrypting certificate is usually shared with relying parties and others to encrypt the claims and tokens using the certificate.

The token signing certificate is required to sign all claims and tokens created by the server. You can have multiple token encrypting and signing certificates for an implementation, and new ones can be added within the AD FS management tool, shown in Figure 6.1.

FIGURE 6.1 Active Directory Federation Certificate Console screen

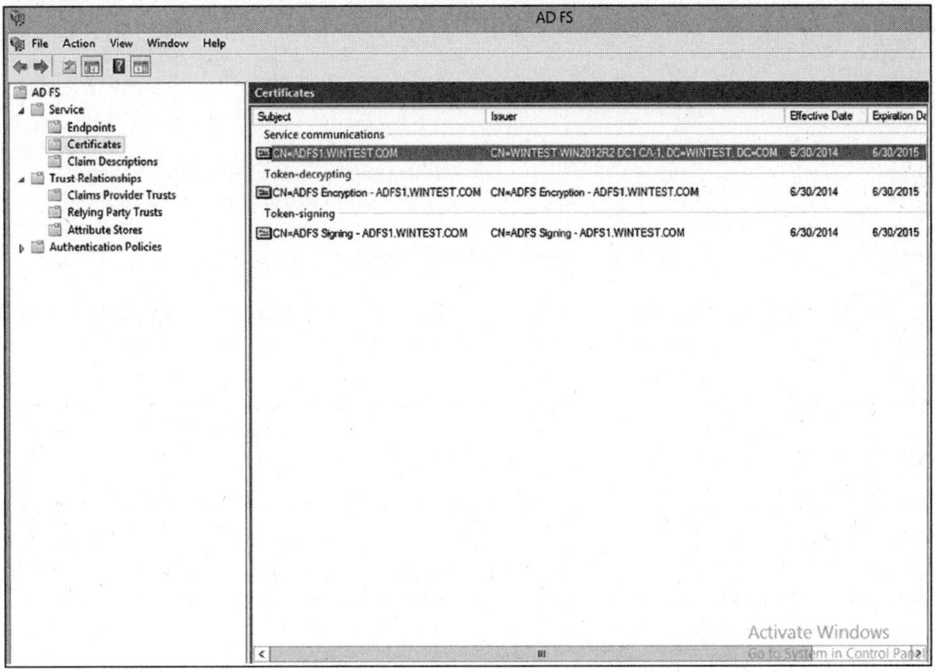

Relying-Party Trust

The federation service name originates from the SSL certificate used for AD FS. The SSL certificate can be template-based and needs to be enrolled and used by IIS.

The next step in setting up AD FS is to configure a relying-party trust. A relying-party trust can be configured with a URL acquired from the relying party. The URL contains the federation metadata used to complete the federation trust configuration. The federation metadata may also be exported to a file that can then be imported into the relying-party trust. There is also a manual option for configuring a relying-party trust.

See Table 6.5 for the Federation Metadata fields.

TABLE 6.5 Federation Metadata Fields

Field	Description
Display Name	This is the friendly display name given to this relying party trust.
Profile	Select AD FS Profile for the standard Windows Server 2012 AD FS, or select AD FS 1.0 And 1.1 Profile for AD FS configurations that need to work with older versions of AD FS.

TABLE 6.5   Federation Metadata Fields *(continued)*

Field	Description
Certificate	This is the optional certificate file from the relying party for token encryption.
URL	This is the URL for the relying party. WS-Federation Passive Protocol URL or SAML 2.0 WebSSO protocols are supported.
Identifiers	This is the unique identifier used for this trust.
Authorization Rules	Selecting this permits all users to access the relying party or denies all users access to the relying party, depending on the needs of this trust.

Configuring Claims Provider and Transform Claims Rules

Claims provider trust rules are configured within the AD FS management console and are configured on a per-trust basis. Planning claims rules involves determining what claims are needed by the relying party to complete the authentication and authorization process and which users will need access to the relying-party trust. The relying party determines what claims need to be received and trusted from the claims provider.

Trust rules start with templates as the basis for the rule. There are different types of claims templates depending on the type of rule being used. The claims rule templates for transforms are described in Table 6.6.

TABLE 6.6   Transform claims rule templates

Template	Description
Send LDAP Attributes as Claims	Attributes found in an LDAP directory (such as Active Directory) can be used as part of the claim.
Send Group Membership as Claim	The group memberships of the logged-in user are sent as part of the claim.
Transform an Incoming Claim	This is used for configuring a rule to change an incoming claim. Changes include both the type and the value of an incoming claim.
Pass Through or Filter an Incoming Claim	This performs an action such as pass-through or filter on an incoming claim based on certain criteria, as defined in the rule.
Send Claims Using a Custom Rule	This creates a rule that's not covered by a predefined template, such as an LDAP attribute generated with a custom LDAP filter.

Defining Windows Authorization Claims in AD FS

Windows Server 2016 stores information that describes Windows authorization claims in the configuration partition of Active Directory. Windows refers to this information as *claim types*; however, Active Directory Federation Services typically refers to this information as claim descriptions (see Figure 6.2). There are more than 40 new claims descriptions available in the AD FS Windows Server 2016 release.

FIGURE 6.2   AD FS claim descriptions

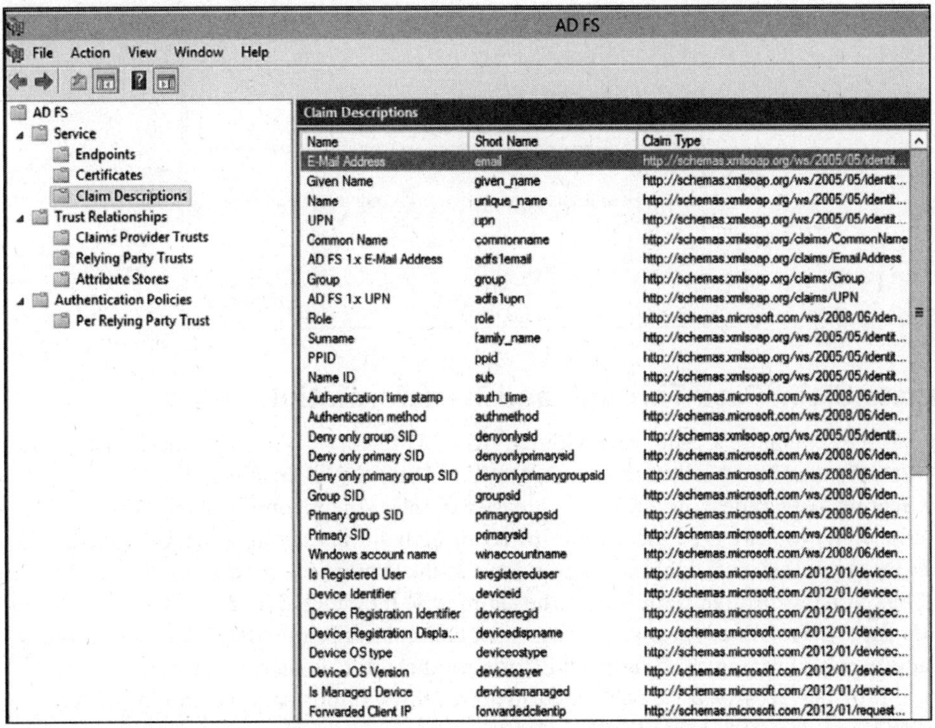

The Active Directory Federation Services role included in Windows Server 2016 lets you configure AD FS to include Windows authorization claims in the AD FS claim pipeline. To simplify this configuration, you can create *claim descriptions* in AD FS. Claim types in Windows authorization claims are analogous to claim descriptions in AD FS. The Windows authorization claim ID maps to the AD FS claim description's claim identifier (see Figure 6.3).

To simplify AD FS configuration using Windows authorization claims, create a claim description in AD FS for each Windows authorization claim you intend to deploy in AD FS.

FIGURE 6.3 Adding a claim description

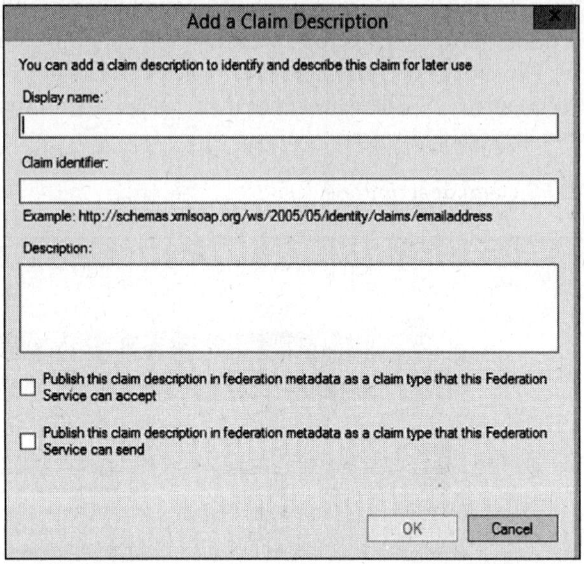

Create Claim Pass-Through and Transformation Rules

You need to configure a claim rule with the Active Directory Claims Provider Trusts Wizard to insert Windows authorization claims into the AD FS claims pipeline.

Creating a claim description makes it easier to select the incoming claim type. Alternatively, you can type the claim type ID directly in the Incoming Claim Type list. A *pass-through claim rule* enables the Windows authorization claim to enter the AD FS claim pipeline. A pass-through claim leaves the claim type ID intact. Therefore, the pass-through claim ID begins with `ad://ext`, whereas most claim description URIs begin with `http://`. In addition, you can create a claim transformation claim rule on the Active Directory Claim Provider Trust Wizard to transform a Windows authorization claim into a well-known claim description (see Figure 6.4).

Creating a claims provider trust claim rule enables the Windows authorization claim to enter the AD FS claim pipeline. However, this does not ensure that AD FS sends the Windows authorization claim. AD FS claim processing begins with the claims provider. This allows the claim to enter the pipeline. Claim processing continues for the targeted relying party—first with the issuance authorization rules and then with the issuance transform rules.

You can configure Windows authorization claims in claims rules configured on a relying party. By default, a relying party does not have any issuance transform rules. Therefore, AD FS drops all claims in the pipeline destined for a relying party when the relying party does not have any rules that pass incoming claims. Additionally, issuance authorization rules determine whether a user can receive claims for a relying party and, therefore, access the relying party.

FIGURE 6.4   Claim transformation claim rule

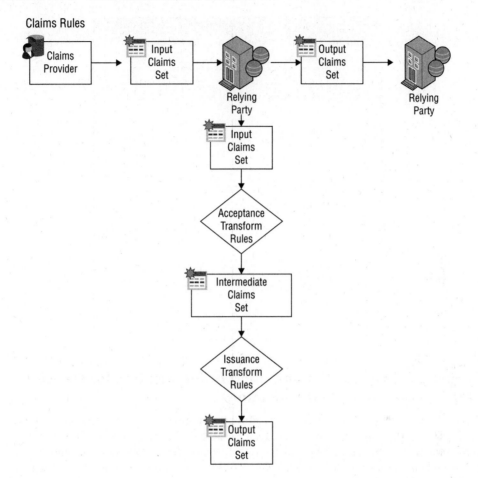

Choose the claims types from the list of inbound rules created in the Active Directory claims provider trust that you want to send to the designated relying party. Then create rules that continue to pass the selected claim types through the pipeline to the relying party. Alternatively, you can create a rule that passes all the inbound claims to the relying party (see Figure 6.5).

The AD FS role in Windows Server 2016 cannot provide claim information when the incoming authentication is not Kerberos. Clients must authenticate to AD FS using Kerberos authentication. If Windows authorization claims are not entering the AD FS claim pipeline, then make sure the client authenticates to AD FS using Kerberos and the correct service principal name is registered on the computer/service account.

FIGURE 6.5 Editing the claims rules

FIGURE 6.5 Editing the claims rules

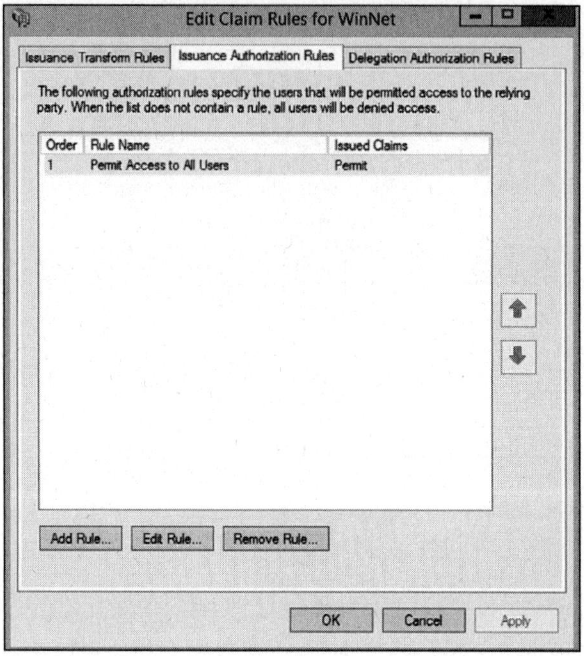

Enabling AD FS to Use Compound Authentication for Device Claims: Compound Authentication

Windows Server 2016 enhances Kerberos authentication by introducing compound authentication. Compound authentication enables a Kerberos TGS request to include two identities: the identity of the user and the identity of the user's device. Windows accomplishes compound authentication by extending Kerberos Flexible Authentication Secure Tunneling (FAST) or Kerberos armoring.

During normal Kerberos authentication, the Kerberos client requesting authentication for a service sends the ticket-granting service (TGS) a request for that service. Using Kerberos armoring, the TGS exchange is armored using the user's ticket-granting ticket (TGT). Prior to sending the ticket-granting service reply (TGS-REP) to the client, the KDC checks the 0x00020000 bit in the value of the msDS-SupportedEncryptionTypes attribute of the security principal's object running the service. An enabled bit means that the service can accept compound authentication. The KDC sends the TGS-REP, which includes the service's ability to support compound authentication.

The Kerberos client receives the ticket-granting service TGS-REP that includes compound authentication information. The Kerberos client then sends another ticket-granting service request (TGS-REQ), with the difference being that this TGS-REQ is armored with the device's TGT rather than the user. This allows the KDC to retrieve authentication information about the principal and the device.

The Active Directory Federation Services role included in Windows Server 2016 automatically enables compound authentication when creating an AD FS web farm. During the creation of the first node in the farm, the AD FS configuration wizard enables the compound authentication bit on the msDS-SupportedEncryptionTypes attribute on the account that you designate to run the AD FS service. If you change the service account, then you must manually enable compound authentication by running the Set-ADUser-compoundIdentitySupported:$true Windows PowerShell cmdlet.

In Exercise 6.3, you will learn how to configure multifactor authentication.

EXERCISE 6.3

Configuring Multifactor Authentication

1. In the AD FS Management Console, traverse to Trust Relationships And Relying Party Trusts.

2. Select the relying party trust that represents your sample application (claimapp) and then either by using the Actions pane or by right-clicking this relying party trust, select Edit Claim Rules.

3. In the Edit Claim Rules For Claimapp window, select the Issuance Authorization Rules tab and click Add Rule.

4. In the Add Issuance Authorization Claim Rule Wizard, on the Select Rule Template screen, select Permit Or Deny Users Based On An Incoming Claim Rule Template and click Next.

5. On the Configure Rule screen, complete all of the following tasks and click Finish.

    a. Enter a name for the claim rule, for example **TestRule**.

    b. Select Group SID As Incoming Claim Type.

    c. Click Browse, type in **Finance** for the name of your AD test group, and resolve it for the Incoming Claim Value field.

    d. Select the Deny Access To Users With This Incoming Claim option.

    e. In the Edit Claim Rules For Claimapp window, make sure to delete the Permit Access To All Users rule that was created by default when you created this relying party trust.

Verify Multifactor Access Control Mechanism

In this phase, you will verify the multifactor access control policy that you set up in the previous phase. You can use the following procedure to verify that a test AD user can access your sample application because the test account belongs to the Finance group. Conversely, you will use the procedure to verify that AD users who do not belong to the Finance group cannot access the sample application.

1. On your client computer, open a browser window and navigate to your sample application: `https://webserv1.contoso.com/claimapp`. This action automatically redirects the request to the federation server, and you are prompted to sign in with a username and password.

2. Type in the credentials of a test AD account to be granted access to the application.

3. Type in the credentials of another test AD account that does not belong to the Finance group.

At this point, because of the access control policy that you set up in the previous steps, an access denied message is displayed for an AD account that does not belong to the Finance group. The default message text is "You are not authorized to access this site. Click here to sign out, and sign in again or contact your administrator for permissions." However, this text is fully customizable.

Workplace Join

Today's employees are mobile and remote, working across a plethora of consumer platforms. The age of bring your own device (BYOD) is here to stay. CIOs, IT security workers, and administrators cringe at the idea of storing company data on unmanaged devices. The Workplace Join feature adds a safety measure to ensure that only registered devices have access to company data.

For Workplace Join to work, a certificate is placed on the mobile device. AD FS challenges the device as a claims-based authentication to applications or other resources without requiring administrative control of the device.

Device Registration Service

Workplace Join is supported by the Device Registration Service (DRS) included with the Active Directory Federation Services role in Windows Server 2016. When a device is set up with Workplace Join, the DRS registers a device as an object in Active Directory and sets a certificate on the consumer device that is used to represent the device identity. The DRS is meant to be both internal and external facing.

DRS requires at least one global catalog server in the forest root domain. The global catalog server is needed to run the PowerShell cmdlet `-Initialize-ADDeviceRegistration` during AD FS authentication.

Workplace Join Your Device

For Workplace Join to succeed, the client computer must trust the AD FS SSL certificate. It must also be able to access and validate revocation information for the certificate from the CRL.

In Exercise 6.4, you will configure the DRS.

EXERCISE 6.4

Workplace Joining a Device

1. Start a Windows PowerShell command window and type

   Initialize-ADDeviceRegistration.

2. When prompted for a service account, type **contoso\fsgmsa$**.

3. On the AD FS server, in the AD FS Management console, navigate to the Authentication Policies tab. Select Edit Global Primary Authentication. Select the Enable Device Authentication check box and click OK.

Finally, you will need to make sure you have the following DNS records for the DRS.

Entry	Type	Address
adfs1	A	IP address of the AD FS server
enterpriseregistration	Alias (CNAME)	adfs1.contoso.com

4. Log on to the client with your Microsoft account.

5. On the Start screen, start the Charms bar and then select the Settings charm. Select Change PC Settings.

6. On the PC Settings screen, select Network and click Workplace.

7. In the Enter Your UserID To Get Workplace Access Or Turn On Device Management box, type the user's UPN or email address—for example, **RobertM@contoso.com**—and click Join.

8. When prompted for credentials, type the user's UPN or email address—for example, **roberth@contoso.com**—and a password such as **P@ssword**. Click OK.

9. You should now see the message "This device has joined your workplace network."

Active Directory Rights Management Services

Active Directory Rights Management Services (AD RMS), included with Microsoft Windows Server 2016, helps safeguard sensitive information created and distributed using AD RMS–enabled applications such as Word, Outlook, or InfoPath, similar to Adobe Acrobat's permissions for print, save, fill-form, and copy functions. Unlike traditional file permission methods, RMS rights stay with the content and ensure exclusive access to the intended recipient.

Application developers may enable their applications to work with RMS extensions. AD RMS uses policies managed from the RMS server to provide a consistent experience for users across the enterprise.

You can enforce AD RMS usage policy templates directly to protect confidential information. You can install AD RMS easily using Server Manager, and you can administer it through the MMC snap-in. These three new administrative roles allow you to delegate AD RMS responsibilities:

- AD RMS Enterprise Administrators
- AD RMS Template Administrators
- AD RMS Auditors

AD RMS integrates with AD FS, which allows two organizations to share information without requiring AD RMS in both organizations.

Self-enrollment AD RMS server enrollment allows for the creation and signing of a server licensor certificate (SLC). This SLC enables the AD RMS server to issue certificates and licenses whenever required.

Considerations and Requirements for AD RMS

Before installing Active Directory Rights Management Services on Windows Server 2016 for the first time, you must meet several requirements:

AD RMS Server   Install the AD RMS server as a member server in the same Active Directory domain as the user accounts that will be using rights-protected content.

AD RMS Service Account   Create a domain user account that has no additional permissions that can be used as the AD RMS service account. I recommend using a group-managed service account to ensure that the account password is managed by Active Directory and that it does not require a manual password change by an administrator.

If you are registering the AD RMS service connection point during installation, the user account installing AD RMS must be a member of the AD DS Enterprise Admins group or equivalent.

Which Database AD RMS Will Store Configuration Data   Microsoft SQL Server 2008 or newer and WID are supported databases for the AD RMS configuration data. Windows Internal Database is more suitable for small and/or test environments. If you are using an external SQL database server for the AD RMS databases, the user account installing AD RMS must have the right to create new databases.

AD RMS URL   Reserve a URL for the AD RMS cluster that will be available throughout the lifetime of the AD RMS installation. Make sure the reserved URL differs from the computer name.

Cryptographic Mode   Mode 1 is composed of RSA 1024-bit keys and SHA-1 hashes. Mode 2 includes RSA 2048-bit keys and SHA-256 hashes for a more secure and recommended option.

Location for Cluster Key Storage By default, the cluster key is stored within AD RMS. You may also deploy a cryptographic service provider to store the cluster key. However, you will have to distribute the key manually when installing additional AD RMS servers.

Cluster Key Password The Cluster Key password helps to encrypt the cluster key, and it must be provided when adding AD RMS servers to the cluster. The Cluster Key password must also be provided when recovering an AD RMS cluster from backup.

Cluster Name Choose the fully qualified domain name to be hosted on the AD RMS server. An SSL certificate should be configured with the FQDN of the AD RMS server. The cluster address and port cannot be changed after AD RMS is deployed. A non-SSL address can be configured, but you will lose the AD RMS with Identity Federation functionality.

AD RMS Add-On for Internet Explorer

The Windows Rights Management Add-on (RMA) for Internet Explorer enables rights-protected content to be viewed only. Because you can only view and not alter these restricted files, this prevents sensitive documents, web-based information, and email messages from being forwarded, edited, or copied by unauthorized individuals. For you to run RMA for Internet Explorer successfully, you must first install the Windows Rights Management (RM) client. The Extensible Rights Markup Language (XrML) is the XML verbiage used by AD RMS to express usage rights for rights-protected content.

AD RMS Requirements

AD RMS requires an AD RMS–enabled client. Windows Vista, Windows 7, and Windows 8/8.1 include the AD RMS client by default. If you are not using Windows Vista, Windows 7, Windows 8/8.1/10 Windows Server 2008, Windows Server 2008 R2, Windows Server 2012/2012 R2, or Windows Server 2016, you can download the AD RMS client for previous versions of Windows from Microsoft's Download Center.

   File System: The NTFS file system is recommended.

   Messaging: Message Queuing.

   Web Services: Internet Information Services (IIS). ASP.NET must be enabled.

Active Directory Domain Services

AD RMS must be installed in an Active Directory domain in which the domain controllers are running Windows Server 2008 or above. All users and groups that use AD RMS to acquire licenses and publish content require an email address configured in Active Directory.

   Database Server: AD RMS requires a SQL database server. Microsoft SQL Server 2005 or above are all supported SQL versions.

The new AD RMS administrative roles are as follows:

AD RMS Service Group   When the AD RMS role is installed onto a server, a local AD RMS service account is created and added to the local AD RMS service group. The server uses the service account to start services at system startup and cannot be the same account used to install the service.

AD RMS Enterprise Administrators   The AD RMS policies and settings are managed by members of the local AD RMS Enterprise Administrators group. When AD RMS is installed onto the server, the user account installing the role is added to the AD RMS Enterprise Administrators group. Only administrators who manage RMS should be added to this group.

AD RMS Template Administrators   Users who belong to the local AD RMS Templates Administrators group are allowed to manage rights policy templates. AD RMS template administrators have the rights to read cluster data, list rights policy templates, create new rights policy templates, modify existing rights policy templates, and export rights policy templates.

AD RMS Auditors   The local AD RMS Auditors role allows administrators who have this right to manage logs and reports. The AD RMS Auditors role is a read-only role that is restricted to running reports available on the AD RMS cluster, reading cluster information, and reading logging settings.

Installing AD RMS

AD RMS deployment is described as a root cluster, which is not used in terms of failover or network balancing clustering. An AD RMS root cluster manages all of the AD RMS licensing and certificate provisions for the forest. There can be only one AD RMS root cluster per AD forest. After a root cluster is deployed, there is the option of installing additional licensing-only clusters, which issue licenses to clients for publishing their content.

Now that you have a basic understanding of AD RMS, let's take the next step and install it. In Exercise 6.5, you will install AD RMS using the Server Manager MMC.

EXERCISE 6.5

Installing an AD RMS Role on the Local Computer Using Server Manager

1. Start Server Manager. Click Manage and then click Add Roles And Features.

2. The Add Roles And Features Wizard shows the Before You Begin screen. Click Next.

3. Select the Active Directory Rights Management Services Role and click Next.

4. Add the required Active Directory Rights Management Services by default and click Add Features.

5. Click Next.

6. On the screen that explains ADRMS, click Next.

7. On the Select Role Services screen, by default Active Directory Rights Management Server is selected. Identity Federation Support uses AD FS federated trust between organizations to establish user identities and provide access to the RMS-protected content across the federation. Click Next.

8. Click Next on the Web Server (IIS) screen.

9. At the confirmation screen, click Install.

10. Once the installation is complete, click Close.

11. While still in Server Manager, click the AD RMS link on the left side.

12. Click the More About The AD RMS Service Account link next to Configuration Required For Active Directory Rights Management Service.

13. Under Action, click the Perform Additional Configuration link.

14. At the AD RMS introduction screen, click Next.

15. On the Create Or Join An AD RMS Cluster screen, choose Create A New AD RMS Cluster. (The other choice will not be available because you are installing the first AD RMS server and must start the cluster.) Click Next.

16. AD RMS uses a database to store configuration and policy information. At the Select Configuration Database screen, choose Use Windows Internal Database on this server. (The other option is to use a third-party database engine or MSSQL.) Click Next.

17. On the Specify Service Account screen, choose the service account that AD RMS will use. Click the Specify button and type in an administrator account and password other than the ones with which you are currently logged in. Click Next.

18. At the Cryptographic Mode screen, choose Cryptographic Mode 2 (RSA 2048-bit keys/SHA-256 hashes) and click Next.

19. At the Configure AD RMS Cluster Key Storage screen, choose Use AD RMS Centrally Managed Key Storage and click Next.

20. Next you will be asked to enter a password in the AD RMS Cluster Key Password field. The AD RMS cluster key password is used to encrypt the AD RMS cluster key that is stored in the AD RMS database. Type **P@ssw0rd**, confirm it, and click Next.

21. On the Select Website screen, click default website and click Next. AD RMS needs to be hosted in IIS. This will set up a default website for AD RMS.

22. On the Specify Cluster Address screen, choose whether to use a secure or a nonse-cure website. Choose the Use An SSL-Encrypted Connection (https://) check box. In the Internal Address box, type in the server name and click the Validate button. After the address is verified, click Next.

EXERCISE 6.5 *(continued)*

23. The Choose A Server Authentication Certificate For SSL Encryption screen appears. If you receive a message stating the certificate for this server is already created, just click Next. If the message doesn't appear, choose one of your certificates and click Next.

24. The Name The Server Licensor Certificate screen appears. Accept the default server and click Next.

25. You have the option to register AD RMS now or later. If you register the server now, AD RMS will take effect immediately. If you register the server later, AD RMS will not work until you register. You will not register during this exercise. Choose Register Later and click Next.

26. At the Configure Identity Federation Support screen, specify the name of the web server that Identity Federation will use and click the Validate button. The Next button will become available once the server is validated. If an error appears during valida-tion, it will not affect this exercise. Click Next.

27. At the Confirm Installation Selections screen, verify all of your settings and click Install.

28. The install progress screen appears. When the install is complete, click Close.

29. Close the Server Manager MMC.

Managing AD RMS: AD RMS Service Connection Point

The *service connection point (SCP)* is used to store the URL of the AD RMS cluster. The SCP is stored as an object in Active Directory. The SCP can be configured when AD RMS is being installed or later through the Active Directory Rights Management Services console. Only one SCP can exist in an Active Directory forest.

The AD RMS SCP can be registered automatically during AD RMS installation, or it can be registered after installation has finished. To register the SCP, you must be a member of the local AD RMS Enterprise Administrators group and the Active Directory Domain Services (AD DS) Enterprise Admins group, or you must have been given the appropriate authority.

Managing the SCP is accomplished on the SCP tab of the AD RMS cluster's Properties dialog box.

> If a client computer is not located within the Active Directory forest, you must use registry keys to point the AD RMS client to the AD RMS cluster. These registry keys are created in HKEY_Local_Machine\Software\ Microsoft\MSDRM\ServiceLocation. Create a key called Activation with the value of http(s)://<your_cluster>/_wmcs/certification, where <your_cluster> is the URL of the root cluster used for certification.

AD RMS Templates

As you know, a template is a mold that you can use over and over again. AD RMS templates are no different. Before you start creating AD RMS templates, you must first create a shared directory where the templates can be stored. An administrator can then create AD RMS rights policy templates on the AD RMS cluster and export those templates to the shared directory. If your users are connected to the company intranet and they are using AD RMS–enabled applications, they can access the AD RMS templates right from the shared directory as long as they have read access to the shared folder. If your users are not connected to the company intranet, just copy the template to their computers, and this will allow AD RMS–enabled applications to continue to function properly.

When publishing protected content, the author selects the rights policy template to apply from the templates that are available on the local computer. Visibility of the templates is controlled via NTFS permissions. If the user does not have NTFS read access, the respective template will not be visible in an RMS-aware application.

When a user attempts to use protected content, the RMS-enabled application obtains the latest version of the rights policy template that was used to publish the content from the configuration database. The RMS-enabled application then applies its settings to the content. When the rights policy template is modified on the RMS server, RMS updates the template accordingly, in both the configuration database and the shared folder.

If a rights policy template is deleted, it is removed from the configuration database and also from the shared folder (that is specified as the file location for storing copies of templates) location when the template is deleted.

When working with rights policy templates, perform the following tasks:

1. Create and edit rights policy templates.

2. When creating a rights policy template, define the users and rights that apply. Also define how the rights policy template is to be applied to content.

3. Edit the rights policy templates later when they need to be updated.

4. Create as many rights policy templates as are required to manage rights in the organization, but consider that some applications are limited in the number of templates that can be displayed in the application's user interface. If more than a few templates are created in a cluster, you might want to scope the different templates to different groups of users by modifying NTFS permissions.

5. When a template is no longer appropriate, archive the rights policy template and update the distribution of the rights policy templates to the clients so that users do not try to protect content with the retired template. Users attempting to use content protected with the template will still be able to do so because the archived template is still accessible to the RMS servers issuing licenses.

6. If usage of all documents protected with a template is no longer desired, you can delete the template instead of archiving it. Make sure you understand that if users try to access data that is from a deleted template, that data will not be accessible because the template is gone.

See Table 6.7 for a description of the RMS template rights.

TABLE 6.7 Description of rights in RMS templates

Right	Description
Full control	If established, this right enables a user to exercise all rights in the license, whether or not the rights are specifically established to that user.
View	If this right is established, the AD RMS client enables protected content to be decrypted. Usually, when this right is established, the RMS-aware application will allow the user to view protected content.
Edit	If this right is established, the AD RMS client enables protected content to be decrypted and re-encrypted by using the same content key. Usually, when this right is established, the RMS-aware application will allow the user to change protected content and then save it to the same file. This right is effectively identical to the Save right.
Save	If this right is established, the AD RMS client enables protected content to be decrypted and then re-encrypted by using the same content key. Usually, when this right is established, the RMS-aware application will allow the user to change protected content and then save it to the same file. This right is effectively identical to the Edit right.
Export (Save As)	If this right is established, the AD RMS client enables protected content to be decrypted and then re-encrypted by using the same content key. Usually, when this right is established, the RMS-aware application will allow the user to use the Save As feature to save protected content to a new file.
Print	Usually when this right is established, the RMS-aware application will allow the user to print protected content.
Forward	Usually when this right is established, the RMS-aware application will allow an email recipient to forward a protected message.
Reply	Usually when this right is established, the RMS-aware application will allow an email recipient to reply to a protected message and include a copy of the original message.
Reply All	Usually when this right is established, the RMS-aware application will allow an email recipient to reply to all recipients of a protected message and include a copy of the original message.
Extract	Usually when this right is established, the RMS-aware application will allow the user to copy and paste information from protected content.

Right	Description
Allow Macros	Usually when this right is established, the RMS-aware application will allow the user to run macros in the document or use an editor to modify macros in the document.
View Rights	If this right is established, the AD RMS client enables a user to view the user rights that are assigned by the license.
Edit Rights	If this right is established, the AD RMS client enables a user to edit the user rights that are assigned by the license.

Backing Up AD RMS

Follow these steps to allow you to recover from any AD rights management server failure:

1. Record your cluster key password and store it in a safe manner.
2. Export the trusted publishing domain (see Exercise 6.8).
3. Create database backups.

Record and Store Your Cluster Key Password

During installation, take note of the cluster key password and securely store it. If you inherited the AD RMS server and the cluster key password hasn't been documented, you should change it before backup. To accomplish this, start the Active Directory Rights Management Services console under ServerName ➤ Security Policies ➤ Cluster Key Password. Click Change Cluster Key Password.

Create a Backup of the AD RMS Database

AD RMS uses three databases in the database server:

Configuration Database   This is a critical component of an AD RMS installation. The database stores, shares, and retrieves all configuration data and other data that the service requires to manage account certification, licensing, and publishing services for a whole cluster.

Directory Services Database   This contains information about users, identifiers (such as email addresses), security IDs, group membership, and alternate identifiers. This information is a cache of directory services data.

Logging Database   This is all of the historical data about client activity and license acquisition. For each root or licensing-only cluster, by default AD RMS installs a logging database in the same database server instance hosting the configuration database.

In Exercise 6.6, we will perform a backup of the RMS database.

EXERCISE 6.6

Backing Up an AD RMS Database

1. Log on to the SQL server.

2. Click Start ➢ All Programs ➢ Microsoft SQL Server and select SQL Server Management Studio. The Connect To Server dialog box will appear. Verify that the server name is correct and that authentication is set for Windows Authentication.

3. Click Connect.

4. Expand the Databases node.

5. Right-click DRMS_Config_rms_domain_com_443, select Tasks, and then select Back Up.

6. Click Add in the Destination section and select the location.

7. Click OK to finish the backup.

8. Repeat these steps to back up the logging and directory services cache database.

 If you cannot restore the configuration database, you can recover your AD RMS infrastructure with the exported TPD and the cluster key password.

AD RMS Trust Policies

Trust policies are implemented to define how content licensing requests are processed throughout the enterprise, including rights-protected content from other AD RMS clusters. Trust policies are defined as follows:

Trusted User Domains   A trusted user domain (TUD) is the boundary mechanism for the AD RMS root cluster to process client licensor certificates or use licenses from users whose rights account certificates (RACs) were issued by another AD RMS root cluster. You must import the server licensor certificate of the AD RMS cluster to be trusted, to define your TUD.

Trusted Publishing Domains   A trusted publishing domain (TPD) is another boundary type for one AD RMS cluster to issue licenses against publishing licenses issued by another AD RMS cluster. You must also import the server licensor certificate and private key of the server to be trusted, to define the TPD.

Windows Live ID   Microsoft offers an online RMS service for an AD RMS user to send rights-protected content to another user with their Windows Live ID. The Windows Live ID recipient is then able to read rights-protected content from the originating AD RMS cluster registered through Microsoft's online RMS service. This extended AD RMS implantation does not allow the Windows Live ID user to create rights-protected content from the on-premise AD RMS cluster.

Federated Trust   With a federated trust established between AD forests, users from one organization can share rights-protected content with another organization without requiring AD RMS implementation on both sides of the trust.

Microsoft Federation Gateway   Microsoft also offers federated trust through the Microsoft Federation Gateway, which is essentially a trusted broker between organizations. Microsoft Federation Gateway handles all of the identity verifications with all participating Microsoft federated organizations. Microsoft federated organizations can take advantage of this gateway by filtering lists to select which domains can receive certificates or licenses from the on-premise AD RMS cluster.

Managing Trusted User Domains   Trusted user domains enable trust between domains running AD RMS, and they are often used to connect users between forests. TUD management is accomplished in the AD RMS Management console. TUD information is exported to a .bin file and then subsequently imported using the Import Trusted User Domain dialog box.

Adding a Trusted User Domain   By default, Active Directory Rights Management Services (AD RMS) will not process requests from users whose rights account certificate was issued by a different AD RMS installation. However, you can add user domains to the list of trusted user domains, which allows AD RMS to process such requests.

For each TUD, you can also add and remove specific users or groups of users. In addition, you can remove a TUD; however, you cannot remove the root cluster for this Active Directory forest from the list of TUDs. Every AD RMS server trusts the root cluster in its own forest. In Exercise 6.7 we'll add a TUD into the test domain.

EXERCISE 6.7

Adding a Trusted User Domain

Before getting started, the TUD of the AD RMS installation should already be exported and available.

1.   Start the Active Directory Rights Management Services console and expand the AD RMS cluster.

2.   In the console tree, expand Trust Policies and click Trusted User Domains.

3.   In the Actions pane, click Import Trusted User Domain.

4.   In the Trusted User Domain File dialog box, type the path to the exported server licensor certificate of the user domain to trust or click Browse to locate it.

5.   In Display Name, type a name to identify this trusted user domain. If you would like to extend this trust to federated users, select Extend Trust To Federated Users Of The Imported Server.

6.   Click Finish.

Exporting the Trusted User Domain

TUDs allow an AD RMS cluster to issue licenses to users whose rights account certificate was established by another server in an AD RMS cluster. Exporting a TUD's key and importing it into another AD RMS cluster allows the cluster to process requests for use licenses from users whose rights account certificates are in a different cluster.

Membership in the local AD RMS Enterprise Admins group, or equivalent, is the minimum required to complete this procedure. In Exercise 6.8, we will export the TUD and store the data in a location you provide.

EXERCISE 6.8

Exporting the Trusted User Domain

1. Start the Active Directory Rights Management Services console and expand the AD RMS cluster.

2. In the console tree, expand Trust Policies and click Trusted User Domains.

3. In the Actions pane, click Export Trusted User Domain.

4. The Save As dialog box appears. I recommend you modify the .bin filename to include the name of your server, such as ADRMS_Cluster1_LicensorCert.bin.

5. Click Save to save the file with the name and location you specified.

Exporting the Trusted Publishing Domain

Unlike a trusted user domain, a trusted publishing domain enables an AD RMS cluster to issue licenses as if it was a different AD RMS cluster. To accomplish this, both the certificate and the private key need to be imported. This is different from a TUD scenario, where only the certificate is imported.

Importing a TPD is accomplished within the AD RMS Management console using the Import Trusted Publishing Domain dialog box. Saving a copy of the trusted publishing domain can be done from within the AD RMS administration console. In Exercise 6.9, we will export the TPD.

EXERCISE 6.9

Exporting the Trusted Publishing Domain

1. Start the AD RMS administration console.

2. In the console tree view, select the Trusted Publishing Domains node.

3. In the details pane on the right, select Export Trusted Publishing Domain. The Export Trusted Publishing Domain dialog box will appear.

4. From the Export Trusted Publishing Domain dialog box, click Save As. The Export Trusted Publishing Domain File Save As dialog box will appear. On the left pane, select the folder you want to save the trusted publishing domain.

5. In File Name enter a filename; then verify the XML File (*.xml) type is selected for Save As Type.

6. Click Save. This will close the Export Trusted Publishing Domain As dialog box.

7. In the Export Trusted Publishing Domain dialog box, enter a password in the Password box.

8. Enter a password again in the Confirm Password dialog box.

9. Click Finish.

Adding a Trusted Publishing Domain

Exercise 6.10 assumes you have exported the trusted publishing domain of another AD RMS cluster (as described in the preceding section). Membership in the local AD RMS Enterprise Admins group, or equivalent, is the minimum required to complete this procedure.

EXERCISE 6.10

Adding the Trusted Publishing Domain

1. Start the Active Directory Rights Management Services console and expand the AD RMS cluster.

2. In the console tree, expand Trust Policies and click Trusted Publishing Domains.

3. In the Actions pane, click Import Trusted Publishing Domain.

4. In the Trusted Publishing Domain File dialog box, type the path to the trusted publishing domain file or click Browse to locate it. This file contains the licensor certificate, private key (if the key is stored in software), and rights policy templates. This file is encrypted.

5. In Password, type the password required to decrypt this file.

6. In Display Name, type a name to identify this trusted user domain.

7. Click Finish.

Managing Distributed and Archived Rights Policy Templates

Rights policy templates are managed in the AD RMS Management console. Planning and overviews of rights policies are available here:

http://technet.microsoft.com/en-us/library/ee221094

http://technet.microsoft.com/en-us/library/dd996658

You can designate the location for the templates as well as set whether the templates can be exported by using the properties of the Rights Policy Template tab.

Configuring a Web Application Proxy

One of the advantages of using the Remote Access role service in Windows Server 2016 is the Web Application Proxy. Normally, your users access applications on the Internet from your corporate network. The *Web Application Proxy* reverses this feature, and it allows your corporate users to access applications from any device outside the network.

Administrators can choose which applications to provide reverse proxy features, and this allows administrators the ability to give access selectively to corporate users for the desired application that you want to set up for the Web Application Proxy service.

The Web Application Proxy feature allows applications running on servers inside the corporate network to be accessed by any device outside the corporate network. The process of allowing an application to be available to users outside of the corporate network is known as *publishing*.

Web Application Proxies work differently than a normal VPN solution because when an administrator publishes applications through Web Application Proxy, end users get access only to applications that the administrator published. Administrators have the ability to deploy the Web Application Proxy alongside a VPN as part of your Remote Access deployment for your organization.

Web Application Proxy can function as an AD FS proxy, and it also preauthenticates access to web applications using Active Directory Federation Services (AD FS).

Publishing Applications

One disadvantage to corporate networks are that the machines that access the network are normally devices issued by the organization. That's where Web Application Proxy publishing can help.

Web Application Proxy allows an administrator to publish an organization's applications, thus allowing corporate end users the ability to access the applications from their own devices. This is becoming a big trend in the computer industry called *bring your own device (BYOD)*.

In today's technology world, users are buying and using many of their own devices, even for business work. Because of this, the users are comfortable with their own devices. Web Application Proxy allows an organization to set up applications and enable their corporate users to use these applications with the devices the users already own, including computers, tablets, and smartphones.

The client side is easy to use as long as the end user has a standard browser or Office client. End users can also use apps from the Microsoft Windows Store that allow the client system to connect to the Web Application Proxy.

Configuring Pass-Through Authentication

Now when setting up the Web Application Proxy (see Figure 6.6) so that your users can access applications, you must have some kind of security or everyone with a device would be able to access and use your applications.

FIGURE 6.6   Example of Web Proxy setup

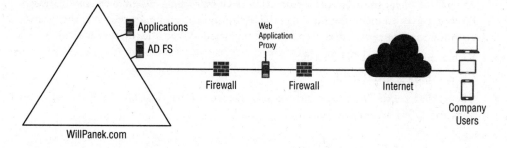

Because of this, Active Directory Federation Services (AD FS) must always be deployed with Web Application Proxy. AD FS gives you features such as single sign-on (SSO). *Single sign-on* allows you to log in one time with a set of credentials and use that set of credentials to access the applications over and over. To use a Web Application Proxy, you should set your firewall to allow for ports 443 and 49443.

When an administrator publishes an application using the Web Application Proxy, the method that users and devices use for authentication is known as preauthentication. The Web Application Proxy allows for two forms of preauthentication:

AD FS Preauthentication   AD FS preauthentication requires the user to authenticate directly with the AD FS server. After the AD FS authentication happens, the Web Application Proxy then redirects the user to the published web application. This guarantees that traffic to your published web applications is authenticated before a user can access it.

Pass-Through Preauthentication   When using Pass-through Preauthentication, a user is not required to enter credentials before they are allowed to connect to published web applications.

Pass-through authentication is truly a great benefit for your end users. Think of having a network where a user has to log in every time that user wants to access an application. The more times you make your end users log into an application, the more chances there are that the end user will encounter possible issues. Pass-through authentication works in the following way:

1. The client enters a URL address on their device, and the client system attempts to access the published web application.

2. The Web Application Proxy sends the request to the proxy server.

3. If the backend server needs the user to authenticate, the end user needs to enter their credentials only once.

4. After the server authenticates the credentials, the client has access to the published web application.

To access applications easily that are published by the Web Application Proxy and use the AD FS preauthentication, end users need to use one of the following types of clients:

- Any HTTP client that supports redirection (web browsers). When Web Application Proxy receives an incoming message, the Web Application Proxy redirects the user to an authentication server and then back to the original web address authenticated.

- Rich clients that use HTTP basic.

- Clients that uses MSOFBA.

- Clients that use the Web Authentication Broker for authentication like Windows Store apps and RESTful applications.

Authentication Capabilities

One of the great advantages of using AD FS for authentication is that your organization gets to also benefit from all of the different features that AD FS provides including:

Workplace Join   This feature in AD FS allows users to join devices to the corporate network that would not normally be domain-joined. An example of this is a user's home computer. Once an administrator enables this feature, the AD FS admin will be able to configure all applications that require devices to be registered before they can gain access to published applications.

Single Sign-On   The Single Sign-On (SSO) feature allows users to enter their credentials only once but then be authenticated to all supported published applications. SSO is a feature that is used heavily when connecting your corporate network to another network (like the cloud). Users sign in once but have access to both networks.

Multifactor Authentication (MFA)   AD FS gives an administrator the ability to require users to authenticate with more than one authentication scheme (smart card).

Multifactor Access Control   Authorization claim rules allow an administrator to control access in AD FS. Once these claim rules are implemented, they are used to issue or deny claims. This will help determine whether a user or a group of users will be allowed to access to the AD FS secured resources. Authorization rules can only be set on relying party trusts.

One thing an administrator should remember, when you decide to publish applications using the Web Application Proxy, an administrator is not required to configure any of the AD FS authentication features mentioned above.

This allows the network administrators to allow access to devices that are not able to join the workplace, or provide additional factors of authentication (kiosk machines).

All of the above features can be combined to allow for stricter security on applications or ignored for less security on applications.

PowerShell Commands

Table 6.8 shows you just some of the available PowerShell commands available for AD FS and the Web Application Proxy.

TABLE 6.8 PowerShell Commands

Command	Description
Add-AdfsAttributeStore	Administrators can use this command to add an attribute store to the Federation Service.
Add-AdfsCertificate	This command allows an administrator to add a new certificate to the AD FS server for signing, decrypting, or securing communications.
Add-AdfsClaimsProviderTrust	Administrators can use this command to add a new claims provider trust to the Federation Service.
Add-AdfsClient	This command allows an admin to register an OAuth 2.0 client with AD FS.
Add-AdfsFarmNode	Administrators can use this command to add a computer to an existing federation server farm.
Add-AdfsNativeClientApplication	This command allows an admin to add a native client application role to an application in AD FS.
Add-AdfsServerApplication	Administrators can use this command to add a server application role to an application in AD FS.
Disable-AdfsCertificateAuthority	This command allows an admin to disable a certificate authority.
Disable-AdfsLocalClaimsProviderTrust	This command allows an administrator to disable a local claims provider trust.
Disable-AdfsRelyingPartyTrust	Administrators can use this command to disable a relying party trust of the Federation Service.
Enable-AdfsApplicationGroup	This command allows an administrator to enable an application group in AD FS.

TABLE 6.8   PowerShell Commands *(continued)*

Command	Description
Enable-AdfsClaimsProviderTrust	Administrators can use this command to enable a claims provider trust in the Federation Service.
Enable-AdfsLocalClaimsProviderTrust	This command allows an administrator to enable a local claims provider trust.
Get-AdfsApplicationGroup	Administrators can use this command to view an application group.
Get-AdfsAttributeStore	This command allows an administrator to view the attribute stores of the Federation Service.
Get-AdfsAuthenticationProvider	Administrators can use this command to view a list of all authentication providers in AD FS.
Get-AdfsCertificate	This command allows an administrator to view the certificates from AD FS.
Get-AdfsCertificateAuthority	Administrators can use this command to view a certificate authority.
Get-AdfsClient	This command allows an administrator to view registration information for an OAuth 2.0 client.
Get-AdfsFarmInformation	Administrators can use this command to view AD FS behavior level and farm node information.
Initialize-ADDeviceRegistration	Admins can use this command to initialize the Device Registration Service configuration in the Active Directory forest.
New-AdfsApplicationGroup	This command creates a new application group.
New-AdfsClaimRuleSet	Administrators can use this command to create a set of claim rules.
New-AdfsOrganization	This command allows an administrator to create a new organization information object.

Command	Description
`Register-AdfsAuthenticationProvider`	Administrators can use this command to register an external authentication provider in AD FS.
`Remove-AdfsApplicationGroup`	This command allows an administrator to remove an application group.
`Set-AdfsFarmInformation`	This command allows an admin to remove a stale or offline farm node from the farm information table.
`Set-AdfsProperties`	Administrators can use this command to set the properties that control global behaviors in AD FS.
`Set-AdfsServerApplication`	This command allows an administrator to modify configuration settings for a server application role of an application in AD FS.
`Set-AdfsWebConfig`	Administrators can use this command to modify web customization configuration settings

Summary

In this chapter, I discussed the Active Directory Federation Services, which provides Internet-based clients with a secure identity access solution that works on both Windows and non-Windows operating systems.

I also talked about Active Directory Rights Management Services. I explained that AD RMS is included with Microsoft Windows Server 2016 and discussed how it allows administrators or users to determine what access to give other users in an organization.

Finally, I talked about the Web Application Proxy. The Web Application Proxy allows an administrator to publish an organization's applications, thus allowing corporate end users the ability to access the applications from their own devices.

Exam Essentials

Understand Active Directory Federation Service.   Active Directory Federation Service gives users the ability to do a single sign-on and access applications on other networks without needing a secondary password. Organizations can set up trust relationships with other trusted organizations so that a user's digital identity and access rights can be accepted without a secondary password.

Know how to install Active Directory Rights Management Services.   Active Directory Rights Management Services, included with Microsoft Windows Server 2016, allows administrators and users to determine what access (open, read, modify, and so on) they give to other users in an organization. This access can be used to secure email messages, internal websites, and documents.

Understand what Web Application Proxy.   The Web Application Proxy allows your corporate users to access applications from any device outside the network.

Review Questions

You can find the answers in the Appendix.

1. ABC Industries wants configuration modifications of the Certification Authority role service to be logged. How would you implement this? (Choose all that apply.)

   A. You should consider enabling auditing of system events.

   B. You should consider enabling logging.

   C. You should consider enabling auditing of object access.

   D. You should consider enabling auditing of privilege use.

   E. You should consider enabling auditing of process tracking.

2. Federation proxy services are installed through which of the following?

   A. Separate Active Directory Federation Proxy install download

   B. Server Manager ➤ Remote Access ➤ Web Proxy

   C. Server Manager ➤ Active Directory Federation Services ➤ Active Directory Proxy services

   D. Windows PowerShell ➤ Install-Windows-Feature Web Proxy

3. The new Workplace Join feature supports which of following? (Choose all that apply.)

   A. Federates an iPhone to the corporate intranet

   B. Allows Windows 8 clients to process claim-based trusts

   C. Allows Windows 8 clients to form claim-based trusts automatically with the home domain

   D. None of the above

4. You install and configure four Windows Server 2016 servers as an AD FS server farm. The AD FS configuration database is stored in a Microsoft SQL Server 2012 database. You need to ensure that AD FS will continue to function in the event of an AD FS server failure. You also need to ensure that all four servers in the AD FS farm will actively perform AD FS functions. What should you include in your solution?

   A. Windows Failover Clustering

   B. Windows Identity Foundation 3.5

   C. Network Load Balancing

   D. Web Proxy Server

5. Your network contains an Active Directory domain named contoso.com. You plan to deploy a Windows 2016 Active Directory Federation Services (AD FS) farm that will contain eight federation servers. You need to identify which technology or technologies must be deployed on the network before you install the federation servers. Which technology or technologies should you identify? (Choose all that apply.)

   A. Network Load Balancing

   B. Microsoft Forefront Identity Manager 2010

   C. Windows Internal Database feature

   D. Microsoft SQL Server 2016

   E. The Windows Identity Foundation 3.5 feature

6. You are the system administrator at JavaCup, which hosts a web RMS-aware application that the JavaCup forest and Boston Tea Company forest users need to access. You deploy a single AD FS server in the JavaCup forest. Which of the following is a true statement about your AD FS implementation? (Choose all that apply.)

    A. You will configure a relying-party server on the JavaCup AD FS server.

    B. The AD FS server in the Boston Tea Company forest functions as the claims provider.

    C. The AD FS server in the Boston Tea Company forest functions as the relying-party server.

    D. You will configure a claims provider trust on the JavaCup AD FS server.

7. You store AD FS servers in an OU named Federation Servers. You want to auto-enroll the certificates used for AD FS. Which certificates should you add to the GPO?

    A. The CA certificate of the forest

    B. The third-party (VeriSign, Entrust) CA certificate

    C. The SSL certificate assigned to the AD FS servers

    D. The Token Signing certificate assigned to the AD FS Servers

8. You plan to implement Active Directory Rights Management Services (AD RMS) across the enterprise. You need to plan the AD RMS cluster installations for the forest. Users in all domains will access AD RMS–protected documents. You need to minimize the number of AD RMS clusters. Which of the following will help you determine how many AD RMS root clusters you require?

    A. You need at least one AD RMS root cluster for the enterprise.

    B. You need at least one AD RMS root cluster per forest.

    C. You need at least one AD RMS root cluster per domain.

    D. You need at least one AD RMS root cluster per Active Directory site.

    E. An AD RMS root cluster is not required.

9. You have a server named Server1 that runs Windows Server 2016. You need to configure Server1 as a Web Application Proxy. Which server role or role service should you install on Server1?

    A. Remote Access

    B. Active Directory Federation Services

    C. Web Server (IIS)

    D. DirectAccess and VPN (RAS)

10. Your network contains an Active Directory forest named WillPanek.com. The forest contains a member server on the perimeter network named Server1 that runs Windows Server 2016.The administrator installs the Active Directory Federation Services server role on Server1 along with the Web Application Proxy. Which two inbound TCP ports should you open on the firewall? Each correct answer presents part of the solution. (Choose two.)

    A. 443

    B. 390

    C. 8443

    D. 49443

Appendix

Answers to Review Questions

Chapter 1: Installing Active Directory

1. **A, B, C, D.** The forest and function levels have to be Windows 2003 or newer to install an RODC.

2. **B.** A domain controller can contain Active Directory information for only one domain. If you want to use a multidomain environment, you must use multiple domain controllers configured in either a tree or a forest setting.

3. **D.** NTFS has file-level security, and it makes efficient usage of disk space. Since this machine is to be configured as a domain controller, the configuration requires at least one NTFS partition to store the Sysvol information.

4. **A, D.** To convert the system partition to NTFS, you must first use the CONVERT command-line utility and then reboot the server. During the next boot, the file system will be converted.

5. **B, E.** The use of LDAP and TCP/IP is required to support Active Directory. TCP/IP is the network protocol favored by Microsoft, which determined that all Active Directory communication would occur on TCP/IP. DNS is required because Active Directory is inherently dependent on the domain model. DHCP is used for automatic address assignment and is not required. Similarly, NetBEUI and IPX/SPX are not available network protocols in Windows Server 2016.

6. **A, C.** The Sysvol directory must be created on an NTFS partition. If such a partition is not available, you will not be able to promote the server to a domain controller. An error in the network configuration might prevent the server from connecting to another domain controller in the environment.

7. **B, C.** You need to run the Adprep command when installing your first Windows Server 2016 domain controller onto a Windows Server 2008 R2 domain. Adprep /rodcprep actually gets the network ready to install a read-only domain controller and not a GUI version.

8. **A.** You'll need to use Active Directory Federation Services (AD FS) in order to implement federated identity management. Federated identity management is a standards-based and information technology process that will enable distributed identification, authentication, and authorization across organizational and platform boundaries. The AD FS solution in Windows Server 2016 helps administrators address these challenges by enabling organizations to share a user's identity information securely.

9. **B.** The HOSTS file is a text-file-based database of mappings between hostnames and IP addresses. It works like a file-based version of DNS. DNS resolves a hostname to an IP address.

10. **A.** You only need to give them rights to the WillPanek.com zone using the DNS snap-in. If they do not have any rights to the WillPanekAD.com zone, they will not be able to configure this zone in any way.

Chapter 2: Administer Active Directory

1. A. A computer account and the domain authenticate each other by using a password. The password resets every 30 days. Since the machine has not connected to the domain for 16 weeks, the computer needs to be rejoined to the domain.

2. C. Checking the box Account Never Expires will prevent this user's account from expiring again.

3. D. The dsadd command allows you to add an object (user's account) to the Active Directory database.

4. A. Distribution groups are for emails only, and distribution groups cannot be assigned rights and permissions to objects.

5. A. Inheritance is the process by which permissions placed on parent OUs affect child OUs. In this example, the permissions change for the higher-level OU (Texas) automatically caused a change in permissions for the lower-level OU (Austin).

6. B, E. Enabling the Advanced Features item in the View menu will allow Isabel to see the LostAndFound and System folders. The LostAndFound folder contains information about objects that could not be replicated among domain controllers.

7. A. Through the use of filtering, you can choose which types of objects you want to see using the Active Directory Users and Computers tool. Several of the other choices may work, but they require changes to Active Directory settings or objects.

8. A. To allow the junior admin to do backups, their account needs to be part of the Backup Operators local group. To add their account to the local group, you need to use Computer Management.

9. A, B, C, D. All of the options listed are common tasks presented in the Delegation of Control Wizard.

10. D. The Delegation of Control Wizard is designed to allow administrators to set up permissions on specific Active Directory objects.

Chapter 3: Maintaining Active Directory

1. B. The NTDS settings for the site level are where you would activate and deactivate UGMC.

2. A. By decreasing the replication interval for the DEFAULTIPSITELINK object, you will decrease the replication latency for all sites using the DEFAULTIPSITELINK.

3. D. In the Active Directory Sites and Services console, the Server NTDS settings are where you would activate and deactivate global catalogs.

4. D. Preferred bridgehead servers receive replication information for a site and transmit this information to other domain controllers within the site. By configuring one server at each site to act as a preferred bridgehead server, Daniel can ensure that all replication traffic between the two sites is routed through the bridgehead servers and that replication traffic will flow properly between the domain controllers.

5. C. By default, connection objects are automatically created by the Active Directory replication engine. You can choose to override the default behavior of Active Directory replication topology by manually creating connection objects, but this step is not required.

6. B. The Knowledge Consistency Checker (KCC) is responsible for establishing the replication topology and ensuring that all domain controllers are kept up-to-date.

7. D. Site link bridges are designed to allow site links to be transitive. That is, they allow site links to use other site links to transfer replication information between sites. By default, all site links are bridged. However, you can turn off transitivity if you want to override this behavior.

8. B. Simple Mail Transfer Protocol was designed for environments in which persistent connections may not always be available. SMTP uses the store-and-forward method to ensure that information is not lost if a connection cannot be made.

9. D. The Directory Service event log contains error messages and information related to replication. These details can be useful when you are troubleshooting replication problems.

10. A, D. By creating new sites, Christina can help define settings for Active Directory replication based on the environment's network connections. She can use connection objects to define further the details of how and when replication traffic will be transmitted between the domain controllers.

Chapter 4: Implementing GPOs

1. C. The Delegation of Control Wizard can be used to allow other system administrators permission to add GPO links.

2. C. The system administrator can specify whether the application will be uninstalled or whether future installations will be prevented.

3. B. You would use GPUpdate.exe/force. The /force switch forces the GPO to reapply all policy settings. By default, only policy settings that have changed are applied.

4. A. You would use the Windows PowerShell Invoke-GPUpdate cmdlet. This PowerShell cmdlet allows you to force the GPO to reapply the policies immediately.

5. D. DVD Present Targeting is not one of the options that you may consider when using item-level targeting.

6. A, B. If you want your clients to be able to edit domain-based GPOs by using the ADMX files that are stored in the ADMX Central Store, you must be using Windows 10, Windows 8, Windows 7, or Windows Server 2008/2008 R2/2012/2012 R2/2016.

7. D. If you assign an application to a user, the application does not get automatically installed. To have an application automatically installed, you must assign the application to the computer account. Since Finance is the only OU that should receive this application, you would link the GPO to Finance only.

8. C. The Resultant Set of Policy (RSoP) utility displays the exact settings that apply to individual users, computers, OUs, domains, and sites after inheritance and filtering have taken effect. Desktop wallpaper settings are under the User section of the GPO, so you would run the RSoP against the user account.

9. B. The Enforced option can be placed on a parent GPO, and this option ensures that all lower-level objects inherit these settings. Using this option ensures that Group Policy inheritance is not blocked at other levels.

10. A. If the data transfer rate from the domain controller providing the GPO to the computer is slower than what you have specified in the slow link detection setting, the connection is considered to be a slow connection, and the application will not install properly.

Chapter 5: Understanding Certificates

1. C. The Add-CATemplate command allows an administrator to add a certificate template to the CA.

2. A, E. Certificate Enrollment Web Services with the Certificate Enrollment Policy Web Server role is the preferred Microsoft solution for issuing certificates through the internet.

3. B. The online responder uses a lightweight HTTP protocol that responds faster and more efficiently than downloading a traditional CRL.

4. B, C. To enable auditing, you must check the boxes for Success Audits and Failure Audits on the Events tab of the Federation Service Properties dialog box. You must also enable Object Access Auditing in Local Policy or Group Policy.

5. A. To configure a server as a stand-alone CA server, you need to be an administrator on that server.

6. B. Since you are planning to issue certificates based on a User certificate template, you need to first copy that template so that you can alter it to the new settings.

7. A. You change the validity period of a certificate template, an administrator needs to modify the validity period setting for the certificate template.

8. C. The reason that you check the Delta CRL is because the Delta CRL shows any changes since the last CRL update. So if you want clients to verify the CRL every 30 minutes, you would want to set the Delta CRL publication interval.

9.   D. Administrators can use the `Get-CACrlDistributionPoint` command to view all the locations set for the CRL distribution point (CDP).

10. A. Administrators can use the `Get-CATemplate` command to view the list of templates set on the CA for issuance of certificates.

Chapter 6: Configure Access and Information Protection Solutions

1.   B, C. To enable AD FS auditing, you must check the boxes for Success Audits and Failure Audits on the Events tab of the Federation Service Properties dialog box. You must also enable Object Access Auditing in Local Policy or Group Policy.

2.   B. Federation Proxy Services are installed under Remote Access as a web application proxy server in Windows Server 2016.

3.   A, B, C. By using Workplace Join, information workers can join their personal devices with their company's workplace computers to access company resources and services. When you join your personal device to your workplace, it becomes a known device and provides seamless second-factor authentication and single sign-on to workplace resources and applications.

4.   C. Network Load Balancing (NLB) is the only support Microsoft solution for providing high availability across an ADFS server farm. Windows Failover Clustering does not currently support ADFS as one master server is allowed to write to the configuration database per farm.

5.   D. The AD FS configuration database stores all of the configuration data. It contains information that a federation service requires to identify partners, certificates, attribute stores, claims, and so forth. You can store this configuration data in either a Microsoft SQL Server 2005 or newer database or the Windows Internal Database feature that is included with Windows Server 2008/2008 R2, Windows Server 2012/2012 R2, and Windows Server 2016. The Windows Internal Database supports only up to five federation servers in a farm.

6.   A, B. The relying-party server is a member of the Active Directory forest that hosts resources that a user in the partner organization wants to access. In this case, the relying party server should be the JavaCup AD FS server. A claims provider provides users with claims. These claims are stored within digitally encrypted and signed tokens. In this case, Boston Tea Party is the claims provider.

7.   A. The Forest CA certificate is the only certificate that is automatically trusted, does not require user interaction and digital signature does not change in this scenario.

8.   B. Licensing Server/Cluster is the component in charge of delivering publishing and use licenses. Several clusters can be installed per forest depending on the technical needs (servers' workload and bandwidth constraints).

9.   A. To use the Web Application Proxy, you must install the Remote Access role.

10. A, D. To use a Web Application Proxy and AD FS, you should set your firewall to allow for ports 443 and 49443.

Index

Comprehensive Online Learning Environment

Register to gain one year of FREE access to the online interactive learning environment and test bank to help you study for your MCSA Windows Server 2016 certification exam—included with your purchase of this book!

The online test bank includes:

- **Assessment Test** to help you focus your study to specific objectives
- **Chapter Tests** to reinforce what you've learned
- **Practice Exams** to test your knowledge of the material
- **Digital Flashcards** to reinforce your learning and provide last-minute test prep before the exam
- **Searchable Glossary** to define the key terms you'll need to know for the exam
- **Videos** created by the author to accompany many of the chapter exercises

Register and Access the Online Test Bank

To register your book and get access to the online test bank, follow these steps:

1. Go to bit.ly/SybexTest.
2. Select your book from the list.
3. Complete the required registration information including answering the security verification proving book ownership. You will be emailed a pin code.
4. Go to http://www.wiley.com/go/sybextestprep and find your book on that page and click the "Register or Login" link under your book.
5. If you already have an account at testbanks.wiley.com, login and then click the "Redeem Access Code" button to add your new book with the pin code you received. If you don't have an account already, create a new account and use the PIN code you received.